YOU ALREADY KNOW

Italian

Learn Italian by speaking English
with 5,000 Italian words and *frasi* that
are nearly *identico* to English

RAYMOND W. LOWRY

New York   Chicago   San Francisco   Lisbon   London   Madrid   Mexico City
Milan   New Delhi   San Juan   Seoul   Singapore   Sydney   Toronto

Library of Congress Cataloging-in-Publication Data

Lowry, Raymond W.
    You already know Italian / by Raymond W. Lowry.
        p.   cm.
    ISBN 0-07-146489-1
    1. Italian language—Textbooks for foreign speakers—English.   2. Italian
language—Self-instruction.   I. Title.

PC1129.E5L69   2006
458.2'421—dc22   2006041868

1 2 3 4 5 6 7 8 9 0   LBM/LBM   0 9 8 7 6

ISBN 0-07-146489-1

Book edited by Generosa Gina Protano
Designed and produced by GGP Publishing, Inc., Larchmont, New York 10538
(www.ggppublishing.com)

CONTENTS

This Book's Purpose and Promise   v

How to Use This Book to Best Advantage   viii

Italian Pronunciation   1

Italian Grammar   19

Lista di termini e frasi familiari

    (List of Familiar Terms and Phrases)   31

Lista di termini identici e simili

    (List of Identical and Similar Terms)   43

Lista di termini "simili falsi"

    (List of "Falsely Similar" Terms)   261

Lista di termini e frasi utili

    (List of Helpful Terms and Phrases)   283

THIS BOOK'S PURPOSE AND PROMISE
An Important Note to Self-Directed Learners

T he thesis that underlies this volume's title is simply stated: unless you've spent your life building sand castles, lazily watching the clouds roll by, or otherwise not paying much attention to the world around you, *you already*—perhaps without being conscious of the fact—*possess an essential familiarity with the Italian language*. Indeed, you already employ a significant number of Italian terms in your everyday speech and understand many more. For in fact, modern English is heavily interlaced with Italian terminology: words that are often incorrectly assumed to be English, while in fact they've been Italian—or, originally, Latin—from the start, drawn into our polyglot tongue by over two millennia of cultural interchange. If you doubt that assertion, it will be demonstrated momentarily.

The purpose of this book is to assist you in readily adding to that preexisting base of acquaintance. To help you, in short, learn *more* Italian, *faster and more thoroughly and confidently*, than you have believed possible. And give you a basic working knowledge of the structure and syntax of Italian as well.

It's probably safe to assume that your interest in broadening your Italian vocabulary arises at least in part from the fact that you're an involved and enthused citizen of our increasingly multicultural world. That is, an individual who has read and been fascinated by, among others, books with Italian settings, subjects, or motifs; an individual who has enjoyed Italian or Italian-themed or -sited films; who has been confronted with Italian menus and reveled in the cuisine offered there; who has at least some acquaintance with popular and / or "serious" Italian music, art, and architecture; and knows at least a bit about Italy's all-important contribution to Western history and culture. And very possibly you have an urge to travel to **bella Italia**—or perhaps have already been there, and long to return to that lovely land and *really* converse with its natives in their own lilting tongue.

If that assumption is correct, then this book's assertive title is almost certainly true: you *do* already own a larger Italian vocabulary than you've imagined, and are especially well positioned to advance more quickly and easily toward a growing mastery of *la lingua italiana* than you've supposed. Here's the promised demonstration: you *do* recognize and understand at least a majority of the following words, don't you?— *amore, antipasto, bambino, bravo, carne, casa, casino, cinema, diva, falsetto, inferno, latte, mafia, mamma, numero, oro, olivo, paradiso, pasta, papà, pizza, prosciutto, quasi, radio, salsa, soprano, terra ferma, vendetta, veranda, vino.* If your answer is in the affirmative, then you're almost certainly well acquainted with a large fraction of the 200-plus words contained in this book's initial word list, *Lista di termini e frasi familiari* (List of Familiar Terms and Phrases), and truly possess a meaningful "head start" in the relatively painless task of building an even more comprehensive Italian vocabulary.

"Relatively painless?" Well, yes! For this book's unique feature is its primary focus on *cognate* English-Italian terminology. That is, words that are either spelled and / or pronounced identically, almost-identically, or with a high degree of similarity in both languages. An English ambulance, for example, is an Italian **ambulanza**; the English term *abbreviation* equates to **abbreviazione** in Italian; and if you've suffered an abrasion in New York, your **abrasione** is no more bothersome than it'd be in **Roma**. In short, cognates are far easier to master than same-meaning words that bear little or no resemblance to one another—and there are literally *thousands* of English / Italian cognates that can be readily incorporated into your basic Italian vocabulary! Many important terms contain no similarity at all across the linguistic divide, of course, and, eventually, many of them will be important for you to learn as well. But they will be far more easily and eagerly mastered once you've got a few hundred cognates securely stowed away in your mental bilingual lexicon.

In short, this book's approach is to work from easy to not so easy, rather than the other way around. Here, we want to start you off *fast*, and let your already possessed and easily broadened vocabulary serve as a base for the more difficult words and grammatical structures that, in time, will round out your learning. If that sounds like a fair and attractive proposition, fellow learner . . . well, read on! And **welcome to the world of easiest-to-master conversational Italian!**

HOW TO USE THIS BOOK
TO BEST ADVANTAGE

Except for the few who are blessed with inborn linguistic superskill, *no* foreign tongue is truly "easy" to learn: all are as complex and internally inconsistent as we humans who invented them. Relatively speaking, however, Italian is by far the easiest of all non-native languages for an English speaker to master. Not only does it have a structural logic less replete with exceptions and self-contradictions than most, but *it's full to overflowing with cognates:* words that are identical or highly similar across the linguistic divide. This is the greatest advantage that any learner of Italian possesses: he or she can amass a relatively vast vocabulary—the essential foundation of language acquisition—with less arduous effort than is required for *any* other tongue! Indeed, most English speakers already know between scores and hundreds of Italian words.

This book, uniquely, is an instructional tool that focuses upon that "easier-ness" of Italian vocabulary acquisition. Like any tool, of course, it can either be utilized skillfully, to the learner's great advantage, or misused and / or underutilized, to his or her loss. The suggestions that follow, then, constitute an "Owner's Manual" on the best-possible usage of this potentially powerful tool.

1. The single greatest assistance the learner can give him- / herself is to get the essentials of *pronunciation* in mind-and-mouth *first*. Before *all* else: before the easiness of cognate-rich vocabulary, even, and certainly before becoming enmeshed in the complexities of grammatical formality and syntactical structure. *First,* learn how the language "sounds and says." You must first train the ears and mind and mouth! It would be impossible to overstress the importance of this: go *first* to this book's pronunciation chapter, and carefully read and heed both its suggestions and detailed descriptions. Only then, *after* absorbing an essential familiarity with Italian's vocal / aural character, actively progress toward the absorption of vocabulary itself. In most cases, a mere four hours or less of listening and practice, as specified in the pronunciation guide, will have you well on your way to really "owning" the basic character of Italian expression. And having gained that, you'll have given yourself a *great* additional boost toward Italian mastery, and be well ahead of those who are ignorant of pronunciation's all-important primacy. Failing to develop accurate pronunciation from the outset, conversely, would be a continual drag upon your progress, and eventually become a handicap in need of difficult unlearning and correction.

2. Then, with the matter of "sound" confidently in ear, you'll be ready to begin absorbing Italian's cognate-rich vocabulary. Not all of the five thousand cognates at the heart of this book will be of need or interest to you, of course. So, especially as you begin to build vocabulary, *be selective!* After you're sure of all the terms in the book's initial list, *Lista di termini e frasi familiari*, turn with highlighter in hand to the main list, *Lista di termini identici e simili,* which constitutes this volume's core. From it select a dozen or two everyday nouns from across its alphabetic spectrum. For example, from **ability** (abilità) and **academy** (accademia), through **discrepancy** (discrepanza), and **nose** (naso), and **recourse** (ricorso), and **student** (studente), on to **zebra** (zebra) and **zone** (zona), and so forth. Then choose another dozen. Then another. Then another . . . , adding a few everyday adjectives to the mix as you go along.

While you can afford to ignore the "*m.,*" "*f.,*" and "*m. & f.*"coding at first, at some point during your buildup of nouns and pronouns you'll need to turn to the chapter on grammar and become comfortable with the wildly irrational issue of noun / adjective "gender." You'll have no choice in that: it must be done. But *don't* immerse yourself in the issue of verbs and conjugations yet! That comes last—and largely outside of this volume—when you've amassed a substantial lexicon of nouns and adjectives, and are *eager* to begin to learn and properly use the "action" words that will make your Italian dance and sing.

Yes, verbs come last. Because they must be conjugated for most effective conversational use, and because conjugation is every language's most tangled morass, verbs are by far the toughest to master. In infinitive form, they're a snap; but in conjugated form—well, that's something else.

But when you've got a hundred or two easy nouns and adjectives in hand, your effort toward verb mastery will seem a worthy price to pay.

3. Finally, as you begin to build and augment your core Italian vocabulary, *do not forget* the time-tested / experience-proven value of a "flash" system of memory-embedding, review, and self-testing! If you're computer adept, you can create such a tool within your PC with either a database or word-processing program, or by using one of the many notebook-type applications widely available. (At least one, in all likelihood, is embedded within your computer's operating system itself.) Alternatively—and portably!—hand-lettered 2x4 cards (English on one side, Italian with pronunciation key, gender code, and perhaps even pluralization on the other) never loses its effectiveness. In either case, the very act of transposing words into such a system is, in and of itself, a valuable aid to learning and retention. And of course, the value of a ready-review tool cannot be overstated.

FORMAT & SYMBOLOGY

All entries in this book follow the same pattern: extra space separates the English from the Italian or the Italian from the English portions of each word set; the English or Italian call word—depending on which word list you're consulting—is *always* shown in boldface roman and its Italian or English counterpart, in lightface roman. A phonetic representation of the Italian term's pronunciation is appended to each entry, within parentheses and in italics.

Throughout, masculine and feminine nouns are signified by an "*m.*" and an "*f.,*" and bigender terms by an "*m. & f.*" Occasionally, you man find an *n.* (for *noun*) to distinguish the noun meaning of the word from that of a different part of speech. Adjectives (always shown in masculine form!) are denoted by "(adj.)," positioned after the adjective itself; and verbs (always shown in infinitive form) by "(to)." Adverbs, conjunctions, pronouns, prepositions, and colloquial expressions are assumed to be self-identifying and / or unimportant to be so distinguished in the present context, and thus bear no such denotations.

In instances where several other noncognate English terms *also directly translate* to the Italian word, they will conjoin the cognate in immediate succession, separated by commas. Thus, the entry

abbreviate, abridge, shorten (to)   abbreviare (*ahb-breh-vee-AHR-reh*)

indicates that in addition to the closely cognate term at the far left, the annexed terms *are also directly translatable* by the Italian word. In more instances than not, a string of English words separated by commas will be closely related and synonymous within itself—*but not always!* For example, the following pair of entries

> **desert, wilderness**   deserto *m.* (*deh-ZEHR-toh*)
> **fund, bottom**   fondo *m.* (*FOHN-doh*)

illustrate that English terms with considerably different meanings can own the same translation in Italian. *The learner must be particularly alert to these word strings,* and remember to make a separate "flash" device entry for each elemental pair!

Similarly, where more than a single *Italian* word is a direct translation of the **English** term(s) at the right, a comma separates them. Again, the diligent student will provide him- / herself with a "flash" device for *every* word-pairing listed!

Symbolic markings in this book are as follows:

• Where a "bomb" (💣) symbol is appended to an entry, it refers to a subtle spelling or pronunciational differentiation between the English and Italian terms that, without remark, might be missed.
• Where space permits, arrows embracing a ➲word or fragment➲ indicate an important similarity (including location of the stressed syllable) between related Italian word forms. Where minor spelling differences are noted, the first character or syllable of a hyphenated -*fragment* is drawn from the original, and subsequent characters indicate the alteration. Thus the line

> **infante**   infante *m.* (*een-FAHN-teh*) ➲*f.* -ta➲

indicates that the noun exists in both genders and that the spelling of the feminine form is ***infanta.*** Similarly, the entry

> **negative**   negativa *f.* (*neh-gah-TEE-vah*) ➲(adj.) -vo➲

indicates that the noun-related English adjective *negative* is, in Italian, spelled ***negativo.*** And the entry

physics   fisica *f.* (*FEE-zee-kah*) ➲**physical** (adj.) -co➲   💣✷

demonstrates that the two entries need not be identical, but rather only closely related to warrant the memory-convenience of single-line placement.

• Arrows embracing an "*m.*," "*f.*," "*m. & f.*," or "(adj.)" denomination signify that the related word they enclose is *identical* to the listed term.

Thus, the entry

human   umano *m.* (*oo-MAH-noh*) ➲(adj.)➲

indicates that the Italian for English adjective ***human*** is spelled and pronounced exactly as is its related.

• In instances where the learner will gain from additional intelligence about a given term or closely related (but not necessarily cognate) term, it will be provided directly below the entry, flagged by the international "Information" symbol, ⓘ. *Because these notes contain an important wealth of "extra" vocabulary, data, and understanding, the learner is urged to pay careful attention to their content.*

ITALIAN PRONUNCIATION

Despite the astonishingly high volume of look- and sound-alike crossover between English and Italian, the two languages take a markedly different approach to some spelling and pronunciational fundamentals. While Italian speech contains virtually every sound present in English, it spells some of those sounds differently, and emphasizes others with greater or lesser intensity than is common in English. Additionally, Italian includes in its vocal repertoire several subtle intonations that are all but unknown in Britain and America—somewhat difficult, at first, for the English-accustomed mouth to effect—and that together produce a more undulant, more "musical" language than we're accustomed to hearing and speaking.

These distinctions and nuances must be understood and absorbed *from the outset* if real linguistic efficiency is to be attained. First, they must be recognized by the ear. Then, because vocabulary needs to be *read* to be most rapidly and deeply absorbed, they must become readily recognized on the printed page. Finally, they must become comfortably familiar and readily reproduced within the new Italian speaker's mouth. It cannot be overemphasized that *if any one of these steps is shortchanged, the learner's eventual conversational efficiency will be severely compromised* by erroneous assumption, misconception, or simple incapacity. An accurate reproduction of the "sound" of Italian *must* be accurately perceived by both the ear and the eye, and then effectively attained by the mouth.

The two-part, several-hour aural, visual, and vocal training program outlined below *will do more to advance the learner toward confident mastery of the sound of Italian than any other action he or she might undertake at this stage of development.* This book's users are urged in the strongest possible terms to follow its prescriptions before undertaking attainment of Italian vocabulary and understanding of the language's underlying grammatical structure. That is, do *not* begin amassing words until you've learned how they actually sound and "say." To do otherwise is to virtually guarantee the much more difficult and time-costly necessity of *un*learning incorrect assumptions and habits.

TRAINING YOUR EAR

From your own audio collection, or from a friend's, or from your local library, or the bookstore where you purchased this book, obtain a tape or CD that contains spoken Italian . . . and *listen* to it. That's all: just listen. Do not at this point try to learn words or phrases, or "understand" anything at all. *Just listen!* Turn off the phone, dim the lights, close your eyes, lean your head back, and simply let the speaker's voice wash over you for thirty minutes at least. Or, better yet, a full hour. Just *hearing* how Italian sounds.

The ideal recording for this ear-training exercise would be one that contains no English at all, but rather is exclusively the recounting, in Italian, of a story, or a news report, or a conversational interchange, or the reading of a book, and so forth. Such all-Italian recordings may be difficult to find in any but the largest metropolitan centers, however. So you'll very possibly end up with an instructional audio in which English words and phrases are spoken first, followed by their Italian translations spoken somewhat more slowly than normal. No matter: you're not now concerned with meaning at all, but rather simply with *sound.* Your sole objective is to become initially familiar with the essential sound, shape, intonation, stress, and rise-and-fall cadence of Italian vocalization. Nothing else.

At the conclusion of your listening session, take an hour's or a day's break, and then return to the recording and listen again. This time, be a bit more attentive not merely to the general sound and flow of Italian, but also to its constituent parts—particularly the "slightly odd" ones. Again, you're not listening to comprehend, but rather to simply hear and *notice*. Begin to notice, for example, both the "vowel breathiness" and consonantal distinctness of the speech . . . the gently rolled

R's . . . the emphasized *S*'s . . . the odd *TS* and "buzzy" *DZ* sounds . . . the often clearly doubled *D, F, K, L, P,* and *T* sounds.

Then listen again. And, if possible, yet again, until you've experienced a total of two to four hours of "immersion" listening. *Every minute you invest in such listening will pay itself back* in time saved from future uncertainty, confusion, and misunderstanding.

Count yourself done with *il pasto completo* ("the whole repast") when the general sound of Italian has begun to become so familiar and well imbedded in your mind that its few "weird" vocalizations cease to seem odd at all, and you can begin to confidently anticipate **both** the sound and the pace and feel of the language as it unfolds from word to word. You're beginning to get bored? Good! You're progressing: it's becoming "old hat!" And with that—*at least four* half- to full-hour listening sessions well embedded in your ear—you're done with initial "ear training," and ready to begin "seeing and saying" Italian.

If you have access to a PBS channel that regularly airs Italian-language news coverage or an Italian instructional series (usually at midnight and / or weekend hours), or to a cable system that offers extensive Italian programming, videotape and watch / listen to several such programs for several half-hour sessions at least. If you continue to do so, or repeatedly listen to your tapes / CDs during your vocabulary-building period, your understanding, competence, and skill will all be steadily strengthened, and your progress accelerated and solidified.

TRAINING YOUR EYES AND MOUTH

Open this book to any two-page spread in its midsection, and there, working at an unhurried pace *and pointedly ignoring* both the leftmost *boldface English word* on each line and the *lightface roman Italian word* that follows it, move slowly from entry to entry, *focusing solely on each term's phonetic representation.* That is, the parenthesized syllable-by-syllable rendition of each line's Italian word. Your objective is to attempt to vocalize that representation in mimicry of the type and quality of sound you've recently heard issue from your loudspeakers.

For now, pay no attention whatsoever to words, their actual spellings, or meanings. Neither should you be concerned with the "why" of any given pronunciation. Your sole concern should be with *sound*. That is, an attempt to match your mouth to the phonetic representation—pointedly including the ALL-CAPS accentuated syllable—given for each entry. It is likely that in some instances, particularly in your first few minutes of trying, your mouth will resist some of the constructions found—many *TS* and *TSY* combinations, for example. But press on: millions of people don't find these sounds arduous at all, and many thousands more successfully learn how to form them every year. There's nothing even vaguely "impossible" here; just a seeming abundance of strangeness and modest difficulty at the start. It will soon abate!

Similarly, do not waylay yourself with curiosity about such things as the overwhelming incidence of "breathy" *-AH* and *-EH* and *-OH* sounds . . . or the seemingly high incidence of doubled *R*'s . . . or the apparently inconsistent wandering of *S*'s back and forth across natural syllabic lines. Resolution of these curiosities will occur in due course; for the time being, simply accept that they're the way Italian actually works, and concentrate on trying to make your eye and mouth make sense of them. A detailed description of the pronunciation of each Italian alphabet character follows later in this chapter, and will be important to review and absorb. For the time being, however, your attention should be focused on whole-syllable sound production. The whys and wherefores of each letter's intonational value can wait a bit longer.

Remaining unhurried—and unconcerned, for the moment, whether you're getting it precisely right (you're almost certainly *not*, at least some of the time)—continue your out loud pronunciational effort from top to bottom of at least two full pages, and preferably three or four. Then call it quits for a while. Total investment thus far: between thirty and forty-five minutes. You may not realize it yet, but you've just made a huge step *into Italian!*

As soon as practicable, return to a spread of pages within this book's *Lista di termini identici e simili* (for variety's sake, pick a different alphabetical section this time) and repeat your out loud enunciation of the phonetics found there. This time, however, you are going to look carefully and repeatedly at the *Italian word* on each line before vocalizing its phonic representation. You still don't care about the word's *meaning* (although in many instances, now, that will be self-evident), but you do want to start to make a firm connection between the word's actual spelling and its phoneticized representation. Between spelling and sound, in short.

Oh oh! You've begun to notice some serious spelling and pronunciational anomalies, haven't you! *Ch-* combinations, for example, that are represented with a wildly un-English hard-*K* sound . . . and *ce-* and *ci-*constructions that move in the opposite direction, yielding an anti-intuitive *CH* sound! And *gh-* spellings that yield a hard-*G* sound without a hint of *H*-like exhalation to them . . . and all those *z*'s that are represented as possessing odd *TS* or *DZ* intonations. Can all this be *right?* Yes, it is . . . and soon enough, you'll begin to recognize the patterns. And soon, as well, understand why.

Continue your reading-and-pronouncing effort for, again, two full pages at least, and preferably several more. By now, you should be beginning to master the production of some of the more difficult sounds specified by the phonetic code. When you're satisfied with your progress (again, a half-hour minimum is advised), take another break before returning to. . . .

Give yourself an initial *acceleration test*. Again selecting a random beginning point and again completely ignoring both the whole-word spelling and the term's meaning, pick a single two- or three-syllable word as your starting point, and rather than merely attempting to pronounce it as the phonetic guide suggests, practice doing so at a faster and faster rate, until it's emerging from your mouth as a unified whole rather than a jerky syllable-by-syllable construction. This may seem particularly difficult at first, especially in the case of words with consonants on both sides of syllabic breaks, *both of which consonants need to be expressed!* And those doubled- and tripled-across-break *R*'s are the typically gentle Italian "roll" or "trill" of that letter, which it would also be good to start trying to master. And the seemingly misplaced *S*'s you've so often noticed are your signal that in Italian that sound often assumes the expressively extended "almost-hiss" you earlier noted in your tape-listening. And those other all-important doubled-across-break consonants are not only a reflection of letter-doubling itself, but also of the fact that Italian distinctly *double-pronounces* such constructions, rather than merely emphasizing them with increased volume as

Italian Pronunciation   5

we generally do in English. Some of these will seem excruciatingly difficult to effectively enunciate "at speed," at first—a set of double-*B*'s, for example, being almost a Mount Everest of oral difficulty! But keep at it, and slowly, surely, you *will* begin to become not only the master of virtually any construction that falls beneath your eye, but moreover a *rapid*-master, capable of expressing whole words rather than slowly enunciated syllable-by-syllable constructs.

Keep at it, on your one chosen word, until a dozen or more increasingly rapid repetitions have forced your mouth into the required shapes and movements to get it spoken with quick confidence. Then move on to another word, and another and another, repeating in each case the same progress from slow / careful pronunciation to confident rapid-fire *expression* of the whole-unit term. That is, with a smoothly ever-diminishing space between syllables. Just as your outloud reading of the words of *this* English paragraph would be, through years of familiarity and everyday practice, essentially without intraword breaks of any kind, so also do you want to attain the point where your expression of Italian terms will be similarly unified and unpaused except between the whole words themselves.

You're undoubtedly some distance from that level of expertise still—but you *are* headed in that direction! One word at a time. Over and over. And soon, you'll find that each new word—even those really difficult five-, six-, and seven-syllable monsters with which Italian is replete—becomes all the easier to attain and really, deeply master. Hard? Not really. All it takes, like any other skill, is *practice . . . practice . . . practice!* For thirty minutes . . . an hour . . . maybe two.

And by that point you really *will* be becoming comfortable and expert—not only beginning to hear Italian words as they're spoken in everyday conversation, but moreover noticing that these pleasing sounds are issuing from *your* mouth and understanding! It's an important point to have achieved!

In sum, in a half-dozen hours or so you've not only *absorbed* a new sound structure, but you've also begun to be comfortable with its use—and you're almost ready, now, to begin building your cognate-based Italian vocabulary with accuracy and confidence. This chapter's next section will finalize and solidify your understanding of the basics of Italian pronunciation, and it will leave you fully ready to begin absorbing *language*.

"SAYING" THE ITALIAN ALPHABET

As you progressed through the foregoing exercises, you noticed numerous spelling and pronunciational oddities that need to be comprehended at "letter-level" to complete your overall understanding of Italian speech. In considerable detail, then, the following will resolve what mysteries remain.

Italian officially possesses, now, precisely the same alphabet as does English, although five of the letters thereof are neither native to the language nor often employed, except in the representation of nonnative words. Specifically, the letters *J, K, W, X,* and *Y* are all but invisible in the Italian lexicon, *although the English-equivalent sounds that we associate with those characters are richly abundant in the language.* As you have begun to appreciate in the course of the foregoing exercises, those sounds are produced, in Italian, by other letters and letter-combinations.

The full Italian alphabet, together with each letter's phonetic name-pronunciation and representative contextual pronunciation(s), is listed below. The listing sequence is from easiest-to-absorb (by an English speaker), through somewhat-trickier, to really problematic, potentially confusing, and most-difficult-to-master.

The 16 "Easy" Letter Sounds

A (*AH*) The Italian alphabet's initial letter yields one of the easiest and least variable of all pronunciations. Simply put, it is *always and everywhere throughout Italy* pronounced like an English "soft *a*," as in English *lava* or *mama*. Italian possesses all the other sounds that we English speakers draw from our widely variable *A* (such as in *bather* and *matter* and *water*), but those sounds are never represented in Italian by the letter *A*. So fix this one easily and firmly in mind: "Italian *A* as in *father*." Always.

B (*BEE*) Another easy one. *B* in Italian is pronounced identically as it is in English, in all circumstances. "Italian *B* as in *baby*."

D (*DEE*) Still easy. *D* in Italian carries precisely the same value as it does in English. "Italian *D* as in *dear*."

F (*EHF-feh*) Easy again! The Italian *F* is identical in value to its English counterpart. "Italian *F* as in *fun*."

J (*ee-LOONG-gah*) This letter has almost disappeared from the native Italian lexicon, and is now used almost exclusively in imported-to-Italian nomenclature. In the rare instances where it is employed, it generally pronounces as it does in the donating tongue. Usually, it is safe to pronounce this letter as in English. Thus: "Italian *J* as in *jazz*."

K (*KAHP-pah*) As with the foregoing, *K* is a rarely seen import to the Italian alphabet. In all cases it pronounces exactly the same way as does its English equivalent. "Italian *K* as in *king*."

L (*EHL-leh*) Widely used in Italian, *L* is pronounced as in English. "Italian *L* as in *love*."

M (*EHM-meh*) As in English. "Italian *M* as in *mother*."

N (*EHN-neh*) As in English. "Italian *N* as in *nannie*."

P (*PEE*) Exactly as in English: lips together, and puff it out! "Italian *P* as in *prince*."

Q (*KOO*) As in English, the Italian *Q* owns an essentially "*K*" sound, and is <u>always</u> found in combination with a *u* plus a second vowel that follows; that is, *qua, que, qui,* or *quo* triplets. In practical terms, these can all be pronounced as in similar English combinations, with a "*KW*" sound blending into the second vowel. Some Italian dialects tend to slightly "break" *qua* and *qui* combinations into a *KOO* + vowel construction, thus pronouncing *quarto* as (*koo-AHR-toh*) rather than (*QWAHR-toh*), and so forth. Said "at speed," however, this is a barely detectable subtlety. So relax with the safe generalization: "Italian *Q* as in *queen*."

T (*TEE*) As in English. Exactly and always. "Italian *T* as in *truth*."

V (*VOO*) Exactly as it is in English. "Italian *V* as in *victory*."

W (*DOHP-pyah-voo*) Nonexistent in the native-Italian lexicon, this letter occurs as an import only. In those rare instances, as throughout most of Europe, it is almost invariably pronounced like an English **V**. Thus a bartender will readily understand a request for *whiskey*, but very probably ask what kind of (*VEE- skee*) you want. "Italian *W* as in '*I vant to show you my etchings*.'"

X (*EEKS*) Nonnative to Italian. Rarely seen except in words derived from Greek or Latin, or, more recently, other tongues. Generally pronounces as in English. "Italian *X* as in *extra*."

Y (*EEP-see-lohn*) Although *Y* now officially "exists" in the Italian alphabet, its use is limited to the spelling of a very few imported words, and pronounced as in the donating tongue.

The 2 "Tricky" Letter Sounds

E (*EH*) The Italian *E* has two sounds: an open and a close (or closed) sound. When the *E* is open, it's pronounced as in English words *bed, met, petty*. Some Italian words with an open *E* are *letto* (*leht-toh*), *bed*; *bello* (*behl-loh*) *beautiful*; *sette* (*seht-teh*), *seven*. When it's close, the *E* is pronounced as in the English word w<u>ai</u>t. Some Italian words with a closed *E* are *bere* (*beh-reh*), *to drink*; *sete* (*seh-teh*), *thirst*; *neve* (*neh-veh*), *snow*. As you can see, we are using the same letters *(EH)* to represent both sounds: one, because the difference between the two sounds is subtle and, therefore, difficult for someone who is having his / her first encounter with the language; two, because the explanation would be too complicated at this stage; three, because open and close pronunciations will start coming automatically by the positioning of the letter in the word. The two sounds are both present in the Italian word *bene* (*beh-neh*), *well*. "Italian *E* as in *bene*."

I (*EE*) Most of the time, the Italian *I* is easy: on its own, when not combined with another vowel, it pronounces like an English "long *e*," as in *lien* or *machine*. Thus: *abilità* (*ah-bee-lee-TAH*), *ability; dissimile* (*dees-SEE-mee-leh*), *dissimilar*.

However, in those instances where an *I* serves as the lead letter of a two-vowel combination (technically, a "diphthong"), significant change occurs. Specifically . . .

• **IA**, in which the two letters combine and condense in a severe way their individual pronunciations (*ee* and *ah*) into a unified single-syllable *yah* intonation. Thus: **academy**—accademia (*ahk-kah-DEH-myah*), NOT (*ahk-kah-deh-MEE-ah*); and **flame**—fiamma (*FYAHM-mah*), NOT (*fee-AHM-mah*)

• **IE** follows the same pattern, yielding *yeh*. Thus: **ambient**—ambiente (*ahm-BYEHN-teh*), NOT (*ahm-bee-EHN-teh*); and **convenience**—convenienza (*kohn-veh-NYEHN-tsah*), NOT (*kohn-veh-nee-EHN-tsah*)

• **IO**, similarly, pronounces *yoh*. As in **decision**—decisione (*deh-chee-SYOH-neh*), NOT (*dee-chee-see-OH-neh*); and **obsession**—ossessione (*ohs-sehs-SYOH-neh*), NOT (*ohs-sehs-see-OH-neh*)

• **IU**, completing the established pattern, pronounces *yoo*. Thus: **refusal**—rifiuto (*ree-FYOO-toh*), NOT (*ree-fee-OO-toh*); and **conjugal**—coniugale (*koh-nyoo-GAH-leh*), NOT (*koh-nee-oo-GAH-leh*)

These diphthong exceptions aside, the "*I* = long *e*" pronunciation is invariably in effect. "Italian *I* as in **bier**."

O (*OH*) The Italian *O*, like the Italian *E,* has both an open and a close (closed) pronunciation. When it's pronounced open, it sounds like the *O* in the English word **strong**. Italian words with an open *O* are **porta** (*pohr-tah*), *door;* **posta** (*poh-stah*), *mail;* **porto** (*pohr-toh*), *harbor.* When it's pronounced closed, it sounds like the *O* in the English word **hope** or **cozy**. For the same reasons as in the case of the letter *E,* above, we are representing both sounds with the letters *OH*. The Italian word **poco** has first an open *O* and then a close one. Thus: "Italian *O* as in **poco**."

R (*EHR-reh*) The Italian *R* is essentially the same as in English, with the notable distinction of often being "rolled" or "trilled," except in some instances where it is immediately followed by a consonant or the vowel *i*. *R*'s in words with one or more *R*'s in differents spots of the word rarely roll more than one or two at most. In most cases, the Italian *R*-roll, while distinct and unmistakable, is softer and "less aggressive" than found in many other European languages; an angry or emphatic Italian will roll his *R*'s with special vigor, however!

Nothing so surely and immediately denotes a nonnative speaker as his or her consistent failure to "roll." As an aid to learning this very fundamental Italian sound and practice, many *R*'s in the phonetic guidance in this book are doubled or tripled, indicating not that they are to be double-pronounced (as are all other double-spelled consonants), but rather "rolled."

U (OO)   The Italian *U* produces, *in most instances*, a sound like an English "double *o*," as in **boot, root,** or **toot.** However, when directly followed by another vowel, the diphthong usually coalesces into a mild English "*w*-flavored" intonation. Thus the all-important **buono** (good) is pronounced (*BWOH-noh*), NOT (*boo-OH-noh*). Another example is the adjective **inadeguato** (inadequate), pronounced (*ee-nah-deh-GWAH-toh*), NOT (*een-ah-deh-goo-AH-toh*). The learner will discover that most such constructions "form themselves" for oral convenience, and that the variation can generally be assumed to be a self-generating exception to the otherwise-reliable "double-*o*" rule.

The 5 "Difficult" Letter Sounds

H (AHK-kah)   The Italian *H* is a uniquely influential letter that needs to be well understood before we progress onward to its coconspirators in complexity, *C* and *G*. Indeed, it can be argued that without "*H*- understanding," a significant fraction of the language's pronunciation will remain a perplexing, paradoxical mystery. This is because, in and of itself, *the widely used Italian H is not a "pronounced" letter at all(!), but rather serves only as a symbolic indicator of the manner in which a consonant that immediately precedes it is to be enunciated.* Read that sentence again, and understand clearly: **by itself, the Italian H is without pronunciational value whatsoever.** It's without sound. Instead, it is a backward-pointing "sign" or "signal" indicative of something other than its own intrinsic sound value. Which is nil.

In Italian, in short, the *H* is always silent. *Always!* Even in imported-into-Italian words such as **hamburger, hobby,** and **hotel**, the letter *H* is without pronunciational value, merit, or effect. For example, the three foregoing words are pronounced by Italians as (*AHM-boor-*

gehr), *(AAH-bee)*, and *(oh-TEL)*. Despite what we'd normally expect in so airy, so heavily aspirated Italian, an *H* does *not* indicate an extra measure of soft breathiness. In an Italian mouth, an *H* remains utterly silent. Completely inert. Wholly without "air." *Without exception!*

Still, for all its silence, it is not without importance. Indeed, it owns a very great significance wherever it occurs in a native Italian word. Simply put, it tells the reader or speaker *how the preceding C or G* (which, except in imported words, are the only two letters that ever precede an *H*) is *to be sounded.* Nothing more. And nothing less.

Repeating for emphasis: the Italian *H* exists solely to "say something" about **another** letter. Specifically, about the *C* or *G* that precedes it. Aside from bearing this "message," it might as well not exist. It has no value of its own. Do NOT express it vocally. Ever!

Alas for English speakers, what the *H* "tells" its reader or speaker about that preceding letter is, for us, often anti-intuitive in the extreme. Viz: *exactly the opposite* of what we'd most readily expect in the generally "soft" Italian context. That is, instead of indicating that the preceding consonant is to be softened or "aerated," the Italian *H* says just the reverse. "Pronounce the *C* or *G* ahead of me with solid firmness and no hint of an airy, hissing, or resounding overtone," it says. "Do *not* give that preceding *C* a *soft-and-breathy C* sound (as in English *champion* or *cheese* or *cherry*), but rather, give it a hard *K*-like pronunciation (as in English *cap* or *cook* or *cuticle*)!" And "Do *not* allow that preceding *G* to get all mushy-gooey-windy, with an English *J*-like sound, but insure that it comes out of your mouth with a firm roof-of-the-mouth *G*-like intonation (as in English **ghastly** or **ghetto** or **ghost**)."

In sum, the Italian *H* directs us to do precisely the opposite of what we'd most often do in English . . . or what we'd *especially* assume so-breathy Italian to do! It tells us (1) to ignore itself completely, and (2) to insure that the preceding consonant is "firm" rather than "soft."

Completing and compounding all the foregoing is the fact that often, when it comes to *C*'s and *G*'s, *the absence of an Italian H very often indicates that an English-like H sound is to be inserted!!!* Thus bringing full circle the complexity alluded to at the outset of this long discussion. It is, at first, a confusingly difficult reversal-of-expectations to get on top of! But once you've got it well and firmly in mind, you can congratulate yourself on having surmounted one of Italian pronunciation's highest hurdles. The additional detail provided at *C* and *G*, below, will complete the circle. . . .

C (*CHEE*) As previously implied, the Italian *C* is a troublesome letter indeed: the producer of one of Italian's most maddeningly variable sounds. And not only variable, but often quite opposite in pronunciational value from that which we assign to this letter in English speech. In summary:

Italian *CA, CO, CU,* and *C-consonant* combinations *including CH* (!), yield an English *K* sound. It's the inclusion of the *CH* combo that is most troublesome to English speakers, of course, who are accustomed to that combination's almost-always production of a soft, aspirated sound (as in *chap, cheap, chip, chop,* and *chum*). In Italian, the *CH* linkup produces **precisely the opposite** of what we're accustomed to: a hard English *K* as in **keep** or **kill**. This sound reversal, in conjunction with the other sound reversals noted directly below, makes the Italian *C* one of the most fundamental of all difficulties faced, and consequently one of the most critical that the learner absorb and incorporate into his consciousness from the outset.

No less "backward" feeling, the Italian *CE* combination yields a surprising English *CH* sound, as exemplified by our **cello**—which of course is not "our" word at all, but rather an Italian term that, amazingly, we have brought into English with its native pronunciation intact. So while anti-intuitive, at least the *CE* combo is easy to keep in mind: "*CE* as in **cello** (*CHEHL-loh*)."

Continuing the anti-intuitive (for us English speakers) theme, Italian *CI* combinations also produce the unexpected *CH* sound! Thus, while we pronounce the word *cinema* as (*SIN-eh-mah*) in English, in Italian the same word is pronounced (*CHEE-neh-mah*) . . . *circa* is our (*SIR-kah*) and an Italian's (*CHEER-kah*), . . . and our *citadel* (*SIT-ah-dell*)is their **cittadella** (*cheet-tah-DEHL-lah*).

The Italian *C*'s final twist regards those instances in which it is doubled. In most instances, the *CC* combination pronounces, as expected, with a distinct double-*K* sound, as in **vecchio** (*VEHK-kyoh*), meaning *old*. But . . .

CCE and *CCI* combinations give the initial *C* a *tee* sound, before adding on the *CH* pronunciation that would otherwise be expected per the citations above. Thus **successo** (*soot-CHEHS-soh*), English *success.*

Because *C* is so widely employed in Italian (as in English), but with a so-often notably different result, the serious learner must make mastery of this letter a primary objective. It is, arguably, the least understood and most often pronunciationally botched of all Italian characters; don't be among the substantial majority of visitors who completely misunderstand its effect!

G (*JEE*) The Italian *G*, bless it's wicked soul, is similar to the *C* in having little reliable personality of its own, and rather being largely at the mercy of its context to "make up its mind" about what it wants to sound like. In a word, it's a problematic letter in the extreme.

Italian *GA*, *GO*, *GU,* and *G-consonant* (including *GH*) combinations pronounce like an ordinary English "firm *g.*" That is, an expulsion formed by the midtongue's stoppage-then-release against the hard palate—as in English **gate**, **gothic**, **gum**, **glove**, **ghetto**, or **ghost**.

In Italian *GE-consonant* and *GI-consonant* combinations, however, the letter *G* assumes an English *J*-like sound, just as it does in many English words—*gem, general, gin* and *giraffe*, for example. In these cases, the *J*-like sound is followed by the succeeding vowel value and it's succeeding consonantal sound. Thus **generico** (*jeh-NEHR-ree-koh*), English *generic*, or **gigante** (*jee-GAHN-teh*), English *giant.* The latter word, note, exemplifies both Italian *G*'s essential sounds.

When a *GI* combination extends to double-vowel length, as in *GIA, GIO*, or *GIU* (i.e., *G* + diphthong: *GIA, GIO,* or *GIU*), however, the *I* value drops out of the *J*-sounding mix, yielding a *JAH, JOH,* or *JOO* sound precedent to the following consonant. Thus the ubiquitous **giorno** (day) does **NOT** include pronunciation of the *I*, but rather comes out as (*JOHR-noh*). This "drop out" is one of the trickiest of Italian pronunciational oddities for many learners to remember, owing to the great frequency and generally immense importance of the *I* in Italian spelling. But it can't be avoided: "*GI* + second vowel = silent *I*."

And we're not done with *G* yet! In the not-uncommon *GL* + *I* combination (*GLI*), it's the *G* itself that disappears from pronunciational effect, yielding only a residual *LYEE* sound, as exemplified by the the sound of the letters -*lli*- in English words **million** and **scallion**. When *GLI* is followed by vowel *a, e,* or *o,* we get sounds *lyah*, *lyeh* and *lyoh*, respectively. Thus **biglietto** (*bee-LYHET-toh*), *ticket*; and **bagaglio** (*bah-GAH-lyoh*), *luggage.*

Similarly, a *GN* combination also results in the *G*'s vocal disappearance, yielding an English "*NY*" sound, as heard in English **onion**. Thus **campagna** (*kahm-PAH-nyah*), *campaign.*

The Italian *G*, alas, is common enough to make early mastery of its variant complexities highly advisable. The latter two problems are relatively easy, but to get the other *G*- complexities well in mind, eye, and mouth will require more effort. Don't delay!

S (*EHS-seh*) In pronunciational terms, the Italian *S* isn't as difficult to master as the two foregoing troublemakers—but it's not far behind! It produces one of two sounds, equivalent to an English "s" or "z," although in many cases real certainty regarding which pronunciation belongs where can only be determined on a word-by-word basis.

Several certainties *do* exist. An Italian double-*S* is *always* reliably "ess-sy" and entirely free of buzzy-**z** intonation. Similarly, an *S* + vowel at the beginning of a word *always* pronounces as in English **safe**, **serene**, **simple**, **soft**, or **supple**. And an *S* followed by -*c, -f, -p, -q,* or -*t*, regardless of where that construct occurs within a word, generates a standard English *S* sound as well. (The learner who creates his/her own c-f-p-q-t acronym as a memory aid will profit well from the exercise; the author's mnemonic in this regard, alas, cannot be cited in polite company!) It is also certain that whenever the Italian sibilant *S* is expressed, regardless of its singular or doubled status within the spelling of the word, it is done with slightly more emphasis than is accorded to any other undoubled Italian consonant except *r*. Thus the "moving around" of *S*'s in many phonetic guides, to whatever syllabic position forces the speaker's mouth toward a "natural" emphasis of this troublesome letter.

Now the difficulties begin! Usually when an Italian *S* immediately precedes a *b, d, g, l, m, n, r,* or *v*, or often when it's followed by a vowel, it is pronounced with a *z* sound, just as that letter pronounces that intonation in such English words as *please, rose,* and *museum.* And Italian nouns and adjectives ending in a *-so, -sa, -se* construct *often* pronounce with a *z* sound as well—e.g., *sposo m.* (*SPOH-zoh*), *spouse / husband;* and *preciso* (adj.) (*preh-CHEE-zoh*), *precise*—although these are notable exceptions to the more common *s* intonation. There is, alas, no reliable rule that governs these variants; the early learner who forgets to substitute a *z* for an *s* sound in one or another of these troublesome instances, or makes an incorrect transposition of sounds, will hardly be held to account by a native Italian, however. Regionalism plays a role here, and even *they* misspeak their language sometimes—as many English speakers garble their own with regularity!

We're not done with our *S* troubles yet, however. For the letter assumes distinctly different (although now, reliably unbuzzed) sounds when immediately followed by a *-c* in combination with various other letters. Thus:

> *SC* + *E* or *SC* + *I* = SH sound
> *SC* + *A, SC* + *O,* or *SC* + *U* = *SK* sound
> *SCH* + *E* or *SCH* + *I* = *SK* sound

Clear as mud? Well, at least there were those sixteen "easy" letters!

Z (*DZEH-tah*) Finally, the important, widely occurring Italian Z (at least fiftyfold more common than in the English lexicon) is another troublesome letter, in that *it rarely pronounces with even a hint of an English "z" sound* (that is, as a simple "buzzing long *e*"), yet doesn't follow an invariably dependable pronunciational rule of its own, either.

In many instances, an Italian Z pronounces, most unexpectedly, like an English *TS* construct, such as is made at the end of (English) words like *forts, meats,* or *weights.* Because this *TS* sound invariably occurs within the body of the Italian word (where such a sound construct *never* occurs in English), it may initially seem quite odd and difficult to master in midword position. A few moments of concentrated practice, however, will make the sound both easy to produce and "natural" feeling in the mouth.

An apt example of this anti-intuitive (to us!) pronunciation can be found within the word *aberrazione* (aberration), which issues from an Italian mouth as (*ah-behr-rah-TSYOH-neh*). No buzz at all, but rather just a "tee-essy" sound. As decidedly un-English as it might be imagined.

It follows, of course, that when an Italian *Z* is doubled—which is very often indeed—it is not an English *z* sound that repeats, but rather the *T* portion of the single-*Z* pronunciation. That is, the first of the *Z* pair is assigned a sharply ending *T* enunciation, with the second *Z* "repeating" in the form of the full *TS* construct described above. The pronunciation of this double-*Z* occurrence is best exemplified by the "universal" word *pizza*—arguably the most widely known Italian term in existence, from Rome to London to Kansas City to Hong Kong. From an Italian's mouth, this delicious word issues as (*PEET-tsah*), which notably includes the millisecond break within the *T* sound that effectively doubles its enunciation. Most Americans and Brits, of course, tend to elide the second *T*, pronouncing a slightly lazier (*PEET-suh*); and a few, yes, pronounce what seems to them a more "logical" (*PEET-zuh*). Still, it's gratifying to hear just how often that word *is* pronounced fully correctly, even thousands of miles from the sunny land where that food originated—and is still and forever a staple, sold out of very nearly as many shops as purvey the pie in New York City!

In other instances, an Italian *Z* will assume a subtle *dz* sound, as in the English word *adz*. This pronunciation is *more often than not* found in Italian terms that begin with *Z*—e.g., **zebra** (*DZEH-brah*)—but it may also occur within a word, both singly and in a doubled form—as in **zanzara** (*dsahn-DSAH-rah*), *gnat;* and **parabrezza** (*pah-rah-BREHD-dzah*), *windshield.*

"SAYING" ITALIAN WORDS

Compared to the complexities encountered immediately above, several summary generalizations about Italian words in general can be easily stated, understood, and mastered.

Letters doubled in Italian spelling are always—*always!!*—doubled in pronunciational value. There are no exceptions to this rule: Italian double letters really "mean" something! While some teachers suggest that doubles must be invariably and distinctly double-*pronounced*, the fact is that many doubles occur amidst constructions that make double-pronunciation almost impossible for the nonnative mouth to produce, without slowing to a near halt. In those instances, a lengthened *emphasis*, at least, must be produced to remain true to the word's actual pronunciational value. A single example will suffice: in an English mouth, the Italian word **mamma** is far more often than not elided to (*MAH-mah*); to an Italian, that is a nonword. Rather, he / she would very distinctly intone (*MAHM-mah*). And while consonants represent at least 90 percent of all double-letter spellings, the rare instances of doubled vowels are also subject to the same rule. Thus **zii** (*TSEE-ee*), plural of **zio** *m.* (uncle); and **veemente** (adj.) (*veh-eh-MEHN-teh*), *vehement,* are definitely nonelided. Yet again: there are *no* exceptions to this rule. It is absolute!

While an Italian word's stressed syllable can occur at any point within its structure, by far the most common accenting occurs in the penultimate—the next-to-last—syllable. The learner who fails to note which words deviate from this standard, and thus blithely pronounces *all* words with stress next-to-the-end, will be a much cruder speaker than need be. But at least he/she will be right more often than not.

Finally, while Italian words, like English, are composed of syllabic subunits, they are in the end organic "whole" things rather than merely a haltingly strung-together assemblage of individual sounds. The learner's objective must always be to *unify* every word by reducing syllabic pausing to a minimum. With extensive "repeat and repeat" practice of every word being brought into his or her new vocabulary, as urged earlier in this chapter, the student will enjoy a steady increase in both competence, comprehension, confidence, and communicability.

ITALIAN GRAMMAR

Simplicity, of course, cannot be expected within any tongue's grammatical makeup, pointedly including Italian's. Between its nonintuitive assignment of noun genders, multiplicity of plural forms, wide variety of general, definite, indefinite, and partitive articles, miniuniverse of pronoun forms, preposition-and-article combinations and condensations, various forms of adverbs, deeply complex and often irregular verb conjugations—and yes, from time to time a flagrant inconsistency and / or self-contradiction—the intricacies of Italian grammar can be almost as taxing to fully master as those of any language extant.

Owing to the complexities just described, it cannot be within the scope of this book—which is, at root, basically an "easy" vocabulary builder rather than a comprehensive instructional text—to offer an all-inclusive, highly detailed analysis of the structure and rules of Italian grammar. Full comprehension of *any* language's convoluted and often-inconsistent architecture can only be gained by intensive study with knowledgeable teachers and / or scholarly texts addressing and illustrating that issue alone. And practice, practice, practice! The latter in the form of real, extended conversational experience—preferably "on the ground," within that tongue's home milieu.

As a guide to understanding Italian's basic grammatical underpinnings, however, a general and necessarily limited overview of its formal edifice is offered on the following pages. Enough, surely, to enable the attentive learner, utilizing the substantial "easy" cognate vocabulary he or she gains from within these pages, to become an *effective* communicator, if not, yet, a fluently "correct" one. To attain the latter status, the ambitious learner's attention must be directed to more comprehensive and detailed instruction than can be afforded here.

NOUNS
Gender

Italian nouns—words that identify persons, places, and things—are unlike those of English only in that the vast majority (better than 99 percent) are mysteriously assigned a "gender." That is, they are identified as either "masculine" or "feminine," with far-reaching implications regarding their proper use, correct pluralization, and the form that attached modifiers must take.

NOUN UNDERSTANDING #1: **Linguistic, or grammar, gender bears no relationship whatsoever to "sexuality"** except in the case of animate entities, where nature and grammar coincide (son—figlio, father—padre, **lupo**—wolf, **gatto**—cat, are masculine; **daughter**—figlia, **mother**—madre, **[she] wolf**—lupa, **[she] cat**—gatta, are feminine), as in Latin, from which Italian derives. However, in all other respects and since Latin, an Italian noun's gender does not arise from any intrinsically "male" or "female" quality owned or implied by the word, but rather is rooted in an abstract, arbitrary, and often illogical-seeming standard lost in the mists of bygone time.

The masculine or feminine designation of a noun, in short, has absolutely nothing to do with "manliness" or "femininity," but rather is merely a convention that the learner must accept and master on a word-by-word basis. To fail to do so is to severely retard his or her advancement toward correct fluency.

NOUN UNDERSTANDING #2: **Neither a noun's spelling or pronunciation is absolutely indicative of its gender.** To be sure, because a preponderance of Italian masculine-singular nouns end with the letter -*o* (e.g., **access**—accesso, **baboon**—babbuino, **cactus**—cacto), it's generally safe to assume an *o*-ending term to be masculine. Similarly, *most* nouns ending in -*a* (e.g., **defense**—difesa, **ecology**—ecologia, **fame**—fama) are feminine. Nouns that conclude with an -*e* can be either masculine or feminine (e.g., **tooth**—dente, **foot**—piede, **sea**—mare, are masculine; **snow**—neve, **ship**—nave, are feminine). These are merely high-odds *likelihoods*, however: enough exceptions exist (e.g., **hand**—mano is feminine; **poet**—poeta is masculine; **ardor**—ardore is masculine) to warrant studious *learning* rather than assuming!

Italian singular nouns that end in -*i* can be either masculine or feminine on a roughly equal basis: only a slight plurality of these are feminine.

Italian nouns ending in -*u* or a *consonant* are extremely rare, are *always* terms imported from other languages (including ancient Latin), and are far more likely than not to have been assigned to the masculine side of the ledger.

Among the large body of "variable" nouns, mostly referent to *people and animals*, that can assume either a masculine or feminine form (and spelling) depending upon their reference to an identifiably male or female person or animal, are words such as a **male professor,** which is *un professore,* while his female counterpart is *una professoressa; a boy baby* is *un bambino,* while his twin sister is *una bambina.* And so on. Even this small island of gender-rationality loses much of its allure, however, in view of the existence of dual-gender (herein, *m., f.*) terms such as **apprentice** (apprendista) and **artist** (artista), which do not assume a different spelling in reference to male or female (although their modifiers must!).

The learner, then, is left with but two options. Either he or she can largely ignore the issue of gender (upon which hangs considerably more than mere "noun correctness" or the lack thereof), and be content to speak a very rough and often-incorrect form of Italian, *or determine to laboriously memorize the gender assigned to each and every noun as it is learned.* The latter course is highly recommended, although it is much more demanding. Only with proper gender well in mouth will real admiration be earned! Graceful fluency *depends* upon noun correctness.

Pluralization

NOUN UNDERSTANDING #3: **In Italian, pluralization is never accomplished by the addition of an -*s*.** Instead, a more complicated schema prevails, requiring consideration of *both the noun's gender and spelling* to achieve a proper plural form. In brief:

• *THE VAST MAJORITY* of Italian masculine nouns pluralize by changing their -*o* ending to the letter -*i*. Thus, (one) **object**—oggetto becomes (plural) **objects**—oggetti; **pagan**—pagano becomes **pagans**—pagani; and **saint**—santo becomes **saints**—santi.

• *VIRTUALLY ALL* Italian feminine singular nouns ending in an unstressed -*a* pluralize by changing that ending to -*e*. Thus (one) **staircase**—scala becomes (plural) **staircases**—scale; **table**—tavola becomes **tables**—tavole; and **urn**—urna becomes **urns**—urne.

• *VIRTUALLY ALL* Italian masculine *and* feminine singular nouns ending in -*e* pluralize by changing the termination to -*i*. Thus **tooth**—dente becomes **teeth**—denti; **foot**—piede becomes **feet**—piedi; and **ship**—nave becomes **ships**—navi, and so forth.

• *VIRTUALLY ALL* Italian single-syllable nouns (which are rare), singulars ending in -*i* (rare) or -*ie*, singulars ending in a stressed -à or –ù, and singulars of foreign origin (rare) *remain unchanged in plural form.*

There are a relatively small number of oddball and anomalous nouns, of course, that "break the rules," and for which pluralization is handled on a different basis than those outlined above. A small body of masculine -*o* enders, for example, pluralize by changing to -*a and becoming feminine* (!), as was exemplified previously in the cases of *egg / eggs* and *fruit / fruits*. Another small number make substantial, whole-syllable spelling changes between singular and plural forms. And some undergo a substantial alteration of stressing between the two forms. For the most part, however, such treatments are rare enough to be ignored in the early stage of learning; excepting only the two pairings noted above, no such terms are included in this book's compendia. In advanced teaching texts and reference works, such atypical pluralizations are pointedly highlighted.

ARTICLES
Definite Articles

Here's another instance of English owning a much simpler linguistic subsystem than prevails in Italian: we simply say "**the**" to indicate a specific person or persons, place or places, thing or things. End of story: a single all-purpose designator covers it all. Italian, however, requires no fewer than seven (!) terms to fulfill the same function, the correct one for any given context depending upon both the gender and singular / plural status of the following noun to which it refers. Thus the following variety:

The One Dual-Gender Definite Article:

- **"The"** preceding masculine singular *or* feminine singular nouns *beginning with a vowel* is: *l'*, without an intervening space. Thus, **the acrobat**—l'acrobato; **the opera**—l'opera.

The Other Masculine Definite Articles:

- **"The"** preceding masculine singular nouns *beginning with any consonant except* z- *or an* s-consonant combination: *il*. Thus, **the bandit**—il bandito; **the navigator**—il navigatore.

- **"The"** preceding masculine singulars *beginning with a* z- *or an* s-consonant combination: *lo*. Thus, **the uncle**—lo zio; **the scandal**—lo scandalo.

- **"The"** preceding masculine plural nouns *beginning with a vowel: gli*. Thus, **the electrodes**—gli elettrodi; **the occupants**—gli occupanti.

NOTE: The once standard practice of employing *gl'* as the definite article preceding masculine plurals beginning with vowel *i* is now considered obsolete.

- **"The"** preceding masculine plurals *beginning with any consonant except* z- *or an* s-consonant combination: *i*. Thus, **the banquets**—i banchetti; **the designers**—i disegnatori.

- **"The"** preceding masculine plurals *beginning with* z- *or an* s-consonant combination: *gli*. Thus, **the scientists**—gli scienziati; **the zephyrs**—gli zeffiri.

The Other Feminine Definite Articles:

- **"The"** preceding feminine singular nouns *beginning with any consonant:* <u>la</u>. Thus, **the candle**—la candela; **the mother**—la madre.

- **"The"** preceding feminine plurals *beginning with consonants or vowels:* <u>le</u>. Thus, **the windows**—le finestre; **the stores**—le botteghe; **the actions**—le azioni; **the objections**—le obiezioni; **the elections**—le elezioni; **the emotions**—le emozioni.

Note: **"The"** = <u>l'</u> (without an intervening space) before feminine plurals beginning with *e* has been falling more and more out of use, and it's by now considered obsolete. Thus: **the elections**— le elezioni (*Not* l'elezioni); **the emotions**—le emozioni (*Not* l'e-mozioni).

All of the foregoing definite articles are subject to contraction when combined with certain prepositions. For example, the preposition **on**—*su* in combination with the definite article form *il* becomes the contraction: *sul*. To fully detail the several dozen variants of this practice, however, is beyond our scope and purpose here; the committed learner will find a full listing of these contractions in any "full-service" instructive textbook.

Indefinite Articles

There's far less complexity in dealing with the Italian equivalents of **"a"** and **"an."** Again, both the gender and the initial letter of the following noun determine the appropriate form of an associated indefinite. Of course, these are linked exclusively with *singular* nouns.

- **"A / an"** preceding masculine singular nouns *except those noted below:* <u>un</u>. Thus, **a crystal**—un cristallo; **a tendon**—un tendine.

- **"A / an"** preceding masculine singulars *beginning with an* s + consonant, *a* ps-consonant combination, *or a* z: *uno*. Thus: **a sculptor**—*uno scultore*; **a pseudonym**—*uno pseudonimo*; **a zero**—*uno zero*.

- **"A / an"** preceding all feminine singular nouns: *una*. Thus, **a festival**—una festa; **a laceration**—una lacerazione.

NOTE: The once standard practice of employing *un'* as the indefinite article preceding feminine singulars beginning with a vowel is now considered obsolete.

Partitive Articles

In Italian, "partitive-sense" articles—designators of nonspecific quantity—are equivalent to the English terms **some** and **any**. Because these are generally linked with article-preposition contractions, (see **NOTE** under Definite Articles), the student must seek detail in this regard from a more comprehensive grammatical text.

General Articles

In English, to say that one "loves cats," "admires architecture," or "wants money" is to imply an all-encompassing embrace of all or every member of *the* class specified by the noun, or *the* class in general, or *the* class as a whole. Similarly, to state that "Fascism is evil," "Gluttony is self-indulgent," or "Men like sports" is again to imply inclusion of *the* whole general category defined by the subject noun. In Italian, such all-inclusive generalizations are not normally made without inclusion of the appropriate *singular definite article* to make the statement grammatically correct. Thus, **I like ballet**—Mi piace il balletto. That is, "I like the ballet."

ADJECTIVES

Adjectival Position

Italian adjective use differs in two important respects from English practice. First, with only the handful of common exceptions listed below, adjectives *follow* the noun that they modify, rather than precede it. Thus, while in English we would say *a fast car*, an Italian would reverse the adjective-noun sequence and say *un auto rapida*. Similarly, an English **barbarous Baptist** would be an Italian *battista barbaro*. This practice is virtually universal throughout Italian speech and writing, *except relative to the dozen very heavily used adjectives listed below, which are usually (but not invariably) placed **before** the noun they modify.*

ancient—antico	**new**—nuovo
bad—cattivo	**old**—vecchio
beautiful—bello	**short** (*in duration*)—breve
good—buono	**small**—piccolo
large—grande	**ugly**—brutto
long—lungo	**young**—giovane

Thus, **beautiful woman**—bella donna; **new book**—nuovo libro; **ugly baron**—brutto barone, and so forth. It must be emphasized, however, that these exceptions are not themselves without exceptions, as anyone who has crossed Firenze's *Ponte Vecchio*, or ridden down Venezia's *Canale Grande* will immediately remember! When special or titular emphasis is needed, these "Exceptional Twelve" Italian adjectives emphasize themselves by moving back into *otherwise-normal* behind-the-noun position. Note also that *grande* is singularly unique in that it abbreviates to *gran* before nouns beginning with a consonant (except *z*- and *s-consonant* combinations), and elides to *grand'* (without an intervening space between the apostrophe and the following word) before nouns beginning with a vowel.

Adjectival Endings

The other way in which Italian adjectives differ from their English counterparts is that they, of course, like definite and indefinite articles, are invariably made to match the gender and singular-or-plural status of the nouns they modify. *Adjectives in the listings in this book (and most other reference books) are uniformly shown in their masculine singular form.* The majority of masculine singular adjectives end with the letter

-*o*; the remaining balance of masculine singulars end with the letter -*e*; *no* masculine singular adjective terminates with the letter -*a*. The great preponderance of feminine-singular adjectives terminate with the letter -*a*. All adjectival endings pluralize by the same rules as apply to nouns.

PRONOUNS

One cannot, of course, speak useful Italian (or any other language) without constant and very substantial use of pronouns. We communicate, after all, at least as much about ourselves and others as about "things."

Unfortunately, Italian pronouns—embracing such varieties as personal, possessive, relative, conjunctive, and disjunctive—constitute one of the language's most complex grammatical subsystems. So much so that, with its scores of contextual variants, any attempt to offer more than the narrowest summary distillation is considerably beyond this book's purview. Thus, save for the listing of conjunctive subject-of-verb personal pronouns below, the learner must direct his or her attention to an instructive text that treats comprehensively this vitally important class of words.

- **I**—io
- **you** (*sing. / familiar—use with friends, family, and children*)—tu

  you (*m. & f. sing. / formal*)—Lei

  you (*pl. / familiar*)—voi

  you (*pl. / formal*)—Loro

- **we**—noi

- **he**—egli
- **he, it**—esso
- **she**—ella
- **she, it**—essa
- **they** (*m.*)—essi
- **they** (*f.*)—esse

The learner is again cautioned that the above listing is but a fractional representation of the Italian pronoun universe, and distinctly limited in terms of correct use. He or she is urged, as soon as sufficient basic vocabulary has been attained to yield a growing sense of strength and confidence, to seek further intelligence elsewhere regarding this vital category of the Italian tongue.

PREPOSITIONS
Full Prepositions

In contrast to the vast complexity referred to immediately above, Italian's small universe of prepositions is—barring the single complication noted at the bottom of this section—relatively easy to master. In brief, the prepositions are:

Contracted Prepositions

As noted above (in section titled Articles), some prepositions are usually conjoined with a definite article and then recast in "contracted" form. A general Italian Grammar will list, define, and offer usage examples of these thirty-plus contractions.

ADVERBS

above—sopra	**in**—in / a
among—fra / tra	**in front of**—davanti a
at—a	**near**—vicino a
behind—dietro	**of**—di
beneath—sotto	**on**—su
between—fra / tra	**over**—sopra
by—da	**to**—*a*
for—per	**under**—sotto
from—da	**with**—con

Italian adverbs, like their English counterparts, modify verbs, adjectives, and sometimes other adverbs by specifying time, place, degree, manner, causation, and so forth. In English, a substantial preponderance of adverbs terminate in an *-ly* construct (***abnormally, bashfully, capriciously, finally***). In Italian, the overwhelming majority of adverbs terminate in a *-mente* construct (*anormalmente, timidamente, capricciosamente, finalmente*). Furthermore, *few Italian words that are not adverbs end in the* -mente *construct*. The few Italian adverbs that do not terminate in *-mente* are almost always multiword adverbial phrases, such as **calmly**—con calmo, **confidentially**—in confidenza, and so forth.

An Italian adverb generally follows the word it modifies.

VERBS

Lastly, we come very briefly to the complicated and ever-troublesome matter of verbs. In Italian, as in many languages, the complexity of verbs is considerable, in that they not only specify an action, but also indicate by one or another "conjugated" form and / or modifier the past, present, variously conditional, ongoing, or future context of that action, its "indicative," "reflexive," or "imperative" mood, the singularity or plurality of the actor(s) or acted-upon, and his / her / their / its sex or inanimate gender. All in a single word or two-word construct, which can assume any one of up to eighty-plus forms!

While it is clearly beyond the scope of the present volume to decipher and teach this complicated tangle of variants, the following basics are offered to give the learner an introductory practical understanding of Italian verb structure and use.

- In Italian as in all languages, the fundamental form of every verb is its *infinitive*. That is, the form that specifies only the verb's essential action ("to abstain," "to eat," "to make," "to speak"), without indication of who or what is executing the action or being acted upon, or the action's "mood" or timeframe. As is common practice in dictionaries and other language compendia, ***all verbs in this book's lists are shown in this infinitive form.*** *The student who learns the most regularly useful of these infinitives will be able to communicate his or her essential needs effectively, if not* with the smooth, polished, and grammatically correct fluency of one who has truly mastered the language.

- The overwhelming majority of Italian verbs terminate, in their infinitive form, in either an -*are*, -*ere,* or -*ire* triplet; immediately preceding that three-letter ending is the verb's "root." It is by a verb's terminating triplet that the basic form of its conjugation is determined, and upon its root that the conjugation is structured. Regular (as opposed to irregular) Italian -*are* verbs, for example, typically form the first-person present indicative by adding an -*o* to the verb's root. Thus, **to arrive**—arrivare becomes **I arrive**—arrivo; **to want**—desiderare becomes **I want**—desidero; **to speak**—parlare becomes **I speak**—parlo; **to wait**—aspettare becomes **I wait**—aspetto; and **to participate**—partecipare becomes **I participate**—partecipo. Several fill-in exercises are offered at the conclusion of this volume to test the learner's understanding of this very basic single-tense handling of regular -*are* verbs in the First Person Present Indicative tense.

Were all Italian verbs as "regular" as are most that end in -*are*, and were there only a handful of contextual variables rather than the fourteen (!!!) that the Romance languages employ (each with six sub-variables!), there would be room in this volume to cover this critical element of Italian grammar with comprehensive thoroughness. Alas, the topic is not so simple, as attested by the many textbooks that focus on nothing but verbs alone! Two that this author has used and can heartily recommend are *Italian Verb Drills,* by Paola Nanni-Tate; and *The Big Green Book of Italian Verbs*, by Katrien Maes-Christie and Daniel Franklin. The former is an easier, more basic treatment, ideal for novices, while the latter is a highly detailed and richly comprehensive technical overview of over five hundred verbs in their multitude of conjugations, variants, and irregularities. The learner is encouraged to rely upon such sources for enlightenment regarding, and mastery of, this complex yet vitally important part of the Italian grammatical structure.

LISTA DI TERMINI E FRASI FAMILIARI
List of Familiar Terms and Phrases

This first word list is composed of words that have been adopted directly into English from Italian (e.g., *brio, casino, veranda*) and of words (e.g., *antipasto, bambino, casa, cinema*) that have become generally familiar throughout the English-speaking world via various cultural media—general and classical music, popular literature, movies, Italian restaurants and cuisine, and so forth. Thus, despite the relatively few cognates within this list, it will be, for most learners, the easiest of the book's three compendia: a helpful reminder / refresher regarding an Italian minivocabulary that, at least subconsciously, is already well known.

In many instances, familiarity with these words is much greater than awareness of their Italian origin. Ask the average American or Briton where the English term *veranda* comes from, for example, and you'll likely be met with a blank stare, suggesting that he or she is wholly unaware of the fact that the word is a direct, intact adoption from the Italian lexicon, and thus every bit as usable in Rome or Milan as in London, New York, Toronto, or Sydney. Very likely you too will find many wholly familiar words here, the Italian source of which will surprise you, and thereby instantly broaden your reading and conversational strength (and confidence!) in the language of Dante, Verdi, and Giovanni Q. Pubblico. Some learners may find this list somewhat more difficult. If you're not the type who's regularly enjoyed Italian or Italian-subject films, and / or have few Italian-speaking friends, and / or don't watch some of television's grittier dramas or broader comedies, and / or seldom venture into an Italian restaurant, and / or are not a classical music buff, opera fan, broad reader or regular museum visitor, or have little or no familiarity with Spanish (which shares many words with Italian) or classical Latin. . . . If, in short, you've thus far led a somewhat nonexpansive life in multicultural terms, then perhaps many of these words will not be familiar to you after all. But they're *very* basic and familiar to many, nonetheless, and should be readily incorporated into your bilingual vocabulary as a starting point.

In many instances, not surprisingly, there needs to be some adjustment of pronunciation. The *circa* that we pronounce as (*SIR-kuh*), for example, issues from an Italian mouth as (*CHEER-kah*), and in most other instances the precise pronunciational value that English speakers assign to any given set of alphabetic symbols is at least minimally at odds with the sounds that Italians see in the same combination of letters. If you've taken the earlier suggestion to make the task of pronunciational understanding your *first and foremost responsibility*, however, you should readily accommodate to that difficulty.

acqua *f.* (*AHK-kwah*)   water

acquavite *f.* (*ahk-kwah VEE-teh*)   brandy

addio *m.* (*ahd-DEE-oh*)   good-bye, farewell

allegro (adj.) (*ahl-LEH-groh*)   cheerful, frisky, jolly, lively, merry

amante *m. & f.* (*ah-MAHN-teh*)   sweetheart, lover

amico *m.* (*ah-MEE-koh*)   friend

amore *m.* (*ah-MOHR-reh*)   love
ⓘ The related but noncognate verbal form of this word is *amare* (*ah-MAHR-reh*), *to love.*

antipasto *m.* (*ahn-tee-PAH-stoh*)   appetizer
ⓘ This term is generally used in the plural: *antipasti.*

aria *f.* (*AHR-ryah*)   air (*atmosphere*), song

arrivederci (*ahr-rree-veh-DEHR-chee*)   farewell, see you again
ⓘ This is a less formal version than *arrivederla.*

avanti (*ah-VAHN-tee*)   forward, onward, ahead
ⓘ Colloquially, this word is used throughout Italy to mean *Come in!*

avemaria *f.* (*ah-veh-mahr-REE-ah*) or **avemmaria** *f.* (*ah-vehm-mahr-REE-ah*) Hail Mary

bambina *f.* (*bahm-BEE-nah*)   baby girl, girl child
bambino *m.* (*bahm-BEE-noh*)   child (*in general*), baby boy, little boy

ⓘ *Bambino* and *bambina* are generally interchangeable with *ragazzo* and *ragazza* in reference to children, although the former terms are more commonly employed regarding preschoolers, and as endearments. *Ragazzo* and *ragazza* are most often used in reference to older children. RELATED: *bambinesco* (adj.) (*bahm-bee-NEH-skoh*), *babyish;* and *bambola f.* (*BAHM-boh-lah*), *doll.* The omnigender term *nipote* (*nee-POH-teh*) can refer to either a grandchild of either sex or to a niece or nephew.

bandito *m.* (*bahn-DEE-toh*) bandit, outlaw

barista *m.* (*bahr-REE-stah*) bartender

baritono *m.* (*bahr-REE-toh-noh*) baritone (*singer & voice of a baritone*) / (adj.) (*mid-to-low male*) voice range

basso *m.* (*BAHS-soh*) bass (*singer & voice of a bass*) / (adj.) low, short, shallow, soft

basta (*BAH-stah*) enough
ⓘ This is the common idiomatic contraction of *abbastanza.*

bello (adj.) (*BEHL-loh*) beautiful, handsome, lovely, fine, pleasing to the eye
ⓘ Most Italian words that relate to beauty begin with the syllable *bel-*. THUS: *bellezza f.* (*behl-LEHT-tsah*), *beauty;* and the adjective *bellino* (*behl-LEE-noh*), meaning *pretty, cute, good-looking.* A snappy dresser is a *bellimbusto m.* (*behl-leem-BOO-stoh*), *dandy.* Even the improving of beauty follows in line: *belletto m.* (*behl-LEHT-toh*) for *makeup* (cosmetics) and *salone di bellezza m.* (*sah-LOH-neh dee* ____) for *beauty parlor.* In reference to the voice *bello* under which this entry appears, it must be remembered that an adjective always matches the gender of the noun it modifies. Thus, one would never refer to a beautiful woman as a *bello donna*, but rather as a *bella donna.* The all-purpose antonym: *brutto* (adj.) (*BROOT-toh*), *ugly.*

benvenuto! (*behn-veh-NOO-toh*) welcome!
ⓘ The foregoing term translates literally as *Good coming!* Most Italian words that relate to "goodness" begin with the syllable *ben-*. Thus, the primary noun of that conceptual series, *bene m.* (*BEH-neh*), *good,* heads a long string of related terms: *benedetto* (adj) (*beh-neh-DEHT-toh*), *blessed; benedire* (*beh-neh-DEER-reh*), *(to) bless; benedizione f.* (*beh-neh-dee-TSYOH-neh*), *benediction, blessing; benefattore m.* (*beh-neh-faht-TOHR-reh*), *benefactor; benefattrice f.* (*beh-neh-faht-TREE-cheh*), *benefactress; beneficare* (*beh-neh-fee-KAHR-reh*), *(to) benefit; beneficiario m.* (*beh-neh-fee-CHAR-ryoh*), *beneficiary; benefico* (adj) (*beh-NEH-fee-koh*), *beneficent; benessere m.* (*beh-nehs-SEHR-reh*), *welfare; benevolenza f.* (*beh-neh-voh-LEHN-tsah*), *benevolence;* the adjective *benevolo* (*beh-neh-VOH-loh*), *benevolent, kindly;* the adverb *benevolmente* (*beh-neh-vohl-*

MEHN-teh), *benevolently;* and the masculine plural noun **beni** (*BEH-nee*), *goods, estate.* The two amazing exceptions to all the foregoing are **bontà** *f.* (*bohn-TAH*), *goodness;* and **buono** (adj) (*BWOH-noh*), *good.*

bianco (adj) (*BYAHN-koh*) white

biscotto *m.* (*beez-KOHT-toh*) cookie, cracker

bocca *f.* (*BOHK-kah*) mouth (anatomy)

bordello *m.* (*bohr-DEHL-loh*) brothel

bottega *f.* (*boht-TEH-gah*) shop, store
ⓘ While the foregoing word is used throughout Italy (and Spain), the terms **negozio** *m.* (*neh-GOH-tsyoh*) and **spaccio** *m.* (*SPAHT-choh*) are more commonly used from Rome northward.

bravo! (*BRAH-voh*) that's very good!
ⓘ Again, the gender complexity arises. When expressing enthusiastic appreciation to or regarding a *female* performer, the word becomes **brava!**

brio *m.* (*BREE-oh*) verve, elan

buon anno! (*bwohn AHN-noh*) **felice Capo d'anno!** (*feh-LEE-cheh KAH-poh dahn-noh*) **buon Capodanno!** (*bwohn KAH-poh dahn-noh*) happy New Year!

buongiorno! *m.* (*bwohn-JOHR-noh*) good morning! hello! good day!

ⓘ This is the common Italian greeting from dawn to midafternoon, at which point the salutation becomes **buonasera!** *f.* (*bwoh-nah-SEH-rah*), *good evening!* The greeting for *good afternoon,* **buon pomeriggio** (*bwohn poh-meh-REED-joh*), has been falling more and more out of use to the point that it's now considered antiquated. NOTE that **buongiorno!** is also used in parting, as "*Have a good day!*" See also *Ciao!*

buon compleanno! (*bwohn kohm-pleh-AHN-noh*) happy birthday!

buon Natale! (*bwohn nah-TAH-leh*) merry Christmas!

buon viàggio! (*bwohn vee-AHD-joh*) have a good trip!

buona fortuna! (*bwoh-nah fohr-TOO-nah*) good luck!

buonanotte! (*bwoh-nah-NOHT-teh*) good night!

buonasera! (*bwoh-nah-SEHR-rah*) good evening!
ⓘ (See Note @ **buongiorno!**)

buono (adj) (*BWOH-noh*) good

caffè *m.* (*kahf-FEH*) coffee, café, coffee shop, small restaurant

calore *m.* (*kah-LOHR-reh*) heat

campagna *f.* (*kahm-PAH-nyah*) rural region, countryside

campanile *m.* (*kahm-pah-NEE-leh*) bell tower

campo *m.* (*KAHM-poh*) field, small plaza (*in Venice*)

cane *m.* (*KAH-neh*) dog

capo *m.* (*KAH poh*) boss, chief, head man, leader

capodanno *m.* (*kah-poh-DAHN-noh*) New Year's Day

capriccio *m.* (*kah-PREET-choh*) caprice, whim

carne *f.* (*KAHR-neh*) meat, flesh

caro (adj) (*KAHR-roh*) dear

casa *f.* (*KAH-zah*) house, home
  ⓘ In Venice only, this sometimes and inconsistently contracts to *Ca'*.

casino *m.* (*kah-ZEE-noh*) casino, gambling establishment

ciao! (*CHOW*) hello! hi! glad to see you! bye-bye! so long! see ya!
  ⓘ This colloquialism is the multiuse equivalent of the Hawaiian *Aloha* or Hebrew *Shalom*: a word that can be used as either a greeting (with slight stressing at the beginning of the word, and the voice rising "happily" through the word's quick enunciation), or a farewell (voice falling "matter-of-factly" or "slightly sadly" through the word's slower expression).

cinema *m.* (*CHEE-neh-mah*) movie, movie house, film industry

circa (CHEER-kah) about, in regard to, approximately
  🖝 Don't mispronounce as *circo* (*CHEER-koh*), which is *circus*.

coda *f.* (*KOH-dah*) (*musical*) ending, (*animal's*) tail

cognoscenti *m.* (*koh-nyoh-SHEN-tee*) connoisseurs, people "in the know"

comandante *m.* (*koh-mahn-DAHN-teh*) commander

con (*kohn*) with

concerto *m.* (*kohn-CHEHR-toh*) concert
  ⓘ In English use, this more precisely signifies *piece for solo instrumentalist + orchestra.*

consigliare (*kohn-see- LYAHR-reh*) (to) counsel, (to) advise

consigliere *m.* (*kohn-see-LYEHR-reh*) counselor, councilman
  ⓘ The variant *consigliatore* (*kohn-see-lyah-TOHR-reh*) is also widely used.

consiglio *m.* (*kohn-SEE-lyoh*) advice

contralto *m.* (*kohn-TRAHL-toh*)   alto (*singer*), (*midrange female*) voice range

cupola *f.* (*KOO-poh-lah*)   dome

diavolo *m.* (*DYAH-voh-loh*)   devil

Dio *m.* (*DEE-oh*)   God

diva *f.* (*DEE-vah*)   very famous female singer or actress

divertimento *m.* (*dee-vehr-tee-MEHN-toh*)   diversion, amusement

dolce *m.* (*DOHL-cheh*)   dessert, candy
> ⓘ This term is commonly found at the bottom of Italian menus in plural form—*dolci* (*DOHL-chee*)—indicating the restaurant's selection of dessert *sweets*. Also closely associated are the terms: *dolce* (adj.) (*DOHL-cheh*), *sweet* (taste or general quality of); and *dolcezza* *f.* (*dohl-CHEHT-tsah*), *sweetness*. The adverb *dolcemente* (*dohl-cheh-MEHN-teh*), *sweetly, soothingly*, also springs from the same root.

domani *m.* (*doh-MAH-nee*)   tomorrow

donna *f.* (*DOHN-nah*)   woman

espresso *m.* (*eh-SPREHS-soh*)   espresso, pressure-steamed coffee
> ♪ In English, this word is commonly misspelled and mispronounced "expresso."

falsetto *m.* (*fahl-SEHT-toh*)   falsetto (*singer*), (*very high male*) voice range

famoso (adj.) (*fah-MOH-soh*)   famous

farina *f.* (*fahr-REE-nah*)   flour

fede *f.* (*FEH-deh*)   faith

fedele (adj.) (*feh-DEH-leh*)   faithful

felice (adj.) (*feh-LEE-cheh*)   glad, happy

fine *f.* (*FEE-neh*)   end

finestra *f.* (*fee-NEH-strah*)   window

fiore *m.* (*FYOHR-reh*)   blossom, flower

fiume *m.* (*FYOO-meh*)   river

formaggio *m.* (*fohr-MAHD-joh*)   cheese

forno *m.* (*FOHR-noh*)   oven

forte (adj.) (*FOHR-teh*)   loud, strong

fortissimo (adj.) (*fohr-TEES-see-moh*)   very loud, loudest

fumare (*foo-MAHR-reh*) (to) smoke

funghi *m.* (*FOON-gee*) mushrooms
☛ Often mispronounced (*FOON-jee*) by inattentive learners. Also note that the singular form *fungo* is almost never used except in general reference to *fungus*.

gamba *f.* (*GHAM-bah*) leg

gatto *m.* (*GAHT-toh*) cat
ⓘ The word for a *small cat* or *kitten* is **gattino** (*gaht-TEE-noh*).

gelato *m.* (*jeh-LAH-toh*) ice cream

ghetto *m.* (*GEHT-toh*) ghetto

grande (adj.) (*GRAHN-deh*) big, great, large, grand
ⓘ Probably not already familiar, and definitely noncognate, are the important antonym adjectives **piccolo** (*PEEK-koh-loh*), *small*; **piccolino** (*peek-koh-LEE-noh*), *tiny;* **piccino** (*peet-CHEE-noh*), *very tiny, wee;* and **poco** (*POH-koh*), *little* (not much). The latter term means *little* (small amount) and as an adverb, *slightly.*

grazie (*GRAH-tsyeh*) thank you
ⓘ This all-important word enjoys a variety of subtle pronunciational variations from place to place in Italy, and from class to class, and time to time. Italy is rich in dialects, a subject too large and too specialized to treat here. (*GRAHT-zee*) and (*GRAH-tsee-ah*) are but two variant examples. The pronunciation given above is the standard one, used by all educated Italians in Italy and outside of Italy. *Tante grazie!* (TAHN-teh____), *Thank you very much! Mille grazie!* (MEEL-leh____), *Many thanks* (literally, "a thousand thanks")!

guerra *f.* (*GWEHR-rrah*) war

inferno *m.* (*een-FEHR-noh*) hell

innamorata *f.* (*een-nah-mohr-RAH-tah*) sweetheart, girlfriend; (adj.) loving, in love, fond of, crazy about

innamorato *m.* (*een-nah-mohr-RAH-toh*) sweetheart, boyfriend; (adj.) loving, in love, fond of, crazy about

latte *m.* (*LAHT-teh*) milk
ⓘ Some English speakers have come to assume that this single word refers to a form of light coffee. *Coffee with milk* ("caffè con latte") in Italy is prepared differently than in the United States, and it's known as *caffellatte* (*kahf-fehl-LAHT-teh*). The adjective form referring to *milk* in Italian is **latteo** (*LAHT-teh-oh*), *milky.*

lento (adj.) (*LEHN-toh*) slow

lingua *f.* (*LEEN-gwah*) tongue (*physical organ*), language

luna *f.* (*LOO-nah*) moon
> ⓘ An important, related term: *chiaro (m.) di luna (KYAHR-roh dee LOO-nah), moonlight*

lupo *m.* (*LOO-poh*) wolf

madre *f.* (*MAH-dreh*) mother

maestro *m.* (*mah-EH-stroh*) master (*great artist*), teacher, advanced artisan

mafia *f.* (*MAH-fyah*) mafia

mal *(m.)* **di mare** (*mahl dee MAH-reh*) seasickness

mamma (*MAHM mah*), mother, mom, mama

mano *f.* (*MAH-noh*) hand

mare *m.* (*MAHR-reh*) sea

mezzo *m.* (*MEHD-dsoh*) half, middle; (adj.) half, mid-, semi-, medium
> ⓘ This important term is the root of many variants, including the preposition *in mezzo di* (*een MEHD-dsoh dee*), *amid, amidst, in the middle of;* and compound words such as *mezzaluna f.* (*mehd-dsah-LOO-nah*), *half moon, crescent;* **mezzanotte** (*mehd-dsah-NOHT-teh*), *midnight;* **mezzeria** (*mehd-dseh-REE-ah*), *centerline;* and **mezzogiorno** (*mehd-dsoh-JOHR-noh*), *noon.* NOTE the distinctly different noun form of *mezzo's* adjectival denotation: *metà f.* (*meh-TAH*), *half;* and its related adverbial form: *metà e metà* (*meh-TAH eh meh-TAH*), *half-and-half.*

mondo *m.* (*MOHN-doh*) world

Natale *m.* (*nah-TAH-leh*) Christmas

no (*noh*) no (*negative response, NOT an indication of nil quantity*)

nonna *f.* (*NOHN-nah*) grandmother

nonni *m.* (*NOHN-nee*) grandparents

nonno *m.* (*NOHN-noh*) grandfather

nord *m.* (*nohrd*) north

notte *f.* (*NOHT-teh*) night

nuovo (adj.) (*NWOH-voh*) new

occupato (adj.) (*ohk-koo-PAH-toh*) occupied, busy, in use

olio *m.* (*OH-lyoh*) oil

opera *f.* (*OH-pehr-rah*) (grand) opera, work

operetta *f.* (*oh-pehr-REHT-tah*) operetta, light opera

oro *m.* (*OHR-roh*) gold

osso *m.* (*OHS-soh*) bone

pace *f.* (*PAH-cheh*) peace

pacifico (adj.) (*pah-CHEE-fee-koh*) peaceable, peaceful

padre *m.* (*PAH-dreh*) father

padrona *f.* (*pah-DROH-nah*) mistress, employer, boss, overseer, landlady
  ✒ The denotation of *mistress*, here, is NOT that of a lover!

padrone *m.* (*pah-DROH-neh*) master, employer, boss, overseer, landlord

pagliaccio *m.* (*pah-LYAHT-choh*) clown
  ① The related adjectival form is: **pagliaccesco** (*pah-lyaht-CHEHS-koh*), *clownish.*

palazzo *m.* (*pah-LAHT-tsoh*) palace

pantaloni *m.* (*pahn-tah-LOH-nee*) trousers

papa *m.* (*PAH-pah*) pope

papà *m.* (*pah-PAH*) daddy

paparazzo *m.* (*pah-pahr-RAHT-tsoh*) photographer (*of celebrities*)
  ① This term is most often seen in the collective plural: **paparazzi.**

passeggiare (*pahs-sehd-JAHR-reh*) (to) stroll

passeggiata *f.* (*pahs-sehd-JAH-tah*) stroll, (pleasure) walk

pasta *f.* (*PAH-stah*) pasta

pensione *f.* (*pehn-SYOH-neh*) boarding house, small and modest hotel, pension

per favore (pehr *fah-VOHR-reh*) please

pesce *m.* (*PEH-sheh*) fish

pianoforte *m.* (*pyah-noh-FOHR-teh*) piano

piazza *f.* (*PYAHT-tsah*) (large) plaza, public square

pietà f. (pyeh-TAH) pity

pietra f. (PYEH-trah) stone

pizza f. (PEET-tsah) pizza

pollo m. (POHL-loh) chicken, fowl (in general)

pomodoro m. (poh-moh-DOHR-roh) tomato

ponte m. (POHN-teh) bridge (span, NOT card game)

postino m. (poh-STEE-noh) postman, mailman

prego! (PREH-goh) you're welcome! don't mention it!
ⓘ **Prego,** which literally translates *I beg you*, is the colloquialism employed throughout Italy in response to expressions of gratitude ("I beg you [not to mention it because it was my pleasure]"), or in request that a courtesy be accepted, such as opening a door and stepping aside for others to pass through ("I beg you [to accept my consideration]").

presto (PREH-stoh) soon, quick, early (for an appointment)

pronto (adj.) (PROHN-toh) prompt, quick, ready, willing
ⓘ Colloquially, this is the standard telephone greeting throughout Italy.

prosciutto m. (proh-SHOOT-toh) cured ham, (food, NOT comic overactor)

quasi (KWAH-zee) almost, nearly

ristorante m. (ree-stohr-RAHN-teh) restaurant

salsa f. (SAHL-sah) sauce
ⓘ The term **sugo** m. (SOO-goh) denotes a heavier, creamier *sauce;* and **sugo di carne** (___dee KAHR-neh), *gravy.*

salute! (sah-LOO-teh) to your health!

scherzo m. (SKEHR-tsoh) jest, joke

secco (adj.) (SEHK-koh) dry

sempre (SEHM-preh) always

sì (see) yes

signora f. (see-NYOHR-rah) lady, Madam, Missus, (married) woman

signore m. (see-NYOHR-reh) man, gentleman, Mister, Sir
ⓘ Thankfully, pictographic symbolism is now widely used on Italian restroom doors, thus minimizing the one-time embarrassment of men walking into the women's room! This misunderstanding arose from the oddity of the

plural of lady (ladies = *signore*) being identical to the singular for man (*signore*). Still, this remains a subtle distinction to be well aware of!

signorina *f.* (*see-nyohr-REE-nah*) Miss (*unmarried female*), young woman

simpatico (adj.) (*seem-PAH-tee-koh*) agreeable, congenial, nice, pleasant
👉 The common English use of this term to connote "bonded" interpersonal affinity, sympathy, and harmony is NOT reflected in Italian use!

sinfonia *f.* (*seen-foh-NEE-ah*) symphony

sole *m.* (*SOH-leh*) sun, sunshine
ⓘ The root "sol" is common to most Italian words that relate to the sun. THUS: *solare* (adj.) (*soh-LARH-reh*), *solar; luce* (*f.*) *del sole* (*LOO-cheh dehl SOH-leh*), *sunlight; solatio* (*soh-lah-TEE-oh*) or *soleggiato* (*soh-lehd-JAH-toh*), both adjectives, *sunny; crema f. solare* (*KREH-mah soh-LAHR-reh*), *suntan lotion.*

soprano *m.* (*sohp-RAH-noh*) soprano (*singer*), high voice range (*female*)

sotto voce (*soht-toh VOH-cheh*) *quietly said* (literally, "under-voice")
ⓘ In Italian, the prefix *sotto* always refers to "underneathness," so to speak. THUS: *sottovalutare* (*soht-toh-vah-loo-TAHR-reh*), *(to) underestimate; sotterraneo* (adj.) (*soht-tehr-RRAH-neh-oh*), *underground; sottolineare* (*soht-toh-lee-neh-AHR-reh*), *(to) underline; sottopassaggio m.* (*soht-toh-pahs-SAHD-joh*), *underpass; sottovesti f.* (*soht-toh-VEH-stee*), *underwear.*

spaghetti *m.* (*spah-GEHT-tee*) spaghetti

stella *f.* (*STEHL-lah*) (*celestial*) star

strada *f.* (*STRAH-dah*) road, street
ⓘ In contemporary usage, "main" roads and streets primarily share this term. A secondary road will often be referred to as *cammino m.* (*kahm-MEE-noh*), and an older and / or narrower street will frequently be called a *via* (*VEE-ah*). A principal *highway, superhighway, expressway,* or *freeway* is known as *autostrada f.* (*ow-toh-STRAH-dah*); and an *avenue* or *boulevard,* as a *viale* (*VYAH-leh*).

svelte (adj.) (*ZVEHL-teh*) svelte, slender
ⓘ With the meaning above, Italian *svelte* is used to refer to more than one woman. The basic adjective from which both Italian *svelte* and English *svelte* come from is *svelto,* meaning *quick* (in movement), *quick-witted* or *smart, slim,* or *slender.*

tenore *m.* (*teh-NOHR-reh*) tenor (*singer*), (adj.) high voice range (*male*)

terra *f.* (*TEHR-rrah*)   ground, land, soil, earth

terra *f.* **ferma** (*tehr-rrah FEHR-mah*)   mainland

testa *f.* (*TEH-stah*)   head (*anatomy*)

topo *m.* (*TOH-poh*)   mouse

toro *m.* (*TOHR-roh*)   bull

torta *f.* (*TOHRR-tah*)   cake, pie, tart

triste (adj.) (*TREE-steh*)   blue, moody, sad

tristezza *f.* (*tree-STEHT-tsah*)   sadness

troppo (*TROHP-poh*)   too (excessive, overly)

tutto (adj.) (*TOOT-toh*)   all, everything, whole

uova *f.* (*WOH-vah*)   eggs
    ⓘ This is one of the very few instances in Italian where a noun's gender also determines its plurality.

uovo *m.* (*WOH-voh*)   egg

vecchio (adj.) (*VEHK-kyoh*)   old, elderly

vendetta *f.* (*vehn-DEHT-tah*)   vengeance, revenge

veranda *f.* (*vehr-RAHN-dah*)   porch

verde (adj.) (*VEHR-deh*)   green

verità *f.* (*vehr-ree-TAH*)   truth

via (*VEE-ah*)   by means of, by way of; *as a feminine noun,* road, street, way
    ⓘ The Italian word for *railroad,* **ferrovia** *f.* (*fehr-rroh-VEE-ah*), literally means *iron road.*

villa *f.* (*VEEL-lah*)   very large urban house, spacious country house

vino *m.* (*VEE-noh*)   wine

virtuoso *m.* (*veer-too-OH-zoh*)   virtuoso

vita *f.* (*VEE-tah*)   life

vivace *adj.* (*vee-VAH-cheh*)   vivacious, lively

voce *f.* (*VOH-cheh*)   voice, rumor

LISTA DI TERMINI IDENTICI E SIMILI
List of Identical and Similar Terms

Now we come to the big list—*la lista grande ed importante*: the register of 5,000-plus words that, because of their high degrees of similarity across the lingual divide, can most readily be absorbed by English-speaking students of contemporary Italian. Even a casual reader's perusal of this immense collection would provide both a substantial increase in the reader's Italian vocabulary and a greatly improved familiarity with Italian pronunciation. And the serious learner who utilizes it as the basis of an ongoing and systematic language-acquisition program will find it both invaluable and continually encouraging. So, let's get to it!

—A—

abacus   abaco *m.* (*AH-bah-koh*)

abandon, relinquish, vacate, forsake, jilt (to)   abbandonare (*ahb-bahn-doh-NAHR-reh*)

abandoned (adj.)   abbandonato (*abh-bahn-doh-NAH-toh*)

abandonment   abbandono *m.* (*ahb-bahn-DOH-noh*)

abdominal (adj.)   addominale (*ahd-doh-mee-NAH-leh*) 💣

aberration   aberrazione *f.* (*ah-behr-rrah-TSYOH-neh*)

abhor (to)   aborrire (*ahb-bohr-RREER-reh*)

ability, adeptness, skill   abilità *f.* (*ah-bee-lee-TAH*)

able, capable, adept, skillful (adj.) abile (*AH-bee-leh*), capace (*kah-PAH-cheh*)

ably abilmente (*ahb-beel-MEHN-teh*)

abnormality anormalità *f.* (*ah-nohr-mah-lee-TAH*) ☝

abnormally anormalmente (*ah-nohr-mahl-MEHN-teh*) ☝

aboard a bordo (*ah BOHR-doh*)

abolish (to) abolire (*ah-boh-LEER-reh*)

abominable, loathsome (adj.) abominévole (*ah-boh-mee-NEH-voh-leh*)

abominate, loathe (to) abominare (*ah-boh-mee-NAHR-reh*)

abomination abominazione *f.* (*ah-boh-mee-nah-TSYOH-neh*)

abortion aborto *m.* (*ah-BOHR-toh*) ⟶**abortive** (adj.) -tivo☉

abound (to) abbondare (*ahb-bohn-DAHR-reh*)

abrasion abrasione *f.* (*ah-brah-ZYOH-neh*)

abrasive (adj.) abrasivo (*ah-brah-SEE-voh*)

abbreviate, abridge, shorten (to) abbreviare (*ahb-breh-vee-AHR-reh*)

abbreviation abbreviazione *f.* (*ahb-breh-vee-ah-TSYOH-neh*)

absence assenza *f.* (*ahs-SEHN-tsah*) ⟶**absent** (adj.) -nte☉

absolute (adj.) assoluto (*ahs-soh-LOO-toh*)

absolutely assolutamente (*ahs-soh-loo-tah-MEHN-teh*)

absolution assoluzione *f.* (*ahs-soh-loo-TSYOH-neh*)

absorb, engross (*physically OR mentally*) (to) assorbire (*ahs-sohr-BEER-reh*)

absorbed (adj.) assorbito (*ahs-sohr-BEE-toh*)

absorbent, absorbing (adj.) assorbente (*ahs-sohr-BEHN-teh*)

abstain (to) astenersi (*ah-steh-NEHR-see*)

abstinence astinenza *f.* (*ah-stee-NEHN-tsah*)

abstract (adj.) astratto (*ah-STRAHT-toh*)

abstraction astrazione *f.* (*ah-strah-TSYOH-neh*)

absurd, preposterous (adj.) assurdo (*ahs-SOOR-doh*)

absurdity assurdità *f.* (*ahs-soor-dee-TAH*)

abundance, plenty abbondanza *f.* (*ahb-bohn-DAHN-tsah*)

abundant, plentiful (adj.) abbondante (*ahb-bohn-DAHN-teh*)

abuse abuso *m.* (*ah-BOO-soh*) Ɔ**abusive** (adj.) -sivoϹ

abuse, misuse (to) abusare (*ah-boo-ZAHR-reh*)

abusively abusivamente (*ah-boo-see-vah-MEHN-teh*)

abyss, chasm abisso *m.* (*ah-BEES-soh*)

academy accademia *f.* (*ahk-kah-DEH-myah*) Ɔ**academic** (adj.) -icoϹ

accelerate (to) accelerare (*aht-cheh-leh-RAHR-reh*)

acceleration accelerazione *f.* (*aht-cheh-leh-rah-TSYOH-neh*)

accent, (*linguistic*) stress accento *m.* (*aht-CHEHN-toh*)

accent, accentuate, stress (to) accentare (*aht-chehn-TAHR-reh*)

accept (to) accettare (*aht-cheht-TAHR-reh*)

acceptability accettabilità *f.* (*aht-cheht-tah-bee-lee-TAH*)

acceptable, OK (adj.) accettabile (*aht-cheht-TAH-bee-leh*)

acceptance accettazione *f.* (*aht-cheht-tah-TSYOH-neh*)

access accesso *m.* (*aht-CHES-soh*)

accessible (adj.) accessibile (*aht-ches-SEE-bee-leh*)

accessory accessorio *m.* (*aht-ches-SOHR-ryoh*) Ɔ(adj.)Ϲ

accident incidente *m.* (*een-chee-DEHN-teh*), accidente *m.* (*aht-chee-DEHN-teh*)

accidental (adj.) accidentale (*aht-chee-dehn-TAH-leh*)

accidentally accidentalmente (*aht-chee-dehn-tahl-MEHN-teh*)

acclamation acclamazione *f.* (*ahk-klah-mah-TSYOH-neh*)

acclimate (to) acclimatare (*ahk-klee-mah-TAHR-reh*)

accolade accollata *f.* (*ahk-kohl-LAH-tah*)

accommodate (*make provision for*) (to) accomodare (*ahk-koh-moh-DAHR-reh*)

accommodation (*generous courtesy*) accomodazione *f.* (*ahk-koh-moh-dah-TSYOH-neh*)

accommodating (adj.) accomodante (*ahk-koh-moh-DAHN-teh*)

accompaniment accompagnamento *m.* (*ahk-kohm-pah-nyah-MEHN-toh*)

accompany (to) accompagnare (*ahk-kohm-pah-NYAHR-reh*)

accord, concord, (*state of*) agreement accordo *m.* (*ahk-KOHR-doh*)

accord (to) accordare (*ahk-kohr-DAHR-reh*)

account (*financial*), bill, count conto *m.* (*KOHN-toh*)

  ⓘ **The check, please.**" "Il conto, per favore." (*eel-KOHN-toh____*)

account, narrative, story, tale racconto *m.* (*rahk-KOHN-toh*)

accumulate (to) accumulare (*ahk-koo-moo-LAHR-reh*)

accumulation accumulazione *f.* (*ahk-koo-moo-lah-TSYOH-neh*)

accuracy accuratezza *f.* (*ahk-koo-rah-TEHT-tsah*)

accurate (adj.) accurato (*ahk-koor-RAH-toh*)

accurately accuratamente (*ahk-koor-rah-tah-MEHN-teh*)

accusation accusa *f.* (*ahk-KOO-zah*)

accuse (to) accusare (*ahk-koo-SAHR-reh*)

accused accusato *m.* (*ahk-koo-SAH-toh*) ⊃*f.* -ta☾ / ⊃(adj.)☾

accuser accusatore *m.* (*ahk-koo-sah-TOHR-reh*) ⊃*f.* -trice☾

ace (*expert or playing card*) asso *m.* (*AHS-soh*)

acerbic (adj.) acerbo (*ah-CHER-boh*)

acid acido *m.* (*AH-chee-doh*) ⊃**acid, acidic, sour** (adj.)☾

acidity acidità *f.* (*ah-chee-dee-TAH*)

acne acne *f.* (*AHK-neh*)

acoustic (adj.) acustico (*ah-KOO-stee-koh*)

acoustics (*science or properties of sound*) acustica *f.* (*ah-KOO-stee-kah*)

acquiesce (to) acquiescere (*ahk-kwee-EH-shehr-reh*)

acquiescence acquiescenza *f.* (*ahk-kwee-eh-SHEHN-tsah*)

acquire (to)   acquistare (*ahk-kwee-STAHR-reh*)

acquisition   acquisto *m.* (*ahk-KWEE-stoh*)

acrid (adj.)   acre (*AH-kreh*)

acrimony   acrimonia *f.* (*ah-kree-MOH-nyah*)

acrobat   acrobato *m.* (*ah-kroh-BAH-toh*) ➲*f.* -ta☯

act, deed   atto *m.* (*AHT-toh*)

act (to)   agire (*ah-JEER-reh*)

action (*deed, NOT movement*)   azione *f.* (*ah-TSYOH-neh*)

activate (to)   attivare (*aht-tee-VAHR-reh*)

active (adj.)   attivo (*aht-TEE-voh*)

activism   attivismo *m.* (*aht-tee-VEEZ-moh*)

activity   attività *f.* (*aht-tee-vee-TAH*)

actor   attore *m.* (*aht-TOHR-reh*) ➲*f.* -trice☯

actual (adj.)   attuale (*aht-TWAH-leh*)

acumen   acume *m.* (*ah-KOO-meh*)

acupuncture   acupuntura *f.* (*ah-koo-poon-TOOR-rah*)

acute, sharp, shrewd (adj.)   acuto (*ah-KOO-toh*)

acutely, sharply   acutamente (*ah-koo-tah-MEHN-teh*)

acuteness, sharpness, shrewdness   acutezza *f.* (*ah-koo-TEHT-tsah*)

adage   adagio *m.* (*ah-DAH-joh*)

adamant (adj.)   adamantino (*ahd-dah-mahn-TEE-noh*)

adapt (to)   addattare (*ahd-daht-TAHR-reh*)

adaptability   adattabilità *f.* (*ah-daht-tah-bee-lee-TAH*)

adaptable   adattabile *f.* (*ah-daht-tah-BEE-leh*)

adaptation   adattamento *m.* (*ah-daht-tah-MEHN-toh*)

adaptive (adj.)   adattevole (*ah-daht-teh-VOH-leh*)

add (*math process*) (to)   addizionare (*ahd-dee-tsyoh-NAHR-reh*)

add (to) aggiungere (*ahd-JOON-jehr-reh*) 🔊

addition (*process of*) addizione *f.* (*ahd-dee-TSYOH-neh*)

additional (adj.) addizionale (*ahd-dee-tsyoh-NAH-leh*)

adequate (adj.) adeguato (*ah-deh-GWAH-toh*)

adequately adeguatamente (*ah-deh-gwah-tah-MEHN-teh*)

adhere, cling, stick to (to) aderire (*ah-deh-REER-reh*)

adherence *f.* aderenza (*ah-dehr-REHN-tsah*)

adherent aderente *m.* (*ah-der-REHN-teh*) ⊃(adj.)⊂

adhesion adesione *f.* (*ah-deh-ZYOH-neh*)

adhesive adesivo *m.* (*ah-deh-SEE-voh*)

adjacent, adjoining (adj.) adiacente (*ah-dyah-CHEN-teh*)

adjective aggettivo *m.* (*ahd-jeht-TEE-voh*) 🔊

adjourn (to) aggiornare (*ahd-johr-NAHR-reh*) 🔊

adjournment aggiornamento *m.* (*ahd-johr-nah-MEHN-toh*) 🔊

adjudicate, judge (to) giudicare (*joo-dee-KAHR-reh*) 🔊

adjust (to) aggiustare (*ahd-joo-STAHR-reh*) 🔊

adjustment aggiustamento *m.* (*ahd-joo-stah-MEHN toh*) 🔊

administer (to) amministrare (*ahm-mee-nee-STRAHR-reh*) 🔊

administration, management amministrazione *f.* (*ahm-mee-nee-strah-TSYOH-neh*), direzione (*deer-reh-TSYOH-neh*)

administrative (adj.) amminstrativo (*ahm-mee-nee-strah-TEE-voh*) 🔊

administrator, manager, executive amministratore *m.* (*ahm-mee-nee-strah-TOHR-reh*), direttore (*deer-reht-TOHR-reh*)

admiration ammirazione *f.* (*ahm-meer-rah-TSYOH-neh*) 🔊

admirable (adj.) ammirabile (*ahm-meer-RAH-bee-leh*) 🔊

admire (to) ammirare (*ahm-meer-RAHR-reh*) 🔊

admirer ammiratore *m.* (*ahm-meer-rah-TOHR-reh*) 🔊

admissible (adj.) ammissibile (*ahm-mees-SEE-bee-leh*) 🔊

admission, admittance (*to place, event*) ammissione *f.* (*ahm-mees-SYOH-neh*), entrata (*ehn-TRAH-tah*)

admit (*to place or event*) (to) ammettere (*ahm-MEHT-tehr-reh*) ⚫︎

adolescence adolescenza *f.* (*ah-doh-leh-SHEHN-tsah*)

adolescent adolescente *m.* (*ah-doh-leh-SHEHN-teh*) ◐(adj.)◖

adopt (to) adottare (*ah-doht-TAHR-reh*)

adoption adozione *f.* (*ah-doh-TSYOH-neh*)

adorable (adj.) adorabile (*ah-dohr-RAH-bee-leh*)

adore, worship (to) adorare (*ah-dohr-RAHR-reh*)

adorn (to) adornare (*ah-dohr-NAHR-reh*)

adorned (adj.) adorno (*ah-DOHR-noh*), adornato (*ah-dohr-NAH-toh*)

adornment adornamento *m.* (*ah-dohr-nah-MEHN-toh*)

adrenaline adrenalina *f.* (*ah-dreh-nah-LEE-nah*)

adult adulto *m.* (*ah-DOOL-toh*) ◐*f.* -ta◖

adult, grown-up (adj.) adulto (*ah-DOOL-toh*)

adulterer adultero *m.* (*ah-DOOL-tehr-roh*) ◐ *f.* -ra◖

adultery adulterio *m.* (*ah-dool-TEHR-ryoh*)

advance (to) avanzare (*ah-vahn-TSAHR-reh*) ◐**advanced** (adj.) -zato◖

advancement avanzamento *m.* (*ah-vahn-tsah-MEHN-toh*) ⚫︎

advantage avvantaggio *m.* (*ahv-vahn-TAHD-joh*), vantaggio *m.* (*vahn-TAHD-joh*) ⚫︎

advantageous (adj.) avvantaggioso (*ahv-vahn-tahd-JOH-soh*) ⚫︎

advantageously avvantaggiosamente (*ahv-vahn-tahd-joh-sah-MEHN-teh*) ⚫︎

adventure avventura *f.* (*ahv-vehn-TOOR-rah*) ⚫︎

adventurer avventuriere *m.* (*ahv-vehn-toor-RYEHR-reh*) ⚫︎

adventurous (adj.) avventuroso (*ahv-vehn-toor-ROH-soh*) ⚫︎

adversary avversario *m.* (*ahv-vehr-SAHR-ryoh*) ⚫︎

adversely avversamente (*ahv-vehr-sah-MEHN-teh*) ⚫︎

adversity, hardship avversità *f.* (*ahv-vehr-see-TAH*) 💣

advisory, notice of, notification avviso *m.* (*ahv-VEE-soh*) 💣

aerial (adj.) aereo (*ah-EH-reh-oh*)

aeronautics aeronautica *f.* (*ah-ehr-roh-NOW-tee-kah*)

aesthetics estetica *f.* (*eh-STEH-tee-kah*) ➲**aesthetic** (adj.) -ico℃

affable (adj.) affabile (*ahf-FAH-bee-leh*)

affably affabilmente (*ahf-fah-beel-MEHN-teh*)

affair (*notable matter or incident*) affare *m.* (*ahf-FAHR-reh*)

affectation affettazione *f.* (*ahf-feht-tah-TSYOH-neh*)

affection affezione *m.* (*ahf-feh-TSYOH-neh*)

affectionate (adj.) affettuoso (*ahf-feht-TWOH-soh*)

affectionately affettuosamente (*ahf-feht-twoh-sah-MEHN-teh*)

affiliation affiliazione *f.* (*ahf-fee-lyah-TSYOH-neh*)
  ⓘ A closely related noncognate is: **membership**—affiliati *m.* (*ahf-fee-LYAH-tee*)

affinity affinità *f.* (*ahf-fee-nee-TAH*)

affirm, state, aver (to) affermare (*ahf-fehr-MAHR-reh*)

affirmation, statement affermazione *f.* (*ahf-fehr-mah-TSYOH-neh*)

affirmative affermativa *f.* (ahf-fehr-mah-TEE-vah)

affirmative (adj.) affermativo (*ahf-fehr-mah-TEE-voh*)

affirmatively affermativamente (*ahf-fehr-mah-tee-vah-MEHN-teh*)

affix (to) affissare (*ahf-fees-SAHR-reh*)

afflict, distress (to) affliggere (*ahf-FLEED-jehr-reh*)

affliction, distress afflizione *f.* (*ahf-flee-TSYOH-neh*)

affront affronto *m.* (*ahf-FROHN-toh*)

agency agenzia *f.* (*ah-jehn-TSEE-ah*)

agent agente *m.* (*ah-JEHN-teh*)

aggravate (to) aggravare (*ahg-grah-VAHR-reh*)

aggravation aggravamento *m.* (*ahg-grah-vah-MEHN-toh*)

aggression aggressione *f.* (*ahg-gres-SYOH-neh*)

aggressive (adj.) aggressivo (*ahg-gres-SEE-voh*)

aggressively aggressivamente (*ahg-gres-see-vah-MEHN-teh*)

aggressiveness aggressività *f.* (*ahg-gres-see-vee-TAH*)

aggressor aggressore *m.* (*ahg-gres-SOHR-reh*)

agile, nimble (adj.) agile (*ah-JEE-leh*)

agility agilità *f.* (*ah-jee-lee-TAH*)

agitate, stir (to) agitare (*ah-jee-TAHR-reh*)

agitation agitazione *f.* (*ah-jee-tah-TSYOH-neh*)

agitated (adj.) agitato (*ah-jee-TAH-toh*)

agitator agitatore *m.* (*ah-jee-tah-TOHR-reh*)

agonize (to) agonizzare (*ah-goh-neet-TSAHR-reh*)

agonizing (adj.) agonizzante (*ah-goh-neet-TSAHN-teh*)

agony agonia *f.* (*ah-goh-NEE-ah*)

agriculture, farming agricoltura *f.* (*ah-gree-kohl-TOOR-rah*)

air (*breathable*), aria (*song*) ària *f.* (*AHR-ryah*)

air conditioning aria condizionata *f.* (*AHR-ryah kohn-dee-tsyoh-NAH-tah*)

airline linea (*f.*) aerea (*LEE-neh-ah ah-EH-reh-ah*)

airmail posta (*f.*) aerea (*POH-stah ah-EH-reh-ah*)

airplane aeroplano *m.* (*ah-eh-roh-PLAH-noh*)

airport aeroporto *m.* (*ah-eh-roh-POHR-toh*)

airy (adj.) arioso (*ahr-RYOH-soh*)

alarm (*fear OR audible alert signal*) allarme *m.* (*ahl-LAHR-meh*)

alarm (to) allarmare (*ahl-lahr-MAHR-reh*)

alarmist allarmista *m.* (*ahl-lahr-MEE-stah*)

album album *m.* (*AHL-boom*)

alcohol alcol *m.* (*AHL-kohl*), alcool *m.* (*AHL-koh-ohl*), alcole *m.* (*AHL-koh-leh*)

ⓘ Related noncognates: **beverage**—bevanda *f.* (*beh-VAHN-dah*); **drink**—bibita *f.* (*BEE-bee-tah*); **soft drink, soda, soda pop**—bibita (*f.*) non alcoolica (___*nohn ahl-KOH-lee-kah*); **(drinking) glass**—bicchiere *m.* (*beek-KYEHR-reh*); **ice**—ghiaccio *m.* (*GYAHT-choh*).

alcove alcova *f.* (*ahl-KOH-vah*)

algebra algebra *f.* (*AHL-jeh-brah*)

alibi alibi *m.* (*AH-lee-bee*)

alien alieno *m.* (*ah-LYEH-noh*)➲*f.* -na☾

alienate, estrange (to) alienare (*ah-lyeh-NAHR-reh*)

align (to) allineare (*ahl-lee-neh-AHR-reh*)

allegation allegazione *f.* (*ahl-leh-gah-TSYOH-neh*)

allege (to) allegare (*ahl-leh-GAHR-reh*)

allergy allergia *f.* (*ahl-lehr-JEE-ah*)

alleviate, relieve (to) alleviare (*ahl-leh-VYAHR-reh*)

almanac almanacco *m.* (*ahl-mah-NAHK-koh*)

along lungo (*LOON-goh*) ♦※

alphabet alfabeto *m.* (*ahl-fah-BEH-toh*) ➲**alphabetical** (adj.) -tico☾

alpine (adj.) alpino (*ahl-PEE-noh*)

Alps Alpi *f.* (*AHL-pee*)

altar altare *m.* (*ahl-TAHR-reh)*

alter (to) alterare (*ahl-tehr-RAHR-reh*)

alteration alterazione *f.* (*ahl-tehr-rah-TSYOH-neh*)

altercation altercazione *f.* (*ahl-tehr-kah-TSYOH-neh*)

alternate (to) alternare (*ahl-tehr-NAHR-reh*)

alternative alternativa *f.* (*ahl-tehr-nah-TEE-vah*) ➲(adj.) -tivo☾

altitude altitudine *f.* (*ahl-tee-TOO-dee-neh*)

aluminum alluminio *m.* (*ahl-loo-MEE-nyoh*)

amass (to) ammassare (*ahm-mahs-SAHR-reh*)

ambassador ambasciatore *m.* (*ahm-bah-shah-TOHR-reh*)

ambassador's office, embassy ambasciata *f.* (*ahm-bah-SHAH-tah*)

amber ambra *f.* (*AHM-brah*)

ambient (adj.) ambiente (*ahm-BYEHN-teh*) ⊃*m.*☾

ambiguity ambiguità *f.* (*ahm-bee-gwee-TAH*)

ambiguous (adj.) ambiguo (*ahm-BEE-gwoh*)

ambition ambizione *f.* (*ahm-bee-TSYOH-neh*)

ambitious (adj.) ambizioso (*ahm-bee-TSYOH-soh*)

ambulance ambulanza *f.* (*ahm-boo-LAHN-tsah*)

ameliorate (to) migliorare (*mee-LYOH-rah-reh*)

amend (to) emendare (*eh-mehn-DAHR-reh*) ☚

amendment emendamento *m.* (*eh-mehn-dah-MEHN-toh*) ☚

amenity amenità *f.* (*ah-meh-nee-TAH*)

America America *f.* (*ah-MEHR-ree-kah*)

American americano *m.* (*ah-mehr-ree-KAH-noh*) ⊃*f.* -na☾

American (adj.) americano (*ah-mehr-ree-KAH-noh*)

amiable (adj.) amabile (*ah-MAH-bee-leh*)

amicable (adj.) amichevole (*ah-mee-KEH-voh-leh*)

amnesia amnesia *f.* (*ahm-neh-ZEE-ah*)

amnesty amnestia *f.* (*ahm-neh-STEE-ah*)

amoral (adj.) amorale (*ah-mohr-RAH-leh*)

amorous (adj.) amoroso (*ah-mohr-ROH-soh*)

amount to (to) ammontare a (*ahm-mohn-TAHR-reh ah*)

amphibian anfibio *m.* (*ahn-FEE-byoh*) ⊃**amphibious** (adj.)☾ ☚

amphitheater anfiteatro *m.* (*ahn-fee-teh-AH-tro*) ☚

ample (adj.) ampio (*AHM-pyoh*)

amplify (to) amplificare (*ahm-plee-fee-KAHR-reh*), ampliare (*ahm-plee-AHR-reh*)

amputate (to) amputare (*ahm-poo-TAHR-reh*)

amputee amputato *m.* (*ahm-poo-TAH-toh*) ⊃**amputated** (adj.)↻

analysis analisi *f.* (*ah-NAH-lee-zee*)

analyst analista *m.* (*ah-nah-LEE-stah*) ⊃**analytic** (adj.) -tico↻

analyze (to) analizzare (*ah-nah-leed-DZAHR-reh*)

anatomical (adj.) anatomico (*ah-nah-TOH-mee-koh*)

anatomist anatomista *m.* (*ah-nah-toh-MEE-stah*)

anatomy anatomia *f.* (*ah-nah-toh-MEE-ah*)

anchor àncora *f.* (*AHN-kohr-rah*)

anchor (to) ancorare (*ahn-kohr-RAHR-reh*)

anchorage ancoraggio *m.* (*ahn-kohr-RAHD-joh*)

anecdote aneddoto *m.* (*ah-NEHD-doh-toh*)

anemia anemia *f.* (*ah-neh-MEE-ah*)

anesthesia anestesia *f.* (*ah-neh-steh-SEE-ah*)

anesthetic anestetico *m.* (*ah-neh-STEH-tee-koh*) ⊃(adj.)↻ 👋

anesthetist anestesista *m.* (*ah-neh-steh-ZEE-stah*)

angel àngelo *m.* (*AHN-jeh-loh*)

angle, corner, street corner angolo *m.* (*AHN-goh-loh*)

anguish angoscia *f.* (*ahn-GOH-shah*)

angular (adj.) angolare (*ahn-goh-LAHR-reh*)

animal animale *m.* (*ah-nee-MAH-leh*) ⊃(adj.)↻

animated (adj.) animato (*ah-nee-MAH-toh*)

animation animazione *f.* (*ah-nee-mah-TSYOH-neh*)

animosity animosità *f.* (*ah-nee-moh-see-TAH*)

anise ànice *m.* (*AH-nee-cheh*)

annex annesso *m.* (*ahn-NEHS-soh*)

anniversary anniversario *m.* (*ahn-nee-vehr-SAHR-ryoh*)

annotate (to)   annotare (*ahn-noh-TAHR-reh*)

annotation   annotazione *f.* (*ahn-noh-tah-TSYOH-neh*)

announce (to)   annunciare (*ahn-noon-CHAR-reh*), annunziare (*ahn-noon-TSYAHR-reh*)

announcement, advertisement   annunzio *m.* (*ahn-NOON-tsyoh*)

annoy, harass (to)   annoiare (*ahn-noh-YAHR-reh*)

annual, yearly (adj.)   annuale (*ahn-NWAH-leh*), annuo (*AHN-woh*)

annually, yearly   annualmente (*ahn-nwahl-MEHN-teh*)

annul, nullify, cancel, efface (to)   annullare (*ahn-nool-LAHR-reh*)

annulment, nullification, cancellation   annullamento *m.* (*ahn-nool-lah-MEHN-toh*)

anomaly   anomalia *f.* (*ah-noh-mah-LEE-ah*)

anonymous (adj.)   anonimo (*ah-NOH-nee-moh*)

antacid   antacido *m.* (*ahn-TAH-chee-doh*)

antagonism   antagonismo *m.* (*ahn-tah-goh-NEEZ-moh*)

antagonist, opponent   antagonista *m.* (*ahn-tah-goh-NEE-stah*)

anthology   antologia *f.* (*ahn-toh-loh-JEE-ah*)

anthropology   antropologia *f.* (*ahn-troh-poh-loh-JEE-ah*)

antibiotic   antibiotico *m.* (*ahn-tee-bee-OH-tee-koh*)

antibody   anticorpo *m.* (*ahn-tee-KOHR-poh*)

anticipate (to)   anticipare (*ahn-tee-chee-PAHR-reh*)

anticipation   anticipazione *f.* (*ahn-tee-chee-pah-TSYOH-neh*)

antidote   antidoto *m.* (*ahn-TEE-doh-toh*)

antipathetic, disagreeable, nasty *(in attitude)* (adj.)   antipatico (*ahn-tee-PAH-tee-koh*)

antipathy, dislike   antipatia *f.* (*ahn-tee-pah-TEE-ah*)

antiquated (adj.)   antiquato (*ahn-tee-KWAH-toh*)

antique *(old object)*   oggetto antico *m.*(*ohd-JEHT-toh AHN-tee-koh*)

antique, ancient (adj.) antico (*ahn-TEE-koh*)

antiquity antichità *f.* (*ahn-tee-kee-TAH*), antiquità (*ahn-tee-kwee-TAH*)

antiseptic antisettico *m.* (*ahn-tee-SEHT-tee-koh*) ➲(adj.)➾

antisocial (adj.) antisociale (*ahn-tee-soh-CHAH-leh*)

anxiety (*nervous tension*) ansia *f.* (*AHN-syah*)

anxiety (*concerned, worried nervousness*) ansietà *f.* (*ahn-syeh-TAH*)

anxious, uneasy (adj.) ansioso (*ahn-SYOH-soh*), inquieto (*een-kwee-EH-toh*)

apart, separated, aside a parte (*ah PAHR-teh*), da parte (*dah PAHR-teh*), in disparte (*een dee-spahr-teh*)

apartment appartamento *m.* (*ahp-pahr-tah-MEHN-toh*)

apathy apatia *f.* (*ah-pah-TEE-ah*)

aperitif aperitivo *m.* (*ah-pehr-reeh-TEE-voh*)

aperture, breach, gap apertura *f.* (*ah-pehr-TOOR-rah*)

aphorism aforismo *m.* (*ahf-fohr-REEZ-moh*)

apology apologia *f.* (*ah-poh-loh-JEE-ah*)

apostle apostolo *m.* (*ah-POH-stoh-loh*)

apparatus apparato *m.* (*ahp-pahr-RAH-toh*)

apparent (adj.) apparente (*ahp-pahr-REHN-teh*)

apparition apparizione *f.* (*ahp-pahr-ree-TSYOH-neh*)

appeal appello *m.* (*ahp-PEHL-loh*)

appeal (to) appellare (*ahp-pehl-LAHR-reh*)

appear (*come into view*) (to) apparire (*ahp-pahr-REER-reh*)

appearance (*look, aspect*) apparenza *f.* (*ahp-pahr-REHN-tsah*)

appendage, appendix appendice *f.* (*ahp-pehn-DEE-cheh*)

appendectomy appendicectomia *f.* (*ahp-pehn-dee-chek-toh-MYAH*)

appendicitis appendicite *f.* (*ahp-pehn-dee-CHEE-teh*)

appetite appetito *m.* (*ahp-peh-TEE-toh*)

applause applauso *m.* (*ahp-PLOW-soh*)

applicable (adj.) applicabile (*ahp-plee-KAH-bee-leh*)

application applicazione *f.* (*ahp-plee-kah-TSYOH-neh*)

apply (to) applicare (*ahp-plee-KAHR-reh*)

appointment, date, tryst (*social engagement*) appuntamento *m.* (*ahp-poon-tah-MEHN-toh*)

appreciate (*understand or value, prize*) (to) apprezzare (*ahp-preht-TSAHR-reh*)

appreciation apprezzamento *m.* (*ahp-preht-tsah-MEHN-toh*)

apprehend (to) apprendere (*ahp-PREHN-dehr-reh*)

apprehension, misgiving apprensione *f.* (*ahp-prehn-SYOH-neh*)

apprentice apprendista *m.* (*ahp-prehn-DEE-stah*)

appropriate (adj.) appropriato (*ahp-proh-pree-AH-toh*)

appropriate (*take possession of*) (to) appropriarsi (*ahp-proh-pree-AHR-see*)

approval approvazione *f.* (*ahp-proh-vah-TSYOH-neh*)

approve (to) approvare (*ahp-proh-VAHR-reh*)

approximate (to) approssimare (*ahp-prohs-see-MAHR-reh*)

approximate (adj.) approssimativo (*ahp-prohs-see-mah-TEE-voh*)

approximately approssimativamente (*ahp-prohs-see-mah-tee-vah-MEHN-teh*)

approximation approssimazione *f.* (*ahp-prohs-see-mah-TSYOH-neh*)

apropos (adj.) a propòsito (*ah-pro-POH-zee-toh*)

aquarium acquario *m.* (*ahk-KWAHR-ryoh*) ♦

aquatic (adj.) acquatico (*ahk-KWAH-tee-koh*) ♦

aqueduct acquedotto *m.* (*ahk-kweh-DOHT-toh*) ♦

Arab arabo *m.* (*AHR-rah-boh*) ➲(adj.)ℂ

arbiter, umpire àrbitro *m.* (*AHR-bee-troh*)

arbitrary, high-handed (adj.) arbitrario (*ahr-bee-TRAHR-ryoh*)

arbitrate (to) arbitrare (*ahr-bee-TRAHR-reh*)

arbitration arbitrato *m.* (*ahr-bee-TRAH-toh*)

arbitrator arbitro *m.* (*AHR-bee-troh*)

arc, arch arco *m.* (*AHR-koh*)

✦ This word is easy to confuse with **arca, ark!**

archaeology archeologia *f.* (*ahr-keh-oh-loh-JEE-ah*)

archaic (adj.) arcaico (*ahr-KAH-ee-koh*)

architect architetto *m.* (*ahr-kee-TEHT-toh*)

architectural (adj.) architettonico (*ahr-kee-teht-TOH-nee-koh*)

architecture architettura *f.* (*ahr-kee-teht-TOOR-rah*)

archive, file (to) archiviare (*ahr-kee-VYAHR-reh*)

archive(s), file(s) archivio *m.* (*ahr-KEE-vyoh*)

Arctic Artico *m.* (*AHR-tee-koh*) ⊃(adj.)**C**

ardor ardore *m.* (*ahr-DOHR-reh*) ⊃**ardent** (adj.) -dente**C**

arduous (adj.) àrduo (*AHR-dwoh*)

area àrea *f.* (*AH-reh-ah*)

arena arena *f.* (*ahr-REH-nah*)

argue (*posit a logical thesis, NOT "quarrel"*) (to) arguire (*ahr-GWEER-reh*)
ⓘ The concept of arguing in a quarrelsome manner is embraced by the noncognates: **quarrel**—lite *f.* (*LEE-teh*); **to quarrel**—litigare (*lee-tee-GAHR-reh*).

argument (*theme of, topic of, or logical position*) argomento *m.* (*ahr-goh-MEHN-toh*)

aristocracy aristocrazia *f.* (*ah-ree-stoh-krah-TSEE-ah*)

aristocrat aristocrate *m.* (*ah-ree-stoh-KRAH-teh*)

aristocratic (adj.) aristocratico (*ah-ree-stoh-KRAH-tee-koh*)

arithmetic aritmetica *f.* (*ah-reet-MEH-tee-kah*)

arm, weapon arma *f.* (*AHR-mah*)

arm (to) armare (*ahr-MAHR-reh*)

armament armamento *m.* (*ahr-mah-MEHN-toh*)

armistice armistizio *m.* (*ahr-mee-STEE-tsyoh*)

armor armatura *f.* (*ahr-mah-TOOR-rah*)

arms (*weaponry*) armi *f.* (*AHR-mee*)

aroma aroma *f.* (*ahr-ROH-mah*)

aromatic (adj.) aromatico (*ahr-roh-MAH-tee-koh*)

arrest arresto *m.* (*ahr-RREH-stoh*)

arrest (to) arrestare (*ahr-rreh-STAHR-reh*)
ⓘ A closely related noncognate is: **to stall**—arrestarsi (*ahr-rreh-STAHR-see*).

arrival arrivo *m.* (*ahr-RREE-voh*)

arrive, **get to**, **reach (*somewhere*)** (to) arrivare (*ahr-rree-VAHR-reh*)

arrogance arroganza *f.* (*ahr-rroh-GAHN-tsah*)

arrogant (adj.) arrogante (*ahr-rroh-GAHN-teh*)

art arte *f.* (*AHR-teh*)

artery arteria *f.* (*ahr-TEHR-ryah*)

arthritis artrite *f.* (*ahr-TREE-teh*)

article (*physical or literary*), item articolo *m.* (*ahr-TEE-koh-loh*)

artifice artificio *m.* (*ahr-tee-FEE-choh*) ➲**artificial** (adj.) -ciale⊂

artificiality artificialità *f.* (*ahr-tee-fee-cha-lee-TAH*)

artisan artigiano *m.* (*ahr-tee-JAH-noh*)

artist artista *m.* & *f.* (*ahr-TEE-stah*)

artistic (adj.) artistico (*ahr-TEE-stee-koh*)

artistry arte *f.* (*AHR-teh*)

ascertain (to) accertarsi (*aht-chehr-TAHR-see*)

ascribe (to) ascrivere (*ah-SKREE-vehr-reh*)

asparagus asparago *m.* (*ah-SPAHR-rah-goh*)

aspect, **appearance of**, **look of** aspetto *m.* (*ah-SPEHT-toh*)

aspire to (to) aspirare a (*ah-spee-RAHR-reh ah*)

aspirin aspirina *f.* (*ah-speer-REE-nah*)

ass asino *m.* (*AH-see-noh*)

assail, **pelt** (to) assalire (*ahs-sah-LEER-reh*)

assailant, attacker assalitore *m.* (*ahs-sah-lee-TOHR-reh*)

assassin, murderer assassino *m.* (*ahs-sahs-SEE-noh*)

assassinate, murder (to) assassinare (*ahs-sahs-see-NAHR-reh*)

assassination, murder assassinio *m.* (*ahs-sahs-SEE-nyoh*)

assault (to) assalire (a*hs-sah-LEER-reh*)

assault assalto *m.* (*ahs-SAHL-toh*)

assembly, meeting assemblea *f.* (*ahs-sehm-BLEH-ah*), congresso *m.*(*kohn-GRES-soh*)

assent assenso *m.* (*ahs-SEHN-soh*)

assent (to) assentire (*ahs-sehn-TEER-reh*)

assert (to) asserire (*ahs-seh-REER-reh*)

assertion asserzione *f.* (*ahs-sehr-TSYOH-neh*)

assign (to) assegnare (*ahs-seh-NYAHR-reh*)

assignation assegnazione *f.* (*ahs-seh-nyah-TSYOH-neh*)

assignment assegnamento *m.* (*ahs-seh-nyah-MEHN-toh*)

assimilate (to) assimilare (*ahs-see-mee-LAHR-reh*)

assimilation assimilazione *f.* (*ahs-see-mee-lah-TSYOH-neh*)

assimilative (adj.) assimilativo (*ahs-see-mee-lah-TEE-voh*)

assist (to) assistere (*ahs-SEE-stehr-reh*)

assistance assistenza *f.* (*ahs-see-STEHN-tsah*)

assistant assistente *m.* & *f.* (*ahs-see-STEHN-teh*)

associate (to) associare (*ahs-soh-CHAR-reh*)

associated (adj.) associato (*ahs-soh-CHAH-toh*)

association (*group organization*) associazione *f.* (*ahs-soh-chah-TSYOH-neh*)

assorted (adj.) assortito (*ahs-sohr-TEE-toh*)

assortment assortimento *m.* (*ahs-sohr-tee-MEHN-toh*)

assume (to) assumere (*ahs-SOO-mehr-reh*)

assurance assicurazione *f.* (*ahs-see-koor-rah-TSYOH-neh*), sicurezza *f.* (*see-koor-REHT-tsa*)

assure, insure (to) assicurare (*ahs-see-koor-RAHR-reh*)
  ① The closely related noncognate: **insurance**—assicurazione *f.* (*ahs-see-koor-rah-TSYOH-neh*)

assured (adj.) assicurato (*ahs-see-koor-RAHT-toh*)

asthma asma *m. & f.* (*AHZ-mah*)

astrology astrologia *f.* (*ah-stroh-LOH-jee-ah*)

astronaut astronauta *m. & f.* (*ah-stroh-NAOW-tah*)

astronomy astronomia *f.* (*ah-stroh-noh-MEE-ah*)

astute (adj.) astuto (*ah-STOO-toh*)

asymmetrical (adj.) asimmetrico (*ah-seem-MEH-tree-koh*)

asymmetry asimmetria *f.* (*ah-seem-meh-TREE-ah*)

athlete atleta *m. & f.* (*ah-TLEH-tah*)

athletic (adj.) atletico (*ah-TLEH-tee-koh*)

athletics atletismo *m.* (*ah-tleh-TEEZ-moh*)

atmosphere atmosfera *f.* (*aht-moh-SFEHR-rah*)

atmospheric (adj.) atmosferico (*aht-moh-SFEHR-ree-koh*)

atom atomo *m.* (*AH-toh-moh*)

atomic (adj.) atomico (*ah-TOH-mee-koh*)

atomic bomb bomba (*f.*) atomica (*BOHM-bah ah-TOH-mee-kah*)

atonal (adj.) atonale (*ah-toh-NAH-leh*)

atrocious, heinous (adj.) atroce (*ah-TROH-cheh*)

atrocity atrocità *f.* (*ah-troh-chee-TAH*)

atrophy atrofia *f.* (*ah-troh-FEE-ah*)

attach, attack (to) attaccare (*aht-tahk-KAHR-reh*)
  💣 NOTE that the English terms are highly dissimilar!

attachment attaccamento *m.* (*aht-tahk-kah-MEHN-toh*)

attack   attacco *m.* (*aht-TAHK-koh*)

attack, attach (to)   attaccare (*aht-tahk-KAHR-reh*)
   👉 NOTE that the English terms are highly dissimilar!

attempt   tentativo *m.* (*tehn-tah-TEE-voh*) 👉

attempt (to)   tentare (*tehn-TAHR-reh*) 👉

attention   attenzione *f.* (*aht-tehn-TSYOH-neh*)

attention!   attenzione! (*aht-tehn-TSYOH-neh*)
   ① A closely related noncognate: **watch out!**—attento! (*aht-TEHN-toh*)

attentive (adj.)   attento (*aht-TEHN-toh*)

attentively   attentamente (*aht-tehn-tah-MEHN-teh*)

attest, vouch for (to)   attestare (*aht-teh-STAHR-reh*)

attract (to)   attrarre (*aht-TRAHR-rreh*)

attraction (*engaging quality*)   attrazione *f.* (*aht-trah-TSYOH-neh*)

attractive (adj.)   attraente (*aht-trah-EHN-teh*)

attribute (to)   attribuire (*aht-tree-BWEER-reh*)

attribute   attributo *m.*(*aht-tree-BOO-toh*)

attrition   attrizione *f.* (*aht-tree-TSYOH-neh*)

audacity   audacia *f.* (*aow-DAH-chee-ah*)

audible (adj.)   udibile (*oo-DEE-bee-leh*) 👉

audition   audizione *f.* (*aow-dee-TSYOH-neh*)

auditor   uditore *m.* (*oo-dee-TOHR-reh*) 👉

auditorium   auditorio *m.* (*aow-dee-TOHR-ryoh*)

aura   aura *f.* (*AOW-rah*)

aureola, halo   aureola *f.* (*aowr-REH-oh-lah*)

austere (adj.)   austero (*aow-STEHR-roh*)

austerity   austerità *f.* (*aow-stehr-ree-TAH*)

authentic (adj.)   autentico (*aow-TEHN-tee-koh*)

authenticity   autenticità *f.* (*aow-tehn-tee-chee-TAH*)

author autore *m.* (*aow-TOHR-reh*)

authoritarian (adj.) autoritario (*aow-toh-ree-TAHR-ryoh*)

authoritative (adj.) autorevole (*aow-tohr-REH-voh-leh*)

authoritatively autorevolmente (*aow-tohr-reh-vohl-MEHN-teh*)

authority autorità *f.* (*aow-toh-ree-TAH*)

authorization autorizzazione *f.* (*aow-toh-reed-dzah-TSYOH-neh*)

authorize (to) autorizzare (*aow-toh-reed-DZAHR-reh*)

autobiography autobiografia *f.* (*aow-toh-byoh-grah-FEE-ah*)

autograph autografo *m.* (*aow-TOH-grah-foh*)

automatic (adj.) automatico (*aow-toh-MAH-tee-koh*)

ATM / automatic teller machine Bancomat® (*BAHN-koh-maht*)

automatically automaticamente (*aow-toh-mah-tee-kah-MEHN-teh*)

automobile automobile *f.* (*aow-toh-MOH-bee-leh*), auto (*AOW-toh*)
  ⓘ While this cognate is widely used, many Italians retain a preference for the word ***macchina*** (*MAHK-kee-nah*), their original term for *automobile*. Related semicognates: **motorist**—autista *m.* (*aow-TEE-stah*) / automobilista *m.* (*aow-toh-moh-bee-LEE-stah*); and **truck**—autocarro *m.* (*aow-toh-KAHR-rroh*).

autonomy autonomia *f.* (*aow-toh-noh-MEE-ah*)

autopsy autopsia *f.* (*aow-tohp-SEE-ah*)

avalanche valanga *f.* (*vah-LAHN-gah*) ☀

avaricious, stingy, miserly (adj.) avaro (*ah-VAHR-roh*)
  ☀ The related noncognate noun is **miser**—avaro *m.*

averse, against, versus avverso (*ahv-VEHR-soh*), contro (*KOHN-troh*)

aversion avversione *f.* (*ahv-vehr-SYOH-neh*)

aviation aviazione *f.* (*ah-vyah-TSYOH-neh*)

aviator, flier aviatore *m.* (*ah-vyah-TOHR-reh*) ➲*f.* -trice◖

avid (adj.) avido (*AH-vee-doh*)

avocado pera (*f.*) avocado (*PEHR-rah ah-voh-KAH-doh*)

axe   ascia *f.* (*AH-shah*)

axis, axle   asse *m.* (*AHS-seh*)

azure (adj.)   azzuro (*ahd-ZOOR-roh*)

—B—

babble   balbettio *m.* (*bahl-BEHT-tyoh*) 💣

babble (to)   balbettare (*bahl-beht-TAHR-reh*) 💣

baboon   babbuino *m.* (*bahb-BWEE-noh*)

baby   baby *m. & f.* (*BAY-bee*)
  ⓘ This direct-from-English import is becoming increasingly common in larger urban centers, in conversation with English speakers. Among Italians themselves, however, the terms **bambino** and **bambina** remain the norm.

babysitter   baby-sitter *m. & f.* (*bay-bee-SEET-teh-reh*)
  ⓘ Another import in polite concession to the needs of non-Italian speaking visitors. As above, however, the term is not used in Italian-to-Italian interchange.

bacteria   batteri *m.* (*baht-TEHR-ree*)

bacteriology   batteriologia *f.* (*baht-tehr-ryoh-loh-JEE-ah*)

baggage, luggage   bagaglio *m.* (*bah-GAH-lyoh*)

balance (*weighing device*)   bilancia *f.* (*bee-LAHN-chah*)

balcony   balcone *m.* (*bahl-KOH-neh*)

ball (*dance*), dancing   ballo *m.* (*BAHL-loh*)

ball (*sphere*)   palla *f.* (*PAHL-lah*)

ballad   ballata *f.* (*bahl-LAH-tah*)

ballerina   ballerina *f.* (*bahl-lehr-REE-nah*) ➲*m.* -rino🅲
  ⓘ These terms apply to dancers in general, rather than simply to performers of "classical" stage works.

ballet   balletto *m.* (*bahl-LEHT-toh*)

balloon   pallone *m.* (*pahl-LOH-neh*) 💣

balm balsamo *m.* (*BAHL-sah-moh*)

balmy (*weather*) (adj.) balsamico (*bahl-SAH-mee-koh*)

balustrade balustrata *f.* (*bah-loo-STRAH-tah*)

bamboo bambù *m.* (*bahm-BOO*)

banal, hackneyed (adj.) banale (*bah-NAH-leh*)

banality, platitude banalità *f.* (*bah-nah-lee-TAH*)

banana banana *f.* (*bah-NAH-nah*)

band (*group of persons*) banda *f.* (*BAHN-dah*)
  ① The instrumental, musical group is a **banda (*f.*) musicale** (*BAHN-dah moo-zee-KAH-leh*).

band (*instrumental*) banda musicale (*BAHN-dah moo-zee-KAH-leh*)

bandage benda (*BHEN-dah*)

bandit bandito *m.* (*bahn-DEE-toh*)

  ① An armed bandit, or a gunman, is a **bandito (*m.*) armato** (*bahn-DEE-toh ahr-MAH-toh*)

bank (*financial institution, NOT embankment*) banca *f.* (*BAHN-kah*)
  ① A **pier** or **(station) platform**—banchina *f.* (*bahn-KEE-nah*)

banker banchiere *m.* (*bahn-KYEHR-reh*)

banknote banconota *f.* (*bahn-koh-NOH-tah*)

banner, flag bandiera *f.* (*bahn-DYEHR-rah*)

banquet banchetto *m.* (*bahn-KEHT-toh*)

baptism battesimo *m.* (*baht-TEH-zee-moh*)

baptistery battistero *m.* (*baht-tee-STEHR-roh*)

bar, saloon bar *m.* (*BAHR-reh*)
  ① This direct-from-English import has been widely adopted even in intra-Italian converse.

bar (*pole*) barra *f.* (*BAHRR-rah*), sbarra *f.* (*SBAHRR-rah*)

barbarian barbaro *m.* (*BAHR-barr-roh*)

barbarism barbarismo *m.* (*bahr-bahr-REEZ-moh*)

barbarity barbarie *f.* (*bahr-BAHR-ryeh*)

barbarous (adj.) barbaro (*BAHR-bahr-roh*)

barbecue barbecue *m.* (*BAHR-beh-koo*)
    ① As both noun and verb, this term has made its way from Haiti into both Spanish and English, and from there into Italian and many other languages. While the general concept is well understood in Italian, there remains considerable disinterest (and lack of polish) in its execution.

barber barbiere *m.* (*bahr-BYEHR-reh*)
    ① Related are: **beard**—barba *f.* (*BAHR-bah*); **bearded** (adj.)—barbuto (*bahr-BOO-toh*); and **shaving cream**—crema (*f.*) da barba (*KREHM-mah dah BAHR-bah*).

barometer barometro *m.* (*bahr-ROH-meh-troh*)

barometric (adj.) barometrico (*bahr-roh-MEH-tree-koh*)

baron barone *m.* (*bahr-ROH-neh*)

baroness baronessa *f.* (*bahr-roh-NEHS-sah*)

baroque (adj.) barocco (*bahr-ROHK-koh*)

barrel, cask barile *m.* (*bahr-REE-leh*)

barricade barricata *f.* (*bahr-rree-KAH-tah*)

barrier barriera *f.* (*bahr-RYEHR-rah*)

barter, swap (to) barattare (*bahr-aht-TAHR-reh*)

base, basis base *f.* (*BAH-zeh*)

base (to) basare (*bah-ZAHR-reh*)

baseball baseball *m.* (*BAHZ-eh-BAHL-leh*)

basic (adj.) basilare (*bah-zee-LAHR-reh*), fondamentale (*fohn-dah-mehn TAH-leh*), basico (*BAH-zee-koh*)

basketball basket-ball *m.* (*BAHZ-skeet-bahl-leh*)

bastard, mongrel bastardo *m.* (*bah-STAHR-doh*) ➲(adj.)Ↄ

battalion battaglione *m.* (*baht-tah-LYOH-neh*)

batter (to) battere (*BAHT-tehr-reh*)

battery (*artillery emplacement* OR *electrical storage*) batteria *f.* (*baht-tehr-REE-ah*)

ⓘ While this word is becoming increasingly familiar in reference to portable electricity storage devices, many Italians still prefer and use their original term: *pila f.* (*PEE-lah*).

battle battaglia *f.* (*baht-TAH-lyah*)
   ⓘ Closely related: (**little**) **battle, squabble**—battibecco *m.* (*baht-tee-BEHK-koh*)

battlefield campo (*m.*) di battaglia (*KAHM-poh dee baht-TAH-lyah*)

bay baia *f.* (*BAH-yah*)

bazaar bazar *m* (*bah-DZAHR*)

beast bestia *f.* (*BEH-styah*)

beat (*rhythmic sound*) battito *m.* (*BAHT-tee-toh*)

beat (*be victorious over*), defeat, beat up (to) battere (*BAHT-tehr-reh*)

beaten (adj.) battuto (*baht-TOO-toh*)

beatify (to) beatificare (*beh-ah-tee-fee-KAHR-reh*)

beefsteak, steak bistecca *f.* (*bee-STEHK-kah*)

beer birra *f.* (*BEERR-rah*)

belligerence belligeranza *f.* (*behl-lee-jehr-RAHN-tsah*)

belligerent (adj.) belligerante (*behl-lee-jehr-RAHN-teh*)
   ⓘ This and the other **bel-** word above are polar opposites of the more prevalent use of **bel-** to denote one or another manifestation of **beauty**. The former category of **bel-** words come from Latin *bellum* (war) and the latter, from Latin *bellu(m)* (carino), which in turn comes from the diminuitive of *bonus* (buono).

benediction, blessing benedizione *f.* (*beh-neh-dee-TSYOH-neh*)

benefactor benefattore *m.* (*beh-neh-faht-TOHR-reh*) ⊃*f.* -trice☾

beneficiary beneficiario *m.* (*beh-neh-fee-CHAHR-ryoh*)

benefit beneficio *m.* (*beh-neh-FEE-choh*)

benevolence benevolenza *f.* (*beh-neh-voh-LEHN-tsah*)

benevolent (adj.) benevolo (*beh-NEH-voh-loh*)

benign (adj.) benigno (*beh-NEE-nyoh*)

beverage   bevanda *f.* (*beh-VAHN-dah*)

Bible   Bibbia *f.* (*BEEB-byah*) ➲**biblical** (adj.) biblico**C**

bibliography   bibliografia *f.* (*bee-blee-oh-grah-FEE-ah*)

bicarbonate   bicarbonato *m.* (*bee-kahr-boh-NAH-toh*)

biceps   bicipite *m.* (*bee-CHEE-pee-teh*)

bicycle   bicicletta f. (*bee-chee-KLEHT-tah*), bici *f.* (*BEE-chee*)

bicyclist   ciclista *m.* & *f.* (*chee-KLEE-stah*) ✹

biennial, biannual (adj.)   biennale (*bee-ehn-NAH-leh*)

bifocal (adj.)   bifocale (*bee-foh-KAH-leh*)

big   big *m.* & *f.* (*BEEG*)
   ⓘ Italians understand and use this word in conversation with English
   speakers, but it remains a distinctly secondary foreign term to them, not
   normal in *their* everyday use. They still prefer *grande*.

bigot   bigotto *m.* (*bee-GOHT-toh*) ➲**bigoted** (adj.)**C**

bigotry   bigotteria *m.* (*bee-goht-tehr-REE-a*h)

bile   bile *f.* (*BEE-leh*)

bilingual (adj.)   bilingue (*bee-LEEN-gweh*)

billiards   biliardo m. (*bee-LYAHR-doh*)

binoculars   binocolo *m.* (*bee-NOH-koh-loh*)
   ⓘ **Binocolo da teatro** (*bee-NOH-koh-loh dah teh-AH-troh*) are *opera
   glasses.*

biochemistry   biochimica *f.* (*byoh-KEE-mee-kah*)

biographer   biografo *m.* (*bee-OH-grah-foh*)

biographical (adj.)   biografico (*byoh-GRAH-fee-koh*)

biography   biografia *f.* (*byoh-gra-FEE-ah*)

biological (adj.)   biologico (*byoh-LOH-jee-koh*)

biology   biologia *f.* (*byoh-loh-JEE-ah*)

biscuit, cookie, cracker   biscotto *m.* (*bee-SKOHT-toh*)

bizarre, strange, weird (adj.)   bizzarro (*beed-DZAHRR-roh*)

bland (adj.) *blando* (*BLAHN-doh*)

blasphemous (adj.) *blasfemo* (*blah-SFEH-moh*)

blasphemy blasfemia *f.* (*blah-SFEH-myah*)

block blocco *m.* (*BLOHK-koh*)

blond (adj.) biondo (*BYOHN-doh*)

blouse blusa *f.* (*BLOO-zah*)

blue (*color,* NOT *mood*) (adj.) blu (*BLOO*), azzurro (*ahd-DZOORR-roh*)

blue jeans blue-jeans *m.* (*BLOO-jeenz*)

bluff (*ploy,* NOT *cliff*) bluff *m.* (*BLOOF-feh*)

bluff (to) bluffare (*bloof-FAHR-reh*)

Bohemian boemo *m.* (*boh-EH-moh*) ⊃(adj.)ℂ

bohemian bohémien *m.* (*boh-eh-mee-EH*)

boil (to) bollire (*bohl-LEER-reh*)

bomb, bombshell bomba *f.* (*BOHM-bah*)

bombard, shell (to) bombardare (*bohm-bahr-DAHR-reh*)

bombardment bombardamento *m.* (*bohm-bahr-dah-MEHN-toh*)

bomber bombardiere *m.* (*bohm-bahr-DYEHR-reh*)

boom (*economic*) boom *m.* (*BOO-meh*)

border bordo *m.* (*BOHR-doh*)

botany botanica *f.* (*boh-TAH-nee-kah*) ⊃**botanical** (adj.) -nicoℂ

bottle bottiglia *f.* (*boht-TEE-lyah*)

Boy Scout boy-scout *m.* (*boh-ee-SKOWT*)

boycott boicottaggio *m.* (*boy-koht-TAHD-joh*)

boycott (to) boicottare (*boy-koht-TAHR-reh*)

bracelet braccialetto m. (*braht-chah-LEHT-toh*)

brandish (to) brandire (*brahn-DEER-reh*)

brandy brandy *m.* (*BRAHN-dee*), acquavite *f.* (*ahk-kwah-VEE-teh*)

bravado bravata *f.* (*brah-VAH-tah*)

breeze brezza *f.* (*BREHD-dzah*)

brevity brevità *f.* (*breh-vee-TAH*)

bridle briglia *f.* (*BREE-lyah*)

brief, short (adj.) breve (*BREH-veh*)

briefly brevemente (*breh-veh-MEHN-teh*)

brilliant (adj.) brillante (*breel-LAHN-teh*)

brio, sprightliness, verve, vim brio (*BREE-oh*)

(with) brio, sprightly (adj.) brioso (*bree-OH-soh*)

British (adj.) britannico (*bree-TAHN-nee-koh*)

Briton bretone *m.* (*BREH-toh-neh*)

brocade broccato *m.* (*brohk-KAH-toh*)

bronchitis bronchite *f.* (*brohn-KEE-teh*)

bronze bronzo *m.* (*BROHN-dzoh*)
   ⓘ The Italian construction *bronz-* is also applied to words that connote the quality of being bronzed. Thus: *abbronzare* (*ahb-brohn-DZAHR-reh*), *(to) sunbathe; abbronzatura f.* (*ahb-brohn-dzah-TOOR-rah*), *sunburn;* and *abbronzato* (*ahb-brohn-DZAH-toh*), *sunburned* (adj.)**.**

brown (adj.) bruno (*BROO-noh*) ➲**brunette** (adj.) -na➲.

brusque (adj.) brusco (*BROO-skoh*)

brutal (adj.) brutale (*broo-TAH-leh*)

brutality brutalità *f.* (*broo-tah-lee-TAH*)

brutalize (to) abbrutire (*ahb-broo-TEER-reh*) ♦※

brute bruto *m.* (*BROO-toh*) ➲(adj.)➲

buffoon, jester buffone *m.* (*boof-FOH-neh*)

bulb (*botanical*) bulbo *m.* (*BOOL-boh*)
   ⓘ An electric **lightbulb** is *lampadina f.* (*lahm-pah-DEE-nah*).

bulletin bollettino *m.* (*bohl-leht-TEE-noh*)

bungalow bungalow *m.* (*boon-gah-LOH*)

burnish (to) brunire (*broo-NEER-reh*)

bus bus *m.* (*BOOS*), autobus *f.* (*AOW-toh-boos*), pullman *m.* (*POOHL-lmahn*)
ⓘ The contraction of the century-old **autobus** to **bus** is a recent development in the larger Northern Italian cities, spreading slowly to outlying areas. The term **pullman** generally refers to larger intercity and modern tour busses, rather than local route vehicles.

bust (*sculpture*) busto *m.* (*BOO-stoh*)

button bottone *m.* (*boht-TOH-neh*)

cabin (*land or shipboard*) cabina *f.* (*kah-BEE-nah*)

cabinet (*governmental, NOT furniture*) gabinetto *m.* (*gah-bee-NEHT-toh*)
ⓘ This term also denotes: **toilet room, small private room, small office, studio.**

cacophony cacofonia *f.* (*kah-koh-foh-NEE-ah*)

cactus cacto *m.* (*KAHK-toh*)

cadaver, corpse cadavere *m.* (*kah-DAH-vehr-reh*)

cadence cadenza *f.* (*kah-DEHN-tsah*)

caffeine caffeina *f.* (*kahf-feh-EE-nah*)

calamitous (adj.) calamitoso (*kah-lah-mee-TOH-soh*)

calamity, woe calamità *f.* (*kah-lah-mee-TAH*)

calcium calcio *m.* (*KAHL-choh*)

calculate (to) calcolare (*kahl-koh-LAHR-reh*)

calculator macchina calcolatrice *f.* (*MAHK-kee-nah kahl-koh-lah-TREE-cheh*)

calculation, calculus calcolo *m.* (*KAHL-koh-loh*)

calligraphy, handwriting calligrafia *f.* (*kahl-lee-GRAH-fyah*)

callous (adj.) calloso (*kahl-LOH-soh*)

calm, stillness calma *f.* (*KAHL-mah*), quiete (*kwee-EH-teh*)

calm, still (adj.)   calmo (*KAHL-moh*)

calm, soothe (to)   calmare (*kahl-MAHR-reh*)

calmative, tranquilizer   calmante *m.* (*kahl-MAHN-teh*)

calmly   con calmo (*kohn KAHL-moh*)

calmness   calma *f.* (*KAHL-mah*)

caloric (adj.)   calorico (*kah-LOHR-ree-koh*)

calorie   caloria *f.* (*kah-lohr-REE-ah*)

camelia   camelia *f.* (*kah-MEH-lyah*)

cameo   cammeo *m.* (*kahm-MEH-oh*)

camp   campo *m.* (*KAHM-poh*), accampamento (*ahk-kahm-pah-MEHN-toh*) 💣

campaign (*military, political,* OR *advertising*)   campagna *f.* (*kahm-PAH-nyah*)

camper   campeggiatore *m.* (*kahm-pehd-jah-TOHR-reh*)

camping   campeggio *m.* (*kahm-PEHD-joh*)

canal, channel   canale *m.* (*kah-NAH-leh*)

canary   canarino *m.* (*kah-nahr-REE-noh*)

cancel, erase (to)   cancellare (*kahn-chel-LAHR-reh*)

cancer   cancro *m.* (*KAHN-kroh*)

candelabrum   candelabro *m.* (*kahn-deh-LAH-bro*)

candid (adj.)   candido (*KAHN-dee-doh*)

candidate, nominee   candidato *m.* (*kahn-dee-DAH-toh*), designato (*deh-zee-NYAHT-toh*)

candidly   candidamente (*kahn-dee-dah-MEHN-teh*)

candied (adj.)   candito (*kahn-DEE-toh*)

candle   candela *f.* (*kahn-DEH-lah*)

candlestick   candeliere *m.* (*kahn-dehl-YEHR-reh*)

candor   candore *m.* (*kahn-DOHR-reh*)

canine (adj.)   canino (*kah-NEE-noh*)

canon (*approved list; law; rule, or musical form*)   canone *m.* (*KAH-noh-neh*)

canon (religious official) canonico *m.* (*kah-NOH-nee-koh*)

canonical (adj.) canonico (*kah-NOH-nee-koh*)

canonize (to) canonizzare (*kah-noh-neet-TSAHR-reh*)

capacity (volume OR ability) capacità *f.* (*kah-pah-chee-TAH*)

(having the) capacity to, able, capable (adj.) capace (*kah-PAH-cheh*)

caper (condiment) cappero *f.* (*KAHP-peh-roh*)

capital (city) capitale *f.* (*kah-pee-TAH-leh*)

capital (money) capitale *m.* (*kah-pee-TAH-leh*)

capitalism capitalismo *m.* (*kah-pee-tah-LEEZ-moh*)

capitalist capitalista *m.* (*kah-pee-tah-LEE-stah*)

capitalistic (adj.) capitalistico (*kah-pee-tah-LEE-stee-koh*)

capitulate (to) capitolare (*kah-pee-toh-LAHR-reh*)

caprice, whim capriccio *m.* (*kah-PREET-choh*)

capricious, temperamental (adj.) capriccioso (*kah-preet-CHOH-soh*)

capsule capsula *f.* (*KAHP-soo-lah*)

captain capitano *m.* (*kah-pee-TAH-noh*)

car (railway, NOT automotive), cart carro *m.* (*KAHRR-roh*)
    ⓘ This term—a form of **carrozza** (carriage)—can apply to virutally any vehicle that conveys a substantial load: a cart, a wagon, a van, a dray, and so forth. Even a chariot falls into the embrace of **carro**! An automobile in Italian, however, is an **automobile**, or **auto**, or **macchina**—NEVER a **carro**.

carafe, decanter caraffa *f.* (*kahr-RAHF-fah*)

caramel caramella *f.* (*kahr-rah-MEHL-lah*)

carat (gold or gem measure) carato *m.* (*kahr-RAH-toh*)

caravan carovana *f.* (*kahr-roh-VAH-nah*)

carbon monoxide monossido (*m.*) di carbonio (*moh-NOHS-see-doh dee kahr-BOH-nyoh*)

carcass carcassa *f.* (*kahr-KAHS-sah*)

carcinogenic (adj.) cancerogeno (*kahn-cheh-ROH-jeh-noh*)

card, paper, map, chart, charter, pass carta *f.* (*KAHR-tah*)
    ⓘ In Italian, the term *carta* embraces many things made of paper or card, or in the form of a card. *Thus*: **credit card**—carta di credito (_____*dee KREH-dee-toh*); **note paper**—carta da lettere (_____*dah LEHT-tehr-reh*); **postcard**—cartolina postale (*kahr-toh-LEE-nah poh-STAHL-leh*); **sign**—cartello (*kahr-TEHL-loh*); **tissue paper**—carta velina (_____*veh-LEE-nah*); **toilet paper**—carta igienica (_____*ee-JEH-nee-kah*); **writing paper**—carta da scrivere (_____*dah SKREE-vehr-reh*). Of course, there's an exception: **business / calling card**—biglietto (*m.*) da visita (*beel-YEHT-toh dah VEE-zee-tah*).

cardiac (adj.) cardiaco (*kahr-DYAH-koh*)

cardinal cardinale *m.* (*kahr-dee-NAH-leh*) ⊃(adj.)⊂

care cura *f.* (*KOOR-rah*) ☙

career carriera *f.* (*kahrr-RYEHR-rah*)

caress carezza *f.* (*kahr-REHT-tsah*)

caress (to) accarezzare (*ahk-kahr-reht-TSAHR-reh*) ☙

cargo carico *m.* (*KAHR-ree-koh*)

caricature caricatura *f.* (*kahr-ree-kah-TOOR-rah*)

carnal (adj.) carnale (*kahr-NAH-leh*)

carnival carnevale *m.* (*kahr-neh-VAH-leh*)

carousel, merry-go-round carosello *m.* (*kahr-roh-ZEHL-loh*)

carriage carrozza *f.* (*kahr-RROHT-tsah*)

carrot carota *f.* (*kahr-ROH-tah*)

carton (*cardboard container*) cartone *m.* (*kahr-TOH-neh*)

cartoon (*drawing*) cartone *m.* (*kahr-TOH-neh*)

cartridge cartuccia *f.* (*kahr-TOOT-chah*)

cascade, waterfall cascata *f.* (*kah-SKAH-tah*)

case (*instance*) caso *m.* (*KAH-zoh*)

case (*container*) cassa *f.* (*KAHS-sah*)

cashier, (bank) teller cassiere *m.* (*kahs-SYEHR-reh*)

cashmere cachemire *m.* (*KASH-meer*)

casino casinò *m.* (*kah-zee-NOH*)

casserole casseruola *f.* (*kahs-sehr-RWOH-lah*)

cassette cassetta *f.* (*kahs-SEHT-tah*)

castigate, chastise (to) castigare (*kah-stee-GAHR-reh*)

castle castello *m.* (*kah-STEHL-loh*)

castrate, geld, emasculate (to) castrare (*kah-STRAHR-reh*)

casual (adj.) casuale (*kah-SWAH-leh*)

casually casualmente (*kah-swahl-MEHN-teh*)

cataclysm cataclisma *m.* (*kah-tah-KLEEZ-mah*)

catacomb catacomba *f.* (*kah-tah-KOHM-bah*)

catalogue catalogo *m.* (*kah-TAH-loh-goh*)

cataract cataratta *f.* (*kah-tahr-RAHT-tah*)

catastrophe catastrofe *f.* (*kah-TAH-stroh-feh*)

category categoria *f.* (*kah-teh-gohr-REE-ah*)

categorical (adj.) categorico (*kah-teh-GOHR-ree-koh*)

cathedral cattedrale *f.* (*kaht-teh-DRAH-leh*)
  ① More modestly, a **church**—chiesa *f.* (*kee-EH-zah*)

Catholic (adj.) cattolico (*kaht-TOH-lee-koh*)

Catholicism cattolicesimo *m.* (*kaht-toh-lee-CHEH-ZEE-moh*)

cause, suit (legal action) causa *f.* (*KOW-zah*)

cause (to) causare (*kow-ZAHR-reh*)

cautious (adj.) cauto (*KOW-toh*)

cavalier, knight cavaliere *m.* (*kah-vah-LYEHR-reh*)
  ① On the chessboard, **knight**—cavallo *m.*

cavalry, chivalry cavalleria *f.* (*kah-vahl-leh-RYAH*)

cavern, cave caverna *f.* (*kah-VEHR-nah*)

cavity cavità *f.* (*kah-vee-TAH*)

cease (to) cessare (*ches-SAHR-reh*)

Lista di termini identici e simili   75

cede, give up, yield, surrender (to) cedere (*CHEH-dehr-reh*)

cedar cedro *m.* (*CHEH-droh*)

celebrant celebrante *m.* (*cheh-leh-BRAHN-teh*)

celebrate (to) celebrare (*cheh-leh-BRAHR-reh*)

celebrated (*honorably famous*) (adj.) celebrato (*cheh-leh-BRAH-toh*), cele-bre (*CHEH-leh-breh*)

celebration celebrazione *f.* (*cheh-leh-brah-TSYOH-neh*)

celebrity celebrità *f.* (*cheh-leh-bree-TAH*)

celestial (adj.) celestiale (*cheh-leh-STYAH-leh*)

celibacy celibato *m.* (*cheh-lee-BAH-toh*)

celibate, unmarried, single, bachelor (adj.) celibe (*CHEH-lee-beh*)

cell (*very small room*) cella *f.* (*CHEL-lah*)

cell (*biological*) cellula *f.* (*CHEL-loo-lah*)

cellular (adj.) cellulare (*chel-loo-LAHR-reh*)

cello violoncello *m.* (*vyoh-lohn-CHEL-loh*)

cement, concrete cemento *m.* (*cheh-MEHN-toh*)

cement (to) cementare (*cheh-mehn-TAHR-reh*)

cemetery cimitero *m.* (*chee-mee-TEHR-roh*) ☛

censor censore *m.* (*chen-SOHR-reh*)

censor (to) censurare (*chen-soor-RAHR-reh*)

censorship censura *f.* (*chen-SOOR-rah*)

census censimento *m.* (*chen-see-MEHN-toh*)

centenary centenario *m.* (*chen-teh-NAHR-ryoh*) ➲(adj.)☾

centennial centennale *m.* (*chen-tehn-NAH-leh*) ➲(adj.)☾

center centro *m.* (*CHEN-troh*)

centigrade (adj.) centigrado (*chen-TEE-grah-doh*)

central (adj.) centrale (*chen-TRAH-leh*)

centralize (to) centralizzare (*chen-tra-leed-DZAHR-reh*)

ceramics ceramica *f.* (*chehr-RAH-mee-kah*) ➲**ceramic** (adj.) -ico➲

cereal cereale *m.* (*chehr-reh-AH-leh*)

cerebral (adj.) cerebrale (*chehr-reh-BRAH-leh*)

ceremonial (adj.) cerimoniale (*chehr-ree-moh-NYAH-leh*)

ceremonious (adj.) cerimonioso (*chehr-ree-moh-NYOH-soh*)

ceremony cerimonia *f.* (*chehr-ree-MOH-nyah*)

certain, sure (adj.) certo (*CHEHR-toh*)

certainly certamente (*chehr-tah-MEHN-teh*)

certainty certezza *f.* (*chehr-TEHT-tsah*)

certificate certificato *m.* (*chehr-tee-fee-KAH-toh*)

certification certificazione *f.* (*chehr-tee-fee-kah-TSYOH-neh*)

certify (to) certificare (*chehr-tee-fee-KAHR-reh*)

cervical cervicale *f.* (*chehr-vee-KAH-leh*)

cervix cervice *f.* (*chehr-VEE-cheh*)

cessation cessazione *f.* (*ches-sah-TSYOH-neh*)

champagne sciampagna *f.* (*sham-PAH-nyah*) ✦

champion campione *m.* (*kahm-PYOH-neh*)

championship campionato *m.* (*kahm-pyoh-NAH-toh*)

chant, song, singing canto *m.* (*KAHN-toh*)

chant, sing (to) cantare (*kahn-TAHR-reh*)

chaos caos *m.* (*KAH-ohs*)

chaotic (adj.) caotico (*kah-OH-tee-koh*)

chapel cappella *f.* (*kahp-PEHL-lah*)

chaplain cappellano *m.* (*kahp-pehl-LAH-noh*)

character (*attributes, NOT eccentric*) carattere *m.* (*kah-RAHT-tehr-reh*)

characteristic (*trait*) caratterristica *f.* (*kah-raht-tehr-RREE-stee-kah*)

characteristic (*typical*) (adj.) caratterristico (*kah-raht-tehr-RREE-stee-koh*)

characterization caratterizzazione *f.* (*kah-raht-tehr-reet-tsah-TSYOH-neh*)

characterize caratterizzare (*kah-raht-tehr-reet-TSAHR-reh*)

charisma carisma *m.* (*kahr-REEZ-mah*)

charitable (adj.) caritatevole (*kahr-ree-tah-TEH-voh-leh*)

charity carità *f.* (*kahr-ree-TAH*)

charlatan ciarlatano *m.* (*char-lah-TAHN-noh*) ✹

chastity castità *f.* (*kah-stee-TAH*)

chemistry chimica *f.* (*KEE-mee-kah*)

chemotherapy chemioterapia *f.* (*keh-myoh-tehr-rah-PEE-ah*)

cherub cherubino *m.* (*kehr-roo-BEE-noh*)

chimpanzee scimpanzé *m.* (*sheehm-pahnt-ZEH*) ✹

chivalrous (adj.) cavalleresco (*kah-vahl-lehr-REH-skoh*)

chocolate cioccolata *f.* (*chohk-koh-LAH-tah*)

choir coro *m.* (*KOHR-roh*)

choral (adj.) corale (*koh-RAH-leh*)

choreographer coreografo *m.* (*kohr-reh-OH-grah-foh*)

choreography coreografia *f.* (*kohr-reh-oh-grah-fee-ah*)

chorus coro *m.* (*KOHR-roh*)

Christ Cristo *m.* (*KREE-stoh*)

Christian cristiano *m.* (*kree-STYAH-noh*) ➲(adj.)◖

Christianity cristianesimo *m.* (*kree-styah-NEH-zee-moh*)

chromatic (adj.) cromatico (*kroh-MAH-tee-koh*)

chromium cromo *m.* (*KROH-moh*)

chromosome cromosoma *m.* (*kroh-moh-ZOH-mah*)

chronic (adj.) cronico (*KROH-nee-koh*)

chronically cronicamente (*kroh-nee-kah-MEHN-teh*)

chronicle cronaca *f.* (*KROH-nah-kah*)

chronological (adj.) cronologico (*kroh-noh-LOH-jee-koh*)

chronology cronologia *f.* (*kroh-noh-loh-JEE-ah*)

chrysanthemum crisantemo *m.* (*kree-sahn-TEH-moh*)

cigar sigaro *m.* (*SEE-gahr-roh*) 🔊

cigarette sigaretta *f.* (*see-gahr-REHT-tah*) 🔊

circle (*geometric*) cerchio *m.* (*CHEHR-kyoh*) 🔊

circle (*of friends*), club circolo *m.* (*CHEER-koh-loh*)

circuit circuito *m.* (*cheer-KWEE-toh*)

circular (*brochure*) circolare *f.* (*cheer-koh-LAHR-reh*)

circulate (to) circolare (*cheer-koh-LAHR-reh*) ⊃**circular** (adj.)⊂

circulation circolazione *f.* (*cheer-koh-lah-TSYOH-neh*)

circulatory (adj.) circolatorio (*cheer-koh-lah-TOHR-ryoh*)

circumference, girth circonferenza *f.* (*cheer-kohn-fehr-REHN-tsah*) 🔊

circumscribe (to) circonscrivere (*cheer-kohn-SKREE-vehr-reh*) 🔊
ⓘ Closely related is the noncognate: **to surround**—circondare (*cheer-kohn-DAHR-reh*).

circumspect (adj.) circospetto (*cheer-koh-SPEHT-toh*) 🔊

circumstance circostanza *f.* (*cheer-koh-STAHN-tsah*) 🔊

circumstantial(adj.) circostanziale (*cheer-koh-stahn-tsee-AH-leh*) 🔊

circumvent (to) circonvenire (*cheer-kohn-veh-NEER-reh*) 🔊

circumvention circonvenzione *f.* (*cheer-kohn-vehn-TSYOH-neh*) 🔊

circus circo *m.* (*CHEER-koh*)

cirrhosis cirrosi *f.* (*cheer-RROH-see*)

cistern cisterna *f.* (*chee-STEHR-nah*)

citadel cittadella *f.* (*cheet-tah-DEHL-lah*)

citation, quotation citazione *f.* (*chee-tah-TSYOH-neh*)

cite, quote (to) citare (*chee-TAHR-reh*)

citizen cittadino *m.* (*cheet-tah-DEE-noh*) ⊃*f.* -na⊂

citizenry cittadinanza *f.* (*cheet-tah-dee-NAHN-tsah*)

citizenship cittadinanza *f.* (*cheet-tah-dee-NAHN-tsah*)

citric (adj.) citrico (*CHEE-tree-koh*)

city, (large) town città *f.* (*cheet-TAH*)

city (*small*) cittadina *f.* (*cheet-tah-DEE-nah*)

city center, downtown centro (*m.*)della città (*CHEN-troh dehl-lah cheet-TAH*)

civic (adj.) civico (*CHEE-vee-koh*)

civil (*courteous* OR *governmental*) (adj.) civile (*chee-VEE-leh*)

civilian civile *m.* (*chee-VEE-leh*) ↻(adj.)↺

civility civiltà *f.* (*chee-veel-TAH*)

civilization civilizzazione *f.* (*chee-vee-leed-dzah-TSYOH-neh*)

civilized (adj.) civilizzato (*chee-vee-leed-DZAH-toh*), civile (*chee-VEE-leh*)

clamor clamore *m.* (*klah-MOHR-reh*)

clan clan *m.* (*KLAHN*)

clandestine (adj.) clandestino (*klahn-deh-STEE-noh*)

clarification chiarificazione *f.* (*kyahr-ree-fee-kah-TSYOH-neh*) 🔊

clarify (to) chiarificare (*kyahr-ree-fee-KAHR-reh*) 🔊

clarinet clarinetto *m.* (*klahr-ree-NEHT-toh*)

clarinetist clarinettista *m.* (*klahr-ree-neht-TEE-stah*)

clarity chiarità *f.* (*kyahr-ree-TAH*) 🔊

class (*qualitative grade, subsection,* OR *learning group*) classe *f.* (*KLAHS-seh*)

classic, classical (adj.) classico (*KLAHS-see-koh*)

classicism classicismo *m.* (*klahs-see-CHEEZ-moh*)

classification classificazione *f.* (*klahs-see-fee-kah-TSYOH-neh*)

classify, grade (to) classificare (*klahs-see-fee-KAHR-reh*)

clause clausola *f.* (*KLOW-zoh-lah*)

claustrophobia claustrofobia *f.* (*klow-stroh-foh-bee-ah*)

clear (*plain, transparent, unobstructed,* OR *good weather*) (adj.) chiaro (*KYAHR-roh*) 💣

clear (*remove obstructions or misunderstanding*) (to) chiarire (*kyahr-REER-reh*) 💣

clearly chiaramente (*kyahr-rah-MEHN-teh*) 💣

clemency clemenza *f.* (*kleh-MEHN-tsah*)

clergy clero *m.* (*KLEHR-roh*)

clerical (adj.) clericale (*klehr-ree-KAH-leh*)

client, customer, hotel guest cliente *m.* & *f.* (*klee-EHN-teh*)

clientele clientela *f.* (*klee-ehn-TEH-leh*)

climate clima *m.* (*KLEE-mah*)

clinic clinica *f.* (*KLEE-nee-kah*) ➲**clinical** (adj.) -co☾

clinically clinicamente (*klee-nee-kah-MEHN-teh*)

closure chiusura *f.* (*kyoo-SOOR-rah*) 💣

club (*social organization or place*) club *m.* (*KLOOB*)

coagulate (to) coagulare (*koh-ah-goo-LAHR-reh*)

coalesce (to) coalizzarsi (*koh-ah-leed-DZAHR-see*), combinarsi (*kohm-bee-NAHR-see*)

coalition coalizione *f.* (*koh-ah-lee-TSYOH-neh*)

coast costa *f.* (*KOH-stah*)

coastal costiero (adj.) (*koh-STYEHR-roh*)

cobra cobra *m.* (*KOH-brah*)

cocaine cocaina *f.* (*koh-kah-EE-nah*)

cocktail cocktail *m.* (*KOHK-tehl*)

cocoa cacao *m.* (*kah-KAH-oh*) 💣

coconut (*tree*) cocco *m.* (*KOHK-koh*); (*fruit*) noce (*f.*) di cocco (*noh-cheh dee____*)

code (*law*) codice *m.* (*koh-DEE-cheh*)

codeine codeina *f.* (koh-deh-EE-nah)

codify (to) codificare (*koh-dee-fee-KAHR-reh*)

coercion coercizione *f.* (*koh-ehr-chee-TSYOH-neh*)

coexist (to) coesistere (*koh-eh-ZEE-stehr-reh*)

cogitate (to) cogitare (*koh-jee-TAHR-reh*)

cognizance conoscenza *f.* (*koh-noh-SHEHN-tsah*)

cognomen, surname, family name cognome *m.* (*koh-NYOH-meh*)

coherent (adj.) coerente (*koh-ehr-REHN-teh*)

cohesion coesione *f.* (*koh-eh-ZYOH-neh*) ⊃**cohesive** (adj.) -sivo☉

coincide (to) coincidere (*koh-een-CHEE-dehr-reh*)

coincidence coincidenza *f.* (*koh-een-chee-DEHN-tsah*)

coincidental (adj.) coincidente (*koh-een-chee-DEHN-teh*)

coincidentally coincidentamente (*koh-een-chee-dehn-tah-MEHN-teh*), per coincidenza (*pehr koh-een-chee-DEHN-tsah*)

collaborate (to) collaborare (*kohl-lah-boh-RAHR-reh*)

collaboration collaborazione *f.* (*kohl-lah-bohr-rah-TSYOH-neh*)

collaborator collaboratore *m.* (*kohl-lah-bohr-rah-TOHR-reh*)

collar (*regular*) colletto *m.* (*kohl-LEHT-toh*)

collar (*priest's or dog's*) collare *m.* (*kohl-LAHR-reh*)

collateral collaterale *m.* (*kohl-lah-tehr-RAH-leh*) ⊃(adj.)☉

colleague collega *m.* (*kohl-LEH-gah*)

collection collezione *f.* (*kohl-leh-TSYOH-neh*)

collective (adj.) collettivo (*kohl-leht-TEE-voh*)

collectively collettivamente (*kohl-leht-tee-vah-MEHN-teh*)

collector (*of art, stamps, and so forth*) collezionista *m.* (*kohl-leh-tsyoh-NEE-stah*)

colloquialism colloquialismo *m.* (*kohl-loh-kwee-ah-LEEZ-moh*)

collusion collusione *f.* (*kohl-loo-ZYOH-neh*)

colonial (adj.)   coloniale (*koh-loh-NYAH-leh*)

colonist, settler   colono *m*. (*koh-LOH-noh*)

colonization   colonizzazione *f*. (*koh-loh-need-dzah-TSYOH-neh*)

colonize (to)   colonizzare (*koh-loh-need-DZAHR-reh*)

colony, settlement   colonia *f*. (*koh-LOH-nyah*)

color, hue, (house or wall) paint, suit (*of cards*)   colore *m*. (*koh-LOHR-reh*)
   ① Related: **complexion**—colorito *m*. (*koh-lohr-REE-toh*); and **without color, colorless**—senza colore (*SEHN-tsah koh-LOHR-reh*). The important noncognate **senza** always means *without*.

coloration   colorazione *f*. (*koh-lohr-rah-TSYOH-neh*)

coloring   coloritura *f*. (*koh-loh-ree-TOOR-rah*)

colossal (adj.)   colossale (*koh-lohs-SAH-leh*)

column   colonna *f*. (*koh-LOHN-nah*)

coma   coma *m*. (*KOH-mah*)

combat, fight, fighting   combattimento *m*. (*kohm-baht-tee-MEHN-toh*)

combat, engage in combat, fight (to)   combattere (*kohm-BAHT-tehr-reh*)

combatant, fighter   combattènte *m*. (*kohm-baht-TEHN-teh*)

combination   combinazione *f*. (*kohm-bee-nah-TSYOH-neh*)

combine (to)   combinare (*kohm-bee-NAHR-reh*)

combustible (adj.)   combustibile (*kohm-boo-STEE-bee-leh*)

combustion   combustione *f*. (*kohm-boo-STYOH-neh*)

comedy   commedia *f*. (*kohm-MEH-dyah*)

comet   cometa *f*. (*koh-MEH-tah*)

comfort   conforto *m*. (*kohn-FOHR-toh*) ♦

comfort (to)   confortare (*kohn-fohr-TAHR-reh*) ♦

comforter (*consoler*)   confortatore *m*. (*kohn-fohr-tah-TOHR-reh*) ♦

comic (*comedian*)   comico *m*. (*KOH-mee-koh*)

comic, comical, funny (adj.)   comico (*KOH-mee-koh*)

command   comando *m*. (*koh-MAHN-doh*)

command (to)   comandare (*koh-mahn-DAHR-reh*)

commander   comandante *m.* (*koh-mahn-DAHN-teh*)

commander in chief   comandante (*m.*) in capo (*koh-mahn-DAHN-teh een KAH-poh*), ____supremo (____*soo-preh-moh*)

commandment   comandamento *m.* (*koh-mahn-dah-MEHN-to*h)

commemorate (to)   commemorare (*kohm-meh-moh-RAHR-reh*)

commemoration   commemorazione *f.* (*kohm-meh-mor-rah-TSYOH-neh*)

commemorative, memorial (adj.)   commemorativo (*kohm-meh-mor-rah TEE-voh*)

commence, begin (to)   cominciare (*koh-meen-CHAHR-reh*)

commencement, beginning   cominciamento *m.* (*koh-meen-chah-MEHN-toh*)

comment   commento *m.* (*kohm-MEHN-toh*)

comment (to)   commentare (*kohm-mehn-TAHR-reh*)

commentary   commentario *m.* (*kohm-mehn-TAHR-ryoh*)

commerce, trade   commercio *m.* (*kohm-MEHRR-choh*)
　ⓘ Closely related noncognates are: **to trade**—commerciare (*kohm-mehr-CHAHR-reh*), and **trader**—commerciante *m.* (*kohm-mehr-CHAHN-teh*).

commercial (adj.)   commerciale (*kohm-mehr-CHAH-leh*)

commercialism   commercialismo *m.* (*kohm-mehr-chah-LEEZ-moh*)

commercialize (to)   commercializzare (kohm-mehr-chah-leed-DZAHR-reh)

commercially   commercialmente (*kohm-mehr-chahl-MEHN-teh*)

commiserate (to)   commiserare (*kohm-mee-zehr-RAHR-reh*)

commission (*committee* OR *percentage*)   commissione *f.* (*kohm-mees-SYOH-neh*)

commissionary, commission agent   commissionario (*kohm-mees-syoh-NAHR-ryoh)*

commissioner   commissario *m.* (*kohm-mees-SAHR-ryoh*)

commit (to)   commettere (*kohm-MEHT-tehr-reh*)

committee   comitato *m.* (*koh-mee-TAH-toh*)

common (adj.)   comune (*koh-MOO-neh*)

commonly comunemente (*koh-moo-neh-MEHN-teh*)

commotion, stir commozione *f.* (*kohm-moh-TSYOH-neh*)

communal (adj.) comunale (*koh-moo-NAH-leh*)

commune (to) comunicare (*koh-moo-nee-KAHR-reh*)

communicable (adj.) comunicabile (*koh-moo-nee-KAH-bee-leh*)

communicant comunicante *m.* (*koh-moo-nee-KAHN-teh*)

communicate (to) comunicare (*koh-moo-nee-KAHR-reh*)

communication (*one-way*) comunicazione *f.* (*koh-moo-nee-kah-TSYOH-neh*)

communication (*interchange*) comunicazioni *f.* (*koh-moo-nee-kah-TSYOH-nee*)

communicative (adj.) comunicativo (*koh-moo-nee-kah-TEE-voh*)

communion comunione *f.* (*koh-moo-NYOH-neh*)

communism comunismo *m.* (*koh-moo-NEEZ-moh*)

communist comunista *m.* & *f.* (*koh-moo-NEE-stah*)

communistic (adj.) comunistico (*koh-moo-NEE-stee-koh*)

community comunità *f.* (*koh-moo-nee-TAH*)

commute (to) commutare (*kohm-moo-TAHR-reh*)

compact (*tightly arranged, NOT small*) (adj.) compatto (*kohm-PAHT-toh*)

compactness compattezza *f.* (*kohm-paht-TEHT-tsah*)

companion, partner compagno *m.* (*kohm-PAH-nyoh*) ➲*f.* -na☾
ⓘ A same-meaning noncognate is: **socio** *m.* (*SOH-choh*), **socia** *f.* (*SOH-chah*).

company (*companionship*) compagnia *f.* (*kohm-pah-NYEE-ah*)

company (*military and commercial*) compagnia *f.* (kohm-pah-NYEE-ah)

comparable (adj.) comparabile (*kohm-pahr-RAH-bee-leh*)

comparative (adj.) comparativo (*kohm-pahr-ah-TEE-voh*)

comparatively comparativamente (*kohm-pah-rah-tee-vah-MEHN-teh*)

compare (to) comparare (*kohm-pah-RAHR-reh*)

compartment compartimento *m.* (*khom-pahr-tee-MEHN-toh*)

compassion compassione *f. (kohm-pahs-SYOH-neh)*

compassionate (adj.) compassionevole *(kohm-pahs-syoh-NEH-voh-leh)*

compassionately compassionevolmente *(kohm-pahs-syoh-neh-vohl-MEHN-teh)*

compatible (adj.) compatibile *(kohm-pah-TEE-bee-leh)*

compatriot, countryman, fellow citizen compatriota *m. (kohm-pah-tree-OH-tah)*

compensate (to) compensare *(kohm-pehn-SAHR-reh)*

compensation compensazione *f. (kohm-pehn-sah-TSYOH-neh)*, compenso *m. (kohm-PEHN-soh)*

compensatory (adj.) compensativo *(kohm-pehn-sah-TEE-voh)*

compete (to) competere *(kohm-PEH-tehr-reh)*

competence competenza *f. (kohm-peh-TEHN-tsah)*

competent (adj.) competente *(kohm-peh-TEHN-teh)*

compile (to) compilare *(kohm-pee-LAHR-reh)*

complement, compliment complemento *m. (kohm-pleh-MEHN-toh)*

complete, thorough, utter (adj.) completo *(kohm-PLEH-toh)*

complete (to) completare *(kohm-pleh-TAHR-reh)*

completely, quite, wholly, utterly, altogether completamente *(kohm-pleh-tah-MEHN-teh)*

completion completamento *m. (kohm-pleh-tah-MEHN-toh)*, completezza *f. (kohm-pleh-teht-tsah)*

complex complesso *m. (kohm-PLES-soh)* ➲(adj.)◖

complexity complessità *f. (kohm-ples-see-TAH)*

complicate (to) complicare *(kohm-plee-KAHR-reh)*

complicated (adj.) complicato *(kohm-plee-KAH-toh)*

complication complicazione *f. (kohm-plee-kah-TSYOH-neh)*

complicity complicità *f. (kohm-plee-chee-TAH)*

compliment (to) complimentare *(kohm-plee-mehn-TAHR-reh)*

component componente *m.* (*kohm-poh-NEHN-teh*) ⟳(adj.)⟲

comport (*oneself*), **behave** (to) comportarsi (*kohm-pohr-TAHR-see*)

comportment comportamento *m.* (*kohm-pohr-tah-MEHN-toh*)

composed of (adj.) composto di (*kohm-POH-stoh dee*)

composer compositore *m.* (*kohm-poh-see-TOHR-reh*)

composition (*created work OR makeup of*) composizione *f.* (*kohm-poh-zee-TSYOH-neh*)

comprehend (to) comprendere (*kohm-PREHN-dehr-reh*), capire (*kah-PEER-reh*)

comprehensible (adj.) comprensibile (*kohm-prehn-SEE-bee-leh*)

comprehension, understanding comprensione *f.* (*kohm-prehn-SYOH-neh*)

comprehensive (adj.) comprensivo (*kohm-prehn-SEE-voh*)

compressed (adj.) compresso (*kohm-PREHS-soh*)

compression compressione *f.* (*kohm-prehs-SYOH-neh*)

compromise compromesso *m.* (*kohm-proh-MEHS-soh*)

computation computazione *f.* (*kohm-poo-tah-TSYOH-neh*)

compute (to) computare (*kohm-poo-TAHR-reh*)

computer computer *m.* (*kohm-POO-tehr-reh*)

ⓘ This recent import into Italian owns the rare distinction of increasingly being heard with English pronunciation. That is, with a (*PYOO*) second syllable and a sharp consonantal ending! Even the term *PC* is fast making its way in, albeit more likely pronounced (*PEE-ZEE*)! Indeed, the original Italian term for computer, the *elaboratore* (*m.*) *elettronico*, has all but disappeared.

comrade camerata *m.* (*kah-mehr-RAH-tah*)

concave (adj.) concavo (*kohn-KAH-voh*)

concede (to) concedere (*kohn-CHEH-dehr-reh*)

conceivable (adj.) concepibile (*kohn-cheh-PEE-bee-leh*)

conceivably concepibilmente (*kohn-cheh-pee-beel-MEHN-teh*)

conceive (to) concepire (*kohn-cheh-PEER-reh*)

concentrate (to)   concentrare (*kohn-chen-TRAHR-reh*)

concentration   concentrazione *f.* (*kohn-chen-tra-TSYOH-neh*)

concept   concetto *m.* (*kohn-CHEHT-toh*)

concession   concessione *f.* (*kohn-chehs-SYOH-neh*)

conciliation   conciliazione *f.* (*kohn-chee-lyah-TSYOH-neh*)

concise (adj.)   conciso (*kohn-CHEE-zoh*)

conclave   conclave *m.* (*kohn-KLAH-veh*)

conclude (to)   concludere (*kohn-KLOO-dehr-reh*)

conclusion, ending   conclusione *f.* (*kohn-kloo-ZYOH-neh*)

conclusive (adj.)   conclusivo (*kohn-kloo-SEE-voh*)

conclusively   conclusivamente (*kohn-kloo-see-vah-MEHN-teh*)

concourse   concorso *m.* (*kohn-KOHRS-soh*)

concrete (adj.)   concreto (*kohn-KREH-toh*)

concurrent (adj.)   concorrente (*kohn-kohr-RREHN-teh*)

concussion   concussione *f.* (*kohn-koos-SYOH-neh*)

condemn (to)   condannare (*kohn-dahn-NAHR-reh*)

condemnation   condannazione *f.* (*kohn-dahn-nah-TSYOH-neh*)

condensation   condensazione *f.* (*kohn-dehn-sah-TSYOH-neh*)

condense (to)   condensare (*kohn-dehn-SAHR-reh*)

condenser   condensatore *m.* (*kohn-dehn-sah-TOHR-reh*)

condiment, relish   condimento *m.* (*kohn-dee-MEHN-toh*)

condition, status, provision, stipulation   condizione *f.* (*kohn-dee-TSYOH-neh*)

condition (to)   condizionare (*kohn-dee-tsyoh-NAHR-reh*)

conditional (adj.)   condizionale (*kohn-dee-tsyoh-NAH-leh*)

conditionally   condizionalmente (*kohn-dee-tsyoh-nahl-MEHN-teh*)

condolence   condoglianza *f.* (*kohn-dohl-YAHN-tsah*)

condominium   condominio *m.* (*kohn-doh-MEE-nyoh*)

condone (to)   condonare (*kohn-dohn-AHR-reh*)

conduct, behavior   condotta *f.* (*kohn-DOHT-tah*)

conduct (to)   condurre (*kohn-DOORR-reh*)

conductive (adj.)   conduttivo (*kohn-doot-TEE-voh*)

conductivity   conduttività *f.* (*kohn-doot-tee-vee-TAH*)

conductor   conduttore *m.* (*kohn-doot-TOHR-reh*)

cone   cono *m.* (*KOH-noh*) ⊃**conical** (adj.) -nico⊂

confection   confetto *m.* (*kohn-FEHT-toh*)

confectioner   confettiere *m.* (*kohn-feht-TYEHR-reh*)

confectionery, candy store   confetteria *f.* (*kohn-feht-tehr-REE-ah*)

confederate   confederato *m.* (*kohn-feh-dehr-RAHT-toh*)

confederate (to)   confederarsi (*kohn-feh-dehr-RAHR-see*)

confederation, confederacy   confederazione *f.* (*kohn-feh-deh-rah-TSYOH-neh*)

confer (upon), bestow (to)   conferire (*kohn-fehr-REER-reh*)

conference   conferenza *f.* (*kohn-fehr-REHN-tsah*)

confess, admit to (to)   confessare (*kohn-fehs-SAHR-reh*)

confession   confessione *f.* (*kohn-fehs-SYOH-neh*)

confessional   confessionale *m.* (*kohn-fehs-syoh-NAH-leh*) ⊃(adj.)⊂

confessor   confessore *m.* (*kohn-fehs-SOHR-reh*)

confidant, confidante   confidente *m. & f.* (*kohn-fee-DEHN-teh*)

confide (to)   confidare (*kohn-fee-DAHR-reh*)

confidence   confidenza *f.* (*kohn-fee-DEHN-tsah*)

confident (adj.)   confidente (*kohn-fee-DEHN-teh*)

confidential (adj.)   confidenziale (*kohn-fee-dehn-TSYAH-leh*)

confidentially   in confidenza (*een kohn-fee-DEHN-tsah*)

confidently   confidentemente (*kohn-fee-dehn-teh-MEHN-teh*)

confine (to)   confinare (*kohn-fee-NAHR-reh*)

confirm (to)   confermare (*kohn-fehr-MAHR-reh*)

confirmation   confermazione *f.* (*kohn-fehr-mah-TSYOH-neh*)

confiscate (to)   confiscare (*kohn-fee-SKAHR-reh*)

confiscation   confiscazione *f.* (*kohn-fee-skah-TSYOH-neh*)

conflagration   conflagrazione *f.* (*kohn-fla-grah-TSYOH-neh*)

conflict, strife   conflitto *m.* (*kohn-FLEET-toh*)

conform (to)   conformarsi (*kohn-fohr-MAHR-rsee*)

conformation   conformazione *f.* (*kohn-fohr-mah-TSYOH-neh*)

conformist   conformista *m.* (*kohn-fohr-MEE-stah*)

conformity   conformità (*kohn-fohr-mee-TAH*)

confound, befuddle, bewilder, confuse (to)   confondere (*kohn-FOHN-dehr-reh*)

confront (to)   confrontare (*kohn-frohn-TAHR-reh*)

confused, addled (adj.)   confuso (*kohn-FOO-soh*)

confusion, mix-up, turmoil   confusione *f.* (*kohn-foo-ZYOH-neh*)

confute, refute, rebut (to)   confutare (*kohn-foo-TAHR-reh*)

confutation, refutation, rebuttal   confutazione *f.* (*kohn-foo-tah-TSYOH-neh*)

congeal, jell (to)   congelare (*kohn-jeh-LAHR-reh*)
   ⓘ Closely related noncognates are: **to freeze**—gelare (*jeh-LAHR-reh*), and **freezing / congealment**—congelamento *m.* (*kohn-jeh-lah-MEHN-toh*).

congenital (adj.)   congenito (*kohn-JEH-nee-toh*)

congestion   congestione *f.* (*kohn-jeh-STYOH-neh*)

conglomerate   conglomerato *m.* (*kohn-gloh-mehr-RAHT-toh*) ➲(adj.)☯

conglomerate (to)   conglomerare (*kohn-gloh-mehr-RAHR-reh*)

conglomeration   conglomerazione *f.* (*kohn-gloh-mehr-rah-TSYOH-neh*)

congratulate (to)   congratulare (*kohn-grah-too-LAHR-reh*)

congratulation   congratulazione *f.* (*kohn-grah-too-lah-TSYOH-neh*)

Congratulations!   Congratulazioni! (*kohn-grah-too-lah-TSYOH-nee*)

congratulatory (adj.)   congratulatorio (*kohn-grah-too-lah-TOHR-ryoh*)

congregate (to) congregarsi (*kohn-greh-GAHR-see*)

congregation congregazione *f.* (*kohn-greh-gah-TSYOH-neh*)

congress, meeting, convention congresso *m.* (*kohn-GREHS-soh*)

conjecture congettura *f.* (*kohn-jeht-TOOR-rah*)

conjecture (to) congetturare (*kohn-jeht-toor-RAHR-reh*)

conjugal (adj.) coniugale (*koh-nyoo-GAH-leh*)

conjugate (to) coniugare (*koh-nyoo-GAHR-reh*)

conjugation coniugazione *f.* (*koh-nyoo-gah-TSYOH-neh*) ✦

conjunction congiunzione *f.* (*kohn-joon-TSYOH-neh*)

conjunctive (adj.) congiuntivo (*kohn-joon-TEE-voh*)

connect (to) connettere (*kohn-NEHT-tehr-reh*)

connection connessione *f.* (*kohn-nehs-SYOH-neh*)

connivance connivenza *f.* (*kohn-nee-VEHN-tsah*)

connoisseur cognoscente *m.* (*koh-nyoh-SHEHN-teh*), conoscitore (*koh-noh-shee-TOHR-reh*)

connotation connotazione *f.* (*kohn-noh-tah-TSYOH-neh*)

connote (to) connotare (*kohn-noh-TAHR-reh*)

conquer (to) conquistare (*kohn-kwee-STAHR-reh*)

conqueror conquistatore *m.* (*kohn-kwee-stah-TOHR-reh*)

conquest conquista *f.* (*kohn-KWEE-stah*)

conscience coscienza *f.* (*koh-SHYEHN-tsah*) ✦

conscientious (adj.) coscienzioso (*koh-shyehn-TSYOH-soh*) ✦

conscientiously coscienziosamente (*koh-shyehn-tsyoh-sah-MEHN-teh*) ✦

conscious, aware (adj.) conscio (*KOHN-shyoh*)

consciously consciamente (*kohn-shyah-MEHN-teh*)

consciousness coscienza *f.* (*koh-SHYEHN-tsah*) ✦

consecrate (to) consacrare (*kohns-ah-KRAHR-reh*)

consecration consacrazione *f.* (*kohn-sah-krah-TSYOH-neh*)

consecutive (adj.) consecutivo (*kohn-seh-koo-TEE-voh*)

consecutively consecutivamente (*kohn-seh-koo-tee-vah-MEHN-teh*)

consensus, consent consenso *m.* (*kohn-SEHN-soh*)

consent, agree to (to) consentire (*kohn-sehn-TEER-reh*)

consequence, aftermath conseguenza *f.* (*kohn-seh-GWEHN-tsah*)

consequential (adj.) consequenziale (*kohn-seh-kwehn-TSYAH-leh*)

consequently conseguentemente (*kohn-seh-gwehn-teh-MEHN-teh*)

conservation, preservation conservazione *f.* (*kohn-sehr-vah-TSYOH-neh*)

conservatism conservatorismo *m.* (*kohn-sehr-vah-tohr-*REEZ-*moh*)

conservative conservatore *m.* (*kohn-sehr-vah-TOHR-reh*)

conservative conservatrice *f.* (*kohn-sehr-vah-TREE-cheh*)

conservative, preservative (adj.) conservativo (kohn-sehr-vah-TEE-voh), conservatore (*kohn-sehr-vah-TOHR-reh*)

conservatory conservatorio *m.* (*kohn-sehr-vah-TOHR-ryoh*)

conserve, store, keep (to) conservare (*kohn-sehr-VAHR-reh*)

consider(to) considerare (*kohn-see-deh-RAHR-reh*)

considerable (*quantity*) (adj.) considerabile (*kohn-see-deh-RAH-bee-leh*)

considerably considerabilmente (*kohn-see-deh-rah-beel-MEHN-teh*)

consideration considerazione *f.* (*kohn-see-dehr-rah-TSYOH-neh*)

consist of (to) consistere in (*kohn-SEE-stehr-reh een*)

consistency consistenza *f.* (*kohn-see-STEHN-tsah*)

consolation, solace consolazione *f.* (*kohn-soh-lah-TSYOH-neh*)

console, (give) solace (to) consolare (*kohn-soh-LAHR-reh*)

consolidate (to) consolidare (*kohn-soh-lee-DAHR-reh*)

consonant consonante *f.* (*kohn-soh-NAHN-teh*)

consort consorte *m. & f.* (*kohn-SOHR-teh*)

consortium, syndicate consorzio *m.* (*kohn-SOHR-tsyoh*)

conspicuous (adj.) cospicuo (*koh-SPEE-kwoh*) 💣

conspicuously cospicuamente (*koh-spee-kwah-MEHN-teh*) ◐※

constancy costanza *f.* (*koh-STAHN-tsah*) ⊃**constant** (adj.) -nte⊃ ◐※

constantly costantemente (*koh-stahn-teh-MEHN-teh*) ◐※

constellation costellazione *f.* (*koh-stehl-lah-TSYOH-neh*) ◐※

consternation costernazione *f.* (*koh-stehr-nah-TSYOH-neh*) ◐※

constituent (adj.) costituente (*koh-stee-too-EHN-teh*) ◐※

constitute (to) costituire (*koh-stee-too-EER-reh*) ◐※

constitution costituzione *f.* (*koh-stee-too-TSYOH-neh*) ◐※

constitutional (adj.) costituzionale (*koh-stee-too-tsyoh-NAH-leh*) ◐※

constraint costrizione *f.* (*koh-stree-TSYOH-neh*) ◐※

construct (to) costruire (*koh-stroo-EER-reh*) ◐※

construction costruzione *f.* (*koh-stroo-TSYOH-neh*) ◐※

constructive (adj.) costruttivo (*koh-stroot-TEE-voh*) ◐※

constructor, builder costuttore *m.* (*koh-stroot-TOHR-reh*) ◐※

consul console *m.* (*KOHN-soh-leh*)

consular (adj.) consolare (*kohn-soh-LAHR-reh*)

consulate consolato *m.* (*kohn-soh-LAH-toh*) -

consult (to) consultare (*kohn-sool-TAHR-reh*)

consultant consultore *m.* (*kohn-sool-TOHR-reh*), consulente (*kohn-soo-LEHN-teh*)

consultation consultazione *f.* (*kohn-sool-tah-TSYOH-neh*)

consume (to) consumare (*kohn-soo-MAHR-reh*)

consumer consumatore *m.* (*kohn-soo-mah-TOHR-reh*)

consummate (adj.) consumato (*kohn-soo-MAH-toh*)

consummation consumazione *f.* (*kohn-soo-mah-TSYOH-neh*)

consumption consumo *m.* (*kohn-SOO-moh*)

contact contatto *m.* (*kohn-TAHT-toh*)

contagious (adj.) contagioso (*kohn-tah-JOH-soh*)

contain (to)   contenere (*kohn-teh-NEHR-reh*)

contaminate, pollute (to)   contaminare (*kohn-tah-mee-NAHR-reh*)

contamination   contaminazione *f.* (*kohn-tah-mee-nah-TSYOH-neh*)

contemplate (to)   contemplare (*kohn-tehm-PLAHR-reh*)

contemplation   contemplazione *f.* (*kohn-tehm-plah-TSYOH-neh*)

contemplative   contemplativo *m.* (*kohn-tehm-plah-TEE-voh*) ⊃(adj.)C

contemporary   contemporaneo *m.* (*kohn-tehm-pohr-RAH-neh-oh*)

contemporary (adj.)   contemporaneo (*kohn-tehm-pohr-RAH-neh-oh*)

contend (*struggle with or against, NOT assert*) (to)   contendere (*kohn-TEHN-dehr-reh*)

contender   contendente *m.* (*kohn-tehn-DEHN-teh*)

content, contented, glad, satisfied (adj.)   contento (*kohn-TEHN-toh*)

content (*oneself or another*) (to)   accontentare (*ahk-kohn-tehn-TAHR-reh*) ♦※

contention   contenzione *f.* (*kohn-tehn-TSYOH-neh*)

contentment, gladness   contentamento *m.* (*kohn-tehn-tah-MEHN-toh*), contentezza (*kohn-tehn-TEHT-tsah*)

contents   contenuto *m.* (*kohn-teh-NOO-toh*)

contest   contesa *f.* (*kohn-TEH-sah*)

contest (to)   contestare (*kohn-teh-STAHR-reh*)

context   contesto *m.* (*kohn-TEH-stoh*)

continent   continente *m.* (*kohn-tee-NEHN-teh*) ⊃(adj.)C

continence   continenza *f.* (*kohn-tee-NEHN-tsah*)

continental (adj.)   continentale (*kohn-tee-nehn-TAH-leh*)

contingency   contingenza *f.* (*kohn-teen-JEHN-tsah*)

contingent (adj.)   contingente (*kohn-teen-JEHN-teh*)

continual, continuous (adj.)   continuo (*kohn-TEE-nwoh*)

continuation   continuazione *f.* (*kohn-tee-nwah-TSYOH-neh*)

continue (to)   continuare (*kohn-tee-NWAHR-reh*)

continuity continuità *f. (kohn-tee-nwee-TAH)*

continuously continuamente *(kohn-tee-nwah-MEHN-teh)*

contort (to) contorcere *(kohn-TOHR-chehr-reh)*
  ① Closely related is the noncognate: **to writhe**—contorcersi *(kohn-TOHR-chehr-see)*.

contortion contorsione *f. (kohn-tohr-SYOH-neh)*

contortionist contorsionista *m. & f. (kohn-tohr-syoh-NEE-stah)*

contour contorno *m. (kohn-TOHR-noh)*

contraband, smuggling contrabbando *m. (kohn-trab-BAHN-doh)*
  ① One who deals in illegal goods: **smuggler**—contrabbandiere *m. (kohn-trahb-bahn-DYEHR-reh)*

contract contratto *m. (kohn-TRAHT-toh)*

contract (to) contrattare *(kohn-traht-TAH-reh)*, *contrarre (kohn-TRAHR-reh)*

contract bridge (*card game*) bridge a contratto *m. (BREE-djeh ah kohn-TRAHT-toh)*

contraction contrazione *f. (kohn-trah-TSYOH-neh)*

contractor contrattatore *m. (kohn-traht-tah-TOHR-reh)*, ⊃*f.* trice❤

contradict (to) contraddire *(kohn-trad-DEER-reh)*

contradictable (adj.) contraddicibile *(kohn-trad-dee-CHEE-bee-leh)*

contradiction contraddizione *f. (kohn-trad-dee-TSYOH-neh)*

contradictory (adj.) contraddittorio *(kohn-trad-deet-TOHR-ryoh)*

contrary contrario *m. (kohn-TRAHR-ryoh)*

contrary (*opposite, NOT ill tempered*) (adj.) contrario *(kohn-TRAHR-ryoh)*

contrast contrasto *m. (kohn-TRAH-stoh)*

contrast (to) contrastare *(kohn-trah-STAHR-reh)*

contravention, misdemeanor contravvenzione *f. (kohn-trahv-vehn-TSYOH-neh)*

contribute (to) contribuire *(kohn-tree-BWEER-reh)*
  ① A related noncognate is: **taxpayer**—contribuente *m. & f. (kohn-tree-BWEHN-teh)*.

contribution contribuzione *f. (kohn-tree-boo-TSYOH-neh)*

contributive (adj.) contributivo (*kohn-tree-boo-TEE-voh*)

contributor contributore *m.* (*kohn-tree-boo-TOHR-reh*)

contributory (adj.) contributorio (*kohn-tree-boo-TOHR-ryoh*)

contrite (adj.) contrito (*kohn-TREE-toh*)

contrition contrizione *f.* (*kohn-tree-TSYOH-neh*)

control, restraint controllo *m.* (*kohn-TROHL-loh*)

control (to) controllare (*kohn-trohl-LAHR-reh*)

controllable (adj.) controllabile (*kohn-trohl-LAH-bee-leh*)

controller controllore *m.* (*kohn-trohl-LOHR-reh*)

controversial (adj.) controverso (*kohn-troh-VEHR-soh*)

controversy controversia *f.* (*kohn-troh-VEHR-syah*)

convalescence convalescenza *f.* (*kohn-vah-leh-SHEHN-tsah*)

convalescent convalescente *m. & f.* (*kohn-vah-leh-SHEHN-teh*) ➲(adj.)➲

convene (to) convenire (*kohn-veh-NEER-reh*)

convenience convenienza *f.* (*kohn-veh-NYEHN-tsah*)

convenient (adj.) conveniente (*kohn-vehn-NYEHN-teh*)

conveniently convenientemente (*kohn-veh-nyehn-teh-MEHN-teh*)

convent convento *m.* (*kohn-VEHN-toh*)

convention (*tradition, NOT meeting*) convenzione *f.* (*kohn-vehn-TSYOH-neh*)

conventional (adj.) convenzionale (*kohn-vehn-tsyoh-NAH-leh*)

converge (to) convergere (*kohn-VEHR-jehr-reh*)

convergence convergenza *f.* (*kohn-vehr-JEHN-tsah*)

convergent (adj.) convergente (*kohn-vehr-JEHN-teh*)

conversation conversazione *f.* (*kohn-vehr-sah-TSYOH-neh*)

conversational (adj.) conversazionale (*kohn-vehr-sah-tsyoh-NAH-leh*), conversevole (*kohn-vehr-SEH-voh-leh*), di conversazione (*dee kohn-vehr-sah-TSYOH-neh*)

conversationalist conversatore *m.* (*kohn-vehr-sah-TOHR-reh*)

converse, talk (to) conversare (*kohn-vehr-SAHR-reh*)

converse (*opposite*) converso *m.* (*kohn-VEHR-soh*) ⊃(adj.)Ⲥ

conversely per converso (*pehr kohn-VEHR-soh*)

convert (to) convertire (*kohn-vehr-TEER-reh*)

converter convertore *m.* (*kohn-verh-TOHR-reh*)

convertible (adj.) convertibile (*kohn-vehr-TEE-bee-leh*)

convex (adj.) convesso (*kohn-VEHS-soh*)

conviction (*belief, NOT legal judgment*) convinzione *f.* (*kohn-veen-TSYOH-neh*)

convince (to) convincere (*kohn-VEEN-chehr-reh*)

convincing (adj.) convincente (*kohn-veen-CHEN-teh*)

convivial (adj.) conviviale (*kohn-vee-VYAH-leh*)

convulsion convulsione *f.* (*kohn-vool-SYOH-neh*)

convulsive (adj.) convulsivo (*kohn-vool-SEE-voh*)

cook, chef cuoco *m.* (*KWOH-koh*)

cooperate (to) cooperare (*koh-oh-pehr-RAHR-reh*)

cooperation cooperazione *f.* (*koh-oh-pehr-rah-TSYOH-neh*)

cooperative cooperativa *f.* (*koh-oh-pehr-raht-TEE-vah*)

cooperative (adj.) cooperativo (*koh-oh-pehr-raht-TEE-voh*)

cooperatively cooperativamente (*koh-oh-pehr-rah-tee-vah-MEHN-teh*)

coordinate (to) coordinare (*koh-ohr-dee-NAHR-reh*)

coordination coordinazione *f.* (*koh-ohr-dee-nah-TSYOH-neh*)

coordinator coordinatore *m.* (*koh-ohr-dee-nah-TOHR-reh*)

copious (adj.) copioso (*koh-PYOH-soh*)

copiously copiosamente (*koh-pyoh-sah-MEHN-teh*)

copy (*duplicate of, NOT textual matter*) copia *f.* (*KOH-pyah*)

copy (*duplicate OR imitate*) (to) copiare (*koh-PYAHR-reh*)

coral corallo *m.* (*kohr-RAHL-loh*)

cord, string, rope corda *f.* (*KOHR-dah*)
    ① A conceptually related noncognate is: **thread, string, wire**—filo *m.* (*FEE-loh*). This term is a more common word for *string* than **corda,** although either will do. Memory aid: think of "little filament."

cordial (*liqueur drink*) cordiale *f.* (*kohr-DYAH-leh*)

cordial, genial (adj.) cordiale (*kohr-DYAH-leh*)

cordiality, geniality cordialità *f.* (*kohr-dyah-lee-TAH*)

cordially cordialmente (*kohr-dyahl-MEHN-teh*)

cornea cornea *f.* (*KOHR-neh-ah*)

cornet cornetta *f.* (*kohr-NEHT-tah*)

cornucopia cornucopia *m.* & *f.* (*kohr-noo-KOH-pyah*)

corollary corollario *m.* (*koh-rrohl-LAHR-ryoh*)

coronary coronario *m.* (*koh-rroh-NAHR-ryoh*) ⊃(adj.)☾

coronate (to) coronare (*kohr-roh-NAHR-reh*)

coronation incoronazione *f.* (e*en-kohr-roh-nah-TSYOH-neh*) ☙

corporate (adj.) corporativo (*kohr-pohr-rah-TEE-voh*)

corporation corporazione *f.* (*kohr-pohr-rah-TSYOH-neh*)

corpse, (*human or other animal*) body corpo *m.* (*KOHR-poh*)

corpulent, portly (adj.) corpulento (*kohr-poo-LEHN-toh*)

correct, right (adj.) corretto (*kohr-RREHT-toh*)

correct (to) correggere (*kohr-RREHD-jehr-reh*)

correction correzione *f.* (*kohr-rreh-TSYOH-neh*)

corrective (adj.) correttivo (*kohr-rreht-TEE-voh*)

correctly correttamente (*kohr-rreht-tah-MEHNT-teh*)

correctness correttezza *f.* (*kohr-rreht-TEHT-tsah*)

correlation correlazione *f.* (*kohr-rreh-lah-TSYOH-neh*)

correspond to (*match, agree with*) (to) corrispondere (*kohr-rree-SPOHN-dehr-reh*)

correspond with (*write*) (to) corrispondere con (*kohr-rree-SPOHN-dehr-reh kohn*)

correspondence (*letters* OR *similarity*) corrispondenza *f.* (*kohr-rree-spohn-DEHN-tsah*)

correspondent (*letter writer*) corrispondente *m.* & *f.* (*kohr-rree-spohn-DEHN-teh*)

corridor, hallway, hall corridoio *m.* (*kohr-rree-DOH-yoh*)

corroborate (to) corroborare (*kohr-rroh-boh-RAHR-reh*)

corroboration corroborazione *f.* (*kohr-rroh-bohr-rah-TSYOH-neh*)

corrode (to) corrodere (*kohr-RROH-dehr-reh*)

corrosion corrosione *f.* (*kohr-rroh-ZYOH-neh*)

corrupter corrutore *m.* (*kohr-rroo-TOHR-reh*)

corruptible (adj.) corruttibile (*kohr-rroot-TEE-bee-leh*)

corruption corruzione *f.* (*kohr-rroo-TSYOH-neh*)

cosmetic cosmetico *m.* (*kohz-MEH-tee-koh*) ⊃(adj.)⊂

cosmetics (*makeup*) cosmetici *m.* (*kohz-MEH-tee-chee*)

cosmic (adj.) cosmico (*KOHZ-mee-koh*)

cosmopolitan (adj.) cosmopolitano (*kohz-moh-poh-lee-TAH-noh*)

cosmos cosmo *m.* (*KOHZ-moh*)

cost costo *m.* (*KOH-stoh*)

cost (to) costare (*koh-STAHR-reh*)

costliness costosità *f.* (*koh-stoh-see-TAH*)

costly, expensive (adj.) costoso (*koh-STOH-soh*)

costume, garb costume *m.* (*koh-STOO-meh*)

cotton cotone *m.* (*koh-TOH-neh*)

council consiglio *m.* (*kohn-SEE-lyoh*)

councilman consigliere *m.* (*kohn-see-LYEHR-reh*)

count (*enumeration*) conto *m.* (*KOHN-toh*)

count (to) contare (*kohn-TAHR-reh*)

count on (*depend, rely upon*) (to) contare su (*kohn-TAHR-reh soo*)

count (*nobleman*) *m.* conte (*KOHN-teh*)

countess contessa *f.* (*kohn-TEHS-sah*)

counterfeit (to) contraffare (*kohn-traf-FAHR-reh*)

counterfeit (adj.) contraffatto (*kohn-trahf-FAHT-toh*), falso (*FAHL-soh*)

counterpart controparte *f.* (*kohn-troh-PAHR-teh*)

county contea *f.* (*kohn-TEH-ah*)

coupon cupone *m.* (*koo-POH-neh*)

courage coraggio *m.* (*kohr-RAHD-joh*)

courageous, brave (adj.) coraggioso (*kohr-rahd-JOH-soh*)

course corso *m.* (*KOHR-soh*)

court (*of building or ruler; NOT of law*) corte *f.* (*KOHR-teh*)

court (to) corteggiare (*kohr-tehd-JAHR-reh*)

courtyard, (enclosed) yard, patio cortile *m.* (*kohr-TEE-leh*)

courteous, polite (adj.) cortese (*kohr-TEH-zeh*)

courtesy, politeness cortesia *f.* (*kohr-teh-ZEE-ah*)

court-martial corte marziale *f.* (*kohr-teh mahr-TSYAH-leh*)

cousin cugino *m.* (*koo-JEE-noh*) ➔*f.* -na☾

coward codardo *m.* (*koh-DAHR-doh*) ☙

cowardice codardia *f.* (*koh-dahr-DEE-ah*) ☙

cowardly (adj.) codardo (*koh-DAHR-doh*)

cowboy cow-boy *m.* (*KAOW-boh-ee*)

cramp crampo *m.* (*KRAHM-poh*)

cranium, skull cranio *m.* (*KRAH-nyoh*)

crater cratere *m.* (*kra-TEHR-reh*)

cravat, necktie cravatta *f.* (*krah-VAH-tah*)

cream crema *f.* (*KREH-mah*)

create (to) creare (*kreh-AHR-reh*)

creation creazione *f.* (*kreh-ah-TSYOH-neh*)

creator creatore *m.* (*kreh-ah-TOHR-reh*) ➲**creative** (adj.) -tivo➲

creature creatura *f.* (*kreh-ah-TOOR-rah*)

credence credenza *f.* (*kreh-DEHN-tsah*)

credentials credenziali *f.* (*kreh-dehn-tsee-AH-lee*)

credibility credibilità *f.* (*kreh-dee-bee-lee-TAH*)

credible, believable (adj.) credibile (*kreh-DEE-bee-leh*)

credit credito *m.* (*KREH-dee-toh*)

credit (*give credence to*), **believe** (to) credere (*KREH-dehr-reh*)
ⓘ Believer—**credente** *m.* (*kreh-DEHN-teh*)

creditor creditore *m.* (*kreh-dee-TOHR-reh*)

credulity credulità *f.* (*kreh-doo-lee-TAH*)

credulous, gullible (adj.) credulo (*KREH-doo-loh*)

creed credo *m.* (*KREH-doh*)

cremate (to) cremare (*kreh-MAHR-reh*)

cremation cremazione *f.* (*kreh-mah-TSYOH-neh*)

crematory *f.* crematorio (*kreh-mah-TOHR-ryoh*)

crepe crespo *m.* (*KREH-spoh*)

crest cresta *f.* (*KREH-stah*)

criminal criminale *m.* (*kree-mee-NAH-leh*) ➲(adj.)➲

criminologist criminologo *m.* (*kree-mee-noh-LOH-goh*)

criminology criminologia *f.* (*kree-mee-noh-loh-JEE-ah*)

crisis crisi *f.* (*KREE-zee*)

criterion criterio *m.* (*kree-TEHR-ryoh*)

critic critico *m.* (*KREE-tee-koh*) ➲**critical** (adj.)➲

criticism, faultfinding critica *f.* (*KREE-tee-kah*)

criticize (to) criticare (*kree-tee-KAHR-reh*)

critique critica *f.* (*KREE-tee-kah*)

croquette crocchetta *f.* (*krok-KEHT-tah*)

cross croce *f.* (*KROH-cheh*)

crown corona *f.* (*kohr-ROH-nah*)

crucial (adj.) cruciale (*kroo-CHAH-leh*)

crucifix crocefisso *m.* (*kroh-cheh-FEES-soh*)

crucifixion crocefissione *f.* (*kroh-cheh-fees-SYOH-neh*)

crucify (to) crocifiggere (*kroh-chee-feed-JEHR-reh*)

crude, raw (adj.) crudo (*KROO-doh*)

crudity crudità *f.* (*kroo-dee-TAH*)

crust, scab crosta *f.* (*KROH-stah*)

crustacean crostaceo *m.* (*kroh-STAH-cheh-oh*)

crusty (adj) crostoso (*kroh-STOH-soh*)

crypt cripta *f.* (*KREEP-tah*)

cryptography crittografia *f.* (*kreet-toh-grah-FEE-ah*)

crystal cristallo *m.* (*kree-STAHL-loh*)

crystalline (adj.) cristallino (*kree-stahl-LEE-noh*)

crystallize (to) cristallizzare (*kree-stahl-leed-DZAHR-reh*)

crystalware, glassware cristallerie *f.* (*kree-stahl-LEHR-ryeh*)

cube cubo *m.* (*KOO-boh*) ➲**cubic** (adj.) -bico☾

cubicle cubicolo *m.* (*koo-BEE-koh-loh*)

cubism cubismo *m.* (*koo-BEE-zmoh*)

cuisine cucina *f.* (*koo-CHEE-nah*)

culinary (adj.) culinario (*koo-lee-NAHR-ryoh*)

culminate (to) culminare (*kool-mee-NAHR-reh*)

culmination culminazione *f.* (*kool-mee-nah-TSYOH-neh*)

culpability, blame, guilt colpabilità *f.* (*kohl-pah-bee-lee-TAH*), colpa (*KOHL-pah*)

culpable, guilty (adj.) colpevole (*kohl-peh-VOH-leh*)

cult culto *m.* (*KOOL-toh*)

cultivate, raise, till (to) coltivare (*kohl-tee-VAHR-reh*)

cultivation coltivazione *f.* (*kohl-tee-vah-TSYOH-neh*)

cultivator, farmer coltivatore *m.* (*kohl-tee-vah-TOHR-reh*), agricoltore (*ah-gree-kohl-TOHR-reh*)

culture cultura *f.* (*kool-TOOR-rah*)

cultural (adj.) culturale (*kool-toor-RAH-leh*)

cultured, cultivated (adj.) colto (*KOHL-toh*)

cumulative (adj.) cumulativo (*koo-moo-lah-TEE-voh*)

cupola (*dome*) cupola *f.* (*KOO-poh-lah*)

curator curatore *m.* (*koor-rah-TOHR-reh*)

cure cura *f.* (*KOOR-rah*)

curiosity curiosità *f.* (*koor-ryoh-see-TAH*)

curious, outlandish (adj.) curioso (*koor-RYOH-soh*)

current corrente *f.* (*kohr-RREHN-teh*)

currently correntemente (*kohr-rrehn-teh-MEHN-teh*)

curriculum curricolo *m.* (*koor-RREE-koh-loh*)

curtain cortina *f.* (*kohr-TEE-nah*)

curvature curvatura *f.* (*koor-vah-TOOR-rah*), curvezza (*koor-VEHT-tsah*)

curve curva *f.* (*KOOR-vah*)

curve, bend, warp, stoop (to) curvare (*koor-VAHR-reh*)

curved, bent, warped, stooped (adj.) curvo (*KOOR-voh*)

cushion cuscino *m.* (*koo-SHEE-noh*)

(small) cushion, pad cuscinetto *m.* (*koo-shee-NEHT-toh*)

custodian, keeper custode *m.* (*koo-STOH-deh*)

custody custodia *f.* (*koo-STOH-dyah*)

(have in) custody, watch over (to) custodire (*koo-stoh-DEER-reh*)

custom costume *m.* (*koh-STOO-meh*) 💣

cuticle cuticola *f.* (*koo-TEE-koh-lah*)

cycle ciclo *m.* (*CHEE-kloh*)

cyclist ciclista *m.* (*chee-KLEE-stah*)

cyclone ciclone *m.* (*chee-KLOH-neh*)

cylinder cilindro *m.* (*chee-LEEN-droh*)

cylindrical (adj.) cilindrico (*chee-LEEN-dree-koh*)

cynic cinico *m.* (*CHEE-nee-koh*) ⊃**cynical** (adj.)⊂

cynicism cinismo *m.* (*chee-NEE-zmoh*)

cypress cipresso *m.* (*chee-PREHS-soh*)

—D—

dagger daga *f.* (*DAH-gah*), stiletto *m.* (*stee-leht-toh*), pugnale *m.* (*poo-nyah-leh*)

damage danno *m.* (*DAHN-noh*) ☛

damask damasco *m.* (*dah-MAHS-koh*)

damnation dannazione *f.* (*dahn-nah-TSYOH-neh*) ☛

dance danza *f.* (*DAHN-tsah*)

dance (to) danzare (*dahn-TSAHR-reh*), ballare (*bahl-LAHR-reh*)

dancing dancing *m.* (DAHN-seeng), ballo *m.* (*BAHL-loh*)

dart dardo *m.* (*DAHR-doh*)

data dati *m.* (*DAH-tee*)
  ☛ Note potential confusion with following word!

date (*re calendar, NOT fruit*) data *f.* (*DAH-tah*)

date (*determine time of occurance*) (to) datare (*dah-TAHR-reh*)

deacon diacono *m.* (*dee-AH-koh-noh*)
  ☛ Note potential confusion with following word!

dean decano *m.* (*deh-KAH-noh*)

debate dibattito *m.* (*dee-BAHT-tee-toh*) ☛

debate (to) dibattere (*dee-BAHT-tehr-reh*) ♦※

debilitate (to) debilitare (*deh-bee-lee-TAHR-reh*)

debilitated, weak (adj.) debole (*DEH-boh-leh*)

debilitation debilitazione *f.* (*deh-bee-lee-tah-TSYOH-neh*)

debit debito *m.* (*DEH-bee-toh*)

debt debito *m.* (*DEH-bee-toh*)

debtor debitore *m.* (*deh-bee-TOHR-reh*)

debut debutto *m.* (*deh-BOOT-toh*)

decadence decadenza *f.* (*deh-kah-DEHN-tsah*)

decadent (adj.) decadente (*deh-kah-DEHN-teh*)

decaffeinated (adj.) decaffeinizzato (*deh-kahf-fay-need-DZAH-toh*)

decapitate (to) decapitare (*deh-kah-pee-TAHR-reh*)

decency (*physical modesty* OR *moral rectitude*) decenza *f.* (*deh-CHEN-tsah*)

decent, modest (*in dress*), **ethical** (adj.) decente (*deh-CHEN-teh*)

decide (to) decidere (*deh-CHEE-dehr-reh*)

decimal (adj.) decimale (*deh-chee-MAH-leh*)

decimate (to) decimare (*deh-chee-MAHR-reh*) ➲**decimated** (adj.) -mato◖

decision decisione *f.* (*deh-chee-SYOH-neh*)

decisive (adj.) decisivo (*deh-CHEE-see-voh*)

declaration dichiarazione *f.* (*dee-kyahr-rah-TSYOH-neh*) ♦※

declare (to) dichiarare (*dee-kyahr-RAHR-reh*) ♦※

decline (*in health or status,* NOT *refuse*) (to) declinare (*deh-klee-NAHR-reh*)

decompose (to) decomporre (*deh-kohm-POHRR-reh*)

decomposition decomposizione *f.* (*deh-kohm-poh-zee-TSYOH-neh*)

decongestant decongestionante *m.* (*deh-kohn-jeh-styoh-NAHN-teh*)

decorate (to) decorare (*deh-kohr-RAHR-reh*)

decoration decorazione *f.* (*deh-kohr-rah-TSYOH-neh*)

decorative (adj.) decorativo (*deh-kohr-rah-TEE-voh*)

decorator decoratore *m.* (*deh-kohr-rah-TOHR-reh*)

decorum decoro *m.* (*deh-KOHR-roh*)

decree decreto *m.* (*deh-KREH-toh*)

decrepit (adj.) decrepito (*deh-KREH-pee-toh*)

dedicate, devote (to) dedicare (*deh-dee-KAHR-reh*)

dedication dedica *f.* (*DEH-dee-kah*)

deduce, deduct (to) dedurre (*deh-DOORR-reh*)

deduction deduzione *f.* (*deh-doo-TSYOH-neh*)

defamatory, libelous (adj.) diffamatorio (*deef-fah-mah-TOHR-ryoh*)

defame, libel, malign (to) diffamare (*deef-fah-MAHR-reh*) ♦

defeat disfatta *f.* (*dees-FAHT-tah*) ♦

defeatism disfattismo *m.* (*dee-sfaht-TEE-zmoh*) ♦

defect, flaw, fault, imperfection difetto *m.* (*dee-FEHT-toh*) ♦

defective (adj.) difettoso (*dee-feht-TOH-soh*) ♦

defend (to) difendere (*dee-FEHN-dehr-reh*) ♦

defender difensore *m.* (*dee-fehn-SOHR-reh*) ♦

defense difesa *f.* (*dee-FEH-sah*)
　ⓘ Of course, **defenseless** (adj.)—senza difesa (*SEHN-tsah dee-FEH-sah*), indifeso (*een-dee-FEH-soh*)

defensible (adj.) difensibile (*dee-fehn-SEE-bee-leh*) ♦

defensive (adj.) difensivo (*dee-fehn-SEE-voh*) ♦

defer (*put off, NOT acquiesce to*) (to) differire (*deef-fehr-REER-reh*) ♦

deference deferenza *f.* (*deh-fehr-REHN-tsah*)

deferential (adj.) deferente (*deh-fehr-REHN-teh*)

deficiency deficienza *f.* (*deh-fee-CHEHN-tsah*)

deficient (adj.) deficiente (*deh-fee-CHEHN-teh*)

deficit (*financial*) deficit *m.* (*DEH-fee-cheet*)

define (to) difinire (*dee-fee-NEER-reh*) ⊃**definite** (adj.) -ito☾ ☙

definitely definitivamente (*deh-fee-nee-tee-vah-MEHN-teh*)

definition definizione *f.* (*deh-fee-nee-TSYOH-neh*)

definitive (adj.) definitivo (*deh-fee-nee-TEE-voh*)

deflate (to) deflazionare (*deh-flah-tsyoh-NAHR-reh*)

deflect (to) deflettere (*deh-fleht-TEHR-reh*)

deform (to) deformarsi (*deh-fohr-MAHR-see*)

deformed (adj.) deforme (*deh-FOHR-meh*)

deformity deformità *f.* (*deh-fohr-mee-TAH*)

defraud (to) defraudare (*deh-fraow-DAHR-reh*), frodare (*froh-DAH-reh*)

degenerate degenerato *m.* (*deh-jeh-neh-RAH-toh*) ⊃(adj.)☾

degenerate (to) degenerare (*deh-jeh-neh-RAHR-reh*)

degeneration degenerazione *f.* (*deh-jeh-neh-rah-TSYOH-neh*)

degradation degradazione *f.* (*deh-grah-dah-TSYOH-neh*)

degrade (to) degradare (*deh-grah-DAHR-reh*)

deify (to) deificare (*day-fee-KAHR-reh*)

deity deità *f.* (*day-TAH*)

delegate delegato *m.* (*deh-leh-GAH-toh*)

delegate (to) delegare (*deh-leh-GAHR-reh*)

delegation delegazione *f.* (*deh-leh-gah-TSYOH-neh*)

deliberate (to) deliberare (*deh-lee-behr-RAHR-reh*) ⊃(adj.) -rato☾

deliberately deliberatamente (*deh-lee-behr-rah-tah-MEHN-teh*)

deliberation deliberazione *f.* (*deh-lee-behr-rah-TSYOH-neh*)

deliberative (adj.) deliberativo (*deh-lee-behr-rah-TEE-voh*)

delicacy delicatezza *f.* (*deh-lee-kah-TEHT-tsah*)

delicate, dainty (adj.) delicato (*deh-lee-KAH-toh*)

delicious (adj.) delizioso (*deh-lee-TSYOH-soh*)

delight diletto *m.* (*dee-LEHT-toh*) ☙

delight (to)   dilettare (*dee-leht-TAHR-reh*) 💣

delightful (adj.)   dilettevole (*dee-leht-TEH-voh-leh*) 💣

delinquency   delinquenza *f.* (*deh-leen-KWEHN-tsah*)

delinquent   delinquente *m.* (*deh-leen-KWEHN-teh*) ⊃(adj.)ℂ

delirious (adj.)   delirante (*deh-leer-RAHN-teh*)

delirium   delirio *m.* (*deh-LEER-ryoh*)

delude, disappoint (to)   deludere (*deh-LOO-dehr-reh*)

deluge   diluvio *m.* (*dee-LOO-vyoh*) 💣

delusion, disappointment   delusione *f.* (*deh-loo-ZYOH-neh*)

deluxe (adj.)   di lusso (*dee LOOS-soh*) 💣

demagogue   demagogo *m.* (*dehm-mah-GOH-goh*)

demand   domanda *f.* (*doh-MAHN-dah*) 💣

demand, ask about (to)   domandare (*doh-mahn-DAHR-reh*) 💣

demented (adj.)   demente (*deh-MEHN-teh*)

democracy   democrazia *f.* (*deh-moh-krah-TSEE-ah*)

democrat   democratico *m.* (*deh-moh-KRAH-tee-koh*)

democratic (adj.)   democratico (*deh-moh-KRAH-tee-koh*)

demolish (to)   demolire (*deh-moh-LEER-reh*)

demolition   demolizione *f.* (*deh-moh-lee-TSYOH-neh*)

demon, fiend   demonio *m.* (*deh-MOH-nyoh*)

demonic, fiendish (adj.)   demoniaco (*dee-moh-NYAH-koh*)

demonstrable (adj.)   dimostrabile (*dee-moh-strah-BEE-leh*) 💣

demonstrate (to)   dimostrare (*dee-moh-STRAHR-reh*) 💣

demonstration   dimostrazione *f.* (*dee-moh-strah-TSYOH-neh*) 💣

demonstrative (adj.)   dimostrativo (*dee-moh-strah-TEE-voh*) 💣

demoralize (to)   demoralizzare (*deh-mohr-rah-leed-DZAHR-reh*)

denial   diniego *m.* (*dee-NYEH-goh*) 💣

denigrate, belittle (to)   denigrare (*deh-nee-GRAHR-reh*)

denomination   denominazione *f.* (*deh-noh-mee-nah-TSYOH-neh*)

denote (to)   denotare (*deh-noh-TAHR-reh*)

denounce (to)   denunciare (*deh-noon-CHAHR-reh*)

dense, thick (adj.)   denso (*DEHN-soh*)

density   densità *f.* (*dehn-see-TAH*)

dental (adj.)   dentale (*dehn-TAH-leh*)

ⓘ Related noncognates are: **tooth**—dente *m.* (*DEHN-teh*) and **toothache**—mal (*m.*) di dente (*MAHL dee DEHN-teh*).

dentifrice, toothpaste   dentifricio *m.* (*dehn-tee-FREE-choh*), pasta (*f.*) dentifricia (*PAH-stah dehn-tee-FREE-chah*)

dentist   dentista *m.* (*dehn-TEE-stah*)

denture   dentiera *f.* (*dehn-TYEHR-rah*)

denunciation   denuncia *f.* (*deh-NOON-chah*)

deodorant   deodorante *m.* (*deh-oh-dohr-RAHN-teh*) ⊃(adj.)Ͼ

deodorize (to)   deodorare (*deh-oh-dohr-RAHR-reh*)

depart, leave, go away (to)   partire (*pahr-TEER-reh*) ♦※

department   dipartimento *m.* (*dee-pahr-tee-MEHN-toh*) ♦※

departmental (adj.)   dipartimentale (*dee-pahr-tee-mehn-TAH-leh*) ♦※

departure   partenza *f.* (*pahr-TEHN-tsah*) ♦※

depend (to)   dipendere (*dee-PEHN-dehr-reh*) ♦※

dependant   dipendente *m.* & *f.* (*dee-pehn-DEHN-teh*) ⊃**dependent** (adj.)Ͼ ♦※

dependence   dipendenza *f.* (*dee-pehn-DEHN-tsah*) ♦※

deplorable (adj.)   deplorevole (*deh-plohr-REH-voh-leh*)

deplore (to)   deplorare (*deh-ploh-RAHR-reh*)

deport (to)   deportare (*deh-pohr-TAHR-reh*)

deportation   deportazione *f.* (*deh-pohr-tah-TSYOH-neh*)

deposit (to)   depositare (*deh-poh-zee-TAHR-reh*)

deposition deposizione *f.* (*deh-poh-zee-TSYOH-neh*)

depositor depositante *m.* (*deh-poh-zee-TAHN-teh*)

depository, warehouse deposito *m.* (*deh-POH-zee-toh*)
   ① At Italian railway stations, the public **storage room for luggage, checkroom**—deposito bagagli (_____*bah-GAH-lyee*)

depravation, depravity depravazione *f.* (*deh-prah-vah-TSYOH-neh*)

depreciate (to) deprezzare (*deh-preht-TSAHR-reh*)

depreciation deprezzamento *m.* (*deh-preht-tsah-MEHN-toh*)

depression depressione *f.* (*deh-pres-SYOH-neh*)

deprivation privazione *f.* (*pree-vah-TSYOH-neh*) ✊

deprive (to) privare (*pree-VAHR-reh*) ✊

deputy, representative deputato *m.* (*deh-poo-TAH-toh*)

derelict (adj.) derelitto (*dehr-reh-LEET-toh*)

deride, ridicule, mock (to) deridere (*dehr-REE-dehr-reh*)

derision, mockery derisione *f.* (*dehr-ree-ZYOH-neh*)

dermatology dermatologia *f.* (*dehr-mah-toh-loh-JEE-ah*)

derogatory (adj.) derogatorio (*dehr-roh-gah-TOHR-ryoh*)

descend (to) discendere (*dee-SHEHN-dehr-reh*) ✊

descendant discendente *m.* (*dee-shehn-DEHN-teh*) ✊

describe (to) descrivere (*deh-SKREE-vehr-reh*)

description descrizione *f.* (*deh-skree-TSYOH-neh*)

descriptive (adj.) descrittivo (*deh-skreet-TEE-voh*)

desecrate (to) desecrare (*deh-seh-KRAHR-reh*)

desert, wilderness deserto *m.* (*deh-ZEHR-toh*)

deserter disertore *m.* (*dee-sehr-TOHR-reh*) ✊

desertion diserzione *f.* (*dee-sehr-TSYOH-neh*) ✊

design, drawing disegno *m.* (*dee-SEH-nyoh*) ✊

design (to) disegnare (*dee-zeh-NYAHR-reh*) ✊

designate (to) designare (*deh-zee-NYAHR-reh*)

designation designazione *f.* (*deh-zee-nyah-TSYOH-neh*)

designer disegnatore *m.* (*dee-zeh-nyah-TOHR-reh*) 💣

desirability desiderabilità *f.* (*deh-see-dehr-rah-bee-lee-TAH*)

desirable (adj.) desiderabile (*deh-see-dehr-RAH-bee-leh*)

desire, wish desiderio *m.* (*deh-see-DEHR-ryoh*)

desire, wish, want (to) desiderare (*deh-see-dehr-RAHR-reh*)
ⓘ The noncognate verb **volere** yields much the same meaning, and is often used.

desirous (adj.) desideroso (*deh-see-dehr-ROH-soh*)

desolate (adj.) desolato (*deh-soh-LAH-toh*)

desolation desolazione *f.* (*deh-soh-lah-TSYOH-neh*)

despair disperazione *f.* (*dee-spehr-rah-TSYOH-neh*) 💣

despair (to) disperare (*dee-spehr-RAHR-reh*) 💣

desperate, hopeless (adj.) disperato (*dee-spehr-RAH-toh*) 💣

desperation, hopelessness disperazione *f.* (*dee-spehr-rah-TSYOH-neh*) 💣

despot despota *m.* (*DEH-spoh-tah*)

despotic (adj.) dispotico (*dee-SPOH-tee-koh*) 💣

despotism dispotismo *m.* (*dee-spoh-TEEZ-moh*) 💣

dessert dessert *m.* (*dehs-SEHR*)

destination destinazione *f.* (*deh-stee-nah-TSYOH-neh*)

destiny destino *m.* (*deh-STEE-noh*)

destitution destituzione *f.* (*deh-stee-too-TSYOH-neh*)

destroy (to) distruggere (*dee-strood-JEHR-reh*) 💣

destruction distruzione *f.* (*dee-stroo-TSYOH-neh*) 💣

destructive (adj.) distruttivo (*dee-stroot-TEE-voh*) 💣

detail dettaglio *m.* (*deht-TAH-lyoh*)

detail (to) dettagliare (*deht-tah-LYAHR-reh*)

detain (to)   detenere (deh-teh-NEHR-reh)

detective   detective *m. (deh-TEHK-tee-veh)*, agente investigativo (*ah-JEHN-teh een-veh-steeh-gah-TEE-voh*), investigatore (*een-veh-steeh-gah-TOHR-reh*)

detention   detenzione *f. (deh-tehn-TSYOH-neh)*

detergent   detergente *m. (deh-tehr-JEHN-teh)*

deteriorate (to)   deteriorare (*deh-tehrr-yohr-RAHR-reh*)

deterioration   deteriorazione *f. (deh-tehrr-yohr-rah-TSYOH-neh)*

determination   determinazione *f. (deh-tehr-mee-nah-TSYOH-neh)*

determine (to)   determinare (*deh-tehr-mee-NAHR-reh*)

determinism   determinismo *m. (deh-tehr-mee-NEEZ-moh)*

detest (to)   detestare (*deh-teh-STAHR-reh*)

detract (to)   detrarre (*deh-TRAHRR-reh*)

detriment   detrimento *m. (deh-tree-MEHN-toh)*

detritis, debris   detriti *m. (deh-TREE-tee)*

devastate (to)   devastare (*deh-vah-STAHR-reh*)

devastation   devastazione *f. (deh-vah-stah-TSYOH-neh)*

deviate (to)   deviare (*deh-VYAHR-reh*)

deviation, detour   deviazione *f. (deh-vyah-TSYOH-neh)*

devious (adj.)   devio (*DEH-vyoh*)

devotion   devozione *f. (deh-voh-TSYOH-neh)*

devoted (adj.)   devoto (*deh-VOH-toh*)

devour (to)   divorare (*dee-vohr-RAHR-reh*) 💣

devout (adj.)   devoto (*deh-VOH-toh*)

diabetes   diabete *m. (dee-ah-BEH-teh)*

diabetic   diabetico *m. (dee-ah-BEH-tee-koh)*

diabolical, diabolic, devilish (adj.)   diabolico (*dyah-BOH-lee-koh*) 💣

diagnosis   diagnosi *f. (dee-AH-nyoh-see)*

diagonal diagonale *m.* (*dee-ah-goh-NAH-leh*) ⊃(adj.)C

diagonally diagonalmente (*dee-ah-goh-nahl-MEHN-teh*)

diagram diagramma *m.* (*dee-ah-GRAHM-mah*)

dialect dialetto *m.* (*dee-ahl-LEHT-toh*)

dialogue dialogo *m.* (*dee-AH-loh-goh*)

diameter diametro *m.* (*dee-AH-meh-troh*)

diamond diamante *m.* (*dee-ah-MAHN-teh*)

diaphragm, midriff diaframma *m.* (*dyah-FRAHM-mah*)

diarrhea diarrea *f.* (*dyahr-RREH-ah*)

diary diario *m.* (*dee-AHR-ryoh*)

dictate (to) dettare (*deht-TAHR-reh*) 💣

dictator dittatore *m.* (*deet-tah-TOHR-reh*)

dictatorial (adj.) dittatoriale (*deet-tah-tohr-RYAH-leh*)

dictatorship dittatura *f.* (*deet-tah-TOOR-rah*)

diction dizione *f.* (*dee-TSYOH-neh*)

dictionary dizionario *m.* (*dee-tsyoh-NAHR-ryoh*)

diet dieta *f.* (*DYEH-tah*)

dietary (adj.) dietetico (*dyeh-TEH-tee-koh*)

dietitian dietista *m. & f.* (*dyeh-TEE-stah*)

differ (to) differire (*deef-fehr-REER-reh*) ⊃**different** (adj.) -renteC

difference differenza *f.* (*deef-fehr-REHN-tsah*)

differentiate (to) differenziare (*deef-fehr-rehn-TSYAHR-reh*)

difficult, tough, hard (*to do*) (adj.) difficile (*dee-FEE-chee-leh*)

difficulty difficoltà *f.* (*deef-fee-kohl-TAH*)

diffuse, widespread (adj.) diffuso (*deef-FOO-soh*)

digest (to) digerire (*dee-jehr-REER-reh*)

digestible (adj.) digeribile (*dee-jehr-REE-bee-leh*)

digestion digestione *f.* (*dee-jeh-STYOH-neh*)

digital (adj.) digitale (*dee-jee-TAH-leh*)

dignified (adj.) dignitoso (*dee-nyee-TOH-soh*)

dignitary dignitario *m.* (*dee-nyee-TAHR-ryoh*)

dignity dignità *f.* (*dee-nyee-TAH*)

digression digressione *f.* (*dee-grehs-see-OH-neh*)

dilapidated (adj.) dilapidato (*dee-lah-pee-DAH-toh*)

dilemma dilemma *m.* (*dee-LEHM-mah*)

dilettante, amateur dilettante *m.* & *f.* (*dee-leht-TAHN-teh*)

diligence diligenza *f.* (*dee-lee-JEHN-tsah*) ➲**diligent** (adj.) -ente☾

dilute (to) diluire (*dee-loo-EER-reh*)

dimension, size (*magnitude*) dimensione *f.* (*dee-mehn-SYOH-neh*)

diminish, abate, lessen, dwindle, subside (to) diminuire (*dee-mee-noo-EER-reh*)

diminution, diminishment, abatement diminuzione *f.* (*dee-mee-noo-TSYOH-neh*)

diminutive diminutivo *m.* (*dee-mee-noo-TEE-voh*) ➲(adj.)☾

dinosaur dinosauro *m.* (*dee-noh-SOWR-roh*)

diocese diocesi *f.* (*dee-OH-cheh-zee*)

diploma diploma *m.* (*dee-PLOH-mah*)

diplomacy diplomazia *f.* (*dee-ploh-MAH-tsyah*)

diplomat diplomatico *m.* (*dee-ploh-MAH-tee-koh*) ➲**diplomatic** (adj.)☾

direct (to) dirigere (*deer-ree-JEHR-reh*)

direct, directed, lineal, right-through (adj.) diretto (*dee-REHT-toh*)

ⓘ An important relative noncognate: **straight** (adj.)—retto (*REHT-toh*)

direction (*leadership, management* OR *line of sight, action*) direzione *f.* (*dee-reh-TSYOH-neh*)

directly, straight(ly) direttamente (*dee-reht-tah-MEHN-teh*), immediatamente (*eem-meh-dyah-tah-MEHN-teh*)

director, (school) principal, manager direttore *m.* (*dee-reht-TOHR-reh*)

disadvantage, handicap svantaggio *m.* (*zvahn-TAHD-joh*)

disapproval disapprovazione *f.* (*dee-sahp-proh-vaht-TSYOH-neh*)

disapprove (to) disapprovare (*dee-sahp-proh-VAHR-reh*)

disaster disastro *m.* (*dee-SAH-stroh*)

disastrous (adj.) disastroso (*dee-sah-STROH-soh*)

discern (to) discernere (*dee-SHEHR-nehr-reh*)

discernment discernimento *m.* (*dee-shehr-nee-MEHN-toh*)

disciple discepolo *m.* (*dee-sheh-POH-loh*)

disciplinary (adj.) disciplinare (*dee-shee-plee-NAHR-reh*)

discipline disciplina *f.* (*dee-shee-PLEE-nah*)

disco disco *m.* (*DEE-skoh*)

discord discordia *f.* (*dee-SKOHR-dyah*)

discordant (adj.) discordante (*dee-skohr-DAHN-teh*)

discourse, address, speech, talk discorso *m.* (*dee-SKOHR-soh*)

discothèque discoteca *f.* (*dee-skoh-TEH-kah*)

discredit discredito *m.* (*dee-SKREH-dee-toh*)

discreet (adj.) discreto (*dee-SKREH-toh*)

discrepancy discrepanza *f.* (*dee-skreh-PAHN-tsah*)

discretion discrezione *f.* (*dee-skreht-TSYOH-neh*)

discriminate (to) discriminare (*dee-skree-mee-NAHR-reh*)

discrimination discriminazione *f.* (*dee-skree-mee-nah-TSYOH-neh*)

discussion discussione *f.* (*dee-skoos-SYOH-neh*)

disfigure (to) disfigurare (*dee-sfee-goor-RAHR-reh*)

disgrace disgrazia *f.* (*dee-ZGRAH-tsyah*)

disgust disgusto *m.* (*dee-ZGOO-stoh*)

disgust (to) disgustare (*dee-zgoos-TAHR-reh*)

disgusting, distasteful, nasty (*in appearance*) (adj.) disgustoso (*dee-zgoos-TOH-soh*), disgustante (*dee-zgoos-TAHN-teh*)

dishonest (adj.) disonesto (*dee-zoh-NEHS-toh*)

dishonesty disonestà *f.* (*dee-zoh-neh-STAH*)

dishonor, disgrace disonore *m.* (*dee-zoh-NOHR-reh*)

dishonor, disgrace (to) disonorare (*dee-zoh-nohr-RAHR-reh*)

dishonorable, disgraceful (adj.) disonorevole (*dee-zoh-nohr-REH-voh-leh*), disonorante (*dee-zoh-nohr-RAHN-teh*)

disillusion disillusione *f.* (*dee-zeel-loo-SYOH-neh*)

disillusion (to) disilludere (*dee-zeel-loo-DEHR-reh*)

disintegrate (to) disintegrare (*dee-seen-teh-GRAHR-reh*)

disinterested (adj.) disinteressato (*dee-seen-tehr-rehs-SAH-toh*)

disk disco *m.* (*DEE-skoh*)

disobedience disubbidienza *f.* (*dee-soob-bee-DYEHN-tsah*) ◆⋇

disobedient (adj.) disubbidiente (*dee-zohb-beh-DYEHN-teh*)

disobey (to) disubbidire (*dee-zoob-beh-DEER-reh*) ◆⋇

disorder disordine *m.* (*dee-ZOHR-dee-neh*)

disorder (to) disordinare (*dee-zohr-dee-NAHR-reh*)

disorderly (adj.) disordinato (*dee-zohr-dee-NAHT-toh*)

disparity disparità *f.* (*dee-spahr-ree-TAH*)

dispense (to) dispensare (*dee-spehn-SAHR-reh*)

dispersal *f.* dispersione (*dee-spehr-SYOH-neh*)

disposition (*mood OR status*) disposizione *f.* (*dee-spoh-zee-TSYOH-neh*)

disputable (adj.) disputabile (*dee-spoo-TAH-bee-leh*)

dispute disputa *f.* (*DEE-spoo-tah*)

dispute (to) disputare (*dee-spoo-TAHR-reh*)

disseminate (to) disseminare (*dees-sehm-mee-NAHR-reh*)

dissension, dissent, disagreement dissenso *m.* (*dees-SEHN-soh*)

dissent, disagree (to) dissentire (*dees-sehn-TEER-reh*)

disservice disservizio *m.* (*dees-sehr-VEE-tsyoh*)

dissimilar, unlike (adj.) dissimile (*dees-SEE-mee-leh*)

dissipate (to) dissipare (*dees-see-PAHR-reh*)

dissolute (adj.) dissoluto (*dees-soh-LOO-toh*)

dissolution dissoluzione *f.* (*dees-soh-loo-TSYOH-neh*)

dissolve (to) dissolvere (*dees-SOHL-vehr-reh*)

dissonance dissonanza *f.* (*dees-soh-NAHN-tsah*)

dissonant (adj.) dissonante (*dees-soh-NAHN-teh*)

distance distanza *f.* (*dee-STAHN-tsah*) ➲distant (adj.) -ante◖

distill (to) distillare (*dee-steel-LAHR-reh*)

distillation distillazione *f.* (*dee-steel-lah-TSYOH-neh*)

distinct (adj.) distinto (*dee-STEEN-toh*)

distinctive (adj.) distintivo (*dee-steen-TEE-voh*)

distinction distinzione *f.* (*dee-steen-TSYOH-neh*)

distinctly distintamente (*dee-steen-tah-MEHN-teh*)

distinguish (to) distinguere (*dee-STEEN-gwehr-reh*)

distort (to) distorcere (*dee-STOHR-chehr-reh*)

distract (to) distrarre (*dee-STRAHRR-reh*)

distracted, absentminded (adj.) distratto (*dee-STRAHT-toh*)

distraction distrazione *f.* (*dee-strah-TSYOH-neh*)

distribute, apportion (to) distribuire (*dee-stree-boo-EE-reh*)

distribution distribuzione *f.* (*dee-stree-boo-TSYOH-neh*)

distributor distributore *m.* (*dee-stree-boo-TOHR-reh*)

district distretto *m.* (*dee-STREHT-toh*)

disturb, bother, trouble (to) disturbare (*dee-stoor-BAHR-reh*)

disturbance, botherment disturbo *m.* (*dee-STOOR-boh*)

divan, sofa, davenport divano *m.* (*dee-VAH-noh*)

diverge (to)   divergere (*dee-VEHR-jehr-reh*)

divergence   divergenza *f.* (*dee-vehr-JEHN-tsah*)

divergent (adj.)   divergente (*dee-vehr-JEHN-teh*)

diverse (adj.)   diverso (*dee-VEHR-soh*)

diversity   diversità *f.* (*dee-vehr-see-TAH*)

divert, amuse, entertain (to)   divertire (*dee-vehr-TEER-reh*)

divide (to)   dividere (*dee-VEE-dehr-reh*)

dividend   dividendo *m.* (*dee-vee-DEHN-doh*)

divine (adj.)   divino (*dee-VEE-noh*)

divinity   divinità *f.* (*dee-vee-nee-TAH*)

division   divisione *f.* (*dee-vee-ZYOH-neh*)

divorce   divorzio *m.* (*dee-VOHR-tsyoh*)

divorcée   divorziata *f.* (*dee-vohr-TSYAH-tah*)

divulge (to)   divulgare (*dee-vool-GAHR-reh*)

doctor (*scholastic*)   dottore *m.* (*doht-TOHR-re*h)

doctor (*medical*)   medico *m.* (*MEH-dee-koh*)

doctorate   dottorato *m.* (*doht-tohr-RAH-toh*)

doctrine   dottrina *f.* (*doht-TREE-nah*)

document   documento *m.* (*doh-koo-MEHN-toh*)

documentary (adj.)   documentario (*doh-koo-mehn-TAHR-ryoh*)

documentation   documentazione *f.* (*doh-koo-mehn-tah-TSYOH-neh*)

dogma   dogma *m.* (*DOHG-mah*)

dogmatic, assertive (adj.)   dogmatico (*dohg-MAH-tee-koh*)
  ⓘ A related noncognate noun is: **assertiveness**—dogmaticità *f.* (*dohg-mah-tee-chee-TAH*).

dogmatism   dogmatismo *m.* (*dohg-mah-TEE-zmoh*)

dollar   dollaro *m.* (*DOHL-lahr-roh*)

domain   dominio *m.* (*doh-MEE-nyoh*)

domestic (*homelike*), local (*not foreign*) (adj.) domestico (*doh-MEH-stee-koh*)

domestic (*household worker*), maid, housemaid, charwoman domestica *f.* (*doh-MEH-stee-kah*)

domestic animal, pet animale (*m.*) domestico (*ah-nee-MAH-leh_____*)

domesticate, tame (to) domesticare (*doh-meh-stee-KAHR-reh*), addomesticare (*ahd-doh-meh-stee-KAHR-reh*)

domesticated, tame (adj.) domesticato (*doh-meh-stee-KAH-toh*), addomesticato (*ahd-doh-meh-stee-KAH-toh*)

dominant (adj.) dominante (*doh-mee-NAHN-teh*)

dominate, sway (to) dominare (*doh-mee-NAHR-reh*)

domination dominazione *f.* (*doh-mee-nah-TSYOH-neh*)

donate (to) donare (*doh-NAHR-reh*)

donation donazione *f.* (*doh-nah-TSYOH-neh*)

dosage (*of medicine*) dosatura *f.* (*doh-sah-TOOR-rah*)

dose (*medicinal quantity*) dose *f.* (*DOH-seh*)

doubt dubbio *m.* (*DOOB-byoh*)
   ⓘ The related adverbial term is **doubtless**—*senza dubbio* (*SEHN-tsah____*). Remember that *senza* always means *without*.

doubt, question (*the accuracy, veracity of*) (to) dubitare (*doo-bee-TAHR-reh*)

doubtful, dubious, questionable (adj.) dubbio (*DOOB-byoh*), dubbioso (*doob-BYOH-soh*)

douche doccia *f.* (*DOHT-chah*)

dozen dozzina *f.* (*dohd-ZEE-nah*)

drainage drenaggio *m.* (*dreh-NAHD-joh*)

drama, play dramma *m.* (*DRAHM-mah*), spettacolo (*speht-TAH-koh-loh*)

dramatic (adj.) drammatico (*drahm-MAH-tee-koh*)

dramatics drammatica *f.* (*drahm-MAH-tee-kah*)

dramatist drammaturgo *m.* (*drahm-mah-TOOR-goh*)

dramatize (to) drammatizzare (*drahm-mah-teed-DZAHR-reh*)

drape, drapery drappeggio *m.* (*drahp-PEHD-joh*)

drastic (adj.) drastico (*DRAH-stee-koh*)

drink (*alcoholic*) drink *m*. (*DREEN-keh*)

drug droga *f*. (*DROH-gah*)

dual (adj.) duale (*doo-AH-leh*)

duchess duchessa *f*. (*doo-KEHS-sah*)

duel duello *m*. (*doo-EHL-loh*)

duel (to) duellare (*doo-ehl-LAHR-reh*)

duet duetto *m*. (*doo-EHT-toh*)

duke duca *m*. (*DOO-kah*)

duplicate (to) duplicare (*doo-plee-KAHR-reh*)

duplicate duplicato *m*. (*doo-plee-KAHT-toh*)

duplication duplicazione *f*. (*doo-plee-kah-TSYOH-neh*)

durability durabilità *f*. (*doo-rah-bee-lee-TAH*)

durable (adj.) durabile (*door-RAH-bee-leh*)

ⓘ Many things are durable because they are (physically, constitutionally) **hard** (adj.)—duro (*DOO-roh*).

duration durata *f*. (*door-RAH-tah*) ➲**during** -anteↃ

dynamic (adj.) dinamico (*dee-NAH-mee-koh*)

dynamo dinamo *f*. (*DEE-nah-moh*)

dynasty dinastia *f*. (*dee-nah-STEE-ah*)

dyslexia dislessia *f*. (*dee-ZLEHS-syah*)

—E—

east *m*. (*direction, NOT global region*) est (*EHST*)

ebony ebano *m*. (*EH-bah-noh*)

eccentric (adj.) eccentrico (*eht-CHEN-tree-koh*)

eccentricity eccentricità *f*. (*eht-chen-tree-chee-TAH*)

ecclesiastic, clergyman ecclesiastico *m.* (*ehk-kleh-zee-AH-stee-koh*)

ecclesiastic, ecclesiastical (adj.) ecclesiastico (*ehk-kleh-zee-AH-stee-koh*)

echo eco *m.* (*EH-koh*)

eclipse eclissi *f.* (*eh-KLEES-see*)

eclipse (to) eclissare (*eh-klees-SAHR-reh*)

ecological (adj.) ecologico (*eh-koh-LOH-jee-koh*)

ecology ecologia *f.* (*eh-koh-loh-JEE-ah*)

economic, economical, cheap (adj.) economico (*eh-koh-NOH-mee-koh*)

economics scienza economica *f.* (*SHEHN-tsah eh-koh-NOH-mee-kah*), economia politica (*eh-koh-noh-MEE-ah poh-LEE-tee-kah*)

economist economista *m.* (*eh-koh-noh-MEE-stah*)

economize (to) economizzare (*eh-koh-no-meed-DZAHR-reh*)

economy, thrift economia *f.* (*eh-koh-noh-MEE-ah*)

ecstasy, rapture estasi *f.* (*EH-stah-see*)

ecumenical (adj.) ecumenico (*eh-koo-MEHN-nee-koh*)

edict editto *m.* (*eh-DEET-toh*)

edifice, building, (architectural) structure edificio *m.* (*eh-dee-FEE-choh*)

edify (to) edificare (*eh-dee-fee-KAHR-reh*)

edition edizione *f.* (*eh-dee-TSYOH-neh*)

editorial (adj.) editoriale (*eh-dee-tohr-RYAH-leh*)

educate (to) educare (*eh-doo-KAHR-reh*)

education, breeding, upbringing, classiness educazione *f.* (*eh-doo-kah-TSYOH-neh*)

educational (adj.) educativo (*eh-doo-kah-TEE-voh*)

educator educatore *m.* (*eh-doo-kah-TOHR-reh*)

effect effetto *m.* (*ehf-FEHT-toh*)

effect (to) effettuare (*ehf-feht-TWAHR-reh*)

(in) effect effettivamente (*ehf-feht-tee-vah-MEHN-teh*)

effective (adj.) effettivo (*ehf-feht-TEE-voh*)

effectively effettivamente (*ehf-feht-tee-vah-MEHN-teh*)

effectiveness efficacia *f.* (*ehf-fee-KAH-chah*)

effeminate (adj.) effeminato (*ehf-feh-mee-NAH-toh*)

efficacy efficacia *f.* (*ehf-fee-KAH-chah*)

efficiency efficienza *f.* (*ehf-fee-CHEN-tsah*)

efficient (adj.) efficiente (*ehf-fee-CHEN-teh*)

efficiently efficientemente (*ehf-fee-chen-teh-MEHN-teh*)

ego ego *m.* (*EH-goh*)

egotism, selfishness egotismo *m.* (*eh-goh-TEEZ-moh*)

egotist egotista *m.* (*eh-goh-TEE-stah*)

egotistical, selfish (adj.) egotistico (*eh-goh-TEE-stee-koh*)

elaborate (to) elaborare (*eh-lah-bohr-RAHR-reh*)

elaborate (adj.) elaborato (*eh-lah-bohr-RAH-toh*)

elastic elastico *m.* (*eh-LAH-stee-ko*h) ⊃(adj.)**C**

elasticity elasticità *f.* (*eh-lah-stee-chee-TAH*)

elect (to) eleggere (*eh-LEHD-jehr-reh*)

election elezione *f.* (*eh-leh-TSYOH-neh*)

elective (adj.) elettivo (*eh-LEHT-tee-voh*)

electric, electrical (adj.) elettrico (*eh-LEHT-tree-koh*)

electrician elettricista *m.* (*eh-leht-treh-CHEE-stah*)

electricity elettricità *f.* (*eh-leht-tree-chee-TAH*)

electrocardiogram, EKG elettrocardiogramma *m.* (*eh-leht-troh-kahr-dyoh-GRAHM-mah*)

electronic (adj.) elettronico (*eh-leht-TROH-nee-koh*)

electronics elettronica *f.* (*eh-leht-TROH-nee-kah*)

elegance eleganza *f.* (*eh-leh-GAHN-tsah*)

elegant, smart (adj.) elegante (*eh-leh-GAHN-teh*)

element elemento *m.* (*eh-leh-MEHN-toh*)

elementary, elemental (adj.) elementare (*eh-leh-mehn-TAHR-reh*)

elementary, grammar school scuola elementare *f.* (*SKWOH-lah ehl-eh-mehn-TAHR-reh*)

elephant elefante *m.* (*eh-leh-FAHN-teh*)

elevate (to) elevare (*eh-leh-VAHR-reh*)

elevated, high, tall (adj.) elevato (*eh-leh-VAH-toh*), alto (*AHL-toh*)

elevation elevazione *f.* (*eh-leh-vah-TSYOH-neh*)

eligibility eleggibilità *f.* (*eh-lehd-jee-bee-lee-TAH*)

eligible (adj.) eleggibile (*eh-lehd-JEE-bee-leh*)

eliminate (to) eliminare (*eh-lee-mee-NAHR-reh*)

elimination eliminazione *f.* (*eh-lee-mee-nah-TSYOH-neh*)

elongate (to) allungare (*ahl-loon-GAHR-reh*) 👆

eloquence eloquenza *f.* (*eh-loh-KWEHN-tsah*)

eloquent (adj.) eloquente (*eh-loh-KWEHN-teh*)

eloquently eloquentemente (*eh-loh-kwehn-teh-MEHN-teh*)

elude, dodge, evade (to) eludere (*eh-LOO-dehr-reh*)

elusive (adj.) elusivo (*eh-loo-SEE-voh*)

embargo embargo *m.* (*ehm-BAHR-goh*)

embark, board, (get) aboard (to) imbarcare (*eem-bahr-KAHR-reh*) 👆

embarrass (to) imbarazzare (*eem-bahr-raht-TSAHR-reh*) 👆

embarrassment imbarazzo *m.* (*eem-bahr-RAHT-tsoh*) 👆

emblem emblema *m.* (*ehm-BLEHM-mah*)

emblematic (adj.) emblematico (*ehm-bleh-MAHT-tee-koh*)

embroil, entangle (to) imbrogliare (*eem-broh-LYAHR-re*h) 👆

embryonic (adj.) embrionale (*ehm-bree-oh-NAH-leh*)

emerald smeraldo *m.* (*zmeh-RAHL-doh*) 👆

emerge (to) emergere (*eh-MEHR-jehr-reh*)

Lista di termini identici e simili 123

emergency emergenza *f.* (*eh-mehr-JEHN-tsah*)

emigrant emigrante *m.* (*eh-mee-GRAHN-teh*) ↄ(adj.)Ↄ

emigrate (to) emigrare (*eh-mee-GRAHR-reh*)

emigration emigrazione *f.* (*eh-mee-grah-TSYOH-neh*)

eminence eminenza *f.* (*eh-mee-NEHN-tsah*) ↄeminent (adj.) -enteↃ

emit (to) emettere (*eh-MEHT-tehr-reh*)

emollient emolliente *m.* (*eh-mohl-LYEHN-teh*) ↄ(adj.)Ↄ

emotion emozione *f.* (*eh-moh-TSYOH-neh*)

emotional (adj.) emotivo (*eh-moh-TEE-voh*)

emphasis enfasi *f.* (*EHN-fah-zee*)

emphatic (adj.) enfatico (*ehn-FAH-tee-koh*)

empire impero *m.* (*eem-PEHR-roh*) 💣

empirical (adj.) empirico (*ehm-PEER-ree-koh*)

empress imperatrice *f.* (*eem-pehr-rah-TREE-cheh*) 💣

emulate (to) emulare (*eh-mooh-LAHR-reh*)

enchant (to) incantare (*een-kahn-TAHR-reh*) 💣

enchanting (adj.) incantevole (*een-kahn-TEH-voh-leh*) 💣

enchantment incanto *m.* (*een-KAHN-toh*) 💣

encounter incontro *m.* (*een-KOHN-troh*) 💣

encounter, (informally) meet (to) incontrare (*een-kohn-TRAHR-reh*) 💣

encourage (to) incoraggiare (*een-koh-rahd-JAHR-reh*) 💣

encouragement incoraggiamento *m.* (*een-kohr-rahd-jah-MEHN-toh*) 💣

encyclopedia enciclopedia *f.* (*ehn-chee-kloh-peh-DEE-ah*)

endure durare (to) (*doohr-RAHR-reh*)

enduring (adj.) durevole (*doohr-REH-voh-leh*) 💣

enemy nemico *m.* (*neh-MEE-koh*) ↄ(adj.)Ↄ 💣

energetic (adj.) energico (*eh-NEHR-jee-koh*)

energy energia *f.* (*eh-nehr-JEE-ah*)

engineer (*technical*, NOT *railway*) ingegnere *m.* (*een-jeh-NYEHR-reh*) ✹

engineering ingegneria *f.* (*een-jeh-nyehr-REE-ah*) ✹

English (*language*) inglese *m.* (*een-GLEH-zeh*) ⊃(adj.)↻ ✹

Englishman, Englishwoman inglese *m.* & *f.* (*een-GLEH-zeh*)

enigma, riddle enimma *m.* (*eh-NEEM-mah*)

enigmatic (adj.) enimmatico (*eh-neem-MAH-tee-koh*)

enormity enormità *f.* (*eh-nohr-mee-TAH*)

enormous, huge (adj.) enorme (*eh-NOHR-meh*)

enter (to) entrare (*ehn-TRAHR-reh*)

enthusiasm, zest entusiasmo *m.* (*ehn-too-ZYAH-zmoh*)

enthusiast entusiasta *m.* & *f.* (*ehn-too-ZYAH-stah*)

enthusiastic (adj.) entusiastico (*ehn-too-ZYAH-stee-koh*)

entrance, entry, entryway entrata *f.* (*ehn-TRAH-tah*), ingresso (*een-GREHS-soh*)
ⓘ **Exit**—uscita *f.* (*oo-SHEE-tah*)

enumerate (to) enumerare (*eh-noo-mehr-RAHR-reh*)

enumeration enumerazione *f.* (*eh-noo-mehr-rah-TSYOH-neh*)

enunciate (to) enunciare (*eh-noon-CHAR-reh*)

enunciation enunciazione *f.* (*eh-noon-chah-TSYOH-neh*)

ephemeral (adj.) effimiro (*ehf-FEE-mehr-roh*)

epic (*poem, novel,* OR *film*) epopea *f.* (*eh-POH-peh-ah*)

epic (adj.) epico (*EH-pee-koh*)

epidemic epidemia *f.* (*eh-pee-deh-MEE-ah*)

epidemic (adj.) epidemico (*eh-pee-DEH-mee-koh*)

epilepsy epilessia *f.* (*eh-pee-lehs-SEE-ah*)

episode episodio *m.* (*eh-pee-SOH-dyoh*)

epitaph epitaffio *m.* (*eh-pee-TAHF-fyoh*)

epithet epiteto *m.* (*eh-PEE-teh-toh*)

epitome epitome *f.* (*eh-PEE-toh-meh*)

epoch epoca *f.* (*EH-poh-kah*)

equable, equitable (adj.) equo (*EH-kwoh*)

equal (adj.) eguale (*eh-GWAH-leh*), uguale (*ooh-GWAH-leh*) 🔊

equal, equate (to) eguagliare (*eh-gwah-LYAHR-reh*), uguagliare (*oo-gwah-LYAHR-reh*) 🔊

equality eguaglianza *f.* (*eh-gwah-LYAHN-tsah*), uguaglianza (*oo-gwahl-YAHN-tsah*) 🔊

equanimity equanimità *f.* (*eh-kwah-nee-mee-TAH*)

equation equazione *f.* (*eh-kwah-TSYOH-neh*)

equator equatore *m.* (*eh-kwah-TOHR-reh*)

equatorial (adj.) equatoriale (*eh-kwah-toh-RYAH-leh*)

equestrian (adj.) equestre (*eh-KWEH-streh*)

equidistant (adj.) equidistante (*eh-kwee-dee-STAHN-teh*)

equilibrium, sense of balance equilibrio *m.* (*eh-kwee-LEE-bryoh*)

equipment equipaggio *m.* (*eh-kwee-PAHD-joh*)

equivalent *(adj.)* equivalente (*eh-kwee-vah-LEHN-teh*)

equivocal (adj.) equivoco (*eh-KWEE-voh-koh*)

era era *f.* (*EHR-rah*)

eradicate (to) sradicare (*zrahd-dee-KAHR-reh*) 🔊

erect (adj.) eretto (*ehr-REHT-toh*)

erect (to) erigere (*ehr-REE-jehr-reh*)

erection erezione *f.* (*ehr-reh-TSYOH-neh*)

erosion erosione *f.* (*ehr-roh-ZYOH-neh*)

erotic (adj.) erotico (*ehr-ROH-tee-koh*)

err, stray (*morally*) (to) errare (*ehr-RRAHR-reh*)

erratic (adj.) erratico (*ehr-RRAH-tee-koh*)

erroneous, incorrect, mistaken, wrong (adj.) erroneo (*ehr-RROH-neh-oh*), errato (*ehr-RRAHT-toh*)

error, blunder errore *m.* (*ehr-RROHR-reh*)

erudition, scholarship erudizione *f.* (*eh-roo-dee-TSYOH-neh*)

ⓘ A closely related non cognate is: **scholar**—erudito *m.* (*ehr-roo-DEE-toh*).

erupt (to) eruttare (*eh-root-TAHR-reh*)

eruption, rash eruzione *f.* (*eh-roo-TSYOH-neh*)

escort scorta *f.* (*SKOHR-tah*) ◆

escort (to) scortare (*skohr-TAHR-reh*) ◆

esoteric (adj.) esoterico (*eh-soh-TEHR-ree-koh*)

especially (adj.) specialmente (*speh-chahl-MEHN-teh*) ◆

essence essenza *f.* (*ehs-SEHN-tsah*)

essential (adj.) essenziale (*ehs-sehn-TSYAH-leh*)

essentially essenzialmente (*ehs-sehn-tsyahl-MEHN-teh*)

establish (to) stabilire (*stah-bee-LEER-reh*) ◆

establishment stabilimento *m.* (*stah-bee-lee-MEHN-toh*) ◆

esteem stima *f.* (*STEE-mah*) ◆

estimate, estimation stima *f.* (*STEE-mah*) ◆

estimate (to) stimare (*stee-MAHR-reh*) ◆

eternal (adj.) eterno (*eh-TEHR-noh*)

eternally, forevermore eternamente (*eh-tehr-nah-MEHN-teh*)

eternity eternità *f.* (*eh-tehr-nee-TAH*)

ethereal (adj.) etereo (*eh-TEHR-reh-oh*)

ethics etica *f.* (*EH-tee-kah*) ⊃**ethical** (adj.) -co𝘊

ethnic (adj.) etnico (*EHT-nee-koh*)

eulogize (to) elogiare (*eh-loh-JAHR-reh*)

eulogy elogio *m.* (*eh-LOH-joh*)

Europe Europa *f.* (*Ehoor-ROH-pah*)

European europeo *m.* (*ehoo-roh-PEH-oh*) ⊃(adj.)☾

evacuate (to)   evacuare (*eh-vah-koo-AHR-reh*)

evaluate (to)   valutare (*vah-loo-TAHR-reh*) ♦※

evaluation   valutazione *f.* (*vah-loo-tah-TSYOH-neh*) ♦※

evangelist   evangelista *m.* (*eh-vahn-jeh-LEE-stah*)

evaporate (to)   evaporare (*eh-vah-poh-RAHR-reh*)

evaporation   evaporazione *f.* (*eh-vah-poh-rah-TSYOH-neh*)

evasion   evasione *f.* (*eh-vah-ZYOH-neh*) ⊃**evasive** (adj.) -sivo☾

event, outcome   evento *m.* (*eh-VEHN-toh*)

evidence   evidenza *f.* (*eh-vee-DEHN-tsah*) ⊃**evident** (adj.) -dente☾

evidently   evidentemente (*eh-vee-dehn-teh-MEHN-teh*)

evolution   evoluzione *f.* (*eh-voh-loo-TSYOH-neh*)

evolve (to)   evolvere (*eh-VOHL-vehr-reh*)
   ♦※ NOTE re English "ex-" words below: Italian rarely utilizes an ex- combination, but rather uses es- almost exclusively.

exact (adj.)   esatto (*eh-ZAHT-toh*) ♦※

exactly   esattamente (*eh-zaht-tah-MEHN-teh*) ♦※

exaggerate (to)   esagerare (*eh-zah-jeh-RAHR-reh*) ♦※

exaggeration   esagerazione *f.* (*eh-zah-jeh-rah-TSYOH-neh*) ♦※

exam, examination, test, quiz   esame *m.* (*eh-ZAH-meh*) ♦※

examine, quiz (to)   esaminare (*eh-zah-mee-NAHR-reh*) ♦※

example   esempio *m.* (*eh-ZEHM-pyoh*) ♦※

exasperation   esasperazione *f.* (*eh-zah-speh-rah-TSYOH-neh*) ♦※

exceed (to)   eccedere (*eht-CHEH-dehr-reh*) ♦※

excel(to)   eccellere (*eht-CHEL-lehr-reh*) ♦※

excellence   eccellenza *f.* (*eht-chel-LEHN-tsah*)

excellent (adj.)   eccellente (*eht-chel-LEHN-teh*) ♦※

exception   eccezione *f.* (*eht-cheh-TSYOH-neh*) ♦※

exceptional (adj.)   eccezionale (*eht-cheh-tsyoh-NAH-leh*) 👆

excess   eccesso *m.* (*eht-CHES-soh*) 👆

excessive (adj.)   eccessivo (*eht-ches-SEE-voh*) 👆

excitable, high-strung, hotheaded (adj.)   eccitabile (*eht-chee-TAH-bee-leh*) 👆

excite (to)   eccitare (*eht-chee-TAHR-reh*) 👆

excitement   eccitamento *m.* (*eht-chee-tah-MEHN-toh*) 👆

exclamation   esclamazione *f.* (*eh-sklah-mah-TSYOH-neh*) 👆

exclude (to)   escludere (*eh-SKLOO-dehr-reh*) 👆

exclusion   esclusione *f.* (*eh-skloo-ZYOH-neh*) 👆

exclusive (adj.)   esclusivo (*eh-skloo-ZEE-voh*) 👆

excrement   escremento *m.* (*ehs-kreh-MEHN-toh*) 👆

excursion, outing, junket   escursione *f.* (*eh-skoor-ZYOH-neh*) 👆

excusable (adj.)   scusabile (*skoo-ZAH-bee-leh*) 👆

excuse   scusa *f.* (*SKOO-zah*) 👆

excuse (to)   scusare (*skoo-ZAHR-reh*) 👆
   ⓘ The related noncognate verb: **to apologize**—scusarsi (*skoo-ZAHR-see*)

execution (*NOT* **capital punishment**), **performance**   esecuzione *f.* (*eh-zeh-koo-TSYOH-neh*) 👆

executive (adj.)   esecutivo (*eh-zeh-koo-TEE-voh*) 👆
   ⓘ A corresponding noun form of this term does not exist. Rather, an Italian **executive** is invariably: amministratore *m.*

executor   esecutore *m.* (*eh-zeh-koo-TOHR-reh*) 👆

exemplify (to)   esemplificare (*eh-zehm-plee-fee-KAHR-reh*) 👆

exercise (*practice, demonstration piece, routine*)   esercizio *m.* (*eh-zehr-CHEE-tsyoh*) 👆

exercise (*physical exertion*)   esercizio (*m.*) fisico (*eh-zehr-CHEE-tsee-oh FEE-zee-koh*) 👆

exercise, exert (to)   esercitare (*eh-zehr-chee-TAHR-reh*) 👆

exhale (to)   esalare (*eh-zahl-AHR-reh*) 👆

exhibition   esibizione *f.* (*eh-zee-bee-TSYOH-neh*) 👆

exhort (to)   esortare (*eh-zohr-TAHR-reh*) 💣

exile, banishment   esilio *m.* (*eh-ZEE-lyoh*) 💣

exile (to)   esiliare (*eh-zee-LYAHR-reh*) 💣

exist (to)   esistere (*eh-ZEE-stehr-reh*) 💣

existence   esistenza *f.* (*eh-zee-STEHN-tsah*) 💣

exorbitant (adj.)   esorbitante (*eh-zohr-bee-TAHNT-teh*) 💣

exotic (adj.)   esotico (*eh-ZOH-tee-koh*) 💣

expand (to)   espandere (*eh-SPAHN-dehr-reh*) 💣

expansion   espansione *f.* (*eh-spahn-SYOH-neh*) 💣

expatriate   espatriato *m.* (*eh-spah-tree-AH-toh*) 💣

expedient   espediente *m.* (*eh-speh-DYEHN-teh*) ⊃(adj.)ℂ 💣

expedition   spedizione *f.* (*speh-dee-TSYOH-neh*) 💣

expel, eject, evict, oust (to)   espellere (*eh-SPEHL-lehr-reh*) 💣

expense   spesa *f.* (*SPEH-sah*)

expensive   costoso (*koh-STOH-soh*) 💣

experience   esperienza *f.* (*eh-spehr-RYEHN-tsah*) 💣

experiment   esperimento *m.* (*eh-spehr-ree-MEHN-toh*) 💣

experiment (to)   sperimentare (*spehr-ree-ment-TAHR-reh*) 💣

experimental (adj.)   sperimentale (*spehr-ree-mehn-TAH-leh*) 💣

expert   esperto *m.* (*eh-SPEHR-toh*) ⊃(adj.)ℂ 💣

expire (to)   espirare (*eh-spee-RAHR-reh*) 💣

expletive (adj.)   espletivo (*eh-spleh-TEE-voh*) 💣

explicit (adj.)   esplicito (*eh-SPLEE-chee-toh*) 💣

explode (to)   esplodere (*eh-SPLOH-dehr-reh*) 💣

exploration   esplorazione *f.* (*eh-sploh-rah-TSYOH-neh*) 💣

exploratory (adj.)   esplorativo (*eh-splohr-rah-TEE-voh*) 💣

explore (to)   esplorare (*eh-sploh-RAHR-reh*) 💣

explorer, scout   esploratore *m.* (*eh-sploh-rah-TOHR-reh*) 💣

explosion esplosione *f.* (*eh-sploh-ZYOH-neh*) 💣

explosive esplosivo *m.* (*eh-sploh-ZEE-voh*) ⊃(adj.)℃ 💣

export, exportation esportazione *f.* (*eh-spohr-tah-TSYOH-neh*) 💣

export (to) esportare (*eh-spohr-TAHR-reh*) 💣

exporter esportatore *m.* (*eh-spohr-tah-TOHR-reh*) 💣

exposition esposizione *f.* (*eh-spoh-zee-TSYOH-neh*) 💣

express espresso *m.* (*eh-SPREHS-soh*) ⊃(adj.)℃ 💣

expression, utterance espressione *f.* (*eh-sprehs-SYOH-neh*) 💣

expressive (adj.) espressivo (*eh-sprehs-SEE-voh*) 💣

expulsion, ejection, eviction espulsione *f.* (*eh-spool-SYOH-neh*) 💣

exquisite (adj.) squisito (*skwee-ZEE-toh*) 💣

extend (to) estendere (*eh-STEHN-dehr-reh*) 💣

extension, extent estensione *f.* (*eh-stehn-SYOH-neh*) 💣

extensive (adj.) esteso (*eh-STEHS-soh*) 💣

exterior, outside esterno *m.* (*eh-STEHR-noh*) ⊃(adj.)℃ 💣

exterior, outer, outward (adj.) esteriore (*eh-stehr-RYOHR-reh*) 💣

extinct (adj.) estinto (*eh-STEEN-toh*) 💣

extinction estinzione *f.* (*eh-steen-TSYOH-neh*) 💣

extinguish (to) estinguere (*eh-STEEN-gwehr-reh*) 💣

extortion estorsione *f.* (*eh-stohr-SYOH-neh*) 💣

extra (adj.) extra (*EKS-trah*)

extract estratto *m.* (*eh-STRAHT-toh*) 💣

extract (to) estrarre (*eh-STRAHRR-reh*) 💣

extraneous (adj.) estraneo (*eh-STRAH-neh-oh*) 💣

extraordinary (adj.) straordinario (*strah-ohr-dee-NAHR-ryoh*) 💣

extravagance stravaganza *f.* (*strah-vah-GAHN-tsah*) 💣

extravagant (adj.) stravagante (*strah-vah-GAHN-teh*) 💣

extreme, utmost (adj.) estremo (*eh-STREH-moh*) 🔊

extremely estremamente (*eh-streh-mah-MEHN-teh*) 🔊

extremity estremità *f.* (*eh-streh-mee-TAH*) 🔊

extrovert estroverso *m.* (*eh-stroh-VEHR-soh*) ⤴(adj.)⊂ 🔊

exuberant (adj.) esuberante (*eh-zoo-behr-RAHN-teh*) 🔊

—F—

fabricate, manufacture, make (to) fabbricare (*fahb-bree-KAHR-reh*)

fabrication fabbricazione *f.* (*fahb-bree-kah-TSYOH-neh*)

fabricator, manufacturer fabbricante *m.* (*fahb-bree-KAHN-teh*)
  ⓘ The related noncognate noun: **factory, plant**—fabbrica *f.* (*FAHB-bree-kah*)

fabulous (adj.) favoloso (*fahv-oh-LOH-soh*) 🔊

façade facciata *f.* (*faht-CHAH-tah*)

face (*anatomical*) faccia *f.* (*FAHT-chah*)

facet faccetta *f.* (*faht-CHEHT-tah*)

facetious, witty, humorous (adj.) faceto (*fah-CHEH-toh*)

facial (adj.) facciale (*faht-CHAH-leh*)

facile, easy (adj.) facile (*fah-CHEE-leh*)
  ⓘ An important related adverb: **easily**—facilmente (*fah-cheel-MEHN-teh*)

facilitate (to) facilitare (*fah-chee-lee-TAHR-reh*)

facility, ease (*of action*), **effortlessness** facilità *f.* (*fah-chee-lee-TAH*)

fact fatto *m.* (*FAHT-toh*) 🔊
  ⓘ The everyday phrase **in fact**—infatti (*een-FAHT-tee*)

factor fattore *m.* (*faht-TOHR-reh*) 🔊

faculty (*ability, talent, OR scholastic staff*), **knack** facoltà *f.* (*fah-kohl-TAH*)

fail (to) fallire (*fahl-LEER-reh*)

fair fiera *f.* (*FYEHR-rah*)

falcon, hawk   falco *m.* (*FAHL-koh*)

fallacy   fallacia *f.* (*fahl-LAH-chah*) ⊃**fallacious** (adj.) -lace⊂

fallible (adj.)   fallibile (*fahl-LEE-bee-leh*)

false, fake, counterfeit, untrue (adj.)   falso (*FAHL-soh*)

falsifier, faker, pretender   falsificatore *m.* (*fahl-see-fee-kah-TOHR-reh*)

falsify, fake (to)   falsificare (*fahl-see-fee-KAHR-reh*)

falsification   falsificazione *f.* (*fahl-see-fee-kah-TSYOH-neh*)

fame   fama *f.* (*FAH-mah*)

famous, famed (adj.)   famoso (*fah-MOH-soh*)

familiar (adj.)   familiare (*fah-mee-LYAHR-reh*)

familiarity   familiarità *f.* (*fah-mee-lyah-ree-TAH*)

familiarize (to)   familiarizzare (*fah-mee-lyahr-reed-DZAHR-reh*)

family, household   famiglia *f.* (*fah-MEE-lyah*)

famished, ravenous (adj.)   affamato (*ahf-fah-MAH-toh*) ☛

famishment, hunger *f.*   fame (*FAH-meh*)

fanatic   fanatico *m.* (*fah-NAH-tee-koh*) ⊃**fanatic, fanatical** (adj.)⊂

fanaticism   fanatismo *m.* (*fah-nah-TEEZ-moh*)

fantastic (adj.)   fantastico (*fahn-TAH-stee-koh*)

fantasy   fantasia *f.* (*fahn-tah-ZEE-ah*)

fascination   fascino *m.* (*FAH-shee-noh*)

fascist   fascista *m.* & *f.* (*fah-SHEE-stah*) ⊃(adj.)⊂

fastidious (adj.)   fastidioso (*fah-stee-DYOH-soh*)

fatal (adj.)   fatale (*fah-TAH-leh*)

fatality   fatalità *f.* (*fah-tah-lee-TAH*)

fatally   fatalmente (*fah-tahl-MEHN-teh*)

fate   fato *m.* (*FAH-toh*)

fatigue   fatica *f.* (*fah-TEE-kah*)

favor favore *m.* (*fah-VOHR-reh*)

favor (to) favorire (*fah-vohr-REER-reh*)

favorable (adj.) favorevole (*fah-vohr-REH-voh-leh*)
  ① The antonym **unfavorable** (adj.)—sfavorevole (*sfah-vohr-REH-voh-leh*)

favorite favorito *m.*(*fah-vohr-REE-toh*) ➲(adj.)☾

favoritism favoritismo *m.* (*fah-voh-ree-TEEZ-moh*)

feast festa *f.* (*FEH-stah*)

feat fatto (insigne) *m.* (*FAHT-toh [een-see-nyeh]*)

feces feci *f.* (*FEH-chee*)

federal (adj.) federale (*feh-dehr-RAH-leh*)

federation federazione *f.* (*fed-deh-rah-TSYOH-neh*)

felicity, happiness felicità *f.* (*feh-lee-chee-TAH*)
  ① Closely related noncognates are **happy** (adj)— felice (*feh-LEE-cheh*);
  happily—felicemente (*feh-lee-cheh-MEHN-teh*); and **unhappy /**
  blue—infelice (*een-feh-LEE-cheh*) / triste (*TREE-steh*).

felon fellone *m.* (*fehl-LOH-neh*)

felony fellonia *f.* (*fehl-loh-NEE-ah*)

female femmina *f.* (*FEHM-mee-nah*)

female, feminine (adj.) femminile (*fehm-mee-NEE-leh*)

femininity femminilità *f.* (*fehm-mee-nee-lee-TAH*)

ferment (*social, political unrest*) fermento *m.* (*fehr-MEHN-toh*)

fermentation fermentazione *f.* (*fehr-mehn-tah-TSYOH-neh*)

ferocity ferocia *f.* (*fehr-ROH-chah*) ➲**ferocious, fierce** (adj.) -oce☾

fertile(adj.) fertile (*FEHR-tee-leh*)

fertility fertilità *f.* (*fehr-tee-lee-TAH*)

fertilizer fertilizzante *m.* (*fehr-tee-leed-DZAHN-teh*)

fervently ferventemente (*fehr-vehn-teh-MEHN-teh*)

fervor fervore *m.* (*fehr-VOHR-reh*) ➲**fervent** (adj.) -vente☾

festival festival *m.* (*FEH-stee-vahl*), festa *f.* (*FEH-stah*)

festive (adj.)   festivo (*feh-STEE-voh*)

festivity   festività *f.* (*feh-stee-vee-TAH*)

fetal (adj.)   fetale (*feh-TAH-leh*)

fetus   feto *m.* (*FEH-toh*)

feud   feudo *m.* (*FEHOO-doh*)

feudal (adj.)   feudale (*fehoo-DAH-leh*)

feudalism   feudalismo *m.* (*fehoo-dah-LEEZ-moh*)

fiasco, flop, (unexpected) failure   fiasco *m.* (*FYAH-skoh*)

fiber   fibra *f.* (*FEE-brah*)

fiction   finzione *f.* (*feen-TSYOH-neh*) 👁

fidelity, faithfulness   fedeltà *f.* (*feh-dehl-TAH*)
   ⓘ Important, closely related noncognates are: **faith**—fede *f.* (*FEH-deh*); **faithful, staunch** (adj.)—fedele (*feh-DEH-leh*); and **faithless** (adj.)—senza fede (*SEHNT-tsah feh-DEH*), infedele (*een-feh-DEH-leh*).

fig   fico *m.* (*FEE-koh*)

figure   figura *f.* (*fee-GOOR-rah*)

figure of speech   figura (*f.*) retorica (*fee-GOOR-rah reh-TOHR-ree-kah*)

figure (*calculate*) (to)   figurare (*fee-goor-RAHR-reh*)

figurine   figurina *f.* (*fee-goor-REE-nah*)

filament   filamento *m.* (*fee-lah-MEHN-toh*)

filigree   filigrana *f.* (*fee-lee-GRAH-nah*)

fillet (*of meat, NOT fish*)   filetto *m.* (*fee-LEHT-toh*)

film (*photographic material*), movie   film *m.* (*FEELM*)

filter   filtro *m.* (*FEEL-troh*)

filter (to)   filtrare (*feel-TRAHR-reh*)

finale   finale *m.* (*fee-NAH-leh*) ➲**final** (adj.)➲

finalist   finalista *m.* (*fee-nah-LEE-stah*)

finally   finalmente (*fee-nahl-MEHN-teh*)

finances   finanze *f.* (*fee-NAHN-tseh*)

financial (adj.)   finanziario (*fee-nahn-TSYAHR-ryoh*)

fine (*very small, NOT quality OR penalty*) (adj.)   fine (*FEE-neh*)

fine arts   belle arti *f.* (*behl-leh AHR-tee*)

finish (*surface appearance*)   finitura *f.* (*fee-nee-TOO-rah*), rifinitura *f.* (*ree-fee-nee-TOO-rah*)

finish, end, ending   fine *f.* (*FEE-neh*)

finish, end (to)   finire (*fee-NEER-reh*), terminare (*tehr-mee-NAHR-reh*)

firm (*not loose*), **fast** (*secure*), **steady** (adj.)   fermo (*FEHR-moh*)

firmness   fermezza *f.* (*fehr-MEHT-tsah*)

first-class (adj.)   di prima classe (*dee PREE-mah KLAHS-seh*)

first-rate, top quality (adj.)   di prima qualità (*dee PREE-mah kwa-hlee-TAH*)

fiscal (adj.)   fiscale (*fee-SKAH-leh*)

fissure, crack, slit, slot   fessura *f.* (*fehs-SOOR-rah*)

fix (*set, NOT repair*) (to)   fissare (*fees-SAHR-reh*)

fixation   fissazione *f.* (*fees-sah-TSYOH-neh*)

fixed (*set, NOT repaired*) (adj.)   fisso (*FEES-soh*)

flagrant (adj.)   flagrante (*flah-GRAHN-teh*)

flagrantly   flagrantemente (*flah-grahn-teh-MEHN-teh*)

flame   fiamma *f.* (*FYAHM-mah*) 🌶

flaming (adj.)   fiammante (*fyahm-MAHN-teh*) 🌶

flannel   flanella *f.* (*flah-NEHL-lah*)

flexibility   flessibilità *f.* (*flehs-see-bee-lee-TAH*)

flexible (adj.)   flessibile (*fles-SEE-bee-leh*)

flirt (to)   flirtare (*fleer-TAHR-reh*)

flirtation   flirt *m.* (*FLEER-teh*)

floral (adj.)   floreale (*flohr-reh-AH-leh*)

florist   fioraio *m.* (*fyohr-RAH-yoh*) 🌶

flower (to)   fiorire (*fyohr-REER-reh*) 🌶

fluctuate (to)   fluttuare (*floot-too-AH-reh*)

fluctuation   fluttuazione *f.* (*floot-twah-TSYOH-neh*)

fluent, glib (adj.)   fluente (*floo-EHN-teh*)

fluid   fluido *m.* (*FLOO-ee-doh*) ⊃(adj.)⊃

fluorescent (adj.)   fluorescente (*flwohr-reh-SHEHN-teh*)

focal (adj.)   focale (*foh-KAH-leh*)

focus   fuoco *m.* (*FWOH-koh*) 💣

foil (*metal*)   foglia *f.* (*FOH-lyah*)

folio   folio *m.* (*FOH-lyoh*)

folklore   folclore *m.* (*fohl-KLOHR-reh*)

folly   follia *f.* (*fohl-LEE-ah*)

football   football *m.* (*FOO-teh-bahl-leh*)

force, strength   forza *f.* (*FOHR-tsah*)

force (to)   forzare (*fohr-TSAHR-reh*)

forcible (adj.)   forzato (*fohr-TSAH-toh*)

forest   foresta *f.* (*fohr-REH-stah*)

fork (*eating utensil*)   forchetta *f.* (*fohr-KEHT-tah*)
   ① Lengthening the English yields shortened Italian: **pitchfork**—forca (*FOHR-kah*).

form, shape   forma *f.* (*FOHR-mah*)

form, shape, mold (to)   formare (*fohr-MAHR-reh*)

formal (adj.)   formale (*forh-MAH-leh*)

formality   formalità *f.* (*fohr-mah-lee-TAH*)

formally   formalmente (*fohr-mahl-MEHN-teh*)

format   formato *m.* (*fohr-MAH-toh*)

formation (*creation*)   formazione *f.* (*fohr-mah-TSYOH-neh*)

formative (adj.)   formativo (*fohr-mah-TEE-voh*)

formula   formula *f.* (*FOHR-moo-lah*)

fort, forte   forte *m.* (*FOHR-teh*)

fortification   fortificazione *f.* (*fohr-tee-fee-kah-TSYOH-neh*)

fortify (to)   fortificare (*fohr-tee-fee-KAHR-reh*)

fortress   fortezza *f.* (*fohr-TEHT-tsah*)

fortuitous (adj.)   fortuito (*fohr-TOO-ee-toh*)

fortunate, lucky (adj.)   fortunato (*fohr-too-NAH-toh*)
ⓘ The antonyms **unfortunate, unlucky** (adj.) are—sfortunato (*sfor-too-NAH-toh*).

fortunately   fortunatamente (*fohr-too-nah-tah-MEHN-teh*)

fortune (*chance OR wealth*), **luck**   fortuna *f.* (*fohr-TOO-nah*)

foundation (*basis, structural base*)   fondamento *m.* (*fohn-dah-MEHN-toh*)

foundation (*organization*)   fondazione *f.* (*fohn-dah-TSYOH-neh*)

founder   fondatore *m.* (*fohn-dah-TOHR-reh*)

fount, source, spring (*of water*)   fonte *f.* (*FOHN-teh*)

fountain   fontana *f.* (*fohn-TAH-nah*)

fraction   frazione *f.* (*frah-TSYOH-neh*)

fracture   frattura *f.* (*fraht-TOOR-rah*)

fracture (to)   fratturare (*fraht-toor-RAHR-reh*)
ⓘ Closely related: **to smash into small pieces**—fracassare (*frah-kahs-SAHR-reh*)

fragile, frail, brittle (adj.)   fragile (*FRAH-jee-leh*)

fragment   frammento *m.* (*frahm-MEHN-toh*) ♠

fragmentary (adj.)   frammentario (*frahm-mehn-TAHR-ryoh*) ♠

fragrance   fragranza *f.* (*frah-GRAHN-tsah*) ➲**fragrant** (adj.) -nte❰

frank, candid, straightforward (adj.)   franco (*FRAHN-koh*)

frankly, candidly   francamente (*frahn-kah-MEHN-teh*)

frankness   franchezza *f.* (*frahn-KEHT-tsah*)

fraternal, brotherly (adj.)   fraterno (*frah-TEHR-noh*)

fraternity   fraternità *f.* (*frah-tehr-nee-TAH*)

ⓘ The closely related noncognate: **brotherhood**—fratellanza *f.* (*frah-tel-LAHN-tsah*)

fraternize (to)   fraternizzare (*frah-tehr-need-DZAHR-reh*)

fraud   frode *f.* (*FROH-deh*) 💧

fraudulent (adj.)   fraudolento (*frow-doh-LEHN-toh*)

fraudulently   fraudolentemente (*frow-doh-lehn-teh-MENH-teh*)

frenzy   frenesia *f.* (*freh-neh-ZEE-ah*)

frequency   frequenza *f.* (*freh-KWEHN-tsah*)

frequent (adj.)   frequente (*freh-KWEHN-teh*)

frequent, haunt (to)   frequentare (*freh-kwehn-TAHR-reh*)

frequently   frequentemente (*freh-kwehn-teh-MEHN-teh*)

fresco (*painting in plaster*)   affresco *m.* (*ahf-FREHS-koh*) 💧

fresh, cool (adj.)   fresco (*FREHS-koh*)
   ⓘ A very basic, very important related noncognate is **cold** (adj.)—freddo (*FREHD-doh*) / (faucet marking) *F.*

freshness   freschezza *f.* (*freh-SKEHT-tsah*)

friction   frizione (*free-TSYOH-neh*)

frigid (adj.)   frigido (*FREE-jee-doh*)

fringe   frangia *f.* (*FRAHN-jah*)

frivolity   frivolezza *f.* (*free-voh-LEHT-tzah*)

frivolous (adj.)   frivolo (*FREE-voh-loh*)

front   fronte *m.* (*FROHN-teh*)

frontal (adj.)   frontale (*frohn-TAH-leh*)

frontier   frontiera *f.* (*frohn-TYEHR-rah*)

frugal (adj.)   frugale (*froo-GAH-leh*)

frugality   frugalità *f.* (*froo-gah-lee-TAH*)

fruit (*plural OR mixed*)   frutta *f.* (*FROOT-tah*)
   ⓘ This is one of the rare, odd instances where an Italian noun in singular form changes both gender and spelling: a single piece of **fruit** is— frutto *m.* (*FROOT-toh*)!

fruitful (adj.) fruttuoso (*froot-TWOH-soh*)

fruition fruizione *f.* (*froo-ee-TSYOH-neh*)

frustrate, foil, thwart (to) frustrare (*froo-STRAHR-reh*)

frustration frustrazione *f.* (*froo-strah-TSYOH-neh*)

fugitive fuggitivo *m.* (*food-jee-TEE-voh*) ⊃(adj.)℃

fumes (*visible*), **smoke** fumo *m.* (*FOO-moh*)

(give off) fumes, smoke, use tobacco (to) fumare (*foo-MAHR-reh*)

function funzione *f.* (*foon-TSYOH-neh*)

function (to) funzionare (*foon-tsyoh-NAHR-reh*)

functional (adj.) funzionale (*foont-tsyoh-NAH-leh*)

fund, bottom fondo *m.* (*FOHN-doh*)

fundamental, basic (adj.) fondamentale (*fohn-dah-mehn-TAH-leh*)

funeral funerale *m.* (*foo-nehr-AH-leh*)

funereal (adj.) funereo (*foo-NEHR-reh-oh*)

fungus fungo *m.* (*FOON-goh*)

furious (adj.) furioso (*foor-ree-OH-soh*)

furnish (to) fornire (*forh-NEER-reh*)

furor, rage, wrath, ire furore *m.* (*foor-ROHR-reh*)

furtive, stealthy (adj.) furtivo (*foor-TEE-voh*)
    ⓘ Closely related but noncognate: **theft**—furto *m.* (*FOOR-toh*)

fury furia *f.* (*FOOR-ryah*)

futile (adj.) futile (*foo-TEE-leh*)

futility futilità *f.* (*foo-tee-lee-TAH*)

future futuro *m.* (*foo-TOOR-roh*) ⊃(adj.)℃

—G—

gaiety gaiezza *f.* (*gah-YEHT-tsah*)

gala gala *f.* (*GAH-lah*)

galaxy galassia *f.* (*gah-LAHS-syah*)

gallant (adj.) galante (*gah-LAHN-teh*)

gallery galleria *f.* (*gahl-lehr-REE-ah*)

gallop galoppo *m.* (*gah-LOHP-poh*)

gangster gangster *m.* (*GAHNG-stehr-reh*)

garage garage *m.* (*gah-RAH-jeh*), autorimessa *f.* (*aow-toh-ree-MEHS-sah*)

garden giardino *m.* (*jahr-DEE-noh*) 🔊
  ⓘ Related: **zoo**—giardino (*m.*) zoologico (*jahr-DEE-noh dzoh-oo-LOH-jee-koh*)

gardener giardiniere *m.* (*jahr-dee-NYEHR-reh*) 🔊

gardenia gardenia *f.* (*gahr-DEH-nyah*)

garland, wreath ghirlanda *f.* (*geer-LAHN-dah*)

garrulous (adj.) garrulo (*gahr-RROO-loh*)

gas (*oxygen, helium, and so forth, NOT gasoline*) gas *m.* (*GAHZ*)
  ⓘ What Americans call **gasoline** and Brits call **petrol,** Italians call—benzina *f.* (*behn-ZEE-nah*).

gaseous (adj.) gassoso (*gahs-SOH-soh*)

gastric (adj.) gastrico (*gah-STREE-koh*)

gastritis gastrite *f.* (*gah-STREE-teh*)

gastronomic (adj.) gastronomico (*gah-stroh-NOH-mee-koh*)

gastronomy gastronomia *f.* (*gah-stroh-noh-MEE-ah*)

gay (*cheerful, merry*) (adj.) gaio (*GAH-yoh*)
  🔊 NOTE: Italians have been adopting more and more English *gay* for *homosexual.*

gelatin, jelly gelatina *f.* (*jeh-lah-TEE-nah*)

gem gemma *f.* (*JEHM-mah*)

gender genere *m.* (*JEH-nehr-reh*)

gene gene m (*JEH-neh*)

genealogical (adj.) genealogico (jeh-neh-ah-LOH-jee-koh)

genealogy genealogia *f.* (*jeh-neh-ah-loh-JEE-ah*)

general generale *m.* (*jeh-nehr-RAH-leh*) ⊃(adj.)↻

generality generalità *f.* (*jeh-neh-rah-lee-TAH*)

generalization generalizzazione *f.* (*jeh-neh-rah-leed-dzah-TSYOH-neh*)

generalize (to) generalizzare (*jeh-neh-rah-leed-DZAHR-reh*)

generally generalmente (*jeh-neh-rahl-MEHN-teh*)

generate, beget, breed(to) generare (*jeh-neh-RAHR-reh*)

generation (*time measure*) generazione *f.* (*jeh-neh-rah-TSYOH-neh*)

generator (*electric*), **breeder** generatore *m.* (*jeh-neh-rah-TOHR-reh*)

generic (adj.) generico (*jeh-NEHR-ree-koh*)

generosity generosità *f.* (*jeh-nehr-roh-see-TAH*)

generous (adj.) generoso (*jeh-nehr-ROH-soh*)

generously generosamente (*jeh-nehr-roh-sah-MEHN-teh*)

genetic (adj.) genetico (*jeh-NEH-tee-koh*)

genetics genetica *f.* (*jeh-NEH-tee-kah*)

genitals genitali *m.* (*jeh-nee-TAH-lee*) ⊃**genital** (adj.) -ale↻

genitor, parent genitore *m.* (*jeh-nee-TOHR-reh*)

genius genio *m.* (*JEH-nyoh*)

genocide genocidio *m.* (*jeh-noh-CHEE-dyoh*)

gentile, non-Jewish gentile *m.* (*jehn-TEE-leh*) ⊃(adj.)↻

gentilesse, kindness gentilezza *f.* (*jehn-tee-LEHT-tsah*)
    ⓘ Related but confusingly noncognate: **gentleness**—tenerezza *f.* (*teh-nehr-REHT-tsah*)

gentle, nice, kind, agreeable (adj.) gentile (*jehn-TEE-leh*)

(very) gentle, nice, kind (adj.) gentilissimo (*jehn-tee-LEES-see-moh*)

gentleman gentiluomo *m.* (*jehn-teel-WHOH-moh*)

gentlemanly (adj.) da gentiluomo (*dah jehn-teel-WHOH-moh*)

genuine (adj.) genuino (*jeh-NWEE-noh*)

genuinely genuinamente (*jeh-nwee-nah-MEHN-teh*)

geographical (adj.) geografico (*jeh-oh-GRAH-fee-koh*)

geography geografia *f.* (*jeh-oh-grah-FEE-ah*)

geology geologia *f.* (*jeh-oh-loh-JEE-ah*)

geometric geometrico (adj.) (*jeh-oh-MEH-tree-koh*)

geometry geometria *f.* (*jeh-oh-meh-TREE-ah*)

geopolitics geopolitica *f.* (*jeh-oh-poh-LEE-tee-kah*)

geranium geranio *m.* (*jehr-RAH-nyoh*)

germ germe *m.* (*JEHR-meh*)
 ① A closely related noncognate: **sprout**—germoglio *m.* (*jehr-MOH-lyoh*)

germinate (to) germinare (*jehr-mee-NAHR-reh*)
 ① Another related noncognate: **to sprout**—germogliare (*jehr-moh-LYAHR-reh*)

gesticulate (to) gesticolare (*jeh-stee-koh-LAHR-reh*)

geyser geyser *m.* (*GHY-sehr*)

gigantic (adj.) gigantesco (*jee-gahn-TEHS-koh*)

gin (*liquor,* NOT *card game*) gin *m.* (*JEEN*)

glacial (adj.) glaciale (*glah-CHAH-leh*)

gladiolus gladiolo *m.* (*glah-dee-OH-loh*)

glandular (adj.) ghiandolare (*gyahn-doh-LAHR-reh*)

glaucoma glaucoma *m.* (*glaow-KOH-mah*)

global (adj.) globale (*gloh-BAH-leh*)

globe globo *m.* (*GLOH-boh*)

glorification glorificazione *f.* (*gloh-ree-fee-kah-TSYOH-neh*)

glorify (to) glorificare (*gloh-ree-fee-KAHR-reh*)

glorious (adj.) glorioso (*glohr-RYOH-soh*)

glory gloria *f.* (*GLOHR-ryah*)

glossary glossario *m.* (*glohs-SAHR-ryoh*)

goal (*soccer score* OR *place of scoring*) goal *m.* (GOHL)

golf golf *m.* (*GOHLF*)

gondolier gondoliere *m.* (*gohn-doh-LYEHR-reh*)

gonorrhea gonorrea *f.* (*goh-nohr-RREH-ah*)

gorilla, bodyguard gorilla *m.* (*gohr-REEL-lah*)

Gothic (adj.) gotico (*GOH-tee-koh*)

govern (to) governare (*goh-vehr-NAHR-reh*)

governess governante *f.* (*goh-vehr-NAHN-teh*)

government governo *m.* (*goh-VEHR-noh*)

governmental (adj.) governativo (*goh-vehr-nah-TEE-voh*)

governor governatore *m.* (*goh-vehr-nah-TOHR-reh*)

grace, gracefulness grazia *f.* (*GRAH-tsyah*)

graceful, pretty, gracious (adj.) grazioso (*grah-TSYOH-soh*)

gracefully graziosamente (*grah-tsyoh-sah-MEHN-teh*)

grade (*quality, status* OR *position,* NOT *incline*) grado *m.* (*GRAH-doh*)

gradual (adj.) graduale (*grah-DWAH-leh*)

gradually gradualmente (*grah-dwahl-MEHN-teh*)

graduate (to) graduare (*grah-DWAHR-reh*)

grain, wheat grano *m.* (*GRAH-noh*)

gram grammo *m.* (*GRAHM-moh*)

grammar grammatica *f.* (*grahm-MAH-tee-kah*)

grammatical (adj.) grammaticale (*grahm-mah-tee-KAH-leh*)

grandiose, imposing, (very) large (adj.) grandioso (*grahn-dee-OH-soh*)

grandly grandiosamente (*grahn-dee-oh-sah-MEHN-teh*)

granite granito *m.* (*grah-NEE-toh*)

granular (adj.) granulare (*grah-noo-LAHR-reh*)

graph grafico *m.* (*GRAH-fee-koh*)

graphic grafico *m.* (*GRAH-fee-koh*) ◖(adj.)◗

grateful, thankful (adj.)   grato (*GRAH-toh*)

gratify (to)   gratificare (*grah-tee-fee-KAHR-reh*)

gratis, cost free, gratuitous (adj.)   gratuito (*gra-TOO-ee-toh*)
  ⓘ An important semirelated noncognate: **gratuity, tip**—mancia *f.* (*MAHN-cha*)

gratitude   gratitudine *f.* (*grah-tee-TOO-dee-neh*)

grave (adj.)   grave (*GRAH-veh*)

gravely   gravemente (*grah-veh-MEHN-teh*)

gravitation   gravitazione *f.* (*grah-vee-tah-TSYOH-neh*)

gravity   gravità *f.* (*grah-vee-TAH*)

gray (adj.)   grigio (*GREE-joh*)

grease, fat   grasso *m.* (*GRAHS-soh*) ⊃**greasy** (adj.)⊂

greatness   grandezza *f.* (*grahn-DEHT-tsah*)

gregarious(adj.)   gregario (*greh-GAHR-ryoh*)

gross (*twelve dozen*)   grossa *f.* (*GROHS-sah*)

gross (*in weight*), **fat** (adj.)   grasso (*GRAHS-soh*)

gross, coarse (adj.)   grossolano (*grohs-soh-LAH-noh*)

grossly   grossolanamente (*grohs-soh-lah-nah-MEHN-teh*)

grotesque (adj.)   grottesco (*groht-TEHS-koh*)

grotto   grotta *f.* (*GROHT-tah*)

group, gang   gruppo *m.* (*GROOP-poh*)

guarantee   garanzia *f.* (*gah-rahn-TSEE-ah*)

guarantee (to)   garantire (*gah-rahn-TEER-reh*)

guarantor   garante *m.* & *f.* (*gah-RAHN-teh*)

guard, guardsman, watch   guardia *f.* (*GWAHR-dyah*)

guard, look at, tend to (to)   guardare (*gwahr-DAHR-reh*)

guarded (adj.)   guardingo (*gwahr-DEEN-goh*)

guardian, watchman, caretaker   guardiano *m.* (*gwahr-DYAH-noh*)

guerilla (*hit-and-hide warfare*)   guerriglia *f.* (*gwehr-RREE-lyah*)

guerilla (*hit-and-hide warrior*)   guerrigliere *m.* (*gwehr-rree-LYEHR-reh*)

guide, guidebook, guidance, directory   guida *f.* (*GWEE-dah*)

guide (to)   guidare (*gwee-DAHR-reh*)

guitar   chitarra *f.* (*kee-TAHRR-rah*)

gulf   golfo *m.* (*GOHL-foh*)

gum   gomma *f.* (*GOHM-mah*)

gummy (adj.)   gommoso (*gohm-MOH-soh*)

guru   guru *m.* (*GOO-roo*)

gustatory (adj.)   gustativo (*goo-stah-TEE-voh*)

gusto, relish (*happy enthusiasm*)   gusto *m.* (*GOO-stoh*)

gymnasium   ginnasio *m.* (*jeen-NAH-zyoh*)

gymnast   ginnasta *m.* (*jeen-NAH-stah*)

gymnastics   ginnastica *f.* (*jeen-NAH-stee-kah*) ➲**gymnastic** (adj.) -co➲

gynecology   ginecologia *f.* (*jee-neh-koh-loh-JEE-ah*)

gyrate, revolve, spin, whirl, turn (to)   girare (*jeer-RAHR-reh*)
  ⓘ Related noncognate: **turn**—giro *m.* (*JEER-oh*)

gyroscope   giroscopio *m.* (jeer-roh-SKO-pyoh)

—H—

  ⓘ Only four native Italian words begins with the letter *h*, and relatively
  few contain it even in a component form—an astonishing fact in view
  of the overwhelming predominance of the aspirated *aah* sound in most
  words in the Italian lexicon. Thus, excepting only a few imports from
  other languages, this entire alphabetic section is notable for the phonetic similarity of terms that uniformly display that one negative characteristic: the missing initial *h*.

habit (*clothing, in general*), **suit** (*of clothes*)   abito *m.* (*AH-bee-toh*) ☙

  ⓘ In reference to a specific garment set, this term can apply to either a
  man's or woman's suit. SEE ALSO **vestments** for further detail.

habitable (adj.) abitabile (*ah-bee-TAH-bee-leh*) ♪

habitation abitazione *f.* (*ah-bee-tah-TSYOH-neh*) ♪

habitual (adj.) abituale (*ah-bee-TWAH-leh*) ♪

habituate (to) abituare (*ah-bee-TWAHR-reh*) ♪

hallucination allucinazione *f.* (*ahl-loo-chee-nah-TSYOH-neh*) ♪

Halt!, Stop! alt! (*AHLT*) ♪

hamburger (sandwich) hamburger *m.* (*AHM-boor-gehr*)

hammock amaca *f.* (*ah-MAH-kah*) ♪

handicapped (adj.) handicappato (*ahn-dee-kahp-PAH-toh*), svantaggiato
(*zvahn-tahd-JAH-toh*)

Harlequin Arlecchino *m.* (*ahr-lehk-KEE-noh*) ♪

harmonic (adj.) armonico (*ahr-MOH-nee-koh*) ♪

harmonica armonica *f.* (*ahr-MOH-nee-kah*) ♪

harmonious, sweet-sounding (adj.) armonioso (*ahr-moh-NYOH-soh*) ♪

harmonize (to) armonizzare (*ahr-moh-need-DZAHR-reh*) ♪

harmony armonia *f.* (*ahr-moh-NEE-ah*) ♪

harp arpa *f.* (*AHR-pah*) ♪

hashish hashish *m.* (*ah-SHEESH*) ♪

hatchet accetta *f.* (*aht-CHEHT-tah*) ♪

have (to) avere (*ah-VEHR-reh*) ♪

headquarters quartiere (*m.*) generale (*kwahr-TYEHR-reh jeh-nehr-RAH-leh*)

Hebrew (person OR language), Jew ebreo *m.* (*eh-BREH-oh*)

hectic (adj.) etico (*EH-tee-koh*) ♪

hedonism edonismo *m.* (*eh-doh-NEEZ-moh*) ♪

helicopter elicottero *m.* (*eh-lee-KOHT-tehr-roh*) ♪

helmet elmetto *m.* (*ehl-MEHT-toh*), elmo (*EHL-moh*) ♪

hemisphere emisfero *m.* (eh-mee-SFEHR-roh) ♪

hemophilia emofilia *f.* (*eh-moh-fee-LEE-ah*) ♪

hemorrhage emorragia *f.* (*eh-mohr-rrah-JEE-ah*) 🔥

hemorrhoid emorroide *f.* (*eh-mohr-RROY-deh*) 🔥

heraldry araldica *f.* (*ahr-RAHL-dee-kah*) 🔥

herb erba *f.* (*EHR-bah*) 🔥

herculean (adj.) erculeo (*ehr-KOO-leh-oh*) 🔥

hereditary (adj.) ereditario (*ehr-reh-dee-TAHR-ryoh*) 🔥

heredity eredità *f.* (*ehr-reh-dee-TAH*) 🔥

heresy eresia *f.* (*ehr-reh-SEE-ah*) 🔥

heretic eretico *m.* (*ehr-REH-tee-koh*) ➲**heretical** (adj.)➜ 🔥

heritage eredità *f.* (*ehr-reh-dee-TAH*) 🔥

hermit eremita *m.* (*eh-reh-MEE-tah*) 🔥

hermitage eremitaggio *m.* (*eh-reh-mee-TAHD-joh*) 🔥

hernia ernia *f.* (*EHR-nee-ah*) 🔥

hero eroe *m.* (*ehr-ROH-eh*) ➲**heroic** (adj.) -oico➜ 🔥

heroically eroicamente (*ehr-roh-ee-kah-MEHN-teh*) 🔥

heroin eroina *f.* (*ehr-roh-EE-nah*) 🔥

heroine eroina *f.* (*ehr-roh-EE-nah*) 🔥

heroism eroismo *m.* (*ehr-roh-EEZ-moh*) 🔥

heron airone *m.* (*ahyr-ROH-neh*) 🔥

herpes erpete *m.* (*EHR-peh-teh*) 🔥

hesitate (to) esitare (*eh-zee-TAHR-reh*) ➲**hesitant** (adj.) -tante➜ 🔥

hesitation esitazione *f.* (*eh-zee-tah-TSYOH-neh*) 🔥

heterosexual eterosessuale *m.* (*eh-tehr-roh-sehs-SWAH-leh*) ➲(adj.)➜ 🔥

hexagon esagono *m.* (*eh-SAH-goh-noh*) 🔥

hibernation ibernazione *f.* (*ee-behr-nah-TSYOH-neh*) 🔥

hibiscus ibisco *m.* (*ee-BEES-koh*) 🔥

hierarchy gerarchia *f.* (*jeh-rahr-KEE-ah*) 🔥

hilarious (adj.) ilare (*ee-LAHR-reh*) ☙

hilarity ilarità *f.* (*ee-lahr-ree-TAH*) ☙

historian storico *m.* (*STOHR-ree-koh*) ⊃**historic / -ical** (adj.)↻ ☙

history storia *f.* (*STOHR-ryah*) ☙

hobby hobby *m.* (*AHB-bee*)

holocaust olocausto *m.* (*oh-loh-KAOW-stoh*) ☙

hologram ologramma *m.* (*oh-loh-GRAHM-mah*) ☙

holography olografia *f.* (*oh-loh-grah-FEE-ah*) ☙

Holy Spirit Spirito (*m.*) Santo (*SPEE-ree-toh SAHN-toh*)

homage omaggio *m.* (*oh-MAHD-joh*) ☙

homicide, manslaughter omicidio *m.* (*oh-mee-CHEE-dyoh*) ☙

homily omelia *f.* (*oh-meh-LEE-ah*) ☙

homogeneous (adj.) omogeneo (*oh-moh-JEH-neh-oh*) ☙

homogenize (to) omogeneizzare (*oh-moh-jeh-nayd-DZAHR-reh*) ☙

homosexual omosessuale *m.* (*oh-moh-sehs-SWAH-leh*) ⊃(adj.)↻ ☙

honest, forthright (adj.) onesto (*oh-NEH-stoh*) ☙

honestly onestamente (*oh-neh-stah-MEHN-teh*) ☙

honesty onestà *f.* (*oh-neh-STAH*) ☙

honor onore *m.* (*oh-NOHR-reh*) ☙

honor (to) onorare (*oh-noh-RAHR-reh*) ☙

honorable (adj.) onorevole (*oh-nohr-REH-voh-leh*) ☙

honorary (adj.) onorario (*oh-nohr-RAHR-ryoh*) ☙

horde orda *f.* (*OHR-dah*) ☙

horizon orizzonte *m.* (*ohr-reed-DZOHN-teh*) ☙

horizontal, level (adj.) orizzontale (*ohr-reed-dzohn-TAH-leh*) ☙

hormone ormone *m.* (*ohr-MOH-neh*) ☙

horoscope oroscopo *m.* (*ohr-ROH-skoh-poh*) ☙

horrendous, gruesome(adj.) orrendo (*ohr-RREHN-doh*) 🌶

horrible (adj.) orribile (*ohr-RREE-bee-leh*) 🌶

horrid (adj.) orrido (*OHRR-ree-doh*) 🌶

horror orrore *m.* (*ohr-RROHR-reh*) 🌶

horticulture orticultura *f.* (*ohr-tee-kool-TOOR-rah*) 🌶

hospitable (adj.) ospitale (*oh-spee-TAH-leh*) 🌶

hospital ospedale *m.* (*oh-speh-DAH-leh*) 🌶

hospitality ospitalità *f.* (*oh-spee-tah-lee-TAH*) 🌶

hospitalization ospedalizzazione *f.* (*oh-speh-dah-leed-dzah-TSYOH-neh*) 🌶

hospitalize (to) ospedalizzare (*oh-speh-dah-leed-DZAHR-reh*) 🌶

host oste *m.* (*OH-steh*) 🌶

hostess ospite *f.* (*OH-spee-teh*) 🌶

hostage ostaggio *m.* (*oh-STAHD-joh*) 🌶

hostel (*inexpensive membership lodging*) ostello *m.* (*oh-STEHL-loh*)

hostile, antagonistic (adj.) ostile (*oh-STEE-leh*) 🌶

hostility ostilità *f.* (*oh-stee-lee-TAH*) 🌶

hotel hotel *m.* (*oh-TEHL*), albergo *m.* (*ahl-BEHR-goh*), locanda *f.* (*loh-KAHN-dah*)
   ⓘ A small, modest, inexpensive, privately owned (nonchain) **hotel**—pensione *f.* (*pehn-SYOH-neh*)

human umano *m.* (*oo-MAH-noh*) ⮑(adj.)C 🌶

humanism umanesimo *m.* (*oo-mah-NEH-zee-moh*) 🌶

humanist umanista *m.* (*oo-mah-NEE-stah*) 🌶

humanitarian umanitario *m.* (*oo-mah-nee-TAHR-ryoh*)

humanitarian, humane (adj.) umanitario (*oo-mah-nee-TAHR-ryoh*) 🌶

humanity, mankind umanità *f.* (*oo-mah-nee-TAH*) 🌶

humanly umanamente (*oo-mah-nah-MEHN-teh*) 🌶

humble, lowly (adj.) umile (*OO-mee-leh*) 🌶

humble (to) umiliare (*oo-mee-LYAHR-reh*) 🌶

humid, moist, damp, wet (adj.)   umido (*OO-mee-doh*) ◆⃰

humidify, moisten, wet (to)   inumidire (*ee-noo-mee-DEER-reh*) ◆⃰

humidity, moisture, dampness   umidità *f.* (*oo-mee-dee-TAH*) ◆⃰

humiliate (to)   umiliare (*oo-mee-LYAHR-reh*) ◆⃰

humiliation   umiliazione *f.* (*oo-mee-lyah-TSYOH-neh*) ◆⃰

humility   umiltà *f.* (*oo-meel-TAH*) ◆⃰

humor (*mood* OR *amusement*)   umore *m.* (*oo-MOHR-reh*) ◆⃰

humorist   umorista *m.* (*oo-mohr-REE-stah*) ◆⃰

humorous, jocular (adj.)   umoristico (*oo-mohr-REE-stee-koh*) ◆⃰
  ⓘ A related noncognate adjective is: **witty** (adj.)—spiritoso (*speer-ree-TOH-soh*).

hurricane   uragano *m.* (*oor-rah-GAH-noh*) ◆⃰

hybrid (adj.)   ibrido (*EE-bree-doh*) ◆⃰

hydraulic (adj.)   idraulico (*ee-DRAOW-lee-koh*) ◆⃰

hydrogen   idrogeno *m.* (*ee-DROH-jeh-noh*) ◆⃰

hydrotherapy   idroterapia *f.* (*ee-droh-tehr-rah-PEE-ah*) ◆⃰

hygiene, sanitation   igiene *f.* (*ee-JEH-neh*)

hygienic (adj.)   igienico (*ee-JEH-nee-koh*) ◆⃰

hymn   inno *m.* (*EEN-noh*) ◆⃰

hymnary   innario *m.* (*een-NAHR-ryoh*) ◆⃰

hypersensitive (adj.)   ipersensitivo (*ee-pehr-sehn-see-TEE-voh*) ◆⃰

hypertension   ipertensione *f.* (*ee-pehr-tehn-SYOH-neh*) ◆⃰

hypnosis   ipnosi *f.* (*eep-NOH-zee*) ◆⃰

hypnotic (adj.)   ipnotico (*eep-NOH-tee-koh*) ◆⃰

hypnotism   ipnotismo *m.* (*eep-noh-TEEZ-moh*) ◆⃰

hypnotize (to)   ipnotizzare (*eep-noh-teed-DZAHR-reh*) ◆⃰

hypochondria   ipocondria *f.* (*ee-poh-kohn-DREE-ah*) ◆⃰

hypochondriac   ipocondriaco *m.* (*ee-poh-kohn-DREE-ah-koh*)

hypocrisy ipocrisia *f. (ee-poh-kree-ZEE-ah)*

hypocrite ipocrita *m. (ee-POH-kree-tah)*

hypocritical (adj.) ipocrito *(ee-POH-kree-toh)*

hypodermic ipodermico *m. (ee-poh-DEHR-mee-koh)*

hypothesis ipotesi *f. (ee-POH-teh-zee)*

hypothetical (adj.) ipotetico *(ee-poh-TEH-tee-koh)*

hysterectomy isterectomia *f. (ee-stehr-ehk-toh-MEE-ah)*

hysteria isterismo *m. (ee-stehr-REEZ-moh)*

hysterical (adj.) isterico *(ee-STEHR-ree-koh)*

hysterics isterismo *m. (ee-stehr-REEZ-moh)*

—I—

icon icona *f. (ee-KOH-nah)*

idea idea *f. (ee-DEH-ah)*

ideal (adj.) ideale *(ee-deh-AH-leh)*

idealism idealismo *m. (ee-deh-ah-LEEZ-moh)*

idealist idealista *m. (ee-deh-ah-LEE-stah)*

idealistic (adj.) idealistico *(ee-deh-ah-LEE-stee-koh)*

idealize (to) idealizzare *(ee-deh-ah-leed-DZAHR-reh)*

ideally idealmente *(ee-deh-ahl-MEHN-teh)*

identical (adj.) identico *(ee-DEHN-tee-koh)*

identification identificazione *f. (ee-dehn-tee-fee-kah-TSYOH-neh)*

identity identità *f. (ee-dehn-tee-TAH)*

ideology ideologia *f. (ee-deh-oh-loh-JEE-ah)*

idiocy idiozia *f. (ee-dyoh-TSEE-ah)*

idiom idioma *m.* (*ee-DYOH-mah*)

idiot idiota *m.* (*ee-DYOH-tah*) ⊃**idiotic** (adj.)⊂

idol idolo *m.* (*EE-doh-loh*)

idolize (to) idolatrare (*ee-doh-lah-TRAHR-reh*)

idyllic (adj.) idillico (*ee-DEEL-lee-koh*)

ignorance ignoranza *f.* (*ee-nyohr-RAHN-tsah*)

ignorant (adj.) ignorante (*ee-nyohr-RAHN-teh*)

ignore (to) ignorare (*ee-nyoh-RAHR-reh*)

illegal (adj.) illegale (*eel-leh-GAH-leh*)

illegible (adj.) illeggibile (*eel-lehd-JEE-bee-leh*)

illegitimate (adj.) illegittimo (*eel-leh-JEET-tee-moh*)

illicit (adj.) illecito (*eel-LEH-chee-toh*)

illogical (adj.) illogico (*eel-LOH-jee-koh*)

illuminate (*physically or mentally*), light, enlighten (to) illuminare (*eel-loo-mee-NAHR-reh*)

illumination illuminazione *f.* (*eel-loo-mee-nah-TSYOH-neh*)

illusion illusione *f.* (*eel-loo-ZYOH-neh*)

illusory (adj.) illusorio (*eel-loo-ZOHR-ryoh*)

illustrate (to) illustrare (*eel-loo-STRAHR-reh*)

illustration illustrazione *f.* (*eel-loo-strah-TSYOH-neh*)

illustrative (adj.) illustrativo (*eel-loo-strah-TEE-voh*)

illustrious (adj.) illustre (*eel-LOO-streh*)

imaginable (adj.) immaginabile (*eem-mah-jee-NAH-bee-leh*)

imaginary (adj.) immaginario (*eem-mah-jee-NAHR-ryoh*)

imagination immaginazione *f.* (*eem-mah-jee-nah-TSYOH-neh*)

imaginative, fanciful (adj.) immaginativo (*eem-mah-jee-nah-TEE-voh*)

imagine (to) immaginare (*eem-mah-jee-NAHR-reh*)

imbecile, moron, half-wit, fool imbecille *m.* & *f.* (*eem-beh-CHEEL-leh*)

imitate, mimic (to)   imitare (*ee-mee-TAHR-reh*)

imitation   imitazione *f.* (*ee-mee-tah-TSYOH-neh*)

imitator, mimic   imitatore *m.* (*ee-mee-tah-TOHR-reh*)

immaculate (adj.)   immacolato (*eem-mah-koh-LAH-toh*)

immanent (adj.)   immanente (*eem-mah-NEHN-teh*)

immaterial (adj.)   immateriale (*eem-mah-tehr-RYAH-leh*)

immature (adj.)   immaturo (*eem-mah-TOOR-roh*)

immediate (adj.)   immediato (*eem-meh-DYAH-toh*)

immediately, instantly, presently   immediatamente (*eem-meh-dyah-tah-MEHN-teh*), subito (*SOO-bee-toh*)

immense, huge (adj.)   immenso (*eem-MEHN-soh*)

immerse (to)   immergere (*eem-MEHR-jehr-reh*)

immigrant   immigrante *m. & f.* (*eem-mee-GRAHN-teh*) ⊃(adj.)◑

immigrate (to)   immigrare (*eem-mee-GRAHR-reh*)

imminent (adj.)   imminente (*eem-mee-NEHN-teh*)

immobile, motionless (adj.)   immobile (*eem-MOH-bee-leh*)

immoderate (adj.)   immoderato (*eem-moh-dehr-RAH-toh*)

immodest (adj.)   immodesto (*eem-moh-DEH-stoh*)

immoral (adj.)   immorale (*eem-mohr-RAH-leh*)

immorality   immoralità *f.* (*eem-mohr-rah-lee-TAH*)

immortal (adj.)   immortale (*eem-mohr-TAH-leh*)

immortality   immortalità *f.* (*eem-mohr-tah-lee-TAH*)

immortalize (to)   immortalare (*ehm-mohr-tah-LAHR-reh*)

immovable (adj.)   immobile (*eem-MOH-bee-leh*)

immune (adj.)   immune (*eem-MOO-neh*)

immunity   immunità *f.* (*eem-moo-nee-TAH*)

immunize (to)   immunizzare (*eem-moo-need-DZAHR-reh*)

impart (to)   impartire (*eem-pahr-TEER-reh*)

impartial (adj.)   imparziale (*eem-pahr-TSYAH-leh*)

impartially   imparzialmente (*eem-pahr-tsyahl-MEHN-teh*)

impatience   impazienza *f.* (*eem-pah-TSYEHN-tsah*)

impatient, eager (adj.)   impaziente (*eem-pah-TSYEHN-teh*)

impatiently   impazientemente (*eem-pah-tsyehn-teh-MEHN-teh*)

impede, hinder, hamper, prevent (to)   impedire (*eem-peh-DEER-reh*)

impediment, hindrance, roadblock   impedimento *m.* (*eem-peh-dee-MEHN-toh*)

impenetrable (adj.)   impenetrabile (*eem-peh-neh-TRAH-bee-leh*)

imperative   imperativo *m.* (*eem-pehr-rah-TEE-voh*) ➲(adj.)☾

imperceptible (adj.)   impercettibile (*eem-pehr-cheht-TEE-bee-leh*)

imperfect (adj.)   imperfetto (*eem-pehr-FEHT-toh*)

imperfection   imperfezione *f.* (*eem-pehr-feh-TSYOH-neh*)

imperial   imperiale *f.* (*eem-pehr-RYAH-leh*)

imperialism   imperialismo *m.* (*eem-pehr-ryah-LEEZ-moh*)

impermeable, waterproof (adj.)   impermeabile (*eem-pehr-meh-AH-bee-leh*)
ⓘ An important related noncognate: **raincoat**—impermeabile *m.* (*eem-pehr-meh-AH-bee-leh*)

impersonal (adj.)   impersonale (*eem-pehr-soh-NAH-leh*)

impersonate (to)   impersonare (*eem-pehr-soh-NAHR-reh*)

impersonator   impersonatore *m.* (*eem-pehr-soh-nah-TOHR-reh*)

impertinence   impertinenza *f.* (*eem-pehr-tee-NEHN-tsah*)

impertinent, sassy, saucy (adj.)   impertinente (*eem-pehr-tee-NEHN-teh*)

impetuous, dashing (adj.)   impetuoso (*eem-peh-TWOH-soh*)

implicate (to)   implicare (*eem-plee-KAHR-reh*)

implication   implicazione *f.* (*eem-plee-kah-TSYOH-neh*)

implicit, implied (adj.)   implicito (*eem-PLEE-chee-toh*)

implore, plead (to)   implorare (*eem-plohr-RAHR-reh*)

imply (to)   implicare (*eem-plee-KAHR-reh*)

import importazione *f.* (*eem-pohr-taht-TSYOH-neh*)

import (to) importare (*eem-pohr-TAHR-reh*)

importance importanza *f.* (*eem-pohr-TAHN-tsah*)

important, momentous (adj.) importante (*eem-pohr-TAHN-teh*)

importer importatore *m.* (*eem-pohr-tah-TOHR-reh*)

imposition imposizione *f.* (*eem-poh-zee-TSYOH-neh*)

impossibility impossibilità *f.* (*eem-pohs-see-bee-lee-TAH*)

impossible (adj.) impossibile (*eem-pohs-SEE-bee-leh*)

impotence impotenza *f.* (*eem-poh-TEHN-tsah*)

impotent, helpless, powerless (adj.) impotente (*eem-poh-TEHN-teh*)

impregnate (to) impregnare (*eem-preh-NYAHR-reh*)

impress (to) impressionare (*eem-prehs-syoh-NAHR-reh*)

impression impressione *f.* (*eem-prehs-SYOH-neh*)

impressive (adj.) impressionante (*eem-prehs-syoh-NAHN-teh*)

imprison (to) imprigionare (*eem-pree-joh-NAHR-reh*)

improbable, unlikely (adj.) improbabile (*eem-proh-BAH-bee-leh*)

improper (adj.) improprio (*eem-PRO-pryoh*)

improvise (to) improvvisare (*eem-prohv-vee-ZAHR-reh*)

imprudent, rash (adj.) imprudente (*eem-proo-DEHN-teh*)

impudent (adj.) impudente (*eem-poo-DEHN-teh*)

impulse impulso *m.* (*eem-POOHL-soh*)

impulsive (adj.) impulsivo (*eem-poohl-SEE-voh*)

impure (adj.) impuro (*eem-POOHR-roh*)

impurity impurità *f.* (*eem-poohr-ree-TAH*)

impute, impeach (to) imputare (*eem-poo-TAHR-reh*)

in, into in (*EEN*)

inactive, dormant (adj.) inattivo (*ee-naht-TEE-voh*)

inadequate (adj.) inadeguato (*ee-nah-deh-GWAH-toh*)

inane (adj.) inane (*ee-NAH-neh*)

inaugural (adj.) inaugurale (*ee-now-goor-RAH-leh*)

inaugurate (to) inaugurare (*ee-now-goor-RAHR-reh*)

inauguration inaugurazione *f.* (*ee-now-goor-rah-TSYOH-neh*)

incandescence, glow incandescenza *f.* (*een-kahn-deh-SHEHN-tsah*)

incandescent, glowing (adj.) incandescente (*een-kahn-deh-SHEHN-teh*)

incantation incantimento *m.* (*een-kahn-tee-MEHN-toh*)
ⓘ An incantation casts a **spell**—incantesimo *m.* (*een-kahn-TEH-zee-moh*).

incapacity incapacità *f.* (*een-kah-pah-chee-TAH*)

incarnation incarnazione *f.* (*een-kahr-nah-TSYOH-neh*)

incense incenso *m.* (*een-CHEN-soh*)

incentive incentivo *m.* (*een-chen-TEE-voh*)

incessant (adj.) incessante (*een-chehs-SAHN-teh*)

incidence incidenza *f.* (*een-chee-DEHN-tsah*)

incident incidente *m.* (*een-chee-DEHN-teh*)

incidental (adj.) incidentale (*een-chee-dehn-TAH-leh*)

incidentally incidentalmente (*een-chee-dehn-tahl-MEHN-teh*)

incision, engraving incisione *f.* (*een-chee-ZYOH-neh*)

incisive (adj.) incisivo (*een-chee-ZEE-voh*)

incite (to) incitare (*een-chee-TAHR-reh*)

inclination, penchant, tendency inclinazione *f.* (*een-klee-nah-TSYOH-neh*)

incline, tend to / toward (to) inclinare (*een-klee-NAHR-reh*)

incline, lean, slant, slope (to) inclinarsi (*een-klee-NAHR-see*)

include (to) includere (*een-KLOO-dehr-reh*)

inclusive (adj.) inclusivo (*een-kloo-ZEE-voh*)

incombustible, fireproof (adj.) incombustibile (*een-kohm-boo-STEE-bee-leh*)

incomparable (adj.) incomparabile (*een-kohm-pahr-RAH-bee-leh*)

incompetent, unqualified (adj.) incompetente (*een-kohm-peh-TEHN-teh*)

inconsiderate, rash (adj.) inconsiderato (*een-kohn-see-dehr-RAH-toh*), sconsiderato (*skohn-see-deh-RAH-toh*)

inconvenience inconvenienza *f.* (*een-kohn-veh-NYEHN-tsah*)

incorporate (to) incorporare (*een-kohr-pohr-RAHR-reh*)

incredible (adj.) incredibile (*een-kreh-DEE-bee-leh*)

incriminate (to) incriminare (*een-kree-mee-NAHR-reh*)

incrimination incriminazione *f.* (*een-kree-mee-nah-TSYOH-neh*)

incur (to) incorrere (*een-KOHRR-rehr-reh*)

incurable (adj.) incurabile (*een-koor-RAH-bee-leh*)

incursion, raid incursione *f.* (*een-koor-ZYOH-neh*)

indebted (adj.) indebitato (*een-deh-bee-TAH-toh*)

indefinite (adj.) indefinito (*een-deh-fee-NEE-toh*)

indefinitely indefinitamente (*een-deh-fee-nee-tah-MEHN-teh*)

independence indipendenza *f.* (*een-dee-pehn-DEHN-tsah*)

independent (adj.) indipendente (*een-dee-pehn-DEHN-teh*)

index indice *m.* (*EEN-dee-cheh*)

indicate (to) indicare (*een-dee-KAHR-reh*)

indication indicazione *f.* (*een-dee-kah-TSYOH-neh*)

indicative indicativo *m.* (*een-dee-kah-TEE-voh*) ➲(adj.)☾

indicator indicatore *m.* (*een-dee-kah-TOHR-reh*)

indifference indifferenza *f.* (*een-deef-fehr-REHN-tsah*)

indifferent (adj.) indifferente (*een-deef-fehr-REHN-teh*)

indigestion indigestione *f.* (*een-dee-jeh-STYOH-neh*)

indignant (adj.) indignato (*een-dee-NYAH-toh*)

indignation indignazione *f.* (*een-dee-nyah-TSYOH-neh*)

indirect (adj.) indiretto (*een-dee-REHT-toh*)

indiscreet (adj.) indiscreto (*een-dee-SKREH-toh*)

indiscretion indiscrezione *f.* (*een-dee-skreh-TSYOH-ne*h)

indispensable (adj.) indispensabile (*een-dee-spehn-SAH-bee-leh*)

indisposed, unwell (adj.) indisposto (*een-dee-SPOH-stoh*)

individual (*particular person*) individuo *m.* (*een-dee-VEE-dwoh*)

individual (adj.) individuale (*een-dee-vee-DWAH-leh*)

individuality individualità *f.* (*een-dee-vee-dwah-lee-TAH*)

individually individualmente (*een-dee-vee-dwahl-MEHN-teh*)

induction induzione *f.* (*een-doo-TSYOH-neh*)

inductive (adj.) induttivo (*een-doot-TEE-voh*)

indulge (to) indulgere (*een-DOOL-jehr-reh*)

indulgence indulgenza *f.* (*een-dool-JEHN-tsah*)

indulgent (adj.) indulgente (*een-dool-JEHN-teh*)

industrial, manufacturing (adj.) industriale (*een-doo-STRYAH-leh*)

industrious (adj.) industrioso (*een-doo-STRYOH-soh*)

industry industria *f.* (*een-DOO-stryah*)

inebriate, intoxicate, get drunk (to) inebriare (*ee-neh-bree-AHR-reh*)

ineligible (adj.) ineleggibile (*ee-neh-lehd-JEE-bee-leh*)

inept (adj.) inetto (*ee-NEHT-toh*)

inevitable (adj.) inevitabile (*ee-neh-vee-TAH-bee-leh*)

inexplicable (adj.) inesplicabile (*ee-neh-splee-KAH-bee-leh*)

in fact infatti (*een-FAHT-tee*)

infallible (adj.) infallibile (*een-fahl-LEE-bee-leh*)

infamy infamia *f.* (*een-FAH-myah*) ➲**infamous** (adj.) infame

infancy, childhood infanzia *f.* (*een-FAHN-tsyah*)

infant infante *m.* & *f.* (*een-FAHN-teh*)

infante infante *m.* (*een-FAHN-teh*) ➲*f.* -ta

infantile, childish, childlike (adj.) infantile (*een-fahn-TEE-leh*)

infatuate (to) infatuare (*een-fah-too-AHR-reh*)

infect (to) infettare (*een-feht-TAHR-reh*)

infected (adj.) infetto (*een-FEHT-toh*)

infection infezione *f.* (*een-feh-TSYOH-neh*)

infectious (adj.) infettivo (*een-feht-TEE-voh*)

infer (to) inferire (*een-fehr-REER-reh*)

inference inferenza *f.* (*een-fehr-REHN-tsah*)

inferior, lower, under (adj.) inferiore (*een-fehr-RYOHR-reh*)

inferiority inferiorità *f.* (*een-fehr-ryohr-ree-TAH*)

infernal, hellish (adj.) infernale (*een-fehr-NAH-leh*)

inferno, hell inferno *m.* (*een-FEHR-noh*)

infest (to) infestare (*een-feh-STAHR-reh*)

infidelity infedeltà *f.* (*een-feh-dehl-TAH*)

infinite infinito *m.* (*een-fee-NEE-toh*) ⊃(adj.)C

infinitesimal (adj.) infinitesimale (*een-fee-nee-teh-zee-MAH-leh*)

infinity infinità *f.* (*een-fee-nee-TAH*)

infirm (adj.) infermo (*een-FEHR-moh*)

infirmity infermità *f.* (*een-fehr-mee-TAH*)

in flames, aflame, ablaze, on fire in fiamme (*een FYAHM-meh*) 🔥

inflammable (adj.) infiammabile (*een-fyahm-MAH-bee-leh*) 🔥

inflammation infiammazione *f.* (*een-fyahm-mah-TSYOH-neh*) 🔥

inflammatory (adj.) infiammatorio (*een-fyahm-mah-TOHR-ryoh*) 🔥

inflation (*economic*) inflazione *f.* (*een-flah-TSYOH-neh*)

inflict (to) infliggere (*een-FLEED-jehr-reh*)

influence influenza *f.* (*een-floo-EHN-tsah*), influsso *m.* (*een-FLOOS-soh*)

influence (to) influenzare (*een-flwehn-TSAHR-reh*)

influential (adj.) influente (*een-floo-EHN-teh*)

inform, apprise (to)   informare (*een-fohr-MAHR-reh*)

information   informazioni *f.* (*een-fohr-mah-TSYOH-nee*)

infuriate (to)   infuriare (*een-foo-RYAH-reh*))

(become) infuriated / enraged, rage (to)   infuriarsi (*een-foor-RYAHR-see*)

ingenious (adj.)   ingegnoso (*een-jeh-NYOH-soh*)

ingenuous, naïve, artless (adj.)   ingenuo (*een-JEH-nwoh*)

ingredient   ingrediente *m.* (*een-greh-DYEHN-teh*)

inhabit, dwell at / in (to)   abitare (*ah-bee-TAHR-reh*) ☛

inhabitant, resident   abitante *m. & f.* (*ah-bee-TAHN-teh*) ☛

inhale (to)   inalare (*ee-nah-LAHR-reh*)

inhibit (to)   inibire (*ee-nee-BEER-reh*)

inhibition   inibizione *f.* (*ee-nee-bee-TSYOH-neh*)

inhuman (adj.)   inumano (*ee-noo-MAH-noh*)

inhumanity   inumanità *f.* (*ee-noo-mah-nee-TAH*)

iniquity   iniquità *f.* (*ee-nee-kwee-TAH*)

initial (*alphabetic symbol re name*)   iniziale *f.* (*ee-nee-TSYAH-leh*)

initial (*first*) (adj.)   iniziale (*ee-nee-TSYAH-leh*)

initiate, start, begin (to)   iniziare (*ee-nee-TSYAHR-reh*), cominciare (*koh-meen-CHAR-reh*)

initiation, start, beginning   iniziazione *f.* (*ee-nee-tsyah-TSYOH-neh*), inizio (*ee-NEE-tsyoh*)

initiative   iniziativa *f.* (*ee-nee-tsyah-TEE-vah*)

injustice   ingiustizia *f.* (*een-joo-STEE-tsyah*)

inner (adj.)   interiore (*een-tehr-RYOHR-reh*), interno (*een-TEHR-noh*)

innocence   innocenza *f.* (*een-noh-CHEN-tsah*) ➲**innocent** (adj.) -nte☾

innocuous, harmless (adj.)   innocuo (*een-NOH-kwoh*)

innovation   innovazione *f.* (*een-noh-vah-TSYOH-neh*)

innumerable, countless (adj.)   innumerevole (*een-noo-mehr-REH-voh-leh*)

inoculation   inoculazione *f.* (*ee-noh-koo-lah-TSYOH-neh*)

insanity   insania *f.* (*een-SAH-nyah*) ⊃**insane** (adj.) -ano☾

inscriber, scribe, writer   scrittore *m.* (*skreet-TOHR-reh*)
  ① Related, but noncognate: **to write**—scrivere (*SKREE-vehr-reh*); and
  writing—scrittura *f.* (*skreet-TOOR-rah*)

inscription   iscrizione *f.* (*ee-skree-TSYOH-neh*) ♦※

insect   insetto *m.* (*een-SEHT-toh*)

insensible (adj.)   insensibile (*een-sehn-SEE-bee-leh*)

insensitive (adj.)   insensibile (*een-sehn-SEE-bee-leh*)

insensitivity   insensibilità *f.* (*een-sehn-see-bee-lee-TAH*)

inseparable (adj.)   inseparabile (*een-seh-pahr-RAH-bee-leh*)

inside   interno *m.* (*een-TEHR-noh*)

insidious (adj.)   insidioso (*een-see-DYOH-soh*)

insignificance   insignificanza *f.* (*een-see-nyee-fee-KAHN-tsah*)

insignificant (adj.)   insignificante (*een-see-nyee-fee-KAHN-teh*)

insinuate (to)   insinuare (*een-see-NWAHR-reh*)

insinuation, inuendo   insinuazione *f.* (*een-see-nwah-TSYOH-neh*)

insist, urge, press (to)   insistere (*een-SEE-stehr-reh*)

insistence   insistenza *f.* (*een-see-STEHN-tsah*)

insistent (adj.)   insistente (*een-see-STEHN-teh*)

insolence   insolenza *f.* (*een-soh-LEHN-tsah*) ⊃**insolent** (adj.) -nte☾

insolvency   insolvenza *f.* (*een-sohl-VEHN-tsah*)

insomnia   insonnia *f.* (*een-SOHN-nyah*)

inspect (to)   ispezionare (*ee-speh-tsyoh-NAHR-reh*) ♦※

inspection   ispezione *f.* (*ee-speh-TSYOH-neh*) ♦※

inspector   ispettore *m.* (*ee-speht-TOHR-reh*) ♦※

inspiration   ispirazione *f.* (*ee-speer-rah-TSYOH-neh*) ♦※

inspire (to)   ispirare (*ee-speer-RAHR-reh*) ♦※

install (to) installare (*een-stahl-LAHR-reh*)

installation installazione *f.* (*een-stahl-lah-TSYOH-neh*)

instance istanza *f.* (*ee-STAHN-tsah*), richiesta (*ree-KYEH-sta*) ♦⁕

instant, jiffy istante *m.* (*ee-STAHN-teh*) ♦⁕

instantaneous (adj.) istantaneo (*ee-stahn-TAHN-neh-oh*) ♦⁕

instill (to) istillare (*ee-steel-LAHR-reh*) ♦⁕

instinct istinto *m.* (*ee-STEEN-toh*)

instinctive (adj.) istintivo (*ee-steen-TEE-voh*) ♦⁕

institution istituzione *f.* (*ee-stee-too-TSYOH-neh*) ♦⁕

instruct (to) istruire (*ee-stroo-EER-reh*) ♦⁕

instruction istruzione *f.* (*ee-stroo-TSYOH-neh*) ♦⁕

instructive (adj.) istruttivo (*ee-stroot-TEE-voh*) ♦⁕

instructor istruttore *m.* (*ee-stroot-TOHR-reh*) ⊃*f.* -trice⊃

instrument strumento *m.* (*stroo-MEHN-toh*) ♦⁕

instrumental (adj.) strumentale (*stroo-mehn-TAH-leh*) ♦⁕

insufficient (adj.) insufficiente (*een-soof-fee-CHEN-teh*)

insulin insulina *f.* (*een-soo-LEE-nah*)

insult insulto *m.* (*een-SOOL-toh*)

insulting (adj.) insultante (*een-sool-TAHN-teh*)

intact (adj.) intatto (*een-TAHT-toh*)

intangible (adj.) intangibile (*een-tahn-JEE-bee-leh*)

integrate (to) integrare (*een-teh-GRAHR-reh*)

integrity integrità *f.* (*een-teh-gree-TAH*)

intellect intelletto *m.* (*een-tehl-LEHT-toh*)

intellectual, highbrow intellettuale *m.* & *f.* (*een-tehl-leht-TWAH-leh*)

intellectual (adj.) intellettuale (*een-tehl-leht-TWAH-leh*)

intelligence, wit intelligenza *f.* (*een-tehl-lee-JEHN-tsah*)

intelligent, brainy, smart (adj.) intelligente (*een-tehl-lee-JEHN-teh*)

intense (adj.) intenso (*een-TEHN-soh*)

intensify (to) intensificare (*een-tehn-see-fee-KAHR-reh*)

intensive (adj.) intensivo (*een-tehn-SEE-voh*)

intent intento *m.* (*een-TEHN-toh*) ➲(adj.)☯

intention intenzione *f.* (*een-tehn-TSYOH-neh*)

intentional (adj.) intenzionale (*een-tehn-tsyoh-NAH-leh*)

intentionally intenzionalmente (*een-tehn-tsyoh-nahl-MEHN-teh*)

interest interesse *m.* (*een-tehr-REHS-seh*)

interest (to) interessare (*een-tehr-rehs-SAHR-reh*)

interesting (adj.) interessante (*een-tehr-rehs-SAHN-teh*)

interference (*physical, NOT interpersonal*) interferenza *f.* (*een-tehr-fehr-REHN-tsah*)

interior interiore *m.* (*een-tehr-RYOHR-reh*)

interior, inside (adj.) interiore (*een-tehr-RYOHR-reh*), interno (*een-TEHR-noh*)

interlude interludio *m.* (*een-tehr-LOO-dyoh*)

intermediary, mediator, go-between intermediario *m.* (*een-tehr-meh-DYAHR-ryoh*)

intermission intermissione *f.* (*een-tehr-mees-SYOH-neh*)

intermittent (adj.) intermittente (*een-tehr-meet-TEHN-teh*)

intern interno *m.* (*een-TEHR-noh*)

internal (adj.) interno (*een-TEHR-noh*)

international (adj.) internazionale (*een-tehr-nah-tsyoh-NAH-leh*)

interpret, construe (to) interpretare (*een-tehr-preh-TAHR-reh*)

interpretation interpretazione *f.* (*een-tehr-preh-tah-TSYOH-neh*)

interpreter interprete *m.* (*een-TEHR-preh-teh*)

interrogate, question, ask about (to) interrogare (*een-tehr-rroh-GAHR-reh*)

interrogation interrogazione *f.* (*een-tehr-rroh-gah-TSYOH-neh*)

interrupt (to)   interrompere (*een-tehr-RROHM-pehr-reh*)

interruption   interruzione *f.* (*een-tehr-rroo-TSYOH-neh*)

intersect (to)   intersecare (*een-tehr-seh-KAHR-reh*)

intersection   intersezione *f.* (*een-tehr-seh-TSYOH-neh*), incrocio *m.* (*een-KROH-choh*)

interval   intervallo *m.* (*een-tehr-VAHL-loh*)

intervene, interfere (to)   intervenire in (*een-tehr-veh-NEER-reh een*)

intervention   intervento *m.* (*een-tehr-VEHN-toh*)

intestines, guts, innards   intestini *m.* (*een-teh-STEE-nee*)

intimacy   intimità *f.* (*een-tee-mee-TAH*)

intimate (adj.)   intimo (*EEN-tee-moh*)

intimidation   intimidazione *f.* (*een-tee-mee-dah-TSYOH-neh*)

intolerant (adj.)   intollerante (*een-tohl-lehr-RAHN-teh*)

intoxication   intossicazione *f.* (*een-tohs-see-kah-TSYOH-neh*)

intrepid, fearless, dauntless (adj.)   intrepido (*een-TREH-pee-doh*)

intrepidity, fearlessness   intrepidezza *f.* (*een-treh-pee-DEHT-tsah*)

intrepidly, fearlessly, dauntlessly   intrepidamente (*een-treh-pee-dah-MEHN-teh*)

intricate (adj.)   intricato (*een-tree-KAH-toh*)

intrinsic (adj.)   intrinseco (*een-TREEN-seh-koh*)

introduce (*things, topics, and so forth*) (to)   introdurre (*een-troh-DOOHRR-reh*)

introduce (*persons*) (to)   presentare (*preh-zehn-TAHR-reh*)

introduction (*of things, topics, and so forth*)   introduzione *f.* (*een-troh-doo-TSYOH-neh*)

introduction (*of persons*)   presentazione *f.* (*preh-zehn-tah-TSYOH-neh*)

introverted (adj.)   introverso (*een-troh-VEHR-soh*)

intrude (to)   intrudere (*een-troo-DEHR-reh*)

intruder   intruso *m.* (*een-TROO-zoh*)

intuit, sense (to)   intuire (*een-too-EER-reh*) 🌶

intuition   intuizione *f.* (*een-twee-TSYOH-neh*)

inundation, flood   inondazione *f.* (*ee-nohn-dah-TSYOH-neh*)

invader   invasore *m.* (*een-vah-ZOHR-reh*)

invalid   invalido *m.* (*een-VAH-lee-doh*) ⊃(adj.)◖

invariable (adj.)   invariabile (*een-vahr-RYAH-bee-leh*)

invasion   invasione *f.* (*een-vah-ZYOH-neh*)

invent (to)   inventare (*een-vehn-TAHR-reh*)

invention   invenzione *f.* (*een-vehn-TSYOH-neh*)

inventor   inventore *m.* (*een-vehn-TOHR-reh*) ⊃**inventive** (adj.) -tivo◖

inventory   inventario *m.* (*een-vehn-TAHR-ryoh*)

invest (to)   investire (*een-veh-STEER-reh*)

investigate (to)   investigare (*een-veh-stee-GAHR-reh*)

investigation   investigazione *f.* (*een-veh-stee-gah-TSYOH-neh*)

investment   investimento *m.* (*een-veh-stee-MEHN-toh*)

invigorate (to)   invigorire (*een-vee-goh-REER-reh*)

invincible (adj.)   invincibile (*een-veen-CHEE-bee-leh*)

> ⓘ Two important, related noncognates are: **victor, winner**—vincitore *m.* / vincitrice *f.* (*veen-chee-TOHR-reh* / ____*TREE-cheh*); and **to be victorious, win**—vincere (*VEEN-chehr-reh*). 🌶

invisible (adj.)   invisible (*een-vee-ZEE-bee-leh*)

invitation   invito *m.* (*een-VEE-toh*)

invite (to)   invitare (*een-vee-TAHR-reh*)

involuntary (adj.)   involontario (*een-voh-lohn-TAHR-ryoh*)

irate (adj.)   irato (*eer-RAH-toh*)

ire   ira *f.* (*EER-rah*)

iris (*flower*)   iris *f.* (EER-ree-seh)

iris (*part of the eye*)   iride (*EE-ree-deh*)

ironic, ironical (adj.) ironico (*eer-ROH-nee-koh*)

irony ironia *f.* (*eer-roh-NEE-ah*)

irrational (adj.) irragionevole (*eer-rrah-joh-NEH-voh-leh*)

irregular, fitful (adj.) irregolare (*eer-rreh-goh-LAHR-reh*)

irregularity *f.* irregolarità (*eer-rreh-goh-lahr-ree-TAH*)

irresistible (adj.) irresistibile (*eer-rreh-see-STEE-bee-leh*)

irresponsible (adj.) irresponsabile (*eer-rreh-spohn-SAH-bee-leh*)

irreverent (adj.) irriverente (*eer-rree-vehr-REHN-teh*)

irrevocable (adj.) irrevocabile (*eer-rreh-voh-KAH-bee-leh*)

irritability irritabilità *f.* (*eer-rree-tah-bee-lee-TAH*)

irritable (adj.) irritabile (*eer-rree-tah-BEE-leh*)

irritant irritante *m.* (*eer-rree-TAHN-teh*)

irritate, vex (to) irritare (*eer-rree-TAHR-reh*)

irritating (adj.) irritante (*eer-rree-TAHN-teh*)

irritation irritazione *f.* (*eer-rree-tah-TSYOH-neh*)

island isola *f.* (*EE-zoh-lah*)

isolate, insulate (to) isolare (*ee-zoh-LAHR-reh*) ☞

isolation, insulation isolamento *m.* (*ee-zoh-lah-MEHN-toh*)

isolationism (*political*) isolazionismo *f.* (*ee-zoh-lah-tsyoh-NEEH-zmoh*)

Italy Italia *f.* (*ee-TAH-lyah*)

Italian (adj.) italiano (*ee-tah-LYAH-noh*)

itinerary itinerario *m.* (*ee-tee-nehr-RAHR-ryoh*)

ivory avorio *m.* (*ah-VOHR-ryoh*) ☞

ⓘ No native Italian word begins with the letter *j*, and relatively few contain it even in component form. Thus, excepting only a few imports from other languages, this entire alphabetic section is notable for the phonetic similarity of terms that uniformly display that one negative characteristic: the missing initial *j*.

jacket   giacca *f.* *(JAHK-kah)* ♦⃰

jade   giada *f.* *(JAH-dah)* ♦⃰

jar   giara *f.* *(JAHR-rah)* ♦⃰

jazz   jazz *m.* *(JAHZ-zeh)*

jealous (adj.)   geloso *(jeh-LOH-soh)* ♦⃰

jealousy   gelosia *f.* *(jeh-loh-ZEE-ah)* ♦⃰

jeans (*denim pants*)   jeans *m.* *(JEENZ)*

jelly   gelatina *f.* *(jeh-lah-TEE-nah)* ♦⃰

Jesuit   gesuita *m.* *(jeh-zoo-EE-tah)* ♦⃰

Jesus   Gesù *m.* *(jeh-ZOO)* ♦⃰

Jesus Christ   Gesù Cristo *m.* *(jeh-ZOO KREE-stoh)* ♦⃰

jet (*aircraft*)   jet *m.* *(JEH-teh)*

jewel   gioiello *m.* *(joh-YEHL-loh)* ♦⃰

jeweler   gioielliere *m.* *(joh-yehl-LYEHR-reh)* ♦⃰

jewelry   gioielli *m.* *(joh-YEHL-lee)* ♦⃰

journal, newspaper   giornale *m.* *(johr-NAH-leh)* ♦⃰
   ⓘ A newspaper gives the **news**—notizie *f.* *(noh-TEE-tsee-eh)*

journalism   giornalismo *m.* *(johr-nah-LEEZ-moh)* ♦⃰

journalist, reporter   giornalista *m.* *(johr-nah-LEE-stah)*, cronista *m.* *(kroh-NEE-stah)* ♦⃰

jovial (adj.)   gioviale *(joh-VYAH-leh)* ♦⃰

joy, glee   gioia *f.* *(JOH-yah)* ♦⃰

joyful, joyous, gleeful (adj.)   gioioso *(joh-YOH-soh)* ♦⃰

jubilant (adj.)   giubilante *(joo-bee-LAHN-teh)* ♦⃰

Judaism   giudaismo *m.* *(joo-dah-EEZ-moh)* ♦⃰

judge   giudice *m.* *(JOO-dee-cheh)* ♦⃰

judge (to) giudicare (*joo-dee-KAHR-reh*) 👄

judgment giudizio *m.* (*joo-DEE-tsyoh*) 👄

judicial (adj.) giudiziario (*joo-dee-TSYAHR-ryoh*) 👄

judicious (adj.) giudizioso (*joo-dee-TSYOH-soh*) 👄

juncture giuntura *f.* (*joon-TOOR-rah*) 👄

jungle giungla *f.* (*JOON-glah*) 👄

Junior (*in family nomenclature*) (adj.) iunior (*yoo-NYOHR*) 👄

jurisprudence giurisprudenza *f.* (*joor-ree-sproo-DEHN-tsah*) 👄

jurist giurista *m.* (*joor-REE-stah*) 👄

juror giurato *m.* (*joor-RAH-toh*) 👄

jury giuria *m.* (*joor-REE-ah*) 👄

just, fair, equitable (adj.) giusto (*JOO-stoh*) 👄

justice giustizia *f.* (*joo-STEE-tsyah*) 👄

justification giustificazione *f.* (*joo-stee-fee-kah-TSYOH-neh*) 👄

justify (to) giustificare (*joo-stee-fee-KAHR-reh*) 👄

juvenile, youthful (adj.) giovanile (*joh-vah-NEE-leh*) 👄
    ⓘ Related noncognates include: **young** (adj.)—giovane (*JOH-vah-neh*) and **youth**—giovinezza *f.* (joh-vee-NEHT-tsah).

—K—

ⓘ No native Italian word begins with the letter *k*, and relatively few contain it even in component form. Thus, excepting only a few imports from other languages, this entire alphabetic section is notable for the phonetic similarity of terms that uniformly display that one negative characteristic: the missing initial *k*.

kaleidoscope caleidoscopio *m.* (*kah-lay-doh-SKO-pyoh*) 👄

karat carato *m.* (*kahr-RAH-toh*) 👄

karate karate *m.* (*kahr-RAH-teh*)

key chiave *f.* (*KYAH-veh*)

khaki cachi *m.* (*KAH-kee*), kaki *m.* (*KAH-kee*) 💣

killer killer *m.* (*KEEL-lehr*)

kilo chilo *m.* (*KEE-loh*) 💣

kilocycle chilociclo *m.* (*kee-loh-CHEE-kloh*), kilociclo *m.* (*kee-loh-CHEE-kloh*) 💣

kilogram chilogrammo *m.* (*kee-loh-GRAHM-moh*), kilogrammo *m.* (*kee-loh-GRAHM-moh*) 💣

kilometer chilometro *m.* (*kee-LOH-meh-troh*), kilometro *m.* (*kee-LOH-meh-troh*) 💣

kilowatt chilowatt *m.* (*kee-loh-VAHT*), kilowatt *m.* (*kee-loh-VAHT*) 💣

kiosk chiosco *m.* (*KYOHS-koh*) 💣

kitchen cucina *f.* (*koo-CHEE-nah*) 💣

knot nodo *m.* (*NOH-doh*) 💣

knuckle nocca *f.* (*NOHK-kah*) 💣

—L—

laboratory laboratorio *m.* (*lah-bohr-rah-TOHR-ryoh*)

laborious (adj.) laborioso (*lah-bohr-RYOH-soh*)

labyrinth, **maze** labirinto *m.* (*lah-beer-REEN-toh*)

laceration lacerazione *f.* (*lah-che-rah-TSYOH-neh*)

lacquer lacca *f.* (*LAHK-kah*)

lactose lattosio *m.* (*laht-TOH-syoh*)

lagoon laguna *f.* (*lah-GOO-nah*)

lake lago *m.* (*LAH-goh*)

lament lamento *m.* (*lah-MEHN-toh*)

lamentable (adj.) lamentevole (*lah-mehn-TEH-voh-leh*)

lamp lampada *f.* (*LAHM-pah-dah*)
   ⓘ Important, related noncognates: **lightbulb**—lampadina *f.* (*lahm-pah-*

DEE-nah); and **flashlight**—lampadina (*f.*) tascabile (*lahm-pah-DEE-nah tah-SKAH-bee-leh*)

languish (to)   languire (*lahn-GWEER-reh*)

lantern   lanterna *f.* (*lahn-TEHR-nah*)

largo (*musical distinction*), broad (adj.)   largo (*LAHR-goh*)

larva   larva *f.* (*LAHR-vah*)

laryngitis   laringite *f.* (*lahr-een-JEE-teh*)

lascivious, lecherous (adj.)   lascivo (*lah-SHEE-voh*)

laser   laser *m.* (*LAH-zehr*)

lassitude   lassitudine *f.* (*lahs-see-TOO-dee-neh*)

latent (adj.)   latente (*lah-TEHN-teh*)

lateral (adj.)   laterale (*lah-tehr-RAH-leh*)

Latin   latino *m.* (*lah-TEE-noh*) ⮑(adj.)☾

latitude   latitudine *f.* (*lah-tee-TOO-dee-neh*)

latrine, toilet, privy   latrina *f.* (*lah-TREE-nah*), toletta *f.* (*toh-LEHT-tah*)
  ⓘ While most Italians will understand that an English speaker's request for a **bathroom** equates to "room with toilet," their term *stanza da bagno* literally means "room with bathtub" (and *probably* a toilet). Most commonly, an Italian toilet room is either a *toletta* or *gabinetto*.

laudable (adj.)   lodevole (*loh-DEH-voh-leh*) ☙

laundry (*commercial cleaner*)   lavanderia *f.* (*lah-vahn-dehr-REE-ah*)
  ⓘ **dry cleaner's**—lavanderia (*f.*) a secco (*lah-vahn-dehr-REE-ah ah sehk-koh*)

laureate (adj.)   laureato (*low-reh-AH-toh*)

lava   lava *f.* (*LAH-vah*)

lavatory, washroom   lavatoio *m.* (*lah-vah-TOH-yoh*)

lavatory, sink, washbasin   lavandino *m.* (*lah-vahn-DEE-noh*)

lave, launder, wash (to)   lavare (*lah-VAHR-reh*)
  ⓘ Closely related noncognate: **to wash onself**—lavarsi (*lah-VAHR-see*)

lavender   lavanda *f.* (*lah-VAHN-dah*)

laxative lassativo *m.* (*lahs-sah-TEE-voh*) ⊃(adj.)Ͻ ♠⁑

leader leader *m.* (*LEE-dehr-reh*)

league lega *f.* (*LEH-gah*)

legal, lawful, licit (adj.) legale (*leh-GAH-leh*)

legalize (to) legalizzare (*leh-gah-leed-DZAHR-reh*)

legend leggenda *f.* (*lehd-JEHN-dah*)

legendary (adj.) leggendario (*lehd-jehn-DAHR-ryoh*)

legible (adj.) leggibile (*lehd-JEE-bee-leh*)

legion legione *f.* (*leh-JOH-neh*)

legislation legislazione *f.* (*leh-jee-zlaht-TSYOH-neh*)
ⓘ The underlying, noncognate noun is: **law**—legge *f.* (*LEHD-jeh*).

legislator legislatore *m.* (*leh-jee-zlah-TOHR-reh*)

legislature legislatura *f.* (*leh-jee-zlah-TOOR-rah*)

legitimate (adj.) legittimo (*leh-JEET-tee-moh*)

lemon limone *m.* (*lee-MOH-neh*) ♠⁑

lemonade limonata *f.* (*lee-moh-NAH-tah*) ♠⁑

length lunghezza *f.* (*loon-GEHT-tsah*) ♠⁑

lesbian lesbica *f.* (*LEHZ-bee-kah*) ⊃(adj.)Ͻ

lesion lesione *f.* (*leh-ZYOH-neh*)

lesson lezione *f.* (*leh-TSYOH-neh*) ♠⁑

lethal (adj.) letale (*leh-TAH-leh*)

lethargic (adj.) letargico (*leh-TAHR-jee-koh*)

lethargy letargia *f.* (*leh-tahr-JEE-ah*)

letter (*alphabetic character* OR *epistle*) lettera *f.* (*LEHT-tehr-rah*)

lettuce lattuga *f.* (*laht-TOO-gah*) ♠⁑

leukemia leucemia *f.* (*lehoo-CHEH-mee-ah*)

level (*construction tool*) livello *m.* (*lee-VEHL-loh*) ♠⁑

level (to) livellare (*lee-vehl-LAHR-reh*) ♠⁑

lever leva *f.* (*LEH-vah*)

lexicon lessico *m.* (*LEHS-see-koh*) 🔊

libel libello *m.* (*lee-BEHL-loh*)

liberal liberale *m. & f.* (*lee-behr-RAH-leh*) ⊃(adj.)C

liberalism liberalismo *m.* (*lee-behr-rah-LEE-zmoh*)

liberality liberalità *f.* (*lee-behr-rah-lee-TAH*)

liberate, free, rescue (to) liberare (*lee-behr-RAHR-reh*)

liberated, unconstrained, unoccupied, free (adj.) libero (*LEE-behr-roh*)

liberation, rescue liberazione *f.* (*lee-behr-rah-TSYOH-neh*)

libertine libertino *m.* (*lee-behr-TEE-noh*)

liberty, freedom libertà *f.* (*lee-behr-TAH*)

libido libido *m.* (*lee-BEE-doh*)

libretto, booklet libretto *m.* (*lee-BREHT-toh*)
  ⓘ A libretto and a booklet are, literally, "little books." In Italian, **book**— libro *m.* (*LEE-broh*).

license (*personal quality, NOT permit certificate*) licenza *f.* (*lee-CHEN-tsah*)

licorice liquirizia *f.* (*lee-kweer-REE-tsyah*) 🔊

lieutenant tenente *m.* (*teh-NEHN-teh*) 🔊

ligament legamento *m.* (*leh-gah-MEHN-toh*) 🔊

lilac lillà *f.* (*leel-LAH*)

limbo limbo *m.* (*LEEM-boh*)

limit (*boundry*) limite *m.* (*LEE-mee-teh*)

limit (to) limitare (*lee-mee-TAHR-reh*)

limitation limitazione *f.* (*lee-mee-tah-TSYOH-neh*)

limousine limousine *f.* (*lee-maow-ZEE-neh*)

line (*graphical mark OR transit route*) linea *f.* (*LEE-neh-ah*)

line (*established policy*) linea (*f.*) di condotta (*LEE-neh-ah dee kohn-DOHT-tah*)

lineage lignaggio *m.* (*lee-NYAHD-joh*) 🔊

linear (adj.)   lineare (*lee-neh-AHR-reh*)

lingerie   lingeria *f.* (*leen-jehr-REE-ah*), lingerie (*LEHNJ-ree*)

linguist   linguista *m.* (*leen-GWEE-stah*)

linguistic (adj.)   linguistico (*leen-GWEE-stee-koh*)

linguistics   linguistica *f.* (*leen-GWEE-stee-kah*)

lion   leone *m.* (*leh-OH-neh*)

liquefy (to)   liquefare (*lee-kweh-FAHR-reh*)

liqueur (*alcoholic cordial*)   liquore *m.* (*lee-KWOHR-reh*)

liquid   liquido *m.* (*LEE-kwee-doh*) ⊃(adj.)C

list   lista *f.* (*LEE-stah*)

litany   litania *f.* (*lee-tah-NEE-ah*)

liter, **litre**   litro *m.* (*LEE-troh*)

literal (adj.)   letterale (*leht-tehr-RAH-leh*) 🔊

literary (adj.)   letterario (*leht-tehr-RAHR-ryoh*) 🔊

literate (adj.)   letterato (*leht-tehr-RAH-toh*) 🔊

literature   letteratura *f.* (*leht-tehr-RAH-toor-rah*) 🔊

lithograph   litografia *f.* (*lee-toh-grah-FEE-ah*)

litigation   litigio *m.* (*lee-TEE-joh*), causa *f.* (*KOW-zah*)

liturgy   liturgia *f.* (*lee-toor-JEE-ah*)

livid (adj.)   livido (*LEE-vee-doh*)

lobe   lobo *m.* (*LOH-boh*)

local (adj.)   locale (*loh-KAH-leh*)

locale, **locality**   località *f.* (*loh-kah-lee-TAH*)

locomotive   locomotiva *f.* (*loh-koh-moh-TEE-vah*)

lodge (*give or rent residential space*) (to)   alloggiare (*ahl-lohd-JAHR-reh*) 🔊

lodging   alloggio *m.* (*ahl-LOHD-joh*) 🔊

loge   loggia *f.* (*LOHD-jah*)

logic   logica *f.* (*LOH-jee-kah*) ⊃**logical** (adj.) -coC

long (adj.) lungo (*LOON-goh*) 💣

longevity longevità *f.* (*lohn-jeh-vee-TAH*)

longitude longitudine *f.* (*lohn-jee-TOO-dee-neh*)

loquacious, talkative (adj.) loquace (*loh-KWAH-cheh*)

lotion lozione *f.* (*loh-TSYOH-neh*)

lottery, raffle lotteria *f.* (*loht-tehr-REE-ah*)

loyal (adj.) leale (*leh-AH-leh*) 💣

loyalist lealista *m.* (*leh-ah-LEE-stah*) 💣

loyalty lealtà *f.* (*leh-ahl-TAH*) 💣

lozenge losanga *f.* (*loh-ZAHN-gah*)

lubricant lubrificante *m.* (*loo-bree-fee-KAHN-teh*)

lubricate, oil, grease (to) lubrificare (*loo-bree-fee-KAHR-reh*)

lucrative (adj.) lucrativo (*loo-krah-TEE-voh*)

luminous, light, bright (adj.) luminoso (*loo-mee-NOH-soh*)

lunar (adj.) lunare (*loo-NAHR-reh*) ⊃moon—luna *f.* ℂ

lunatic lunatico *m.* (*loo-nah-TEE-koh*) ⊃(adj.)ℂ

luster lustro *m.* (*LOO-stroh*)

luxurious (adj.) lussuoso (*loos-SWOH-soh*)

luxury *m.* lusso (*LOOS-soh*)

lyric lirico *m.* (*LEER-ree-koh*)

lyricism liricismo *m.* (*lee-ree-CHEEZ-moh*)

—M—

macaroni maccheroni *m.* (*mahk-kehr-ROH-nee*)

machine macchina *f.* (*MAHK-kee-nah*)

machinery macchinario *m.* (*mahk-kee-NAHR-ryoh*), meccanismo *m.* (*mehk-kah-NEEZ-moh*)

machinist macchinista *m.* (*mahk-kee-NEE-stah*)

magazine, storage, warehouse, storehouse magazzino *m.* (*mah-gahd-DZEE-noh*)
> ☛ This term does not in ANY instance refer to a published **periodical**!

magic magia *f.* (*mah-JEE-ah*)

magic (adj.) magico (*MAH-jee-koh*)

magician mago *m.* (*MAH-goh*)

magistrate magistrato *m.* (*mah-jee-STRAH-toh*)

magnanimous (adj.) magnanimo (*mah-NYAH-nee-moh*)

magnet magnete *m.* (*mah-NYEH-teh*)

magnetic (adj.) magnetico (*mah-NYEH-tee-koh*)

magnificence magnificenza *f.* (*mah-nyee-fee-CHEN-tsah*)

magnificent, palatial (adj.) magnifico (*mah-NYEE-fee-koh*)

maintain (to) mantenere (*mahn-teh-NEHR-reh*)

maintenance mantenimento *m.* (*mahn-teh-nee-MEHN-toh*)

major, elder, senior maggiore *m.* (*mahd-JOHR-reh*)
> ⓘ Italian ***maggiore*** also translates the following adjectives: **greater, greatest; elder, eldest; oldest.**

majority maggioranza *f.* (*mahd-johr-RAHNT-zah*)

malady, ailment, disease malattia *f.* (*mah-laht-TEE-ah*)

malaria malaria *f.* (*mah-LAHR-ryah*)
> ⓘ Far more often than not, the Italian prefix ***mal-*** connotes the quality of **evil, wickedness, pain.** *Malaria,* for example, translates literally as "evil air," which was originally believed to cause the disease now described by that term. In addition to the several ***mal-*** cognates immediately below, noncognates in this category include: **evil, pain, ache, hurt**—male *m.* (*MAHL-leh*); **accursed** (adj.)—maledetto (*mah-leh-DEHT-toh*); **to curse**—maledire (*mah-leh-DEER-reh*); **curse**—maledizione *f.* (*mah-leh-dee-TSYOH-neh*); **headache**—mal (*m.*) di testa (*mahl dee TEH-stah*), mal (*m.*) di capo (*mahl dee KAH-poh*); **ill, sick, ailing** (adj.)—malato (*mah-LAH-toh*); **ill omen, jinx**—malaugurio *m.* (*mah-low-GOOR-ryoh*); **illness**—malore *m.* (*mah-LOHR-reh*); **mischievous** (adj.)—malizioso (*mah-lee-TSYOH-soh*); **ruffian**—malfattore *m.*

(*mahl-faht-TOHR-reh*); **scandal**—maldicenza *f.* (*mahl-dee-CHEN-tsah*); **seasickness**—mal (*m.*) di mare (*mahl dee MAHR-reh*); **wicked** (adj.)—malvagio (*mahl-VAH-joh*); **wickedness**—malvagità *f.* (*mahl-vah-jee-TAH*); **(the) underworld**—malavita *f.* (*mah-lah VEE-tah*).

malevolence (adj.)   malevolenza (*mah-leh-voh-LEHN-tsah*)

malevolent (adj.)   malevolo (*mah-LEH-voh-loh*)

malice, mischief   malizia *f.* (*mah-LEEH-tsyah*)

malignant (adj.)   maligno (*mah-LEE-nyoh*)

maltreat, mistreat (to)   maltrattare (*mahl-traht-TAHR-reh*)

mammary gland, breast   mammella *f.* (*mahm-MEHL-lah*)

manager   manager *m.* (*mah-nah-JEHR-reh*), direttore *m.* (*dee-reht-TOHR-reh*)

mandate, warrant   mandato *m.* (*mahn-DAH-toh*)

mandolin   mandolino *m.* (*mahn-doh-LEE-noh*)

maneuver   manovra *f.* (*mah-NOH-vrah*)

maneuver (to)   manovrare (*mah-noh-VRAR-reh*)

mania, fad   mania *f.* (*mah-NEE-ah*)

maniac   maniaco *m.* (*mah-NEE-ah-koh*)

manicure   manicure *f. (OR m.)* (*mah-nee-KOOR-reh*)

manifest (to)   manifestare (*mah-nee-feh-STAHR-reh*)

manifesto   manifesto *m.* (*mah-nee-FEH-stoh*) ➲**manifest** (adj.)➦

manipulate (to)   manipolare (*mah-nee-poh-LAHR-reh*)

manner, way of, fashion of   maniera *f.* (*mah-NYEHR-rah*)

mannerism   manierismo *m.* (*mah-nyehr-REEZ-moh*)

manners (*personal style, deportment*)   maniere *f.* (*mah-NYEHR-reh*)

manual, handbook   manuale *m.* (*mah-NWAH-leh*)

manual (*by hand*) (adj.)   manuale (*mah-NWAH-leh*)

manuscript   manoscritto *m.* (*mah-noh-SKREET-toh*)

many (adj.)   molti (*MOHL-tee*) ♦※

marble (*stone, NOT game piece*)   marmo *m.* (*MAHR-moh*)

march marcia *f.* (*MAHR-chah*)

march (to) marciare (*mahr-CHAR-reh*)

margarine margarina *f.* (*mahr-gahr-REE-nah*)

margin margine *f.* (*MAHR-jee-neh*)

marijuana marihuana *f.* (*mahr-ree-WHAN-nah*), marijuana *f.* (*mahr-ree-WHAN-nah*)

marinate (to) marinare (*mahr-ree-NAHR-reh*)

marine (*military sailor*), **navy** marina *f.* (*mahr-REE-nah*)

marine (adj.) marino (*mahr-REE-noh*)

mariner, sailor, seafarer marinaio *m.* (*mah-ree-NAH-yoh*)

marionette marionetta *f.* (*mahr-ryoh-NEHT-tah*)

marital (adj.) maritale (*mahr-ree-TAH-leh*)

maritime (adj.) marittimo (*mah-REET-tee-moh*)

mark (to) marcare (*mahr-KAHR-reh*)

market mercato *m.* (*mehr-KAH-toh*) 💧
  ⓘ An Italian open-air **marketplace**—piazza (*f.*) del mercato (*pee-AHT-tsah dehl____*). The **black market**—mercato (*m.*) nero (____*NEHR-roh*)

marmalade, jam, preserves marmellata *f.* (*mahr-mehl-LAH-tah*)

maroon (*color*) marrone *m.* (*mahr-RROH-neh*)

martyr martire *m.* (*MAHR-teer-reh*)

martyrdom martirio *m.* (*mahr-TEER-ryoh*)

marvel, wonder meraviglia *f.* (*meh-rah-VEE-lyah*) 💧

marvelous, wondrous, wonderful (adj.) meraviglioso (*meh-rah-vee-LYOH-soh*) 💧

masculine (adj.) maschile (*mah-SKEE-leh*)
  ⓘ Closely related, but hardly cognate: **male**—maschio *m.* (*MAH-skyoh*)

mask maschere *f.* (*MAH-skehr-reh*)

mask (to) mascherare (*mah-skehr-RAHR-reh*)

masquerade mascherata *f.* (*mah-skehr-RAH-tah*)

masquerade (to) mascherarsi (*mah-skehr-RAHR-see*)

mass (*large quantity*), hoard massa *f.* (*MAHS-sah*), ammasso *m.* (*ahm-MAHS-soh*)

mass (*matter*) massa *f.* (*MAHS-sah*)

mass (*religious service*) messa *f.* (*MEHS-sah*) ♠※

massacre massacro *m.* (*mahs-SAH-kroh*)

massage massaggio *m.* (*mahs-SAHD-joh*)

massage (to) massaggiare (*mahs-sahd-JAHR-reh*)

masseur massaggiatore *m.* (*mahs-sahd-jah-TOHR-reh*)

massive (adj.) massiccio (*mahs-SEET-choh*)

match (*sports, esp. boxing*) match *m.* (*MAH-cheh*), partita (*pahr-tee-tah*)

material materiale *m.* (*mah-tehr-RYAH-leh*) ⊃(adj.)C

materialism materialismo *m.* (*mah-tehr-ryah-LEEZ-moh*)

maternal, motherly (adj.) materno (*mah-TEHR-noh*)

maternity maternità *f.* (*mah-tehr-nee-TAH*)

mathematical (adj.) matematico (*mah-teh-MAH-tee-koh*)

mathematics matematica *f.* (*mah-teh-MAH-tee-kah*)

matinee mattinata *f.* (*maht-tee-NAH-tah*)

matriarchy matriarcato *m.* (*mah-tryahr-KAH-toh*)

matrimony, marriage, wedding matrimonio *m.* (*mah-tree-MOH-nyoh*), sposalizio *m.* (*spoh-zah-LEE-tsyoh*)

matter, thing materia *f.* (*mah-TEHR-ryah*), cosa *f.* (*KOH-sah*)

mattress materasso *m.* (*mah-tehr-RAHS-soh*)

mature, ripen (to) maturare (*mah-toor-RAHR-reh*)

mature, grown, ripe (adj.) maturo (*mah-TOOR-roh*)

maturity maturità *f.* (*mah-toor-ree-TAH*)

mausoleum mausoleo *m.* (*mow-zoh-LEH-oh*)

maximum massimo *m.* (*MAHS-see-moh*) ⊃(adj.)◖

mayonnaise maionese *f.* (*mah-yoh-NEH-zeh*)

meager (adj.) magro (*MAH-groh*) ◗※

measure, size (*of clothing*) misura *f.* (*mee-ZOOR-rah*) ◗※

measure (to) misurare, (*mee-zoor-RAHR-reh*) ◗※

measurement misura *f.* (*mee-ZOO-rah*), misurazione *f.* (*mee-zoo-rah-TSYOH-neh*), misuramento *m.* (*mee-zoor-rah-MEHN-toh*) ◗※

mechanic meccanico *m.* (*mehk-KAH-nee-koh*)

mechanical (adj.) meccanico (*mehk-KAH-nee-koh*)

mechanism meccanismo *m.* (*mehk-kah-NEEZ-moh*)

medal (*award*) medaglia *f.* (*meh-DAH-lyah*)

mediator, ombudsman mediatore *m.* (*meh-dyah-TOHR-reh*)

medic, doctor, physician medico *m.* (*MEH-dee-koh*)

medical (adj.) medico (*MEH-dee-koh*)

medicate (to) medicare (*meh-dee-KAHR-reh*)

medicine (*science and practice of*) medicina *f.* (*meh-dee-CHEE-nah*)

medicine (*healing compound*) medicamento *m.* (*meh-dee-kah-MEHN-toh*)

medieval (adj.) medioevale (*meh-dyoh-eh-VAH-leh*)

mediocre (adj.) mediocre (*meh-DYOH-kreh*)

mediocrity mediocrità *f.* (*meh-dyoh-kree-TAH*)

meditate, muse (to) meditare (*meh-dee-TAHR-reh*)

meditation meditazione *f.* (*meh-dee-tah-TSYOH-neh*)

medium (adj.) medio (*MEH-dyoh*)

melancholy malinconia *f.* (*mah-leen-koh-NEE-ah*) ◗※

melancholy, dismal (adj.) melanconico (*meh-lahn-KOH-nee-koh*)

melodious, tuneful (adj.) melodioso (*meh-loh-DYOH-soh*)

melodrama melodramma *m.* (*meh-loh-DRAHM-mah*)

melody, tune melodia *f.* (*meh-loh-DEE-ah*)

melon melone *m.* (*meh-LOH-neh*)

member (*of group* OR *anatomical part*) membro *m.* (*MEHM-broh*)

memoir memoria *f.* (*meh-MOHR-ryah*)

memorable (adj.) memorabile (*meh-mohr-RAH-bee-leh*)

memorandum memorandum *m.* (*meh-mohr-RAHN-doom*)

memorial memoriale *m.* (*meh-mohr-RYAH-leh*)

memory (*specific recollection* OR *facility of recall*) memoria *f.* (*meh-MOHR-ryah*)

menace minaccia *f.* (*mee-NAHT-chah*) ✐

mendicant, beggar mendicante *m.* (*mehn-dee-KAHN-teh*)

menopause menopausa *f.* (*meh-noh-POWH-zah*)

menstruation mestruazione (*meh-strwah-TSYOH-neh*)

mental (adj.) mentale (*mehn-TAH-leh*)
ⓘ The related noncognate: **mind**—mente *f.* (*MEHN-teh*)

mentality mentalità *f.* (*mehn-tah-lee-TAH*)

menthol mentolo *m.* (*mehn-TOH-loh*)

mention menzione *f.* (*mehn-TSYOH-neh*)

mention (to) menzionare (*mehn-tsyoh-NAHR-reh*)

menu menu *m.* (*MEH-noo*), lista (*f.*) delle vivande (*LEE-stah dehl-leh vee-VAHN-deh*)

mercantile (adj.) mercantile (*mehr-kahn-TEE-leh*)

merchandise, wares mercanzia *f.* (*mehr-kahn-TSEE-ah*), merce *f.* (*MEHR-cheh*)

merchant mercante *m.* (*mehr-KAHN-teh*)

mercury mercurio *m.* (*mehr-KOOR-ryoh*)

mere (adj.) mero (*MEHR-roh*)

merely meramente (*mehr-rah-MEHN-teh*)

meringue meringa *f.* (*mehr-REEN-gah*)

merit merito *m.* (*MEHR-ree-toh*)

merit, deserve (to)   meritare (*mehr-ree-TAHR-reh*)

meriting, deserving (adj.)   meritevole (*mehr-ree-TEH-voh-leh*)

message   messaggio *m.* (*mehs-SAHD-joh*), comunicazione *f.* (*koh-moo-nee-kah-TSYOH-neh*)

messenger   messaggero *m.* (*mes-sahd-JEHR-roh*)

metabolism   metabolismo *m.* (*meh-tah-boh-LEEZ-moh*)

metal   metallo *m.* (*meh-TAHL-loh*)

metallic (adj.)   metalico (*meh-TAHL-lee-koh*)

meteor   meteora *f.* (*meh-TEH-OHR-rah*)

meteorology   meteorologia *f.* (*meh-teh-oh-roh-loh-JEE-ah*)

meter, metre   metro *m.* (*MEH-troh*)

method   metodo *m.* (*MEH-toh-doh*)

meticulous (adj.)   meticoloso (*meh-tee-koh-LOH-soh*)

metric (adj.)   metrico (*MEH-tree-koh*)

metropolis   metropoli *f.* (*meh-TROH-poh-lee*)

metropolitan (adj.)   metropolitano (*meh-troh-poh-lee-TAH-noh*)

mezzanine   mezzanino *m.* (*mehd-dzah-NEE-noh*)

microbe   microbo *m.* (*MEE-kroh-boh*)

microfilm   microfilm *m.* (*MEE-kroh-feelm*)

microphone   microfono *m.* (*mee-KROH-foh-noh*)

microscope   microscopio *m.* (*mee-kroh-SKO-pyoh*)

microscopic (adj.)   microscopico (*mee-kroh-SKO-pee-koh*)

mid- (adj.)   medio (*MEH-dyoh*)

middle   mezzo *m.* (*MEHD-dzoh*), medio *m.* (*MEH-dyoh*), intermedio *m.* (*een-tehr-MEH-dyoh*)

middle, half (adj.)   mezzo (*MEHD-dzoh*)

Middle Ages   medioevo *m.* (*meh-dyoh-EH-voh*)

Middle East   Medio Oriente *m.* (*MEH-dyoh Ohr-ree-EHN-teh*)

middle class classe media *f.* (*KLAHS-seh MEH-dyah*) ➲(adj.)ℂ

migrate (to) migrare (*mee-GRAHR-reh*)

migration migrazione *f.* (*mee-grah-TSYOH-neh*)

migratory (adj.) migratorio (*mee-grah-TOHR-ryoh*)

militant (adj.) militante (*mee-lee-TAHN-teh*)

militarism militarismo *m.* (*mee-lee-tahr-REEZ-moh*)

military (adj.) militare (*mee-lee-TAHR-reh*)

militia milizia *f.* (*mee-LEE-tsyah*)

millimeter millimetro *m.* (*meel-LEE-meh-troh*)

millionaire milionario *m.* (*mee-lyoh-NAHR-ryoh*)

mind mente *f.* (*MEHN-teh*) ✋

mineral, ore minerale *m.* (*mee-nehr-RAH-leh*)

miniature miniatura *f.* (*mee-nee-ah-TOOR-rah*) ➲(adj.) -roℂ

miniaturize (to) miniaturizzare (*mee-nee-ah-too-reed-DZYAHR-reh*)

minimum, least minimo *m.* (*MEE-nee-moh*) ➲(adj.)ℂ

miniscule, tiny (adj.) minuscolo (*mee-NOOS-koh-loh*)

minister ministro *m.* (*mee-NEE-stroh*)

ministry ministero *m.* (*mee-nee-STEHR-roh*)

minor (*nonadult person*) minorenne *m.* & *f.* (*mee-nohr-REHN-neh*)

minor (*lesser*), **junior** (*younger of two or more*) (adj.) minore (*mee-NOHR-reh*)

minority (*smaller number*) minoranza *f.* (*mee-nohr-RAHN-tsah*)

minority (*state of nonadulthood*) minorità *f.* (*mee-nohr-ree-TAH*)

minstrel minestrello *m.* (*mee-neh-STREHL-loh*)

mint (*plant* AND *confection*) menta *f.* (*MEHN-tah*) ✋

minus meno (*MEH-noh*) ✋

minute (*tiny*) (adj.) minuto (*mee-NOO-toh*)

miracle miracolo *m.* (*meer-RAH-koh-loh*)

miraculous (adj.) miracoloso (*meer-rah-koh-LOH-soh*)

mirage miraggio *m.* (*meer-RAHD-joh*)

miscellaneous (adj.) miscellaneo (*mee-shel-LAH-neh-oh*)

miserable, wretched (adj.) misero (*MEE-zehr-roh*)

misery miseria *f.* (*mee-ZEHR-ryah*)

misfortune sfortuna *f.* (*sfor-TOO-nah*) 💣

missile missile *m.* (*mees-SEE-leh*)

mission missione *f.* (*mees-SYOH-neh*)

missionary missionario *m.* (*mees-syoh-NAHR-ryoh*)

mix (to) mischiare (*mee-SKYAHR-reh*)

mixed (adj.) misto (*MEE-stoh*)

mixture mistura *f.* (*mee-STOOR-rah*)

mobile, movable (adj.) mobile (*MOH-bee-leh*)

mobilize (to) mobilitare (*moh-bee-lee-TAHR-reh*)

mode moda *f.* (*MOH-dah*)

model, pattern modello *m.* (*moh-DEHL-loh*)

model (to) modellare (*moh-dehl-LAHR-reh*)

moderate (to) moderare (*moh-dehr-RAHR-reh*) ⊃**moderate** (adj.) -ato⊂

moderation moderazione *f.* (*moh-dehr-rah-TSYOH-neh*)

modern (adj.) moderno (*moh-DEHR-noh*)

modernize, renovate (to) rimodernare (*ree-moh-dehr-NAHR-reh*) 💣

modest, demure (adj.) modesto (*moh-DEH-stoh*)

modesty modestia *f.* (*moh-DEH-styah*)

modify (to) modificare (*moh-dee-fee-KAHR-reh*)

molar molare *m.* (*moh-LAHR-reh*)

molecule molecola *f.* (*moh-LEH-koh-lah*)

molest (to) molestare (*moh-leh-STAHR-reh*)

momentary (adj.) momentaneo (*moh-mehn-TAH-neh-oh*)

monarch monarca *m.* (*moh-NAHR-kah*)

monastery monastero *m. (moh-nah-STEHR-roh)*

money (*coinage*) moneta *f. (moh-NEH-tah)*, soldi *m. (SOHL-dee)*
ⓘ Italian currency (bills) is commonly **denaro** *m. (deh-NAHR-roh)* or
valuta *f.* (vah-LOO-tah).

monitor monitore *m. (moh-nee-TOHR-reh)*

monk monaco *m. (MOH-nah-koh)*

monopolize (to) monopolizzare *(moh-noh-poh-leed-DZAHR-reh)*

monotonous, humdrum (adj.) monotono *(moh-NOH-toh-noh)*

monotony, dullness monotonia *f. (moh-noh-toh-NEE-ah)*

monster mostro *m. (MOH-stroh)* 🌶

monstrosity mostruosità *f. (moh-strwoh-see-TAH)* 🌶

monstrous (adj.) mostruoso *(moh-stroo-OH-soh)* 🌶

monument, landmark monumento *m. (moh-noo-MEHN-toh)*

monumental (adj.) monumentale *(moh-noo-mehn-TAH-leh)*

moral (*ethical point OR thrust*) morale *f. (mohr-RAH-leh)*

moral (adj.) morale *(mohr-RAH-leh)*

morale morale *m. (mohr-RAH-leh)*

moralist moralista *m. (mohr-rah-LEE-stah)*

morality moralità *f. (mohr-rah-lee-TAH)*

morally moralmente *(mohr-rahl-MEHN-teh)*

morbid (adj.) morboso *(mohr-BOH-soh)*

morphine morfina *f. (mohr-FEE-nah)*

mortal, deadly, deathly (adj.) mortale *(mohr-TAH-leh)*
ⓘ Italian uses the **mort-** syllable in virtually all terms relating to mortality. THUS: **to die**—morire *(moh-REER-reh)*; **death**—morte *f. (MOHR-
teh)*; **dead** (adj.)—morto *(MOHR-toh)*; **to deaden**—ammortire *(ahm-
mohr-TEER-reh)*; and **coffin**—cassa *(f.)* da morto *(KAHS-sah dah
MOHR-toh)*.

mortality mortalità *f. (mohr-tah-lee-TAH)*

mortify (to) mortificare *(mohr-tee-fee-KAHR-reh)*

mortuary mortuario *m.* (*mohr-too-AHR-ryoh*)

mosaic mosaico *m.* (*moh-ZAH-ee-koh*)

motion (*through space, time*) moto *m.* (*MOH-toh*), movimento *m.* (*moh-vee-MEHN-toh*)

motion (*parliamentary*) mozione *f.* (*moh-TSYOH-neh*) 💣

motivate (to) motivare (*moh-tee-VAHR-reh*)

motive motivo *m.* (*moh-TEE-voh*)

motor motore *m.* (*moh-TOHR-reh*)

motorcycle motocicletta *f.* (*moh-toh-chee-KLEHT-tah*)

motto motto *m.* (*MOHT-toh*)

mount (to) montare (*mohn-TAHR-reh*)

Mount____ (*mountain of specific name*) Monte____ *m.* (*MOHN-teh____*)

mountain montagna *f.* (*mohn-TAH-nyah*)

mountaineer montanaro *m.* (*mohn-tahn-AHR-roh*)

mountainous (adj.) montagnoso (*mohn-tah-NYOH-soh*)

move (*shift position of something*) (to) muovere (*MWOH-vehr-reh*)

move (*one's own position*) (to) muoversi (*MWOH-vehr-see*)

movement movimento *m.* (*moh-vee-MEHN-toh*)

mucus muco *m.* (*MOO-koh*)

multicolored (adj.) multicolore (*mool-tee-koh-LOHR-reh*)

multinational (adj.) multinazionale (*mool-tee-nah-tsyoh-NAH-leh*)

multiple (adj.) multiplo (*MOOL-tee-ploh*)

multiplication moltiplicazione *f.* (*mohl-tee-plee-kah-TSYOH-neh*) 💣

multiply (*mathematical operation*) (to) moltiplicare (*mohl-tee-plee-KAHR-reh*) 💣

multiply (*grow numerous*) (to) moltiplicarsi (*mohl-tee-plee-KAHR-see*) 💣

multitude moltitudine *f.* (*mohl-tee-TOO-dee-neh*) 💣

municipal (adj.) municipale (*moo-nee-chee-PAH-leh*)

mural murale *m.* (*moor-RAH-leh*)

muscle muscolo *m.* (*MOO-skoh-loh*)

muscular (adj.) muscolare (*moo-skoh-LAH-reh*)

museum museo *m.* (*moo-ZEH-oh*)

music musica *f.* (*MOO-zee-kah*)

musical (adj.) musicale (*moo-zee-KAH-leh*)

musician musicista *m.* (*moo-zee-CHEE-stah*)

mustard mostarda *f.* (*moh-STAHR-dah*) ◐⁕

mutable, changeable (adj.) mutevole (*moo-TEH-voh-leh*)

mute muto (adj.) (*MOO-toh*)

mutual (adj.) mutuo (*MOO-twoh*)

my, mine (adj.) mio (*MEE-oh*) ➔*f.* -ia☾

myopia miopia (*mee-oh-PEE-ah*)

myopic, nearsighted (adj.) miope (*mee-OH-peh*)

mysterious (adj.) misterioso (*mee-stehr-RYOH-soh*)

mystery mistero *m.* (*mee-STEHR-roh*)

mystic, mystical (adj.) mistico (*MEE-stee-koh*)

mystify (to) mistificare (*mee-stee-fee-KAHR-reh*)

myth mito *m.* (*MEE-toh*)

mythical (adj.) mitico (*MEE-tee-koh*)

mythology mitologia *f.* (*mee-toh-loh-JEE-ah*)

—N—

name nome *m.* (*NOH-meh*) ◐⁕

(family) name cognome *m.* (*koh-NYOH-meh*)

narcotic narcotico *m.* (*nahr-KOH-tee-koh*) ➔(adj.)☾

narrate, relate (to) narrare (*nahr-RRAHR-reh*)

narration narrazione *f.* (*nahr-rrah-TSYOH-neh*)

narrative (adj.) narrativo (*nahr-rrah-TEE-voh*)

narrative (*account of*) racconto *m.* (*rahk-KOHN-toh*)

nasal (adj.) nasale (*nah-SAH-leh*)

nation nazione *f.* (*nah-TSYOH-neh*) 🔊

national (adj.) nazionale (*nah-tsyoh-NAH-leh*) 🔊

nationalism nazionalismo *m.* (*nah-tsyoh-nah-LEEZ-moh*) 🔊

nationality nazionalità *f.* (*nah-tsyoh-nah-lee-TAH*) 🔊

nativity natività *f.* (*nah-tee-vee-TAH*)

natural (adj.) naturale (*nah-toor-RAH-leh*)

naturalist naturalista *m.* (*nah-toor-rah-LEE-stah*)

naturally naturalmente (*nah-toor-rahl-MEHN-teh*)

nature natura *f.* (*nah-TOOR-rah*)

nausea nausea *f.* (*NAOW-zeh-ah*)

nauseating (adj.) nauseante (*naow-zeh-AHN-teh*)

nautical (adj.) nautico (*NAOW-OO-tee-koh*)

naval (adj.) navale (*nah-VAH-leh*)

naval vessel, ship nave *f.* (*NAH-veh*)

nave navata *f.* (*nah-VAH-tah*)

navigable (adj.) navigabile (*nah-vee-gah-BEE-leh*)

navigate (to) navigare (*nah-vee-GAHR-reh*)

navigation navigazione *f.* (*nah-vee-gah-TSYOH-neh*)

navigator navigatore *m.* (*nah-vee-gah-TOHR-reh*)

nebulous, misty (adj.) nebuloso (*neh-boo-LOH-soh*)

necessary, required (adj.) necessario (*neh-ches-SAHR-ryoh*)

necessity necessità *f.* (*neh-ches-see-TAH*)

negative negativa *f.* (*neh-gah-TEE-vah*) ➲(adj.) -vo❤

negligence, oversight negligenza *f.* (*neh-glee-JEHN-tsah*)

negligent, remiss (adj.) negligente (*neh-glee-JEHN-teh*), trascurato (*trah-skoo-RAH-toh*)

negotiate (to) negoziare *(neh-goh-TSYAHR-reh)*

negotiation negoziazione *f. (neh-goh-tsyah-TSYOH-neh)*

nemesis, foe nemico *m. (neh-MEE-koh)*

neon neon *m. (NEH-ohn)*

nerve (*anatomical*) nervo *m. (NEHR-voh)*

nervous, jittery (adj.) nervoso *(nehr-VO-soh)*

net (*of calculation*), **clean, clear-cut** (adj.) netto *(NEHT-toh)*

net (*object made of netting, OR network*) rete *f. (REH-teh)* ☞✦

neurology neurologia *f. (nehoor-roh-loh-JEE-ah)*

neurotic (adj.) nevrotico *(nehv-ROH-tee-koh)* ☞✦

neutral, nonpartisan (adj.) neutrale *(nehoo-TRAH-leh)*, neutro *(neh-OO-troh)*

neutrality neutralità *f. (nehoo-trahl-lee-TAH)*

new (adj.) nuovo *(NWOH-voh)*
   ⓘ Two related terms are semicognate: **to renew**—rinnovare *(reen-noh-VAHR-reh)*, and **renewal**—rinnovamento *m. (reen-noh-vah-MEHN-toh)*

nicotine nicotina *f. (nee-koh-TEE-nah)*

no, not any, none (adj.) non *(NOHN)*, nessuno *(nehs-SOO-noh)*

nobility nobiltà *f. (noh-beel-TAH)*

noble nobile *m. (NOH-bee-leh)* ➲(adj.)☾

nobleman nobiluomo *m. (noh-beel-WOH-moh)*

nocturnal, overnight (adj.) notturno *(noht-TOOR-noh)*

nominal (adj.) nominale *(moh-mee-NAH-leh)*

norm, standard norma *f. (NOHR-mah)*

normal, standard (adj.) normale *(nohr-MAH-leh)*

normally normalmente *(nohr-mahl-MEHNT-teh)*

north nord *m. (NOHRD)*

northeast nord-est *m. (nohrd-EHST)*

northwest nord-ovest *m. (nohrd-OH-vehst)*

nose naso *m.* (*NAH-soh*) 💣

nostalgia, homesickness nostalgia *f.* (*noh-stahl-JEE-ah*)

nostalgic (adj.) nostalgico (*noh-STAHL-jee-koh*)

not non (*NOHN*)

notable, remarkable (adj.) notevole (*noh-TEH-voh-leh*)

note (*musical, NOT correspondence*) nota *f.* (*NOH-tah*)

> ⓘ An Italian written **note**—biglietto *m.* (*bee-LYEHT-toh*). Curiously, this word also means **ticket**.

note (to) notare (*noh-TAHR-reh*)

noted, well-known (adj.) noto (*NOH-toh*)

noticeable (adj.) notevole (*noh-TEH-voh-leh*)

notification notificazione *f.* (*noh-tee-fee-kah-TSYOH-neh*)

notify (to) notificare (*noh-tee-fee-KAHR-reh*)

notion nozione *f.* (*noh-TSYOH-neh*) 💣

notoriety notorietà *f.* (*noh-tohr-ryeh-TAH*)

notorious (adj.) notorio (*noh-TOHR-ryoh*), malfamato (*mahl-fah-MAH-toh*)

notwithstanding (*nonetheless*) nonostante (*noh-noh-STAHN-teh*) 💣

nourish(to) nutrire (*noo-TREER-reh*)

nourishment nutrimento *m.* (*noo-tree-MEHN-toh*)

novelty novità *f.* (*noh-vee-TAH*)

nude, naked, bare, undressed (adj.) nudo (*NOO-doh*)

null, void (adj.) nullo (*NOOL-loh*)

nullity, nonentity nullità *f.* (*nool-lee-TAH*)

number, numeral, shoe size numero *m.* (*NOO-mehr-roh*)

number (to) numerare (*noo-mehr-RAHR-reh*)

numerical (adj.) numerico (*noo-MEHR-ree-koh*)

numerous (adj.) numeroso (*noo-mehr-ROH-soh*)

nutrition nutrizione *f.* (*noo-tree-TSYOH-neh*)

nutritious (adj.) nutriente (*noo-tree-EHN-teh*)

nylon nailon *m.* (*NAI-lohn*)

—O—

obedience ubbienza *f.* (oob-bee-*DYEHN-tsah*) OR obbedienza *f.* (*ohb-beh-DYEHN-tsah*)

obedient, dutiful (adj.) ubbidiente (*oob-bee-DYEHN-teh*) OR obbediente (*ohb-beh-DYEHN-teh*)

obelisk obelisco *m.* (*oh-beh-LEE-skoh*)

obese (adj.) obeso (*oh-BEH-zoh*), grasso (*GRAHS-soh*)
ⓘ A related noncognate is: **chubby, plump** (adj.)—grassetto (*grahs-SEHT-toh*).

obey to (to) ubbidire a (*oob-bee-DEE-reh ah*) OR obbedire a (*ohb-beh-DEER-reh ah*)

object oggetto *m.* (*ohd-JEHT-toh*) ☙

object(to) obiettare (*oh-byeht-TAHR-reh*)

objection obiezione *f.* (*oh-byeh-TSYOH-neh*)

objective oggettivo *m.* (*ohd-jeht-TEE-voh*) ☙

obligation obbligazione *f.* (*ohb-blee-gah-TSYOH-neh*)

obligatory, mandatory, binding (adj.) obbligatorio (*ohb-blee-gah-TOHR-ryoh*)

oblique, slanted (adj.) obliquo (*oh-BLEE-kwoh*)

oblivion oblio *m.* (*oh-BLEE-oh*)

oblong oblungo *m.* (*oh-BLOON-goh*) ᗒadj.ᗢ

obscene (adj.) osceno (*oh-SHEH-noh*) ☙

obscure (adj.) oscuro (*oh-SKOOR-roh*) ☙

obscurity, darkness oscurità *f.* (*oh-skoor-ree-TAH*) ☙

observance osservanza *f.* (*ohs-sehr-VAHN-tsah*) ☙

observation, remark osservazione *f.* (*ohs-sehr-vah-TSYOH-neh*) ☙

observatory   osservatorio *m.* (*ohs-sehr-vah-TOHR-ryoh*) 💣⃰

observe, notice, remark about (to)   osservare (*ohs-sehr-VAHR-reh*) 💣⃰

observer   osservatore *m.* (*ohs-sehr-vah-TOHR-reh*) 💣⃰

obsession   ossessione *f.* (*ohs-sehs-SYOH-neh*) 💣⃰

obstacle   ostacolo *m.* (*oh-STAH-koh-loh*) 💣⃰

obstruct (to)   ostruire (*oh-stroo-EER-reh*) 💣⃰

obstruction   ostruzione *f.* (*oh-stroo-TSYOH-neh*) 💣⃰

obtain, get (*by own action*) (to)   ottenere (*oht-teh-NEHR-reh*) 💣⃰

obtuse, (mentally) dense, stodgy (adj.)   ottuso (*oht-TOO-zoh*)

obvious (adj.)   ovvio (*OHV-vyoh*) 💣⃰

occasion   occasione *f.* (*ohk-kah-ZYOH-neh*)

occasional (adj.)   occasionale (*ohk-kah-zyoh-NAH-leh*)

occult (adj.)   occulto (*ohk-KOOL-toh*)

occupant   occupante *m.* (*ohk-koo-PAHN-teh*)

occupation, job   occupazione *f.* (*ohk-koo-pah-TSYOH-neh*)

occupied, engaged, busy, in use (adj.)   occupato (*ohk-koo-PAH-toh*)
   ⓘ Although the Italian term for employed (*addetto*) is not a cognate, its
   antonym **unemployed** (adj.)—disoccupato (*dee-zohk-koo-PAH-toh*) can
   be termed a "synonymous cognate."

(be) occupied by, engaged in (to)   occuparsi di (*ohk-koo-PAHR-see dee*)

occupy (*hold space or time*) (to)   occupare (*ohk-koo-PAHR-reh*)

ocean   oceano *m.* (*oh-CHEH-ah-noh*)

odious, obnoxious, hateful (adj.)   odioso (*oh-DYOH-soh*)

odor, scent, smell   odore *m.* (*oh-DOHR-reh*)

(sense an) odor, smell (to)   odorare (*oh-dohr-RAHR-reh*)

offend (to)   offendere (*ohf-FEHN-dehr-reh*)

offender   offensore *m.* (*ohf-fehn-SOHR-reh*)

offense (*transgression*)   offesa *f.* (*ohf-FEH-sah*) 💣⃰

offense (attack) offensiva *f.* (*ohf-fehn-SEE-vah*)

(take) offense (to) offendersi di (*ohf-FEHN-dehr-see dee*)

offensive, objectionable (adj.) offensivo (*ohf-FEHN-see-voh*)

offer offerta *f.* (*ohf-FEHR-tah*)

offer (to) offrire (*ohf-FREER-reh*)

office (*business quarters* OR *elected appointed position*) ufficio *m.* (*oof-FEE-choh*) ♠

official, officer ufficiale *m. & f.* (*oof-fee-CHAH-leh*) ⊃(adj.)↺ ♠

officiate (to) officiare (*ohf-fee-CHAR-reh*)

oily (adj.) oleoso (*oh-leh-OH-soh*)

OK OK (*oh-KAY*), d'accordo (*dahk-KOHR-doh*)

olive oliva *f.* (*oh-LEE-vah*)
  ⓘ An *oliva* grows on an **olive tree**—olivo *m.* (*oh-LEE-voh*) and can be pressed to give **olive oil**—olio (*m.*) d'oliva (*OH-lyoh doh-LEE-vah*).

omission omissione *f.* (*oh-mees-SYOH-neh*)

omit (to) omettere (*oh-MEHT-tehr-reh*)

opal opale *m.* (*oh-PAH-leh*)

opaque (adj.) opaco (*oh-PAH-koh*)

operate (*perform surgery*) (to) operare (*oh-pehr-RAHR-reh*)

operation (*surgical* OR *practical*), transaction operazione *f.* (*oh-pehr-rah-TSYOH-neh*)

operator operatore *m.* (*oh-pehr-rah-TOHR-reh*)

opinion, belief opinione *f.* (*oh-pee-NYOH-neh*)

oppose (to) opporre (*ohp-POHRR-reh*)

opposite opposto *m.* (*ohp-POH-stoh*) ⊃(adj.)↺

opposition opposizione *f.* (*ohp-poh-zee-TSYOH-neh*)

oppressed, downtrodden (adj.) oppresso (*ohp-PRES-soh*)

oppression oppressione *f.* (*ohp-prehs-SYOH-neh*)

oppressive (adj.) oppressivo (*ohp-prehs-SEE-voh*)

optician ottico *m*. (*OHT-tee-koh*) 🌢

optics ottica *f*. (*OHT-tee-kah*) ⊃**optic** (adj.) -co☾ 🌢

optimism ottimismo *m*. (*oht-tee-MEEZ-moh*) 🌢

optimistic (adj.) ottimistico (*oht-tee-MEE-stee-koh*)

option opzione *f*. (*ohp-TSYOH-neh*)

optometry optometria *f*. (*ohp-toh-meh-TRREE-ah*)

opulence, affluence opulenza *f*. (*ohp-oo-LEHN-tsah*)

opulent, affluent (adj.) opulento (*ohp-oo-LEHN-toh*)

oral (adj.) orale (*oh-RAH-leh*)

orange (*fruit*) arancia *f*. (*ahr-RAHN-chah*) 🌢

orange (*color*) (adj.) arancione (*ahr-rahn-CHOH-neh*) 🌢

oration orazione *f*. (*ohr-rah-TSYOH-neh*)

orator, speaker oratore *m*. (*ohr-rah-TOHR-reh*)

oratory oratoria *f*. (*ohr-rah-TOHR-ryah*)

orchestra orchestra *f*. (*ohr-KEH-strah*)

orchid orchidea *f*. (*ohr-kee-DEH-ah*)

ordeal ordalia *f*. (*ohr-DAH-lyah*), prova (*PROH-vah*)

order (to) ordinare (*ohr-dee-NAHR-reh*)

order (*command, neatness, OR sequence*) ordine *m*. (*OHR-dee-neh*)

orderly (adj.) ordinato (*ohr-dee-NAH-toh*)

ordinance ordinanza *f*. (*ohr-dee-NAHN-tsah*)

ordinary (adj.) ordinario (*ohr-dee-NAHR-ryoh*)

organ (*bodily OR musical*) organo *m*. (*OHR-gah-noh*)

organic (adj.) organico (*ohr-GAH-nee-koh*)

organist organista *m*. (*ohr-gah-NEE-stah*)

organization (*formal body*) organizzazione *f*. (*ohr-gah-neet-tsah-TSYOH-neh*)

organize (to) organizzare (*ohr-gah-neet-TSAHR-reh*)

orgasm orgasmo *m.* (*ohr-GAHZ-moh*)

orient (to) orientare (*ohrr-yehn-TAHR-reh*)

Orient, (the) East (*global region*) Oriente *m.* (*ohr-RYEHN-teh*)

Oriental, Eastern (*Asian*), **eastern** (*generally*) (adj.) orientale (*ohr-ryehn-TAH-leh*)

orientation orientazione *f.* (*ohrr-yehn-tah-TSYOH-neh*)

origin origine *f.* (*ohr-REE-jee-neh*)

original, novel (adj.) originale (*ohr-ree-jee-NAH-leh*)

originality originalità *f.* (*ohr-ree-jee-nah-lee-TAH*)

ornament ornamento *m.* (*ohr-nah-MEHN-toh*)

ornamental (adj.) ornamentale (*ohr-nah-mehn-TAH-leh*)

ornate (adj.) ornato (*ohr-NAH-toh*)

orthodox (adj.) ortodosso (*ohr-toh-DOHS-soh*)

orthopedic (adj.) ortopedico (*ohr-toh-PEH-dee-koh*)

oscillate, sway (to) oscillare (*oh-sheel-LAHR-reh*)

ostentatious (adj.) ostentato (*oh-stehn-TAH-toh*)

outrage oltraggio *m.* (*ohl-TRAHD-joh*)

outrageous (adj.) oltraggioso (*ohl-trahd-JOH-zoh*) 🌶

oval ovale *m.* (*oh-VAH-leh*) ➲(adj.)🄲

ovary ovaia *f.* (*oh-VAH-yah*)

ovation ovazione *f.* (*oh-vah-TSYOH-neh*)

oxygen ossigeno *m.* (*ohs-SEE-jeh-noh*) 🌶

—P—

pace passo *m.* (*PAHS-soh*) 🌶

Pacific Ocean Oceano Pacifico *m.* (*oh-cheh-AH-noh pah-CHEE-fee-koh*)

pacifier pacificatore *m.* (*pah-chee-fee-kah-TOHR-reh*)

pacifism pacifismo *m.* (*pah-chee-FEEZ-moh*)

pacifist pacifista *m.* (*pah-chee-FEE-stah*)

pack, packet, package, parcel pacco *m.* (*PAHK-koh*)

pact patto *m.* (*PAHT-toh*) ☙

pagan, heathen pagano *m.* (*pah-GAH-noh*) ⊃(adj.)C

page (*book leaf*) pagina *f.* (*PAH-jee-nah*)

page (*servant*) paggio *m.* (*PAHD-joh*)

pain pena *f.* (*PEH-nah*), dolore *m.* (*doh-LOHR-reh*)

pair paio *m.* (*PAH-yoh*)

pajamas pigiama *m.* (*pee-JAH-mah*)

palace, mansion palazzo *m.* (*pah-LAHT-tsoh*)

palace of justice, courthouse palazzo (*m.*) di giustizia (_____*dee joo-STEE-tsyah*)

pallid, pale, pasty (adj.) pallido (*PAHL-lee-doh*)

palm (*tree*) palma *f.* (*PAHL-mah*)

palm (*of hand*) palmo *m.* (*PAHL-moh*)

panorama panorama *m.* (*pah-noh-RAH-mah*)

pantomime pantomima *f.* (*pahn-toh-MEE-mah*)

pants pantaloni *m.* (*pahn-tah-LOH-nee*)

Papa, Pappa, Dad papà *m.* (*pah-PAH*), (*more familiarly*) babbo (*BAHB-boh*), (*most endearingly*) babbino (*bahb-BEE-noh*)

papal (adj.) papale (*pah-PAH-leh*)

par pari *f.* (*PAHR-ree*)

parade parata *f.* (*pahr-RAH-tah*), sfilata (*sfee-LAH-tah*)

paradise paradiso *m.* (*pahr-rah-DEE-soh*)

paradox paradosso *m.* (*pahr-rah-DOHS-soh*)

parallel parallelo *m.* (*pahr-rahl-LEH-loh*) ⊃(adj.)C

paralysis paralisi *f.* (*pahr-RAH-lee-zee*)

paralyze (to) paralizzare (*pahr-rah-leet-TSAHR-reh*)

paramedic paramedico *m.* (*pahr-rah-MEH-dee-koh*), assistente medico (*ahs-see-STEHN-teh MEH-dee-koh*)

paraphrase parafrasi *f.* (*pahr-RAH-frah-see*)

paraphrase (to) parafrasare (*pahr-rah-frah-ZAHR-reh*)

parasite parassita *m.* (*pahr-rahs-SEE-tah*)

parcel post pacco (*m.*) postale (*PAHK-koh poh-STAH-leh*)

pardon, forgiveness perdono *m.* (*pehr-DOH-noh*)

pardon, forgive (to) perdonare (*pehr-doh-NAHR-reh*)

park parco *m.* (*PAHR-koh*)

park (to) parcheggiare (*pahr-kehd-JAHR-reh*)

parliament parlamento *m.* (*pahr-lah-MEHN-toh*)

parochial (adj.) parrocchiale (*pahr-rrohk-KYAH-leh*)

part, leave, go away (to) partire (*pahr-TEER-reh*)

part, share parte *f.* (*PAHR-teh*)

partial (*incomplete OR favoring*) (adj.) parziale (*pahr-TSYAH-leh*)

partiality parzialità *f.* (*pahr-tsyah-lee-TAH*)

partially parzialmente (*pahr-tsyahl-MEHN-teh*)

participant partecipante *m.* (*pahr-teh-chee-PAHN-teh*)

participate (to) partecipare (*pahr-teh-chee-PAHR-reh*)

participation partecipazione *f.* (*pahr-teh-chee-pah-TSYOH-neh*)

particle particella *f.* (*pahr-tee-CHEL-lah*)

particular (*specific one*) (adj.) particolare (*pahr-tee-koh-LAHR-reh*)

partisan partigiano *m.* (*pahr-tee-JAH-noh*) ⊃(adj.)⊂

partly in parte (*een-PAHR-teh*)

party (*political, NOT social gathering or person*) partito *m.* (*pahr-TEE-toh*)

party (*social function, NOT person or political group*) party (*PAHR-tee*), festa *f.* (*FEH stah*)

pass (*permitting document*) passo *m.* (*PAHS-soh*)

pass (*overtake*) (to)   passare (*pahs-SAHR-reh*)

pass (*time*) (to)   passare (*pahs-SAHR-reh*)

pass (*go beyond, exeeed expectations*) (to)   oltrepassare (*ohl-treh-pahs-SAHR-reh*)

passable (*acceptable*) (adj.)   passabile (*pahs-SAH-bee-leh*)

passage (*movement*), **passageway, aisle**   passaggio *m.* (*pahs-SAHD-joh*)

   ⓘ Two closely related noncognates are: **walk, stroll**—passeggiata *f.* (*pahs-sehd-JAH-tah*); and **to walk**—passeggiare (*pahs-sehd-JAHR-reh*).

passenger   passeggero *m.* (*pahs-sehd-JEHR-roh*)

passerby   passante *m.* (*pahs-SAHN-teh*)

passion, hobby   passione *f.* (*pahs-SYOH-neh*)

passionate (adj.)   appassionato (*ahp-pahs-syoh-NAH-toh*) 🌶

passive (adj.)   passivo (*pahs-SEE-voh*)

passport   passaporto *m.* (*pahs-sah-POHR-toh*)

past   passato *m.* (*pahs-SAH-toh*) ⊃**past, bygone** (adj.)⊂

paste, pasta   pasta *f.* (*PAH-stah*)

pastime   passatempo *m.* (*pahs-sah-TEHM-poh*)

pastor, shepherd   pastore *m.* (*pah-STOHR-reh*)

patch   pezzo *m.* (*PEHT-tsoh*) 🌶

paternal, fatherly (adj.)   paterno (*pah-TEHR-noh*)

paternity, parentage, fatherhood   paternità *f.* (*pah-tehr-nee-TAH*)

pathetic (adj.)   patetico (*pah-TEH-tee-koh*)

pathology   patologia *f.* (*pah-toh-loh-JEE-ah*)

patience, forbearance   pazienza *f.* (*pah-TSYEHN-tsah*)

patient (*medical client*)   paziente *m. & f.* (*pah-TSYEHN-teh*)

patient (*calm, stoical, unexcited, and so forth*) (adj.)   paziente (*pah-TSYEHN-teh*)

patriot   patriota *m.* (*pah-tree-OH-tah*)
   ⓘ A related noncognate: **homeland, native land**—patria *f.* (*PAH-tryah*)

patriotic (adj.) patriottico (*pah-TRYOHT-tee-koh*)

patriotism patriottismo *m.* (*pah-tryoht-TEE-zmoh*)

patron patrono *m.* (*pah-TROH-noh*)

patronage patronato *m.* (*pah-troh-NAH-toh*)

pause pausa *f.* (*PAOW-sah*)

pave (to) pavimentare (*pah-vee-mehn-TAHR-reh*)

pavement, floor pavimento *m.* (*pah-vee-MEHN-toh*)

pavilion padiglione *m.* (*pah-dee-LYOH-neh*) 💣

PC (*personal computer*) PC *m.* (*PEE-ZEE*)
ⓘ This direct import is not yet ubiquitous in Italy, but is spreading fast!

peach (*fruit*) pesca *f.* (*PEH-skah*)
ⓘ A *pesca*—prounced with an open *e*—grows on a **peach tree**—pesco *m.* **Pesca**—pronounced with a closed *e*—means **fishing**. One fishes for *pesce*—**fish.** 💣

peak picco *m.* (*PEEK-koh*) 💣

pear (*fruit*) pera *f.* (*PEHR-rah*)
ⓘ A *pera* grows on a **pear tree**—pero *m.* (*PEHr-roh*).

pearl perla *f.* (*PEHR-lah*)

peculiar (*special*) (adj.) peculiare (*peh-koo-LYAHR-reh*)

peculiar (*odd, weird*) (adj.) strano (*STRAH-noh*)

peculiarity peculiarità *f.* (*peh-koo-lyahr-ree-TAH*)

pedestal piedestallo *m.* (*pyeh-deh-STAHL-loh*) 💣

pedestrian (*walker*) pedone *m.* (*peh-DOH-neh*)

pediatrician pediatra *m.* (*peh-DYAH-trah*)

peel (to) pelare (*peh-LAHR-reh*)

pen (*writing instrument*) penna *f.* (*PEHN-nah*)

penalty pena *f.* (*PEH-nah*)

pendant pendente *m.* (*pehn-DEHN-teh*)

pending (adj.) pendente (*pehn-DEHN-teh*)

penetrate (to)   penetrare (*peh-neh-TRAHR-reh*)

penetration (*physical or mental*), insight   penetrazione *f.* (*peh-neh-trah-TSYOH-neh*)

penicillin   penicillina *f.* (*peh-nee-cheel-LEE-nah*)

peninsula   penisola *f.* (*peh-NEE-zoh-lah*)

penitent   penitente *f.* (*peh-nee-TEHN-teh*) ⊃(adj.)C

pensive, thoughtful (adj.)   pensoso (*pehn-SOH-soh*)
   ⓘ Three related but noncognate terms are: **thought**—pensiero *m.* (*pehn-SYEHR-roh*); **to think**—pensare (*pehn-SAHR-reh*); and **thinker**—pensatore *m.* (*pehn-sah-TOHR-reh*).

people (the) (*civic or national populace*), **folk**   popolo *m.* (*POH-poh-loh*) 💧

people, persons, folks   gente *f.* (*JEHN-teh*)

pepper (*seasoning*)   pepe *m.* (*PEH-peh*)

pepper (*vegetable, NOT sausage*)   peperone *m.* (*peh-pehr-ROH-neh*)

per, for, through, by   per (*PEHR*)

percent   percento *m.* (*pehr-CHEN-toh*)

percentage, royalty (*fee*)   percentuale *f.* (*pehr-chehn-TWAH-leh*)

perception   percezione *f.* (*pehr-cheh-TSYOH-neh*)

perfect, flawless (adj.)   perfetto (*pehr-FEHT-toh*)

perfect (to)   perfezionare (*pehr-feh-tsyoh-NAHR-reh*)

perfectly, flawlessly   perfettamente (*pehr-feht-tah-MEHN-teh*)

perfection   perfezione *f.* (*pehr-feh-TSYOH-neh*)

performance   performance *m.* (*pehr-FOHR-mahn-seh*)

perfume   profumo *m.* (*proh-FOO-moh*) 💧

peril   pericolo *m.* (*pehr-REE-koh-loh*)

perilous (adj.)   pericoloso (*peh-ree-koh-LOH-soh*)

period (*of time OR term of duration*)   periodo *m.* (*pehr-REE-oh-doh*)

periodic, periodical (adj.)   periodico (*pehr-RYOH-dee-koh*)

periodical, magazine   periodico *m.* (*pehr-RYOH-dee-koh*)

periphery, outskirts periferia *f.* (*pehr-ree-fehr-REE-ah*)

permanent, ongoing, standing (adj.) permanente (*pehr-mah-NEHN-teh*)

permissible (adj.) permissibile (*pehr-mees-SEE-bee-leh*)

permission, permit (*documentary*) permesso *m.* (*pehr-MEHS-soh*)

permit, let, allow (to) permettere (*pehr-MEHT-tehr-reh*)

perpendicular (adj.) perpendicolare (*pehr-pehn-dee-koh-LAHR-reh*)

perpetrate (to) perpetrare (*pehr-peh-TRAHR-reh*)

perpetual (adj.) perpetuo (*pehr-PEH-twoh*)

perplexity, quandry perplessità *f.* (*pehr-plehs-see-TAH*)

perseverance perseveranza *f.* (*pehr-seh-vehr-RAHN-tsah*)

persevere (to) perseverare (*pehr-seh-vehr-RAHR-reh*)

persist (to) persistere (*pehr-SEE-stehr-reh*)

persistent (adj.) persistente (*pehr-see-STEHN-teh*)

person persona *f.* (*pehr-SOH-nah*)

personal (adj.) personale (*pehr-soh-NAH-leh*)

personality personalità *f.* (*pehr-soh-nah-lee-TAH*)

personally personalmente (*pehr-soh-nahl-MEHN-teh*)

personnel, staff personale *m.* (*pehr-soh-NAH-leh*), staff (*STAHF-feh*)

perspective prospettiva *f.* (*proh-speht-TEE-vah*) ✒

persuade (to) persuadere (*pehr-swah-DEHR-reh*)

persuasive (adj.) persuasivo (*pehr-swah-SEE-voh*)

pertinent, relevant (adj.) pertinente (*pehr-tee-NEHN-teh*)

perturb (to) perturbare (*pehr-toor-BAHR-reh*)

perverse (adj.) perverso (*pehr-VEHR-soh*)

perversion perversione *f.* (*pehr-vehr-ZYOH-neh*)

pervert (to) pervertire (*pehr-vehr-TEER-reh*)

pessimism pessimismo *m.* (*pehs-see-MEEZ-moh*)

pessimistic (adj.) pessimistico (*pehs-see-MEE-stee-koh*)

pest peste *f.* (*PEH-steh*)

petition petizione *f.* (*peh-tee-TSYOH-neh*)

petroleum petrolio *m.* (*peh-TROH-lyoh*)

petulant (adj.) petulante (*peh-too-LAHN-teh*)

pharmacist, druggist farmacista *m.* (*fahr-mah-CHEE-stah*) 🔊

pharmacy, drug store farmacia *f.* (*fahr-mah-CHEE-ah*) 🔊

phase, stage fase *f.* (*FAH-zeh*) 🔊

phenomenal (adj.) fenomenale (*feh-noh-meh-NAH-leh*) 🔊

phenomenon fenomeno *m.* (*feh-NOH-meh-noh*) 🔊

philanthropy filantropia *f.* (*fee-lanh-troh-PEE-ah*) 🔊

philosopher filosofo *m.* (*fee-LOH-soh-foh*) 🔊

philosophical (adj.) filosofico (*fee-loh-SOH-fee-koh*) 🔊

philosophy filosofia *f.* (*fee-loh-soh-FEE-ah*) 🔊

phobia fobia *f.* (*foh-BEE-ah*) 🔊

phonetic (adj.) fonetico (*foh-NEH-tee-koh*) 🔊

phonograph fonografo *m.* (*foh-NOH-grah-foh*) 🔊

photo, snapshot foto *f.* (*FOH-toh*), ____istantanea (____*ee-stahn-TAH-neh-ah*)

photocopier fotocopiatore *m.* (*foh-toh-koh-pyah-TOHR-reh*) 🔊

photocopy fotocopia *f.* (*foh-toh-KOH-pyah*) 🔊

photogenic (adj.) fotogenico (*foh-toh-JEH-nee-koh*) 🔊

photograph fotografia *f.* (*foh-toh-grah-FEE-ah*) 🔊

photograph (to) fotografare (*foh-toh-grah-FAHR-reh*) 🔊

photographer fotografo *m.* (*foh-TOH-grah-foh*) 🔊

photography fotografia *f.* (*foh-toh-grah-FEE-ah*) 🔊
  ⓘ It follows from the above: **camera**—macchina (*f.*) fotografica (*MAHK-kee-nah foh-toh-GRAH-fee-kah*). The word ***camera*** is widely known in Italy, however, and increasingly used by the Italians themselves.

phrase, sentence frase *f.* (*FRAH-zeh*) 🔊

physicist fisico *m.* (*FEE-zee-koh*)

physics fisica *f.* (*FEE-zee-kah*) ⊃(adj.) **physical** -co☾ ♦※

physiology fisiologia *f.* (*fee-zyoh-loh-JEE-ah*) ♦※

physiotherapy fisioterapia *f.* (*fee-zyoh-tehr-rah-PEE-ah*) ♦※

physique fisico *m.* (*FEE-zee-koh*) ♦※

pianist pianista *m.* (*pyah-NEE-stah*)

pickle (*trouble,* NOT *edible*) impiccio *m.* (*eem-PEET-choh*) ♦※

picnic picnic *m.* (*PEEK-neek*)

picture, painting pittura *f.* (*peet-TOOR-rah*)

picturesque (adj.) pittoresco (*pee-tohr-REH-skoh*) ♦※

piece pezzo *m.* (*PEHT-tsoh*) ♦※

pig, hog, swine porco *m.* (*POHR-koh*) ♦※
  ⓘ This Italian term is only "logically similar" to its English equivalent, rather
  than actually cognate. Still, it offers opportunity to treat two other related
  memory-trick words at the same time. If one will think of the filthy condi-
  tions in which most pigs live, it's easy to learn **dirty, soiled** (adj.)—sporco
  (*SPOHRR-koh*). [An even stronger connotation of **filthy, foul** (adj.) is
  given by *sudicio* (*SOO-dee-choh*)]. Similarly, albeit in a diametrically
  opposed manner, one can make a mental anticonnection between **clean**
  (adj.) and its Italian equivalent—pulito (*poo-LEE-toh*).

pigeon piccione *m.* (*peet-CHOH-neh*) ♦※

pilgrimage pellegrinaggio *m.* (*pehl-leh-gree-NAHD-joh*) ♦※

pill pillola *f.* (*PEEL-loh-lah*)

pilaster, pillar pilastro *m.* (*pee-LAH-stroh*)

pilot (*aviator* OR *nautical steersman*) pilota *m.* (*pee-LOH-tah*)

pilot (to) pilotare (*pee-loh-TAHR-reh*)

pine (*tree*) pino *m.* (*PEE-noh*)

pinnacle pinnacolo *m.* (*peen-NAH-koh-loh*)

pioneer pioniere *m.* (*pyoh-NYEHR-reh*)

pious (adj.) pio (*PEE-oh*)

pipe (*for tobacco*)   pipa *f.* (*PEE-pah*)

pipe (*for liquid or gas transport*)   tubo *m.* (*TOO-boh*)

pistol   pistola *f.* (*pee-STOH-lah*)

pitiful (adj.)   pietoso (*pyeh-TOH-soh*)

placate, appease (to)   placare (*plah-KAHR-reh*)

placid (adj.)   placido (*PLAH-chee-doh*)

plane (*level surface,* NOT *aircraft*)   piano *m.* (*PYAH-noh*) ♦※
   ① This term is used throughout Italy to indicate **floor level.**

plant (*flora*)   pianta *f.* (*PYAHN-tah*) ♦※

plant (to)   piantare (*pyahn-TAHR-reh*) ♦※

plasma   plasma *m.* (*PLAHZ-mah*)

plastic   plastica *f.* (*PLAH-stee-kah*) ⊃(adj.) -co℃

plate   piatto *m.* (*PYAHT-toh*) ♦※
   ① On an Italian menu, this term also denotes a meal's serving sequence, as in **first course**—primo piatto (*literally "first plate"*), and so forth. Two closely related noncognate terms are: **saucer**—piattino *m.* (*pyaht-TEE-noh*); and **platter**—piatto (*m.*) grande.

platform, dais   piattaforma *f.* (*pyaht-tah-FOHR-mah*) ♦※

platinum   platino *m.* (*PLAH-tee-noh*)

plausible (adj.)   plausibile (*plow-ZEE-bee-leh*)

plaza (*small*)   piazzetta *f.* (*pyaht-TSEHT-tah*), campo (*dialect*) *m.* (*KAHM-poh*)

plaza (*large*)   piazzale *f.* (*pyaht-TSAH-leh*) ♦※
   ① In Venice, curiously, the very large St. Mark's Square is NOT known as a *piazzale,* but rather simply as *Piazza San Marco.* And in Rome, the even larger *Piazza Navonna* also eschews the *-ale* designation.

plural   plurale *m.* (*ploor-RAH-leh*) ⊃(adj.)℃

pneumatic (adj.)   pneumatico (*pnehoo-MAH-tee-koh*) ♦※
   ① Also, an Italian (**vehicular**) **tire**—pneumatico *m.* (*pnehoo-MAH-tee-koh*)

pneumonia   pneumonia *f.* (*pnehoo-moh-NEE-ah*), polmonite (*pohl-moh-NEE-teh*) ♦※

poet poeta *m.* (*poh-EH-tah*) ➲*f.* -tessa☾

poetic (adj.) poetico (*poh-EH-tee-koh*)

poetry, poem poesia *f.* (*poh-eh-ZEE-ah*)

point, dot punto *m.* (*POON-toh*) ♠※

point (*tip* OR *sharp end*) punta *f.* (*POON-tah*) ♠※

pointed (adj.) a punta (*ah POON-tah*), acuto (*ah-KOO-toh*)

pole (*geographic* OR *electrical*) polo *m.* (*POH-loh*)

pole (*post*) palo *m.* (*PAH-loh*) ♠※

pole (*rod*) pertica *f.* (*pehr-TEE-kah*) ♠※

police polizia *f.* (*poh-LEE-tsyah*)

policeman, cop poliziotto *m.* (*poh-lee-tsee-OHT-toh*)

policy (*insurance*) polizza *f.* (*poh-LEET-tsah*)

policy (*official, political, governmental*) politica *f.* (*poh-LEE-tee-kah*)

political (adj.) politico (*poh-LEE-tee-koh*)

political science scienza (*f.*) politica (*SHEHN-tsah poh-LEE-tee-kah*)

politician politico *m.* (*poh-LEE-tee-koh*)

politics politica *f.* (*poh-LEE-tee-kah*)

pollen polline *m.* (*pohl-LEE-neh*)

pomp pompa *f.* (*POHM-pah*)

pompous (adj.) pomposo (*pohm-POH-soh*)

ponder (to) ponderare (*pohn-dehr-RAHR-reh*)

pontiff pontefice *m.* (*pohn-TEH-fee-cheh*)

pop (*music* OR *culture*) pop *m.* (*POHP*)

pope papa (*PAH-pah*)

populace popolo *m.* (*POH-poh-loh*)

popular (adj.) popolare (*poh-poh-LAHR-reh*)

popularity popolarità *f.* (*poh-poh-lahr-ree-TAH*)

population popolazione *f.* (*poh-poh-lah-TSYOH-neh*)

porcelain porcellana *f.* (*pohr-chel-LAH-nah*)

pore poro *m.* (*POHR-roh*)

pornography pornografia *f.* (*pohr-noh-grah-FEE-ah*)

porous (adj.) poroso (*pohr-ROH-soh*)

port, harbor, haven porto *m.* (*POHR-toh*)

portable (adj.) portatile (*pohr-TAH-tee-leh*)

portal portale *m.* (*pohr-TAH-leh*)
   ⓘ An important, related noncognate: **door, gate, gateway**—porta *f.*
   (*POHR-tah*)

porter portiere *m.* (pohr-TYEHR-reh)
   ⓘ This word applies to "high-status" luggage carriers, such as are
   employed in hotels. A baggage handler who serves a more general clientele at railway stations, airports, and bus terminals is generally referred
   to as a *portabagagli* (*pohr-tah-bah-GAH-lyee*) or *facchino* (*fahk-KEE-
   noh*). The latter will never object to being referred to as *un portiere*, but
   the reverse is not the case!

portfolio portafoglio *m.* (*pohr-tah-FOH-lyoh*)

portico, porch (*of church or public building*) portico *f.* (*POHR-tee-koh*)

   ⓘ ALSO SEE **veranda**.

portion porzione *f.* (*pohr-TSYOH-neh*)

pose posa *f.* (*POH-sah*)

pose (to) posare (*poh-SAHR-reh*)

position, stand, stance posizione *f.* (*poh-zee-TSYOH-neh*)

positive (adj.) positivo (*poh-see-TEE-voh*)

possess, own (to) possedere (*pohs-seh-DEHR-reh*)
   ⓘ The related noncognate adjective: **own** (adj.)—proprio (*PROH-pree-oh*)

possession possessione *f.* (*pohs-sehs-SYOH-neh*)

possessive (adj.) possessivo (*pohs-sehs-SEE-voh*)

possessor, owner possessore *m.* (*pohs-sehs-SOHR-reh*)

possibility possibilità *f.* (*pohs-see-bee-lee-TAH*)

possible (adj.) possibile (*pohs-SEE-bee-leh*)
 ⓘ The important question of situational possibility, as expressed by the terms **May I?** (**have, do,** and so forth) and **Can I?**, in Italian is expressed by *Posso* (*POHS-soh*)?

possibly possibilmente (*pohs-see-beel-MEHN-teh*)

post (*place or position,* NOT *pole*) posto *m.* (*POH-stoh*)

post, mail, postal service, postal system posta *f.* (*POH-stah*)

post (*send by mail*) (to) impostare (*eem-poh-STAHR-reh*) 👈

post office ufficio postale *m.* (*oof-FEE-choh poh-STAH-leh*)

postal (adj.) postale (*poh-STAH-leh*)

posterior (adj.) posteriore (*poh-stehr-RYOHR-reh*)

posterity posterità *f.* (*poh-stehr-ree-TAH*)

postpone (to) posporre (*poh-SPOHRR-reh*) 👈

postscript poscritto *m.* (*poh-SKREET-toh*)

potato patata *f.* (*pah-TAH-tah*) 👈

potent, mighty (adj.) potente (*poh-TEHN-teh*)

potential potenziale *m.* (*poh-tehn-TSYAH-leh*) ⊃(adj.)C

potion pozione *f.* (*poh-TSYOH-neh*)

poverty povertà *f.* (*poh-vehr-TAH*)

poverty-stricken, impoverished, poor (adj.) povero (*POH-vehr-roh*)

practicable, passable (*unobstructed*) praticabile (*prah-tee-KAH-bee-leh*)

practical, hardheaded (adj.) pratico (*PRAH-tee-koh*)

practically praticamente (*prah-tee-kah-MEHN-teh*)

practice pratica *f.* (*PRAH-tee-kah*)

practice, put into practice (to) praticare (*prah-tee-KAHR-reh*)

pragmatic (adj.) pragmatico (*prahg-MAH-tee-koh*)

precarious (adj.) precario (*preh-KAHR-ryoh*)

precaution precauzione *f.* (*preh-kow-TSYOH-neh*)

precede, outrank (to) precedere (*preh-CHEH-dehr-reh*)

precedence precedenza *f.* (*preh-cheh-DEHN-tsah*)

precedent precedente *m.* (*preh-cheh-DEHN-teh*)

precept precetto *m.* (*preh-CHEHT-toh*)

precinct precinto *m.* (*preh-CHEEN-toh*)

precious (adj.) prezioso (*preh-TSYOH-soh*)

precise (adj.) preciso (*preh-CHEE-zoh*)

precision precisione *f.* (*preh-chee-ZYOH-neh*)

preclude (to) precludere (*preh-KLOO-dehr-reh*)

precursor, harbinger precursore *m.* (*preh-koor-SOHR-reh*)

predatory (adj.) predatorio (*preh-dah-TOHR-ryoh*)

predecessor predecessore *m.* (*preh-deh-ches-SOHR-reh*)

predict, foretell (to) predire (*preh-DEER-reh*)

predilection predilezione *f.* (*preh-dee-leh-TSYOH-neh*)

predispose (to) predisporre (*preh-dee-SPOHRR-reh*)

predisposition predisposizione *f.* (*preh-dee-spoh-seet-TSYOH-neh*)

predominant (adj.) predominante (*preh-doh-mee-NAHNT-teh*)

prefer (to) preferire (*preh-fehr-REER-reh*)

preferable (adj.) preferibile (*preh-fehr-REE-bee-leh*)

preference preferenza *f.* (*preh-fehr-REHN-tsah*)

prejudice pregiudizio *m.* (*preh-joo-DEE-tsyoh*)

prejudiced (adj.) pregiudicato (*preh-joo-dee-KAH-toh*)

preliminary (adj.) preliminare (*preh-lee-mee-NAHR-reh*)

premature (adj.) prematuro (*preh-mah-TOOR-roh*)

premiere prima *f.* (*PREE-mah*) 🔊

premise premessa *f.* (*preh-MEHS-sah*)

premium, bonus, prize premio *m.* (*PREH-myoh*)

premonition premonizione *f.* (*preh-moh-nee-TSYOH-neh*)

preoccupation, worry preoccupazione *f.* (*preh-ohk-koo-pah-TSYOH-neh*)

preoccupied, worried, anxious (adj.) preoccupato (*preh-ohk-koo-PAH-toh*)

(be) preoccupied, worried about (to) preoccuparsi di (*preh-ohk-koo-PAHR-see dee*)

preoccupy, worry (to) preoccupare (*preh-ohk-koo-PAH-reh*)

preparation preparazione *f.* (*preh-pahr-rah-TSYOH-neh*)

prepare (to) preparare (*preh-pahr-RAHR-reh*)

prerequisite requisito *m.* (*reh-KWEE-see-toh*)

prescribe (to) prescrivere (*preh-SKREE-vehr-reh*)

prescription prescrizione *f.* (*preh-skree-TSYOH-neh*)

presence presenza *f.* (*preh-ZEHN-tsah*)

present (adj.) presente (*preh-ZEHN-teh*), attuale (*aht-too-AH-leh*), corrente (*kohr-REHN-teh*)

   ⓘ **To be present**—essere presente (*EHS-seh-reh preh-ZEHN-teh*); and to say *Here!* in reply to a roll call—Presente!

present (*time*) presente *m.* (*preh-ZEHN-teh*)

presentable (adj.) presentabile (*preh-zehn-TAH-bee-leh*)

presentation (*personal introduction*) presentazione *f.* (*preh-zehn-tah-TSYOH-neh*)

present to (*introduce, make acquainted*) (to) presentare a (*preh-zehn-TAHR-reh ah*)

   ⓘ In Italian, the related concept: **to present (*someone*) with (*a gift, honor, award, and so forth*)** utilizes the very noncognate verb—regalare (*reh-gah-LAHR-reh*); a **present (*gift*)**—regalo *m.* (*reh-GAH-loh*).

preserve (to) preservare (*preh-sehr-VAHR-reh*)

presidency presidenza *f.* (*preh-zee-DEHN-tsah*)

president, presiding official, speaker presidente *m.* & *f.* (*preh-see-DEHN-teh*)

press pressa *f.* (*PREHS-sah*), stampa *f.* (*journalists, publishers*) (*STAHM-pah*)

pressure pressione *f.* (*pres-SYOH-neh*)

prestige prestigio *m.* (*preh-STEE-joh*)

presumption presunzione *f.* (*preh-zoon-TSYOH-neh*)

pretend (*falsely claim*, NOT *fantasize*) (to) pretendere (*preh-TEHN-dehr-reh*)

pretension pretesa *f.* (*preh-TEH-sah*)

pretentious (adj.) pretensioso (*preh-tehn-SYOH-soh*)

pretext pretesto *m.* (*preh-TEH-stoh*)

prevail (to) prevalere (*preh-vah-LEHR-reh*)

prevalent (adj.) prevalente (*preh-vah-LEHN-teh*)

prevention, deterrence prevenzione *f.* (*preh-vehn-TSYOH-neh*), preventivo *m.* (*preh-vehn-TEE-voh*)

price prezzo *m.* (*PREHT-tsoh*) ♦⋯

   ⓘ To express that something is, or was, "cheap" without implying shoddiness—**A buon prezzo!**

priest prete *m.* (*PREH-teh*) ♦⋯

primary (adj.) primario (*pree-MAHR-ryoh*)

primate primate *m.* (*pree-MAH-teh*)

prime, first (adj.) primo (*PREE-moh*)

prime minister primo ministro *m.* (*PREE-moh-mee-NEE-stroh*)

primitive (adj.) primitivo (*pree-mee-TEE-voh*)

prince principe *m.* (*PREEN-chee-peh*)

princess principessa *f.* (*preen-chee-PEHS-sah*)

principal, chief, main (adj.) principale (*preen-chee-PAH-leh*)

principally, primarily, chiefly, mainly principalmente (*preen-chee-pahl-MEHN-teh*)

principle (*fundamental truth* OR *ethical precept*) principio *m.* (*preen-CHEE-pyoh*)

priority priorità *f.* (*pree-ohr-ree-TAH*)

prison, jail prigione *f.* (*pree-JOH-neh*)

prisoner, captive prigioniero *m. (pree-joh-NYEHR-roh)*

private (adj.) privato *(pree-VAH-toh)*

privilege privilegio *m. (pree-vee-LEH-joh)*

probability, likelihood, odds probabilità *f. (proh-bah-bee-lee-TAH)*

probable, likely (adj.) probabile *(proh-bah-BEE-leh)*

problem problema *m. (proh-BLEH-mah)*

procedure procedimento *m. (proh-cheh-dee-MEHN-toh)*

proceed (to) procedere *(proh-CHEH-dehr-reh)*

process processo *m. (proh-CHES-soh)*

proclamation proclamazione *f. (proh-kla-mah-TSYOH-neh)*

procrastinate (to) procrastinare *(proh-krah-stee-NAHR-reh)*

procrastination procrastinazione *f. (proh-krah-stee-nah-TSYOH-neh)*

prodigious, prodigal, lavish (adj.) prodigo *(PROH-dee-goh)*

prodigy prodigio *m. (proh-DEE-joh)*

product prodotto *m. (proh-DOHT-toh)*

production, output, yield produzione *f. (proh-doo-TSYOH-neh)*

productive (adj.) produttivo *(proh-doot-TEE-voh)*

profane (adj.) profano *(proh-FAH-noh)*

profane (to) profanare *(proh-fah-NAHR-reh)*

profession professione *f. (proh-fehs-see-OH-neh)*

professional (adj.) professionale *(proh-fehs-syoh-NAH-leh)* ➲professionista
m. (proh-fehs-syoh-nee-stah)➾

professor professore *m. (proh-fehs-SOHR-reh)*

profile profilo *m. (proh-FEE-loh)*

profit profitto *m. (proh-FEET-toh)*

profit (to) approfittare *(ahp-proh-feet-TAHR-reh)* ☛

profitable (adj.) profittevole *(proh-feet-TEH-voh-leh)*

profound, deep (adj.) profondo *(proh-FOHN-doh)*

profoundly, deeply profondamente (*proh-fohn-dah-MEHN-teh*)

profundity, depth profondità *f.* (*proh-fohn-dee-TAH*)

prognosis prognosi *f.* (*proh-NYOH-zee*)

prognosticate, forecast (to) pronosticare (*proh-noh-stee-KAHR-reh*)

prognoticator, forecaster pronosticatore *m.* (*proh-noh-stee-kah-TOHR-reh*)

program programma *m.* (*pro-GRAHM-mah*)

progress, headway progresso *m.* (*proh-GREHS-soh*)

progressive (adj.) progressivo (*proh-grehs-SEE-voh*)

prohibit, forbid, ban (to) proibire (*proh-EE-beer-reh*)

prohibited, forbidden, banned (adj.) proibito (*proh-ee-BEE-toh*)

prohibition, ban proibizione *f.* (*proh-ee-bee-TSYOH-neh*)

prohibitive (adj.) proibitivo (*proh-ee-bee-TEE-voh*)

project, plan, scheme progetto *m.* (*proh-JEHT-toh*)

project (*plan OR envision*) (to) progettare (*proh-jeht-TAHR-reh*)

projection proiezione *f.* (*proh-yeh-TSYOH-neh*) 💣※

prolific (adj.) prolifico (*proh-LEE-fee-koh*)

prolong (to) prolungare (*proh-loon-GAHR-reh*)

prominent (adj.) prominente (*proh-mee-NEHN-teh*)

promise promessa *f.* (*proh-MEHS-sah*)

promise (to) promettere (*proh-MEHT-tehr-reh*)

promote (to) promuovere (*proh-MWOH-vehr-reh*)

promotion (*advance, NOT ad campaign*) promozione *f.* (*proh-moh-TSYOH-neh*)

promptly, readily prontamente (*prohn-tah-MEHN-teh*)

pronounce (to) pronunziare (*proh-noon-TSYAHR-reh*)
   ⓘ The antonym: **to mispronounce**—pronunziar male (*pro-noon-TSYAHR MAH-leh*)

pronunciation pronuncia *f.* (*proh-NOON-chah*)

proof prova *f.* (*PROH-vah*)

propensity propensione *f.* (*proh-pehn-SYOH-neh*)

proper (adj.) proprio (*PROH-pryoh*)

property proprietà *f.* (*proh-pryeh-TAH*)

prophecy profezia *f.* (*proh-feh-TSEE-ah*)

prophesy (to) profetizzare (*proh-feh-teehd-DZAHR-reh*)

prophet profeta *m.* (*proh-FEH-tah*)

prophetic (adj.) profetico (*proh-FEH-tee-koh*)

proponent proponente *m.* (*proh-poh-NEHN-teh*)

proportion proporzione *f.* (*proh-pohr-TSYOH-neh*)

proportionate (adj.) proporzionato (*proh-pohr-tsyoh-NAH-toh*)

proposal, proposition proposta *f.* (*proh-POH-stah*)

propose (to) proporre (*proh-POHRR-reh*)

proprietor proprietario *m.* (*proh-pryeh-TAHR-ryoh*)

prose prosa *f.* (*PROH-zah*)

prospect (*thing or condition expected*) prospetto *m.* (*proh-SPEHT-toh*)

prospective (adj.) prospettivo (*proh-speht-TEE-voh*)

prosper, thrive (to) prosperare (*proh-spehr-RAHR-reh*)

prosperity prosperità *f.* (*proh-spehr-ree-TAH*)

prosperous (adj.) prospero (*PROH-spehr-roh*)

prostitute prostituta *f.* (*proh-stee-TOO-tah*)

protection protezione *f.* (*proh-teh-TSYOH-neh*)

protective (adj.) protettivo (*proh-teht-TEE-voh*)

protector protettore *m.* (*proh-teht-TOHR-reh*)

protein proteina *f.* (*proh-teh-EE-nah*)

protest protesta *f.* (*proh-TEH-stah*)

protest (to) protestare (*proh-teh-STAHR-reh*)

Protestant protestante *m. & f.* (*proh-teh-STAHN-teh*) ⊃(adj.)℃

protocol protocollo *m.* (*proh-toh-KOHL-loh*)

protracted (adj.) protratto (*proh-TRAHT-toh*)

protuberance, bulge protuberanza *f.* (*proh-too-behr-RAHN-tsah*)

prove (to) provare (*proh-VAHR-reh*)

proverb, saying proverbio *m.* (*proh-VEHR-byoh*)

proverbial (adj.) proverbiale (*proh-vehr-BYAH-leh*)

provide, supply (to) provvedere (*prohv-veh-DEHR-reh*)

providence provvidenza *f.* (*prohv-vee-DEHN-tsah*)

province (*geographic political unit*) provincia *f.* (*proh-VEEN-chah*)

provincial (adj.) provinciale (*proh-veen-CHAH-leh*)

provision(s), stock (of), store (of), supply (of) provvista *f.* (*prohv-VEE-stah*)

provisory, provisional, temporary (adj.) provvisorio (*prohv-vee-ZOHR-ryoh*)

provocation provocazione *f.* (*proh-voh-kah-TSYOH-neh*)

proximity, (physical) closeness, nearness prossimità *f.* (*prohs-see-mee-TAH*)

prudence prudenza *f.* (*proo-DEHN-tsah*) ➲**prudent** (adj.) -nte☾

psalm salmo *m.* (*SAHL-moh*) ☛

psychedelic (adj.) psichedelico (*psee-keh-DEHL-lee-koh*)

psychiatrist psichiatra *m.* (*psee-KYAH-trah*)

psychiatry psichiatria *m.* (*psee-kyah-TREE-ah*)

psychoanalysis psicoanalisi *f.* (*psee-koh-ah-NAH-lee-zee*)

psychological (adj.) psicologico (*psee-koh-LOH-jee-koh*)

psychology psicologia *f.* (*psee-koh-loh-JEE-ah*)

psychosis psicosi *f.* (*psee-KOH-zee*)

ptomaine ptomaina *f.* (*ptoh-mah-EE-nah*)

public pubblico *m.* (*POOB-blee-koh*) ➲(adj.)☾

publication pubblicazione *f.* (*poob-blee-kah-TSYOH-neh*)

publicity pubblicità *f.* (*poob-blee-chee-TAH*)

publish (to) pubblicare (*poob-blee-KAHR-reh*)

pugilism, boxing pugilato *m.* (*poo-jee-LAH-toh*)

pugilist, boxer pugilatore *m.* (*poo-jee-lah-TOHR-reh*)

pullover (*sweater*) pullover *m.* (*pool-OH-vehr-reh*)

pulmonary (adj.) polmonare (*pohl-moh-NAHR-reh*) ♦⁂
  ① An important, related noncognate: **pneumonia**—polmonite *f.* (*pohl-moh-NEE-teh*)

pulpit pulpito *m.* (*POOL-pee-toh*)

pulsate (to) pulsare (*pool-SAHR-reh*)

pulse, wrist polso *m.* (*POHL-soh*) ♦⁂

pump pompa *f.* (*POHM-pah*) ♦⁂

pump (to) pompare (*pohm-PAHR-reh*) ♦⁂

punctual, prompt (adj.) puntuale (*poon-TWAH-leh*)

punctually, promptly puntualmente (*poon-twahl-MEHN-teh*)

puncture puntura *f.* (*poon-TOOR-rah*)

pungent (adj.) pungente (*poon-JEHN-teh*)

punishment punizione *f.* (*poo-nee-TSYOH-neh*)

punitive (adj.) punitivo (*poo-nee-TEE-voh*)

pupil (*of eye*) pupilla *f.* (*poo-PEEL-lah*)

pure (adj.) puro (*POOR-roh*)

purge (to) purgare (*poor-GAHR-reh*)

purify (to) purificare (*poo-ree-fee-KAHR-reh*)

puritanical (adj.) da puritano (*dah poor-ree-TAH-noh*)

purity purità *f.* (*poor-ree-TAH*)

putrefaction, putrefication, rot putrefazione *f.* (*poo-treh-fah-TSYOH-neh*)

putrid, rotten (adj.)   putrido (*POO-tree-doh*)

pyramid   piramide *f.* (*peer-RAH-mee-deh*) 💣

—Q—

quadrangle   quadrangolo *m.* (*kwah-DRAHN-goh-loh*)

ⓘ Closely related noncognates are: **square (*geometric figure*)**—quadrato *m.* (*kwah-DRAH-toh*); **square (*equilaterally four-sided*)** (adj.)—quadrato (*kwah-DRAH-toh*); **to square (*mathematical operation*)**—quadrare (*kwah-DRAHR-reh*); and **quadraphonic** (adj.)—quadrafonico (*kwah-drah-FOH-nee-koh*).

qualification (adj.)   qualificazione (*kwah-lee-fee-kah-TSYOH-neh*)

qualify (to)   qualificare (*kwah-lee-fee-KAHR-reh*)

quality   qualità *f.* (*kwah-lee-TAH*)

quantity, amount, sum   quantità *f.* (*kwahn-tee-TAH*), somma (*SOHM-mah*)

quarter (*one fourth*)   quarto *m.* (*KWAHR-toh*)

quarter (*region OR mercy*)   quartiere *m.* (*kwahr-TYEHR-reh*)

quarter (*of year*)   trimestre *m.* (*tree-MEH-streh*)

quartet   quartetto *m.* (*kwahr-TEHT-toh*)

quartz   quarzo *m.* (*KWAHR-tsoh*)

question (*inquiry*)   questione *f.* (*kweh-STYOH-neh*), domanda (*doh-MAHN-dah*) 💣

questionnaire   questionario *m.* (*kweh-styoh-NAHR-ryoh*)

quiet (*silence OR stillness*)   quiete *f.* (*kwee-EH-teh*)

quiet (*without motion*) (adj.)   quieto (*kwee-EH-toh*)

quintet   quintetto *m.* (*kween-TEHT-toh*)

quota   quota *f.* (*KWOH-tah*)

quotation (*price*)   quotazione *f.* (*kwoh-tah-TSYOH-neh*)

—R—

rabbi rabino *m.* (*rah-BEE-noh*)

radial (adj.) radiale (*rah-DYAH-leh*)

radiant (adj.) radiante (*rah-DYAHN-teh*), raggiante (*rahd-JAHN-teh*) ✒

radiate (to) irradiare (*eer-rrah-DYAHR-reh*) ✒

radiation radiazione *f.* (*rah-dyah-TSYOH-neh*)

radiator radiatore *m.* (*rah-dyah-TOHR-reh*)

radical (*political*) radicale *m.* (*rah-dee-KAH-leh*) ⊃(adj.)C

radio, radium radio *f.* (*RAH-dyoh*)

radio (adj.) radiofonico (*rah-dyoh-FOHN-nee-koh*)

radioactive (adj.) radioattivo (*rah-dyoh-aht-TEE-voh*)

radioactivity radioattività *f.* (*rah-dyoh-aht-tee-vee-TAH*)

radius raggio *m.* (*RAHD-joh*) ✒

rancid (adj.) rancido (*rahn-CHEE-doh*)

rank rango *m.* (*RAHN-goh*)

rapid, fast, speedy, quick (adj.) rapido (*RAH-pee-doh*), presto (*PREH-stoh*)

rapidly, quickly rapidamente (*rah-pee-dah-MEHN-teh*)

rare (adj.) raro (*RAHR-roh*)

rarely, seldom raramente (*rahr-rah-MEHN-teh*)

rat ratto *m.* (*RAHT-toh*)

ratify (to) ratificare (*rah-tee-fee-KAHR-reh*)

ration razione *f.* (*rah-TSYOH-neh*) ✒

ration (to) razionare (*rah-tsyoh-NAHR-reh*) ✒

rational (adj.) razionale (*rah-tsyoh-NAH-leh*) ✒

rayon raion *or* rayon *m.* (*RAH-yohn*) ✒

razor rasoio *m.* (*rah-ZOH-yoh*) ✒

react (to)   reagire (*reh-AHD-jeer-reh*)

reaction   reazione *f.* (*reh-ah-TSYOH-neh*)

reactionary   reazionario *m.* (*reh-ah-tsyoh-NAHR-ryoh*) ➲(adj.)Ç

reactor   reattore *m.* (*reh-aht-TOHR-reh*)

real (adj.)   reale (*reh-AH-leh*)

realist   realista *m.* (*reh-ah-LEE-stah*)

reality   realtà *f.* (*reh-ahl-TAH*)

realization   realizzazione *f.* (*reh-ah-leed-dzah-TSYOH-neh*)

realize (*make real, NOT become aware*) (to)   realizzare (*reh-ah-leed-DZAHR-reh*)

really   realmente (*reh-ahl-MEHN-teh*), in realtà (*een reh-ahl-TAH*), veramente (*veh-rah-MEHN-teh*)

realm   reame *m.* (*reh-AH-meh*) ♦※

reason   ragione *f.* (*rah-JOH-neh*) ♦※

reason (to)   ragionare (*rah-joh-NAHR-reh*) ♦※

reasonable (adj.)   ragionevole (*rah-joh-NEH-voh-leh*) ♦※

reassure (to)   rassicurare (*rahs-see-koor-RAHR-reh*) ♦※

rebel   ribelle *m.* (*ree-BEHL-leh*) ➲rebellious (adj.)Ç ♦※

rebel (to)   ribellarsi (*ree-behl-LAHR-see*) ♦※

rebellion   ribellione *f.* (*ree-behl-LYOH-neh*) ♦※

recapitulate (to)   ricapitolare (*ree-kah-peet-toh-LAHR-reh*) ♦※

recede (to)   recedere (*reh-CHEH-dehr-reh*)

receive, get (*passively, by others' actions*), **host** (to)   ricevere (*ree-CHEH-vehr-reh*) ♦※

receiver   ricevitore *m.* (*ree-cheh-vee-TOHR-reh*) ♦※

recent (adj.)   recente (*reh-CHEN-teh*)

recently, lately   recentemente (*reh-chen-teh-MEHN-teh*)

receptacle   ricettacolo *m.* (*ree-cheht-TAH-koh-loh*) ♦※

receptive (adj.)   ricettivo (*ree-cheht-TEE-voh*) ♦※

recipient ricevente *m.* (*ree-cheh-VEHN-teh*) 👆

recitation recitazione *f.* (*reh-chee-tah-TSYOH-neh*)

recite (to) recitare (*reh-chee-TAHR-reh*)

recline (to) reclinare (*reh-klee-NAHR-reh*)

recognition riconoscimento *m.* (*reeh-koh-noh-shee-MEHN-toh*)

recognize (to) riconoscere (*reeh-koh-NOH-shehr-reh*)

recommend (to) raccomandare (*rahk-koh-mahn-DAHR-reh*) 👆

recommendation raccomandazione *f.* (*rahk-koh-mahn-dah-TSYOH-neh*) 👆

recompense, reward ricompensa *f.* (*ree-kohm-PEHN-sah*) 👆

recompense, reward (to) ricompensare (*ree-kohm-pehn-SAHR-reh*)

reconcile (to) riconciliare (*ree-kohn-cheel-YAHR-reh*) 👆

reconstruct, rebuild (to) ricostruire (*ree-koh-stroo-EER-reh*) 👆

record (*written account*) ricordo *m.* (*ree-KOHR-doh*) 👆

record (*phonographic*) disco *m.* (*DEE-skoh*)

recount (*narrative*) racconto *m.* (*rahk-KOHN-toh*) 👆

recount, tell, tell about (to) raccontare (*rahk-kohn-TAHR-reh*) 👆

recourse ricorso *m.* (*ree-KOHR-soh*) 👆

rectangle rettangolo *m.* (*reht-TAHN-goh-loh*) 👆

rectify (to) rettificare (*reht-tee-fee-KAHR-reh*) 👆

recuperate, recover (to) ricuperare (*ree-koo-pehr-RAHR-reh*) 👆

recuperation, recovery ricupero *m.* (*ree-KOO-pehr-roh*)

recur (to) ricorrere (*ree-KOHRR-reh-reh*) 👆

recycle (to) riciclare (*ree-chee-KLAHR-re*h) 👆

red (adj.) rosso (*ROHS-soh*) 👆

ⓘ **pink** (adj.)—rosa (*ROH-zah*)

redeem (to) redimere (*reh-DEE-mehr-reh*)

redeemer redentore *m.* (*reh-dehn-TOHR-reh*)

redemption   redenzione *f.* (*reh-dehn-TSYOH-neh*)

reduce (to)   ridurre (*ree-DOOHRR-reh*) 🔊

reduction   riduzione *f.* (*ree-doo-TSYOH-neh*) 🔊

refer (to)   riferire (*ree-feh-REER-reh*) 🔊

refine (to)   raffinare (*rahf-fee-NAHR-reh*) 🔊

refinement   raffinatezza *f.* (*rahf-fee-nah-TEHT-tsah*) 🔊

reflect, think about (to)   riflettere (*ree-FLEHT-tehr-reh*) 🔊

reflection (*in or by mirror or water*)   riflessione *f.* (*ree-flehs-SYOH-neh*) 🔊

reflex   riflesso *m.* (*ree-FLEHS-soh*) 🔊

reform, reformation   riforma *f.* (*ree-FOHR-mah*) 🔊

reform (to)   riformare (*ree-fohr-MAHR-reh*) 🔊

refresh (to)   rinfrescare (*reen-freh-SKAHR-reh*) 🔊

refreshments   rinfreschi *m.* (*reen-FREH-skee*) 🔊

refrigerator, freezer   frigorifero *m.* (*free-goh-REE-fehr-roh*)

refuge   rifugio *m.* (*ree-FOO-joh*) 🔊

(take) refuge (to)   rifugiarsi (*ree-foo-JAHR-see*) 🔊

refugee   rifugiato *m.* (*ree-foo-JAH-toh*) 🔊

refusal   rifiuto *m.* (*ree-FYOO-toh*) 🔊

refuse (to)   rifiutare (*ree-fyoo-TAHR-reh*) 🔊

refuse (*waste material*)   rifiuti *m.* (*ree-FYOO-tee*) 🔊

regal (adj.)   regale (*reh-GAH-leh*)

regality, royalty   regalità *f.* (*reh-gah-lee-TAH*)

regent   reggente *m.* (*rehd-JEHN-teh*)
  ⓘ Related noncognates: **king**—re *m.* (*REH*) and **queen**—regina *f.* (*reh-JEE-nah*)

regard   riguardo *m.* (*ree-GWAHR-doh*) 🔊

regarding (adj.)   riguardo a (*ree-GWAHR-doh ah*) 🔊

regime   regime *m.* (*reh-JEE-meh*)

regiment reggimento *m.* (*rehd-jee-MEHN-toh*)

region regione *f.* (*reh-JOH-neh*)

register registro *m.* (*reh-JEE-stroh*)

register, enroll, record (to) registrare (*reh-jee-STRAHR-reh*)

registration, enrollment registrazione *f.* (*reh-jee-strah-TSYOH-neh*)

registry, records registri *m.* (*reh-JEE-stree*)

regularity regolarità *f.* (*reh-goh-lahr-ree-TAH*)

regulate (to) regolare (*reh-goh-LAHR-reh*) ⊃**regular** (adj.)⊂ ♦✲

regulation regolamento *m.* (*reh-goh-lah-MEHN-toh*)

regulator regolatore *m.* (*reh-goh-lah-TOHR-reh*)

rehabilitate (to) riabilitare (*ree-ah-bee-lee-TAHR-reh*)

reign regno *m.* (*REH-nyoh*) ♦✲

reign (to) regnare (*reh-NYAHR-reh*) ♦✲

reimburse, repay (to) rimborsare (*reem-bohr-SAHR-reh*) ♦✲

reimbursement rimborso *m.* (*reem-BOHR-soh*) ♦✲

reincarnation reincarnazione (*reh-een-kahr-nah-TSYOH-neh*)

reinforce (to) rinforzare (*reen-fohr-TSAHR-reh*) ♦✲
　ⓘ An important, related noncognate is: **to strengthen**—rafforzare (*rahf-fohr-TSAHR-reh*).

reinforcement rinforzo *m.* (*reen-FOHR-tsoh*) ♦✲

reiterate (to) reiterare (*reh-ee-teh-RAHR-reh*)

reject (to) rigettare (*ree-jeht-TAHR-reh*) ♦✲

rejuvenate (to) ringiovanire (*reen-joh-vah-NEER-reh*) ♦✲

relation relazione *f.* (*reh-lah-TSYOH-neh*)

relations (*dealings with*) relazioni *f.* (*reh-lah-TSYOH-nee*)

relative (*connected with, compared to*) (adj.) relativo (*reh-lah-TEE-voh*)

relativism relativismo *m.* (*reh-lah-tee-VEEZ-moh*)

relativity relatività *f.* (*reh-lah-tee-vee-TAH*)

release (to)   rilasciare (*ree-lah-SHAHR-re*h) 👆

relevant, germane (adj.)   rilevante (*ree-leh-VAHN-teh*) 👆

relic (*of religious nature*)   reliquia *f.* (*reh-LEE-kwee-ah*)

religion   religione *f.* (*reh-lee-JOH-neh*) ➲**religious** (adj.) -gioso◖

reluctance   riluttanza *f.* (*ree-loot-TAHN-tsah*) 👆

reluctant (adj.)   riluttante (*ree-loot-TAHN-teh*) 👆

remain (to)   rimanere (*ree-mah-NEHR-reh*) 👆

remedy   rimedio *m.* (*ree-MEH-dyoh*) 👆

reminiscence   reminiscenza *f.* (*reh-mee-nee-SHEN-tsah*)

remnant   rimanente *m.* (*ree-mah-NEHN-teh*) 👆

remorse   rimorso *m.* (*ree-MOHR-soh*) 👆

remote (adj.)   remoto (*reh-MOH-toh*)

removable (adj.)   amovibile (*ah-moh-VEE-bee-leh*), rimovibile (*ree-moh-VEE-bee-leh*) 👆

removal   rimozione *f.* (*ree-moh-TSYOH-neh*) 👆

remove (to)   rimuovere (*ree-MWOH-vehr-reh*) 👆

renaissance   rinascimento *m.* (*ree-nah-shee-MEHN-toh*) 👆

render (to)   rendere (*REHN-dehr-reh*)

renounce (to)   rinunciare (*ree-noon-CHAR-reh*) 👆

repair   riparazione *f.* (*ree-pahr-rah-TSYOH-neh*)

repair, fix (to)   riparare (*ree-pahr-RAHR-reh*) 👆

repatriate (to)   rimpatriare (*reem-pah-TRYAHR-reh*) 👆

repeat (to)   ripetere (*ree-PEH-tehr-reh*) 👆

repeatedly, over and over   ripetutamente (*ree-peh-too-tah-MEHN-teh*) 👆

repercussion   ripercussione *f.* (*ree-pehr-koos-SYOH-neh*) 👆

repertoire   repertorio *m.* (*reh-pehr-TOHR-ryoh*)

repetition   ripetizione *f.* (*ree-peh-tee-TSYOH-neh*) 👆

report   rapporto *m.* (*rahp-POHR-toh*) 👆

repose, rest, quiet relaxation riposo *m.* (*ree-POH-so*h) 💣

repose, rest (to) riposarsi (*ree-poh-SAHR-see*) 💣
   ⓘ And again, a closely related noncognate: **restful** (adj.)—riposante (*ree-poh-SAHN-teh*)

reprehensible (adj.) riprensibile (*ree-prehn-SEE-bee-leh*) 💣

represent (to) rappresentare (*rahp-preh-zehn-TAHR-reh*) 💣

representation rappresentazione *f.* (*rahp-preh-zehn-tah-TSYOH-neh*) 💣

representative rappresentante *m. & f.* (*rahp-preh-zehn-TAHN-teh*) 💣, deputato *m.* (*deh-poo-TAHT-toh*)

representative (adj.) rappresentativo (*rahp-preh-zehn-tah-TEE-voh*) 💣

repression repressione *f.* (*reh-prehs-SYOH-neh*)

reproduce (to) riprodurre (*ree-proh-DOOHRR-reh*) 💣

reproduction riproduzione *f.* (*ree-proh-doo-TSYOH-neh*) 💣

reptile rettile *m.* (*REHT-tee-leh*) 💣

republic repubblica *f.* (*reh-POOB-blee-kah*)

republican (adj.) repubblicano (*reh-poob-blee-KAH-noh*)

repudiate (to) ripudiare (*ree-poo-dee-AHR-reh*) 💣

repudiation ripudio *m.* (*ree-POO-dyoh*) 💣

repugnance, abhorrence, loathing ripugnanza *f.* (*ree-poo-NYAHN-tsah*)

repugnant, abhorrent (adj.) ripugnante (*ree-poo-NYAHN-teh*) 💣

repulse, rebuff ripulsa *f.* (*ree-POOL-sah*)

reputation, standing reputazione *f.* (*reh-poo-tah-TSYOH-neh*) 💣

repute (to) reputare (*reh-poo-TAHR-reh*) 💣

request richiesta *f.* (*ree-KYEH-stah*) 💣

request (to) richiedere (*ree-KYEH-dehr-reh*) 💣

requisite requisito *f.* (*reh-kwee-ZEE-toh*) 💣

requisition requisizione *f.* (*reh-kwee-zee-TSYOH-neh*)

requisition (to) requisire (*reh-kwee-ZEER-reh*)

research ricerche *f.* (*ree-CHEHR-keh*) 💣

resemble (to) rassomigliare (*rahs-soh-mee-LYAHR-reh*) 💣

reservation (*uncertainty,* NOT *prebooking*) riserva *f.* (*ree-SEHR-vah*) 💣

reserve riserva *f.* (*ree-SEHR-vah*) 💣

reserve (to) riservare (*ree-sehr-VAHR-reh*) 💣

reside (to) risiedere (*ree-SYEH-dehr-reh*)

residence residenza *f.* (*reh-see-DEHN-tsah*)

resident (adj.) residente (*reh-see-DEHN-teh*)

ⓘ A **resident**—abitante *m.* (*ah-bee-TAHN-teh*)

residue residuo *m.* (*reh-ZEE-dwoh*)

resign (*oneself,* NOT *one's position*) (to) rassegnarsi (*rahs-seh-NYAHR-see*) 💣

resignation (*loss of hope*) rassegnazione *f.* (*rahs-seh-nyah-TSYOH-neh*) 💣

resist (to) resistere (*reh-SEE-stehr-reh*)

resistance resistenza *f.* (*reh-see-STEHN-tsah*) ➲**resistant** (adj.) -nte☯

resolute, resolved, determined, intent upon (adj.) risoluto (*ree-soh-LOO-toh*) 💣

resolution risoluzione *f.* (*ree-soh-loo-TSYOH-neh*) 💣

resolve (to) risolvere (*ree-ZOHL-vehr-reh*) 💣

resonance risonanza *f.* (*ree-soh-NAHN-tsah*) 💣

resound (to) risonare (*ree-soh-NAHR-reh*) ➲**resonant** (adj.) -nante☯ 💣

resource risorsa *f.* (*ree-SOHR-sah*) 💣

respect rispetto *m.* (*ree-SPEHT-toh*) 💣

respect (to) rispettare (*ree-speht-TAHR-reh*) 💣

respectable (adj.) rispettabile (*ree-speht-TAH-bee-leh*) 💣

respectful (adj.) rispettoso (*ree-speht-TOH-soh*) 💣

respective (adj.) rispettivo (*ree-speht-TEE-voh*) 💣

respiration, breath respirazione *f.* (*reh-spee-rah-TSYOH-neh*), respiro *m.* (*reh-SPEER-roh*)

respire, breathe (to) respirare (*reh-speer-RAHR-reh*)

respond, answer, reply (to) rispondere (*ree-SPOHN-dehr-reh*) ♦※

response, answer, reply risposta *f.* (*ree-SPOH-stah*) ♦※

responsibility, liability responsabilità *f.* (*reh-spohn-sah-bee-lee-TAH*)

responsible, liable, answerable (adj.) responsabile (*reh-spohn-SAH-bee-leh*)

responsive (adj.) responsivo (*reh-spohn-SEE-voh*)

rest, remainder resto *m.* (*REH-stoh*)

restitution restituzione *f.* (*reh-stee-too-TSYOH-neh*)

(make) restitution, refund (to) restituire (*reh-stee-too-EE-reh*)

restoration restaurazione *f.* (*reh-stah-oo-rah-TSYOH-neh*)

restore, refresh (to) ristorare (*ree-stohr-RAHR-reh*) ♦※
    ⓘ From the above comes the noncognate **refreshment**—ristoro (*ree-STOHR-roh*).

restrict (to) restringere (*reh-STREEN-jehr-reh*)

restriction restrizione *f.* (*reh-stree-TSYOH-neh*)

result, outgrowth risultato *m.* (*ree-sool-TAH-toh*) ♦※

result (to) risultare (*ree-sool-TAHR-reh*) ♦※

resume (to) riassumere (*ree-ahs-SOO-mehr-reh*) ♦※

resurrection risurrezione *f.* (*ree-soor-rreh-TSYOH-neh*) ♦※

retain (to) ritenere (*ree-TEH-nehr-reh*) ♦※

retard, delay (to) ritardare (*ree-tahr-DAHR-reh*) ♦※

retarded (*in time*), delayed (adj.) in ritardo (*een-ree-TAHR-doh*)

retention ritenzione *f.* (*ree-tehn-TSYOH-neh*) ♦※

reticence reticenza *f.* (*reh-tee-CHEN-tsah*) ➲**reticent** (adj.) -cente❍

retina retina *f.* (*REH-tee-nah*)

retire (*from work OR scene*), withdraw (to) ritirarsi (*ree-teer-RAHR-see*) ♦※

retract (*withdraw completely*) (to) ritrattare (*ree-traht-TAHR-reh*) ♦※

retract (*pull back*) (to) ritrarre (*ree-TRAHRR-reh*) ♦※

retreat ritirata *f.* (*ree-teer-RAH-tah*) ♦

retreat (to) ritirarsi (*ree-tee-RAHR-see*) ♦

retribution retribuzione *f.* (*reh-tree-boo-TSYOH-neh*)

retroactive (adj.) retroattivo (*reh-troh-aht-TEE-voh*)

retrospective (adj.) retrospettivo (*reh-troh-speht-TEE-voh*)

return ritorno *m.* (*ree-TOHR-noh*) ♦

return (to) ritornare (*ree-tohr-NAHR-reh*) ♦

reunion riunione *f.* (*ryoo-NYOH-neh*) ♦

reunite, bring together (to) riunire (*ryoo-NEER-reh*) ♦

reveal, disclose (to) rivelare (*ree-veh-LAHR-reh*) ♦

revelation, disclosure rivelazione *f.* (*ree-veh-lah-TSYOH-neh*) ♦

reverberate (to) riverberare (*ree-vehr-behr-RAHR-reh*) ♦

revere (to) riverire (*ree-vehr-REER-reh*) ♦

reverence riverenza *f.* (*ree-vehr-REHN-tsah*) ➲**reverent** (adj.) -nte€

reverse rovescio *m.* (*roh-VEH-shoh*) ♦

reverse (to) rovesciare (*roh-veh-SHAHR-reh*) ♦

revision revisione *f.* (*reh-vee-ZYOH-neh*)

revival ravvivamento *m.* (*rahv-vee-vah-MEHN-toh*) ♦

revive (to) ravvivare (*rahv-vee-VAHR-reh*) ♦

revoke (to) revocare (*reh-voh-KAHR-reh*)

revolt rivolta *f.* (*ree-VOHL-tah*) ♦

revolt (to) rivoltare (*ree-vohl-TAHR-reh*) ♦

revolution rivoluzione *f.* (*ree-voh-loo-TSYOH-neh*) ♦

revolutionary (adj.) rivoluzionario (*ree-voh-loo-tsyoh-NAHR-ryoh*) ♦

revolver (*gun*) rivoltella *f.* (*ree-vohl-TEHL-lah*), revolver *m.* (*reh-VOHL-vehr*) ♦

rhyme rima *f.* (*REE-mah*) ♦

rhyme (to) rimare (*ree-MAHR-reh*) ♦

rhythm ritmo *m.* (*REET-moh*) ⊃**rhythmical** (adj.) -mico☾ ☀

rice riso *m.* (*REE-soh*)

rich, wealthy (adj.) ricco (*REEK-koh*)

riches, wealth ricchezza *f.* (*reek-KEHT-tsah*)

ridicule ridicolo *m.* (*ree-DEE-koh-loh*)

ridiculous, ludicrous, laughable (adj.) ridicolo (*ree-DEE-koh-loh*)

rigid, stiff (adj.) rigido (*REE-jee-doh*)

rigidity, stiffness rigidità *f.* (*ree-jee-dee-TAH*), rigidezza (*ree-jee-DEHT-tsah*)

rigor rigore *m.* (*ree-GOHR-reh*)

rigorous, stringent (adj.) rigoroso (*ree-goh-ROH-soh*)

risk, hazard rischio *m.* (*REE-skyoh*)

risk, hazard (to) rischiare (*ree-SKYAHR-reh*)

risky, hazardous (adj.) rischioso (*ree-SKYOH-zoh*)

rite rito *m.* (*REE-toh*)

ritual rituale *m.* (*ree-too-AH-leh*) ⊃(adj.)☾

rival rivale *m.* (*ree-VAH-leh*) ⊃(adj.)☾

rivalry rivalità *f.* (*ree-vah-lee-TAH*)

roast arrosto *m.* (*ahr-RROH-stoh*) ⊃(adj.)☾ ☀

roast (to) arrostire (*ahr-rroh-STEER-reh*)

roasted (adj.) arrostito (*ahr-rroh-STEE-toh*)

rob, steal (to) rubare (*roo-BAHR-reh*) ☀

robust, hale, hardy, able-bodied, stalwart (adj.) robusto (*roh-BOO-stoh*)

robustness, hardiness robustezza *f.* (*roh-boo-STEHT-tsah*)

rock (*stone*) roccia *f.* (*ROHT-chah*)

rock, rocky, of rock (adj.) roccioso (*roht-CHO-soh*)

rock (*music*) rock *f.* (*RROK*)

rock-and-roll rock and roll *m.* (*rrok-ahnd-ROHL*)

rodent roditore *m.* (*roh-dee-TOHR-reh*)

role (*assigned part* OR *list of members, attendees, and so forth*)   ruolo *m.*
(*RWOH-loh*) 💣

roll (*shaped object*, NOT *food*), **scroll**   rotolo *m.* (*ROH-toh-loh*)

roll (to)   rotolare (*roh-toh-LAHR-reh*)

roller   rullo *m.* (*ROOL-loh*), rotella *f.* (*roh-TEHL-lah*) 💣

romance (*emotional connection*), **novel** (*fiction*)   romanzo *m.* (*roh-MAHN-zoh*)

romantic (adj.)   romantico (*roh-MAHN-tee-koh*)

ⓘ A related noncognate: **novelist**—romanziere *m.* (*roh-mahn-TSYEHR-reh*)

rosary   rosario *m.* (*roh-ZAHR-ryoh*)

rose (*flower*)   rosa *f.* (*ROH-zah*)

rosy (adj.)   roseo (*ROH-zeh-oh*)

rotate (to)   rotare (*roh-TAHR-reh*)

ⓘ Related: **wheel**—ruota *f.* (*RWOH-tah*)

rotation   rotazione *f.* (*roh-tah-TSYOH-neh*)

rouge, lipstick   rossetto *m.* (*rohs-SEHT-toh*)

round (adj.)   rotondo (*roh-TOHN-doh*)

royal (adj.)   reale (*reh-AH-leh*) 💣

ruby   rubino *m.* (*roo-BEE-noh*)

rude (adj.)   rude (*ROO-deh*)

rudiment   rudimento *m.* (*roo-dee-MEHN-toh*)

ruin   rovina *f.* (*roh-VEE-nah*) 💣

ruin (to)   rovinare (*roh-vee-NAHR-reh*) 💣

ruinous (adj.)   rovinoso (*roh-vee-NOH-soh*) 💣

rule (*usual case* OR *command, control*)   regola *f.* (*REH-goh-lah*) 💣

rule (to)   regolare (*reh-goh-LAHR-reh*) 💣

rum   rum *m.* (*ROOM*)

rumor   rumore *m.* (*roo-MOHR-reh*), voce (*VOH-cheh*)

rural (adj.) rurale (*roor-RAH-leh*)

rustic rustico *m.* (*ROO-stee-koh*) ⊃(adj.)Ↄ

—S—

sabotage sabotaggio *m.* (*sah-boh-TAHD-joh*)

sabotage (to) sabotare (*sah-boh-TAHR-reh*)

saboteur sabotatore *m.* (*sah-boh-tah-TOHR-reh*)

saccharine saccarina *f.* (*sahk-kahr-REE-nah*) ⊃(adj.) -noↃ

sack sacco *m.* (*SAHK-koh*) ⊃bag (*paper OR plastic*) sacchetto *m.* (*sahk-KEHT-toh*)Ↄ

sacrament sacramento *m.* (*sah-krah-MEHN-toh*)

sacred (adj.) sacro (*SAH-kroh*)

sacrifice sacrificio *m.* (*sah-kree-FEE-choh*)

sacrifice (to) sacrificare (*sah-kree-fee-KAHR-reh*)

sacrilege sacrilegio *m.* (*sah-kree-LEH-joh*)

sacrilegious (adj.) sacrilego (*sah-KREE-leh-goh*)

safeguard salvaguardia *f.* (*sahl-vah-GWAHR-dyah*) 👆

safeguard (to) salvaguardare (*sahl-vah-gwahr-DAHR-reh*) 👆

sagacious, sage, wise (adj.) saggio (*SAHD-joh*)

sagacity, wisdom saggezza *f.* (*sahd-JEHT-tsah*)

sage, wise person saggio *m.* (*SAHD-joh*)

saint santo *m.* (*SAHN-toh*) ⊃saintly, holy (adj.)Ↄ

salad insalata *f.* (*een-sah-LAH-tah*) 👆

salary, wages salario *m.* (*sah-LAHR-ryoh*)

saliva saliva *f.* (*sah-LEE-vah*)

salmon salmone *m.* (*sahl-MOH-neh*)

salon salone *m.* (*sah-LOH-neh*)

salt   sale *m.* (*SAH-leh*)

salt (to)   salare (*sah-LAHR-reh*)

salty (adj.)   salato (*sah-LAH-toh*), salso (*SAHL-soh*)

salutation   salutazione *f.* (*sah-loo-tah-TSYOH-neh*)

salute, greeting   saluto *m.* (*sah-LOO-toh*)

salute, greet (to)   salutare (*sah-loo-TAHR-reh*)
   ① Closely, albeit "oppositely" related, is: **to snub**—non salutare (*nohn sah-loo-TAHR-reh*), fare un affronto (*fah-reh oon ahf-frohn-toh*).
   ☛Do not confuse either of the foregoing with **"To your health!"** (*traditional toast*)—Alla salute! (*ah-lah sah-LOO-teh*), which embraces the term for **health**—*salute f.*

salvage (to)   salvare (*sahl-VAHR-reh*)

salvation   salvezza *f.* (*sahl-VEHT-tsah*)

sanatorium   sanatorio *m.* (*sah-nah-TOHR-ryoh*)

sanctify (to)   santificare (*sahn-tee-fee-KAHR-reh*)

sanction (to)   sanzionare (*sahn-tsyoh-NAHR-reh*)

sanctity   santità *f.* (*sahn-tee-TAH*)

sanctuary   santuario *m.* (*sahn-too-AHR-ryoh*)

sandal   sandalo *m.* (*SAHN-dah-loh*)

sandwich   sandwich (*SAHN-dweech*), panino *m.* (*pah-NEE-noh*), tramezzino (*trah-mehd-DZEE-noh*)

sane (adj.)   sano (*SAH-noh*)

sanitary (adj.)   sanitario (*sah-nee-TAHR-ryoh*), igienico (*ee-JEH-nee-koh*)

sanity   sanità *f.* (*sah-nee-TAH*)

sapphire   zaffiro *m.* (*dzahf-FEER-roh*) ☛

sarcasm   sarcasmo *m.* (*sahr-KAH-zmoh*)

sarcastic (adj.)   sarcastico (*sahr-KAH-stee-koh*)

satellite   satellite *m.* (*sah-TEHL-lee-teh*)

satire   satira *f.* (*SAH-teer-rah*)

satirical (adj.)   satiresco (*sah-tee-REH-skoh*)

satisfaction   soddisfazione *f.* (*sohd-dee-sfah-TSYOH-neh*) 👄

satisfactory (adj.)   soddisfacente (*sohd-dee-sfah-CHEN-teh*) 👄

satisfied (adj.)   soddisfatto (*sohd-dee-SFAHT-toh*) 👄

satisfy (to)   soddisfare (*sohd-dee-SFAHR-reh*) 👄

saturated (adj.)   saturo (*sah-TOOR-roh*)

saturation   saturazione *f.* (*sah-toor-rah-TSYOH-neh*)

sausage   salsiccia *f.* (*sahl-SEET-chah*) 👄

save (*rescue* OR *preserve*, NOT *economize*) (to)   salvare (*sahl-VAHR-reh*) 👄

savior   salvatore *m.* (*sahl-vah-TOHR-reh*) 👄

saxophone   sassofono *m.* (*sahs-SOH-foh-noh*) 👄

scale (*scope* OR *hardened residue*), **staircase**   scala *f.* (*SKAH-lah*)
ⓘ This Italian term is most important in its noncognate denotation, as a **stairway**. Closely related noncognates are **elevator**—ascensore *m.* (*ah-shen-SOHR-reh*); and **escalator**—scala mobile (_____*MO-bee-leh*).

scale (*weighing device*)   bilancia *f.* (*bee-LAHN-chah*)

scandal   scandalo *m.* (*SKAHN-dah-loh*)

scandalous (adj.)   scandaloso (*skahn-dah-LOH-soh*)

scarce, scant, meager (adj.)   scarso (*SKAHR-soh*)

scarcity   scarsità *f.* (*skahr-see-TAH*)

scarf   sciarpa *f.* (*SHAHR-pah*)

scarlet (adj.)   scarlatto (*skahr-LAHT-toh*)

scenario (*dramatic outline*)   scenario *m.* (*sheh-NAHR-ryoh*)

scene (*section of drama*, NOT *vista*)   scena *f.* (*SHEHN-ah*)

scholar   scolaro *m.* (*skoh-LAHR-roh*) ➲*f.* -ra🔊; erudito *m.* (*ehr-roo-DEE-toh*) ➲*f.* -ta 🔊; studioso *m.* (*stoo-DYOH-soh* ➲*f.* -sa🔊

school, schoolhouse   scuola *f.* (*SKWOH-lah*)

science   scienza *f.* (*SHEHN-tsah*)

scientific (adj.)   scientifico (*shehn-TEE-fee-koh*)

scientist   scienziato *m.* (*shehn-TSYAH-toh*)

scintillate, sparkle, glitter (to) scintillare (*sheen-teel-LAHR-reh*)

scripture scrittura *f.* (*skreet-TOOR-rah*)

scruple scrupolo *m.* (*SKROO-poh-loh*)

scrupulous scrupoloso (*skroo-poh-LOH-soh*)

scrutinize (to) scrutare (*skroo-TAHR-reh*)

sculptor scultore *m.* (*skool-TOHR-reh*)

sculpture scultura *f.* (*skool-TOOR rah*)

seal (*security closure, NOT sea mammal*) sigillo *m.* (*see-JEEL-loh*) 💣※

second (adj.) secondo (*seh-KOHN-doh*)

secondary (adj.) secondario (*seh-kohn-DAHR-ryoh*)

secret segreto *m.* (*seh-GREH-toh*) ➲(adj.)ℭ 💣※

secretary segretario *m.* (*seh-greh-TAHR-ryoh*) ➲*f. -ia*ℭ

section sezione *f.* (*seh-TSYOH-neh*) 💣※

secular (adj.) secolare (*seh-koh-LAHR-reh*)

secure, safe, sure (of) (adj.) sicuro (*see-KOOR-roh*) 💣※

(absolutely) secure, foolproof (adj.) assolutamente sicuro (*ahs-soh-loo-tah-MEHN-teh___*)

security, safety, surety sicurezza *f.* (*see-koor-REHT-tsah*) 💣※

sedative sedativo *m.* (*seh-dah-TEE-voh*) ➲(adj.)ℭ

seduce (to) sedurre (*seh-DOOHRR-reh*)

seductive (adj.) seducente (*seh-doo-CHEN-teh*)

segment segmento *m.* (*sehg-MEHN-toh*)

segregate (to) segregare (*seh-greh-GAHR-reh*)

select (to) scegliere (*sheh-LYEHR-reh*) 💣※

selection selezione *f.* (*seh-leh-TSYOH-neh*)

selective (adj.) selettivo (*seh-leht-TEE-voh*)

self-service self-service *m.* (*sehlf-sehr-VEES*)

semantic (adj.) semantico (*seh-MAHN-tee-koh*)

semantics semantica *f.* (*seh-MAHN-tee-kah*)7

semester semestre *m.* (*seh-MEH-streh*)

semicircle semicerchio *m.* (*seh-mee-CHEHR-kyoh*)

seminary seminario *m.* (*seh-mee-NAHR-ryoh*)

senate senato *m.* (*seh-NAH-toh*)

senator senatore *m.* (*seh-nah-TOHR-reh*)

senile (adj.) senile (*seh-NEE-leh*)

sensation sensazione *f.* (*sehn-sah-TSYOH-neh*)

sensational (adj.) sensazionale (*sehn-sah-tsyoh-NAH-leh*)

sense (*faculty of sensation* OR *feeling* OR *impression*) senso *m.* (*SEHN-soh*)

sense (*intelligence*) senno *m.* (*SEHN-noh*)

sensible (adj.) sensibile (*sehn-SEE-bee-leh*)

sensitive (adj.) sensitivo (*sehn-see-TEE-voh*)

sensual (adj.) sensuale (*sehn-soo-AH-leh*)

sentiment, feeling sentimento *m.* (*sehn-tee-MEHN-toh*)

sentimental (adj.) sentimentale (*sehn-tee-mehn-TAH-leh*)

separate (*not joined*) (adj.) separato (*seh-pahr-RAH-toh*)

separate (*disconnect by external force*) (to) separare (*seh-pahr-RAHR-reh*)

separate (*come apart from internal stress*) (to) separarsi (*seh-pahr-RAHR-see*)

separation, parting separazione *f.* (*seh-pahr-rah-TSYOH-neh*)

serenade serenata *f.* (*sehr-reh-NAH-tah*)

serene (adj.) sereno (*sehr-REH-noh*)

series, sequence, set, suite (*matched group*) serie *f.* (*SEHR-ryeh*)

serious, earnest (adj.) serio (*SEHR-ryoh*)

sermon sermone *m.* (*sehr-MOH-neh*)

serpent, snake serpente *m.* (*sehr-PEHN-teh*)

servant servo *m.* (*SEHR-voh*), domestico *m.* (*doh-MEH-stee-koh*) ➔ *f.* -ca➔

serve (to)   servire (*sehr-VEER-reh*)

service   servizio *m.* (*sehr-VEE-tsyoh*)

servile, subservient (adj.)   servile (*sehr-VEE-leh*)

servitude, servants (*collectively*)   servitù *f.* (*sehr-vee-TOO*)

session   sessione *f.* (*sehs-SYOH-neh*)

severe, stern, strict (adj.)   severo (*seh-VEHR-roh*)

severity   severità *f.* (*seh-vehr-ree-TAH*)

sex   sesso *m.* (*SEHS-soh*) 🌢

sexism   sessismo *m.* (*sehs-SEEZ-moh*) 🌢

sexist   sessista *m.* (*sehs-SEE-stah*) ⇨(adj.)↻ 🌢

sexual (adj.)   sessuale (*sehs-soo-AH-leh*) 🌢

sexy (adj.)   sexy (*SEK-see*)

shampoo   sciampò *m.* (*shahm-POH*) 🌢

shawl   scialle *m.* (*SHAHL-leh*) 🌢

sherbet   sorbetto *m.* (*sohr-BEHT-toh*) 🌢

shopping   shopping *m.* (*SHOHP-peeng*)

sign (*indication*)   segno *m.* (*SEH-nyoh*) 🌢

signal   segnale *m.* (*seh-NYAH-leh*) 🌢

signal (to)   segnalare (*seh-nyah-LAHR-reh*) 🌢

significance, meaning of   significato *m.* (*see-nyee-fee-KAH-toh*)

significant (adj.)   significativo (*see-nyee-fee-kah-TEE-voh*)

signify (to)   significare (*see-nyee-fee-KAHR-reh*)

silence   silenzio *m.* (*see-LEHN-tsyoh*)

silent, noiseless (adj.)   silenzioso (*see-lehn-TSYOH-soh*)

similar, like, alike (adj.)   simile (*SEE-mee-leh*)

similarity   similarità *f.* (*see-mee-lahr-ree-TAH*)

similarly, likewise   similmente (*see-meel-MEHN-teh*)

simple, no-frills (adj.)   semplice (*sehm-PLEE-cheh*) 🌢

simplicity semplicità *f.* (*sehm-plee-chee-TAH*) 💣

simplify (to) semplificare (*sehm-plee-fee-KAHR-reh*) 💣

simply semplicemente (*sehm-plee-cheh-MEHN-teh*) 💣

simultaneous (adj.) simultaneo (*see-mool-TAH-neh-oh*)

sincere, heartfelt (adj.) sincero (*seen-CHEHR-roh*)

sincerely sinceramente (*seen-chehr-rah-MEHN-teh*)

sincerity sincerità *f.* (*seen-chehr-ree-TAH*)

single (adj.) singolo (*seen-GOH-loh*), solo (*SOH-loh*), unico (*OO-nee-koh*)

singular (adj.) singolare (*seen-goh-LAHR-reh*)

sinister (adj.) sinistro (*see-NEE-stroh*)

siren sirena *f.* (*seer-REH-nah*)

site sito *m.* (*SEE-toh*)

situate (to) situare (*see-too-AHR-reh*)

situation situazione *f.* (*see-twah-TSYOH-neh*)

skeleton scheletro *m.* (*SKEH-leh-troh*) 💣

skeptic scettico *m.* (*SHEHT-tee-koh*) ➲**skeptical** (adj.)➳ 💣

ski sci *m.* (*SHEE*) 💣

ski (to) sciare (*shee-AHR-reh*) 💣

sled, sleigh slitta *f.* (*ZLEET-tah*)

slogan slogan *m.* (*ZLOH-gah-nah*)

smog smog *m.* (*ZMOH-gah*)

smoggy (adj.) smoggy (*ZMOHG-ee*)

snob snob *m.* (*ZNOH-beh*)

~~**soap** sapone *m.* (*sah-POH-neh*)~~ 💣

sober, somber (adj.) sobrio (*SOH-bryoh*)

sober (*not drunk*) (adj.) sobrio (*SOH-bryoh*), non ubriaco (*nohn oo-bree-AH-koh*)

sociable, companionable (adj.) socievole (*soh-CHEH-voh-leh*)

social (adj.)   sociale (*soh-CHAH-leh*)

social assistance, social work   assistenza (*f.*) sociale (*ahs-sees-TEHN-tsah soh-CHAH-leh*)

socialism   socialismo *m.* (*soh-chah-LEE-zmoh*)

socialist   socialista *m.* & *f.* (*soh-chah-LEE-stah*) ➲(adj.)☾

society   società *f.* (*soh-cheh-TAH*)

sociology   sociologia *f.* (*soh-choh-loh-JEE-ah*)

soda (*chemical compound*)   soda *f.* (*SOH-dah*)

soda, soft drink   soda *f.* (*SOH-dah*), bibita non alcolica (*bee-BEE-tah nohn ahl-KOH-lee-kah*)

sofa   sofà *m.* (*soh-FAH*)

soft (adj.)   soffice (*SOHF-fee-cheh*)

soil   suolo *m.* (*SWOH-loh*) ☙

sojourn   soggiorno *m.* (*sohd-JOHR-noh*) ☙

sojourn (to)   soggiornare (*sohd-johr-NAHR-reh*) ☙

solar (adj.)   solare (*soh-LAHR-reh*)

soldier   soldato *m.* (*sohl-DAH-toh*)

sole (*of foot or shoe*)   suola *f.* (*SWOH-lah*) ☙

sole, only, single, alone (adj.)   solo (*SOH-loh*)

solely, only   solamente (*soh-lah-MEHN-teh*)

solemn (adj.)   solenne (*soh-LEHN-neh*)

solemnity   solennità *f.* (*soh-lehn-nee-TAH*)

solicit (to)   sollecitare (*sohl-leh-chee-TAHR-reh*)

solicitous (adj.)   sollecito (*sohl-LEH-chee-toh*)

solid   solido *m.* (*SOH-lee-doh*) ➲(adj.)☾

solidify (to)   solidificare (*soh-lee-dee-fee-KAHR-reh*)

solidity   solidità *f.* (*soh-lee-dee-TAH*)

solitary, lone, unaccompanied, lonely, lonesome (adj.) solitario (*soh-lee-TAHR-ryoh*)

solitude, loneliness solitudine *f.* (*soh-lee-TOO-dee-neh*)

solo assolo *m.* (*ahs-SOH-loh*) 🌶

soloist soloista *m. & f.* (*soh-loh-EE-stah*)

solution (*re liquid and problem*) soluzione *f.* (*soh-loo-TSYOH-neh*)

solve (to) risolvere (*ree-SOHL-vehr-reh*) 🌶

sophisticated (adj.) sofisticato (*soh-fee-stee-KAH-toh*)

sordid (adj.) sordido (*SOHR-dee-doh*)

sort (*kind, type*) sorta *f.* (*SOHR-tah*)

sort (to) assortire (*ahs-sohr-TEER-reh*) 🌶

soup zuppa *f.* (*DZOOP-pah*), minestra *f.* (*mee-NEH-strah*)
   ⓘ The cognate above refers to markedly thick, rich soups, while a *minestra* is more "ordinary" in consistency (although, in Italy, never less than long-cooked delicious!). A thin, brothlike soup is *brodo m.* (*BROH-doh*); and *stew* is *stufato m.* (*stoo-FAH-toh*).

spa spa (*SPAH*), stazione (*f.*) climatica (*stah-TSYOH-neh klee-MAH-tee-kah*)

space (*area*), room for spazio *m.* (*SPAH-tsyoh*)

spacious (adj.) spazioso (*spah-TSYOH-soh*)

span (*distance,* NOT *bridge*) spanna *f.* (*SPAHN-nah*)

spasm, pang spasimo *m.* (*SPAH-see-moh*)

spatter spuzzo *m.* (*SPOOT-tsoh*) 🌶

spatter (to) spuzzare (*spoot-TSAHR-reh*) 🌶

special (adj.) speciale (*speh-CHAH-leh*)

~~specialist~~ specialista *m.* (*speh-chah-LEE-stah*)

specially specialmente (*speh-chahl-MEHN-teh*)

specialty specialità *f.* (*speh-chah-lee-TAH*)

species (*kind, sort*) specie *f.* (*SPEH-cheh*)

specific (adj.)   specifico (*speh-CHEE-fee-koh*)

specify (to)   specificare (*speh-chee-fee-KAHR-reh*)

spectacle   spettacolo *m.* (*speht-TAH-koh-loh*) ♠️

spectacular (adj.)   spettacolare (*speht-tah-koh-LAHR-reh*) ♠️

spectator, bystander   spettatore *m.* (*speht-tah-TOHR-reh*) ♠️

speculate (to)   speculare (*speh-koo-LAHR-reh*)

speculation   speculazione *f.* (*speh-koo-lah-TSYOH-neh*)

spend (*money*) (to)   spendere (*SPEHN-dehr-reh*)

spend (*time*) (to)   passare (*pahs-SAHR-reh*) ♠️

sphere   sfera *f.* (*SFEHR-rah*) ♠️

spice   spezia *f.* (*SPEH-tsyah*) ♠️

spinach   spinaci *m.* (*spee-NAH-chee*)

spine, thorn   spina *f.* (*SPEE-nah*)

spine, spinal cord   spina (*f.*) dorsale (*SPEE-nah dohr-SAH-leh*)

spiral   spirale *f.* (*speer-RAH-leh*)   ⊃(adj.)℃

spirit, wit   spirito *m.* (*SPEER-ree-toh*)

spiritual (adj.)   spirituale (*speer-ree-TWAH-leh*)

spit (to)   sputare (*spoo-TAHR-reh*) ♠️

splendid, gorgeous (adj.)   splendido (*SPLEHN-dee-doh*)

splendor, (physical) brilliance   splendore *m.* (*splehn-DOHR-reh*)

spontaneity   spontaneità *f.* (*spohn-tah-nay-TAH*)

spontaneous (adj.)   spontaneo (*spohn-TAH-neh-oh*)

sporadic (adj.)   sporadico (*spohr-RAH-dee-koh*)

sport   sport *m.* (*SPOHR-teh*)

sportsman, outdoorsman, hunter   sportivo *m.* (*spohr-TEE-voh*)

sporty (adj.)   sportivo (*spohr-TEE-voh*)

spouse, husband, groom, bridegroom   sposo *m.* (*SPOH-zoh*)

spouse, wife, bride   sposa *f.* (*SPOH-zah*)

sputum, spit, spittle sputo *m. (SPOO-toh)* 💣

squad, team squadra *f. (SKWAH-drah)*

squalor squallore *m. (skwahl-LOHR-reh)* ⊃**squalid** (adj.) -llido⊂

stability stabilità *f. (stah-bee-lee-TAH)*

stabilize (to) stabilizzare *(stah-bee-leed-DZAHR-reh)*

stable (adj.) stabile *(STAH-bee-leh)*

stadium stadio *m. (STAH-dyoh)*

stall (*small enclosure, NOT stoppage*) stallo *m. (STAHL-loh)*
ⓘ The related noncognate: **stable** (*horse barn*)—stalla *f. (STAHL-lah)*

standardize (to) standardizzare *(stahn-dahr-deed-DZAHR-reh)*

star (*of film or stage*) star *f. (STAHR-reh)*

star (*celestial*) stella *f. (STEHL-lah)*

state (*political entity*) stato *m. (STAH-toh)*

static (*stationary*) (adj.) statico *(STAH-tee-koh)*

station (*railway OR bus depot*) stazione *f. (stah-TSYOH-neh)*

stationary (adj.) stazionario *(stah-tsyoh-NAHR-ryoh)*

statistics (*data*) statistiche *f. (stah-TEE-stee-keh)*

statistics (*mathematical, anayltical science*) statistica *f. (stah-TEE-stee-kah)*

statue statua *f. (STAH-twah)*

steak (*beef*) bistecca *f. (bee-STEHK-kah)*

stellar (adj.) stellare *(stehl-LAHR-reh)*

stenographer stenografa *f. (steh-NOH-grah-fah)*

stenography, shorthand stenografia *f. (steh-noh-grah-FEE-ah)*

stereotype stereotipia *f. (stehr-ree-oh-tee-PEE-ah)*

sterility, barrenness sterilità *f. (stehr-ree-lee-TAH)*

sterilize (to) sterilizzare *(stehr-ree-leed-DZHR-reh)*

stewardess stewardess *f. (stoo-vahr-DEHS-seh)*

stimulant stimolante *m. (stee-moh-LAHN-teh)*

stimulate (to)   stimolare (*stee-moh-LAHR-reh*)

stimulus   stimolo *m.* (*STEE-moh-loh*)

stipend   stipendio *m.* (*stee-PEHN-dyoh*)

stipulate (to)   stipulare (*stee-poo-LAHR-reh*)

stoic   stoico *m.* (*STOH-ee-koh*) ➲**stoical** (adj.)➋

stole   stola *f.* (*STOH-lah*)

stomach   stomaco *m.* (*STOH-mah-koh*)

stove   stufa *f.* (*STOO-fah*), fornello *m.* (*fohr-NEHL-loh*)
   ① An Italian **oven**—forno *m.* (*FOHR-noh*); the same term also means **bakery.**

strange, odd, weird, outlandish, queer (adj.)   strano (*STRAH-noh*)

strange, foreign (adj.)   straniero (*strah-NYEHR-roh*)

stranger, foreigner   straniero *m.* (*strah-NYEHR-roh*), estraneo (*eh-STRAH-neh-oh*) ➍

strategic (adj.)   strategico (*strah-TEH-jee-koh*)

strategy   strategia *f.* (*strah-teh-JEE-ah*)

streak   stria *f.* (*STREE-ah*)

strenuous (adj.)   strenuo (*STREH-nwoh*)

strident (adj.)   stridente (*stree-DEHN-teh*), stridulo (*STREE-doo-loh*)

structure   struttura *f.* (*stroot-TOOR-rah*)

stucco   stucco *m.* (*STOOK-koh*)

student, pupil   studente *m.* (*stoo-DEHN-teh*) ➲*f.* -tessa➋

studio, study (*room* OR *field or focus of learning*)   studio *m.* (*STOO-dyoh*)

studious (adj.)   studioso (*stoo-dee-OH-soh*)

study (to)   studiare (*stoo-DYAHR-reh*)

stupefy, daze, amaze, astonish (to)   stupire (*stoo-PEER-reh*)

stupendous (adj.)   stupendo (*stoo-PEHN-doh*)

stupid (adj.)   stupido (*stoo-PEE-doh*)

stupidity   stupidità *f.* (*stoo-pee-dee-TAH*)

stupor, stupefacation, daze, amazement, astonishment stupore *m.* (*stoo-POHR-reh*)

style stile *m.* (*STEE-leh*) ♠

subconscious subcosciente *m.* (*soob-koh-SHEHN-teh*) ↄ(adj.)ↄ

subject (*topic, NOT ruled citizen*) soggetto *m.* (*sohd-JEHT-toh*) ♠

subjective (adj.) soggettivo (*sohd-jeht-TEE-voh*) ♠

sublime (adj.) sublime (*soo-BLEE-meh*)

submerge (to) sommergere (*sohm-mehr-JEHR-reh*) ♠

submersion sommersione *f* (*sohm-mehr-SYOH-neh*) ♠

submission sottomissione *f.* (*soht-toh-mees-SYOH-neh*) ♠

submit (to) sottomettere (*soht-toh-MEHT-tehr-reh*) ♠

subordinate subordinato *m.* (*soo-bohr-dee-NAH-toh*) ↄ(adj.)ↄ

subsequent (adj.) susseguente (*soos-seh-GWEHN-teh*) ♠

subsidy sussidio *m.* (*soos-SEE-dyoh*) ♠

substance sostanza *f.* (*soh-STAHN-tsah*)

substantial (adj.) sostanziale (*soh-stahn-tsee-AH-leh*)

substitute sostituto *m.* (*soh-stee-TOO-toh*) ♠

substitute (to) sostituire (*soh-stee-TWEER-reh*) ♠

substitution sostituzione *f.* (*soh-stee-too-TSYOH-neh*) ♠

subtle (adj.) sottile (*soht-TEE-leh*) ♠

subtract (to) sottrarre (*soht-TRAHRR-reh*) ♠

suburb sobborgo *m.* (*sohb-BOHR-goh*) ♠

subversive sovversivo *m.* (*sohv-vehr-SEE-voh*) ↄ(adj.)ↄ ♠

subvert (to) sovvertire (*sohv-vehr-TEER-reh*) ♠

succeed (*follow, NOT attain goal*) (to) succedere (*soot-CHEH-dehr-reh*)

success successo *m.* (*soot-CHEHS-soh*)
ⓘ The related antonyms: **failure**—insuccesso *m.* (*een-soot-CHEHS-soh*), fiasco *m.* (*FYAH-skoh*)

succession successione *f.* (*soot-chehs-see-OH-neh*)

successive (adj.) successivo (*soot-chehs-SEE-voh*)

successor successore *m.* (*soot-chehs-SOHR-reh*)

succinct (adj.) succinto (*soot-CHEEN-toh*)

succumb (to) soccombre (*sohk-KOHM-breh*) ♠⁂

suck (to) succhiere (*sook-KYEHR-reh*)

suffer (to) soffrire (*sohf-FREER-reh*) ♠⁂

suffering sofferenza *f.* (*sohf-fehr-REHN-tsah*) ♠⁂

sufficient, enough (adj.) sufficiente (*soof-fee-CHYEN-teh*)

suffocate, smother, stifle, choke (to) soffocare (*sohf-foh-KAHR-reh*) ♠⁂

suggest (to) suggerire (*sood-jehr-REER-reh*)

suggestion suggerimento *m.* (*sood-jehr-ree-MEHN-toh*)

suicide suicidio *m.* (*soo-ee-CHEE-dyoh*)

sum soma *f.* (*SOHM-mah*) ♠⁂

summary sommario *m.* (*sohm-MAHR-ryoh*) ⊃(adj.)⊂ ♠⁂

summit, top sommità *m.* (*sohm-mee-TAH*) ♠⁂

sumptuous (adj.) sontuoso (*sohn-TWOH-soh*) ♠⁂

superb (adj.) superbo (*soo-PEHR-boh*)

superficial (adj.) superficiale (*soo-pehr-fee-CHAH-leh*)

ⓘ The related noncognate: **surface**—superficie *f.* (*soo-pehr-FEE-cheh*)

superfluous (adj.) superfluo (*soo-PEHR-floo-oh*)

superintendent sovrintendente *m.* (*sohv-reen-tehn-DEHN-teh*) ♠⁂

superior, upper (adj.) superiore (*soo-pehr-YOHR-reh*)

superiority superiorità *f.* (*soo-pehr-yohr-ee-TAH*)

superlative (adj.) superlativo (*soo-pehr-lah-TEE-voh*)

supermarket supermercato *m.* (*soo-pehr-mehr-KAH-toh*)

supernatural (adj.) soprannaturale (*soh-prahn-nah-toor-RAH-leh*) ♠⁂

superstar superstar *m. & f. (soo-pehr-STAHR-reh)*

superstition superstizione *f. (soo-pehr-stee-TSYOH-neh)*

superstitious (adj.) superstizioso *(soo-pehr-stee-TSYOH-soh)*

supplement supplemento *m. (soop-pleh-MEHN-toh)*

supplementary (adj.) supplementare *(soop-pleh-mehn-TAHR-reh)*

supplicate, beseech, entreat, plead (to) supplicare *(soop-plee-KAHR-reh)*

supplication, entreaty supplica *f. (SOOP-plee-kah)*

suppose (to) supporre *(soop-POHRR-reh)*

supposition, assumption supposizione *f. (soop-poh-zee-TSYOH-neh)*

suppression soppressione *f. (sohp-prehs-SYOH-neh)* ♦※

supreme, paramount (adj.) supremo *(soo-PREH-moh)*

surmount (to) sormontare *(sohr-mohn-TAHR-reh)* ♦※

surpass (to) sorpassare *(sohr-pahs-SAHR-reh)* ♦※

surprise sorpresa *f. (sohr-PREH-sah)* ♦※

surprise (to) sorprendere *(sohr-PREHN-dehr-reh)* ♦※

surrender (*yield* OR *give self up*) (to) arrendersi *(ahr-RREHN-dehr-see)* ♦※

susceptible (adj.) suscettibile *(soo-sheht-TEE-bee-leh)*

suspect sospetto *m. (soh-SPEHT-toh)* ⊃(adj.)℃ ♦※

suspect (to) sospettare *(soh-speht-TAHR-reh)* ♦※

suspend, discontinue (to) sospendere *(soh-SPEHN-dehr-reh)* ♦※

suspend, hang (to) appendere (ahp-PEHN-dehr-reh), stendere (STEHN-dehr-reh) ♦※

suspended (adj.) sospeso *(soh-SPEH-soh)* ♦※

suspension, discontinuance sospensione *f. (soh-spehn-SYOH-neh)* ♦※

suspicion sospetto *m. (soh-SPEHT-toh)* ♦※

suspicious (*passively*), suspect, doubtful (adj.) sospetto *(soh-SPEHT-toh)*

suspicious (*actively*), mistrustful (adj.) sospettoso *(soh-speht-TOH-soh)* ♦※

sustain, support, uphold, back (to) sostenere *(soh-steh-NEHR-reh)* ♦※

sustainer, supporter, upholder, backer   sostenitore *m.* (*soh-steh-nee-TOHR-reh*)

sustenance, support   sostegno *m.* (*soh-STEH-nyoh*) 💣

sweater   sweater *m.* (*ZWEH-tehr*)

syllable   sillaba *f.* (*SEEL-lah-bah*) 💣

symbol   simbolo *m.* (*seem-BOH-loh*) 💣

symbolic (adj.)   simbolico (*seem-BOH-lee-koh*) 💣

sympathize (to)   simpatizzare (*seem-pah-teed-DZAHR-reh*) 💣

sympathy (*accord* AND *compassion*)   simpatia *f.* (*seem-pah-TEE-ah*) 💣

symphonic (adj.)   sinfonico (*seen-FOH-nee-koh*) 💣

symphony orchestra   orchestra sinfonica *f.* (*ohr-KEH-strah seen-FOH-nee-kah*)

symptom   sintomo *m.* (*SEEN-toh-moh*) 💣

symptomatic (adj.)   sintomatico (*seen-toh-MAH-tee-koh*) 💣

syndrome   sindrome *f.* (*SEEN-droh-meh*) 💣

synonym   sinonimo *m.* (*see-NOH-nee-moh*)

synonymous (adj.)   sinonimo (*see-NOH-nee-moh*)

synthetic (adj.)   sintetico (*seen-TEH-tee-koh*) 💣

syringe   siringa *f.* (*see-REEN-gah*) 💣

syrup   sciroppo *m.* (*sheer-ROHP-poh*) 💣

system   sistema *m.* (*see-STEH-mah*) 💣

systematic (adj.)   sistematico (*see-steh-MAH-tee-koh*) 💣

—T—

table   tavola *f.* (*TAH-voh-lah*) 💣
   ① Both a (**small**) **table** and **tablet**, **writing pad**—tavoletta *f.* (*tah-voh-LEHT-tah*)

table tennis, **ping-pong**   tennis da tavola *m.* (*tehn-NEE-seh dah TAH-voh-lah*)

tablecloth   tovaglia *f.* (*toh-VAH-lyah*) 💣

tact tatto *m.* (*TAH-toh*) 💣

talent talento *m.* (*tah-LEHN-toh*)

talented (adj.) di talento (*dee tah-LEHN-toh*)

tangible (adj.) tangibile (*tahn-JEE-bee-leh*)

tapestry tappezzeria *f.* (*tahp-peht-TSEHR-ryah*)

tardy, late (adj.) tardo (*TAHR-doh*), in ritardo (*een ree-TAHR-doh*) ➲late (adv.) tardi↻

tariff tariffa *f.* (*tahr-REEF-fah*)

tavern taverna *f.* (*tah-VEHRR-nah*), osteria (*oh-stehr-REE-ah*)

tax tassa *f.* (*TAHS-sah*), imposta *f.* (*eem-POH-stah*)

taxi, cab, taxicab tassì *m.* (*tahs-SEE*) 💣

taxi driver tassista *m.* (*tahs-SEE-stah*) 💣

tea tè *m.* (*TEH*)

teapot teiera *f.* (*teh-YEHR-rah*)

technical (adj.) tecnico (*TEHK-nee-koh*)

technique tecnica *f.* (*TEHK-nee-kah*)

tedious (adj.) tedioso (*teh-dee-OH-soh*)

tedium tedio *m.* (*TEH-dyoh*)

teenager teen-ager *m.* (*TEE-nay-gehr-reh*)

telephone telefono *m.* (*teh-LEH-foh-noh*)

telephone (to) telefonare (*teh-leh-foh-NAHR-reh*)

telephone call telefonata *f.* (*teh-leh-foh-NAH-tah*)

telescope telescopio *m.* (*teh-leh-SKOH-pyoh*)

television televisione *f.* (*teh-leh-vee-ZYOH-neh*)

television set televisore *f.* (*teh-leh-vee-ZOHR-reh*)

temperament temperamento *m.* (*tehm-pehr-rah-MEHN-toh*)

temperate (adj.) temperato (*tehm-pehr-RAH-toh*)

temperature temperatura *f. (tehm-pehr-rah-TOOR-rah)*

tempest, storm, gale tempesta *f. (tehm-PEH-stah)*

tempestuous, stormy, gusty (adj.) tempestoso *(tehm-peh-STOH-soh)*

temple (*anatomy*) tempia *f. (TEHM-pyah)*

temple (*religious building*) tempio *m. (TEHM-pyoh)*

temporary "fix," stopgap measure temporaneo *m. (tehm-pohr-RAH-neh-oh)*

tempt (to) tentare *(tehn-TAHR-reh)* 💣

temptation tentazione *f. (tehn-tah-TSYOH-neh)* 💣

tend (*be inclined to, NOT watch over*) (to) tendere *(TEHN-dehr-reh)*

tendency, trend tendenza *f. (tehn-DEHN-tsah)*

tender (adj.) tenero *(TEH-nehr-roh)*

tenderly teneramente *(teh-nehr-rah-MEHN-teh)*

tenderness (*physical*) tenerezza *f. (teh-nehr-REHT-tsah)*

tendon tendine *m. (TEHN-dee-neh)*

tennis tennis *m. (TEHN-nees)*

tense (adj.) teso *(TEH-soh)* 💣

tension, strain, stress tensione *f. (tehn-SYOH-neh)*

tentative (adj.) tentativo *(tehn-tah-TEE-voh)*

term (*word, expression*) termine *m. (TEHR-mee-neh)*

term (*re school*) trimestre *m. (tree-MEH-streh)*

terminal (adj.) terminale *(tehr-mee-NAH-leh)*

terminate (*bring to an end, close, finish*) (to) terminare *(tehr-mee-NAHR-reh)*

terminate (*come to end, reach finish*) (to) terminarsi *(tehr-mee-NAHR-see)*

terminus, end, deadline, abutment termine *m. (TEHR-mee-neh)*

terrace terrazza *f. (tehr-RRAHT-tsah)*

terrible, awful, dreadful (adj.) terribile *(tehr-RREE-bee-leh)*

terribly, awfully, dreadfully terribilmente *(tehr-rree-beel-MEHN-teh)*

territory territorio *m.* (*tehr-rree-TOHR-ryoh*)

terror terrore *m.* (*tehr-RROHR-reh*)

testament, will testamento *m.* (*teh-stah-MEHN-toh*)

testify (to) testimoniare (*teh-stee-moh-NYAHR-reh*)

testimony testimonianza *f.* (*teh-stee-moh-NYAHN-tsah*)

text testo *m.* (*TEH-stoh*) ☛
☛ Don't confuse with **test**!

texture tessitura *f.* (*tehs-see-TOOR-rah*) ☛

theatre teatro *m.* (*teh-AH-troh*) ☛

theme tema *m.* (*TEH-mah*) ☛

theology teologia *f.* (*teh-oh-loh-JEE-ah*) ☛

theory teoria *f.* (*teh-ohr-REE-ah*) ⊃(adj.) **theoretical** -rico⊂ ☛

therapy terapia *f.* (*tehr-rah-PEE-ah*) ☛

thermometer termometro *m.* (*tehr-MOH-meh-troh*) ☛

throne trono *m.* (*TROH-noh*) ☛

timid, bashful, shy (adj.) timido (*TEE-mee-doh*)

timidity, bashfulness, shyness timidezza *f.* (*tee-mee-DEHT-tsah*)

timidly, bashfully, shyly timidamente (*tee-mee-dah-MEHN-teh*)

timor, fear timore *m.* (*tee-MOHR-reh*)

timorous, fearful (adj.) timoroso (*tee-mohr-ROH-soh*)

tint tinta *f.* (*TEEN-tah*)

title titolo *m.* (*TEE-toh-loh*)

tobacco tabacco *m.* (*tah-BAHK-koh*) ☛

tobacco shop tabaccheria *m.* (*tah-bahk-kehr-REE-ah*) ☛

tolerance tolleranza *f.* (*tohl-lehr-RAHN-tsah*) ⊃**tolerant** (adj.) -ante⊂

tolerate (to) tollerare (*tohl-lehr-RAHR-reh*)

tomb, grave tomba *f.* (*TOHM-bah*)

tone tono *m.* (*TOH-noh*)

tonic tonico *m.* (*TOH-nee-koh*) ⊃(adj.)⊂

tonsil tonsilla *f.* (*tohn-SEEL-lah*)

tonsillitis tonsillite *f.* (*tohn-seel-LEE-teh*)

torch torcia *f.* (*TOHR-chah*)

torment tormento *m.* (*tohr-MEHN-toh*)

torment, nag, tease (to) tormentare (*tohr-mehn-TAHR-reh*)

torrent torrente *m.* (*tohr-RREHN-teh*)

torture tortura *f.* (*tohr-TOOR-rah*)

torture (to) torturare (*tohr-toor-RAHR-reh*)

total totale *m.* (*toh-TAH-leh*) ⊃(adj.)⊂

totality, entirety totalità *f.* (*toh-tah-lee-TAH*)

touch tocco *m.* (*TOHK-koh*) 💧⃰

touch (to) toccare (*tohk-KAHR-reh*) 💧⃰

tourism, sightseeing turismo *m.* (*toor-REEZ-moh*) 💧⃰

tourist turista *m. & f.* (*toor-REE-stah*) ⊃(adj.) -tico⊂

tower torre *f.* (*TOHRR-reh*) 💧⃰

trademark, brand marca *f.* (*MAHR-kah*)

tradition tradizione *f.* (*trah-dee-TSYOH-neh*)

traditional (adj.) tradizionale (*trah-dee-tsyoh-NAH-leh*)

traffic (*vehicular flow*) traffico *m.* (*TRAHF-fee-koh*)

tragedy tragedia *f.* (*trah-JEH-dyah*)

tragic (adj.) tragico (*TRA-jee-koh*)

train (*of railway,* NOT *garment*) treno *m.* (*TREH-noh*)

tram, trolley, streetcar tram *m.* (*TRAHM*)

trampoline, springboard trampolino *m.* (*trahm-poh-LEE-noh*)

tramway (*streetcar line* OR *tracks*) tramvia *f.* (*trahm-VEE-ah*)

tranquil, peaceful (adj.) tranquillo (*trahn-KWEEL-loh*)

tranquillity   tranquillità *f.* (*trahn-kweel-lee-TAH*)

transfer   trasferimento *m.* (*trahs-fehr-ree-MEHN-toh*) 🕭

transfer (to)   trasferire (*trahs-fehr-REER-reh*) 🕭

transform (to)   trasformare (*trahs-fohr-MAHR-reh*) 🕭

transfusion   trasfusione *f.* (*trahs-foo-ZYOH-neh*) 🕭

transit (*passage*)   transito *m.* (*TRAHN-see-toh*)

transition   transizione *f.* (*trahn-zee-TSYOH-neh*)

transmission (*electronic*), **broadcast**   trasmissione *f.* (*trahz-mees-SYOH-neh*)

transmit, convey (*electronically*) (to)   trasmettere (*trah-ZMEHT-tehr-reh*) 🕭

transparent (adj.)   trasparente (*trah-spahr-REHN-teh*) 🕭

transport, transportation   trasporto *m.* (*trahs-POHR-toh*) 🕭

transport, convey (*move*) (to)   trasportare (*trah-spohr-TAHR-reh*) 🕭

transvestite   travestito *m.* (*trah-veh-STEE-toh*)

trap, snare, pitfall   trappola *f.* (*TRAHP-poh-lah*)

traverse, crossing   traversata *f.* (*trah-vehr-SAH-tah*)

traverse (to)   traversare (*trah-vehr-SAHR-reh*)

treasure   tesoro *m.* (*teh-ZOHR-roh*) 🕭

treasury (*governmental office or building*)   tesoro *m.* (*teh-ZOHR-roh*) 🕭

treat (to)   trattare (*traht-TAHR-reh*)

   ⓘ The antoynom: **to mistreat**—maltrattare (*mahl-traht-TAHR-reh*)

treatment   trattamento *m.* (*traht-tah-MEHN-toh*)

treaty   trattato *m.* (*traht-TAH-toh*)

tremble, shake, quake, quiver, shiver (to)   tremare (*treh-MAHR-reh*)

tremendous (adj.)   tremendo (*treh-MEHN-doh*)

triangle (*geometric*)   triangolo *m.* (*tree-AHN-goh-loh*)

tribunal   tribunale *m.* (*tree-boo-NAH-leh*)

tributary   tributario *m.* (*tree-boo-TAHR-ryoh*) ➲(adj.)➪

tribute   tributo *m.* (*tree-BOO-toh*)

trick   trucco *m.* (*TROOK-koh*) 💣

triple (adj.)   triplice (*TREE-plee-cheh*)

triple (to)   triplicare (*tree-plee-KAHR-reh*)

trite (adj.)   trito (*TREE-toh*)

triumph   trionfo *m.* (*tree-OHN-foh*)

triumph (to)   trionfare (*tree-ohn-FAHR-reh*)

triumphal (adj.)   trionfale (*tree-ohn-FAH-leh*)

triumphant (adj.)   trionfante (*tree-ohn-FAHN-teh*)

trophy   trofeo *m.* (*troh-FEH-oh*)

tropics   tropico *m.* (*TROH-pee-koh*) ⊃(adj.) **tropical**☾

trot   trotto *m.* (*TROHT-toh*)

trot (to)   trottare (*troh-TAHR-reh*)

trumpet   tromba *f.* (*TROHM-bah*)

trunk (*tree*), stem (*plant*)   tronco *m.* (*TROHN-koh*) 💣

tube, (plumbing) pipe   tubo *m.* (*TOO-boh*)
   ⓘ **hose**—tubo flessibile *m.* (___*flehs-see-BEE-leh*). A **(small) tube (*of toothpaste, and so forth*)**—tubetto (*too-BEHT-toh*)

tuberculosis   tubercolosi *f.* (*too-behr-koh-LOH-see*)

tulip   tulipano *m.* (*too-lee-PAH-noh*)

tumor   tumore *m.* (*too-MOHR-reh*)

tumult, hubbub, riot   tumulto *m.* (*too-MOOL-toh*)
   ⓘ Closely related, but noncognate: **to riot**—tumultare (*too-mool-TAHR-reh*)

tuna   tonno *m.* (*TOHN-noh*) 💣

turban   turbante *m.* (*toor-BAHN-teh*)

turbine   turbine *f.* (*toor-BEE-nah*)
   ⓘ Related noncognates: **whirlwind**—turbine *m.* (*TOOR-bee-neh*); **to swirl**—turbinare (*toor-bee-NAHR-reh*)

tweed tweed *m.* (*teh-WEE-deh*)

type (*kind OR sort, NOT print face*) tipo *m.* (*TEE-poh*) ⊃**typical** (adj.) - pico⊂

tyranny tirannia *f.* (*teer-rahn-NEE-ah*) 🔊

tyrant tiranno *m.* (*teer-RAHN-noh*) 🔊

—U—

ulcer ulcera *f.* (*OOL-chehr-rah*)

ultimate, last (adj.) ultimo (*OOL-tee-moh*)

umbrella ombrello *m.* (*ohm-BREHL-loh*) 🔊

umbilical knot, navel, belly button ombellico *m.* (*ohm-behl-LEE-koh*)

unable, unfit, incapable (adj.) inable (*ee-NAH-bee-leh*), incapace (*een-kah-PAH-cheh*)

unanimous (adj.) unanime (*oo-NAH-nee-meh*)

uncertain (adj.) incerto (*een-CHEHR-toh*) 🔊

uncertainty incertezza *f.* (*een-chehr-TEHT-tsah*) 🔊

unconditional (adj.) incondizionato (*een-kohn-dee-tsyoh-NAH-toh*)

unconscious (adj.) inconscio (*een-KOHN-shoh*) 🔊

undecided (adj.) indeciso (*een-deh-CHEE-soh*), incerto (*een-CHER-toh*) 🔊

undoubtedly indubbiamente (*een-doob-byah-MEHN-teh*) 🔊

unequal (adj.) ineguale (*ee-neh-GWAH-leh*) 🔊

unexpected (adj.) inaspettato (*ee-nah-speht-TAH-toh*) 🔊

unexpectedly inaspettatamente (*ee-aah-speht-tah-tah-MEHN-teh*) 🔊

unfruitful, fruitless, unsuccessful (adj.) infruttuoso (*een-froot-TWOHS-soh*) 🔊

unguent, ointment, salve unguento *m.* (*oon-GWEHN-toh*)

uniform (*official garb*) uniforme *f.* (*oo-nee-FOHR-meh*)

uniform, even (*in consistency or quality*) (adj.) uniforme (*oo-nee-FOHR-meh*)

uniformity, evenness uniformità *f.* (*oo-nee-fohr-mee-TAH*)

unilateral, one-sided (adj.) unilaterale (*oo-nee-lah-tehr-RAH-leh*)

union (*association, NOT labor organization*) unione *f.* (*oo-NYOH-neh*)

unique (adj.) unico (*OO-nee-koh*)

unisex (adj.) unisessuale (*oo-nee-sehs-SWAH-leh*)

unit unità *f.* (*oo-nee-TAH*)

unite (to) unire (*oo-NEER-reh*)

unity unità *f.* (*oo-nee-TAH*)

universe universo *m.* (*oo-nee-VEHR-soh*)

universal (adj.) universale (*oo-nee-verh-SAH-leh*)

university, college università *f.* (*oo-nee-vehr-see-TAH*)

unjust, unfair (adj.) ingiusto (*een-JOO-stoh*) ♠

unjustified, unwarranted (adj.) ingiustificato (*een-joo-stee-fee-KAH-toh*) ♠

unservicable, unusable (adj.) inservibile (*een-sehr-VEE-bee-leh*) ♠

unstable, unsteady (adj.) instabile (*een-STAH-bee-leh*) ♠

urban (adj.) urbano (*oor-BAH-noh*)

urgency urgenza *f.* (*oor-JEHN-tsah*) ➲(adj.) **urgent, pressing** -nte↻

urinal orinatoio *m.* (*ohr-ree-nah-TOH-yoh*) ♠

urinate (to) orinare (*ohr-ree-NAHR-reh*) ♠

urine orina *f.* (*ohr-REE-nah*) ♠

urn urna *f.* (*OOR-nah*)

usage uso *m.* (*OO-zoh*), usanza *f.* (*oo-ZAHN-tsah*)

use uso *m.* (*OO-zoh*)

use (to) usare (*oo-ZAHR-reh*)

user utente *m.* (*oo-TEHN-teh*) ♠

usual (adj.) usuale (*oo-zoo-AH-leh*)

usually usualmente (*oo-swahl-MEHN-teh*)

usurp, encroach upon(to)   usupare (*oo-zoo-PAHR-reh*)

utensil, tool   utensile *m.* (*oo-tehn-SEE-leh*)

uterus, womb   utero *m.* (*OO-tehr-roh*)

utile, utilitarian, useful, helpful (*re thing, NOT person*) (adj.)   utile (*OO-tee-leh*)
   ⓘ The antonym: **useless** (adj.)—inutile (*ee-NOO-tee-leh*)

utility   utilità *f.* (*oo-tee-lee-TAH*)

utilize (to)   utilizzare (*oo-tee-leed-DZAHR-reh*)

—V—

vacant (adj.)   vacante (*vah-KAHN-teh*)

vacation   vacanze *f.* (*vah-KAHN-tseh*)

vaccination   vaccinazione *f.* (*vaht-chee-nah-TSYOH-neh*)

vaccine   vaccino *m.* (*vaht-CHEE-noh*)

vacillating (adj.)   vacillante (*vah-cheel-LAHN-teh*)

vagina   vagina *f.* (*vah-JEE-nah*)

vaginal (adj.)   vaginale (*vah-jee-NAH-leh*)

vague (adj.)   vago (*VAH-goh*)

vain (*futile*) (adj.)   vano (*VAH-noh*)

vain (*conceited*) (adj.)   vanitoso (*vah-nee-TOH-soh*)

(in) vain   in vano (*een VAH-noh*)

valid (adj.)   valido (*VAH-lee-doh*)

valise, suitcase   valigia *f.* (*vah-LEE-jah*)

valley   valle *f.* (*VAHL-leh*)
   ⓘ A **(small) valley, dale, glen**—valleta (*vahl-LEH-tah*)

valor, value, worth   valore *m.* (*vah-LOHR-reh*)

valorous, valiant (adj.)   valoroso (*vah-lohr-ROH-soh*)

valuation   valutazione *f.* (*vah-loo-tah-TSYOH-neh*)

value (to)   valutare (*vah-loo-TAHR-reh*)

(of) value, valuable (adj.)   di valore (*dee vah-LOHR-reh*)
  ① Note this antonym in particular: **worthless** (adj.)—senza valore
  (*SEHN-tsah vah-LOHR-reh*). In Italian, the preposition *senza* always
  means *without*.

vandal   vandalo *m.* (*VAHN-dah-loh*)

vanilla   vaniglia *f.* (*vah-NEE-lyah*)

vanity, conceit   vanità *f.* (*vah-nee-TAH*)

vapor, steam   vapore *m.* (*vah-POHR-reh*)

variation   variazione *f.* (*vahr-ryah-TSYOH-neh*)

varied (adj.)   svariato (*zvahr-RYAH-toh*) 🔥

variety   varietà *f.* (*vahr-ryeh-TAH*)

various (adj.)   vario (*VAHR-ryoh*)

vary (to)   variare (*vahr-RYAHR-reh*)

vase   vaso *m.* (*VAH-zoh*)

vast (adj.)   vasto (*VAH-stoh*)

vehemence   veemenza *f.* (*veh-eh-MEHN-tsah*) ➲**vehement** (adj.) -nte ℃

vehicle   veicolo *m.* (*veh-EE-koh-loh*)

veil   velo *m.* (*VEH-loh*)

vein (*anatomical, botanical*)   vena *f.* (*VEH-nah*)

velocity, speed   velocità *f.* (*veh-loh-chee-TAH*)

(with great) velocity, swift, speedy (adj.)   veloce (*veh-LOH-cheh*)

velvet   velluto *m.* (*vehl-LOO-toh*) ➲**velvet** (adj.) di velluto℃

vend, sell (to)   vendere (*VEHN-dehr-reh*)

vendition, sale   vendita *f.* (*VEHN-dee-tah*)

vendor   venditore *m.* (*vehn-dee-TOHR-reh*)

ventilate (to)   ventilare (*vehn-tee-LAHR-reh*)

ventilation   ventilazione *f.* (*vehn-tee-lah-TSYOH-neh*)

ventilator, (electric) fan, louver ventilatore *m.* (*vehn-tee-lah-TOHR-reh*)

venture ventura *f.* (*vehn-TOOR-r*ah)

venturesome (adj.) avventuroso (*ahv-vehn-toor-ROH-zoh*) ✒

veranda, porch (*of house, villa, hotel, and so forth*) veranda *f.* (*vehr-RAHN-dah*)

verb verbo *m.* (*VEHR-boh*)

verbose, wordy (adj.) verboso (*vehr-BOH-soh*)

verbal (adj.) verbale (*vehr-BAH-leh*)

verdict verdetto *m.* (*vehr-DEHT-toh*)

verdure, greenery verde *m.* (*VEHR-deh*), verzura (*literary*) *f.* (*vehr-ZOOR-rah*), verdura (*rare*) (*vehr-DOOR-rah*)

verify (to) verificare (*vehr-ree-fee-KAHR-reh*)

verily, truly veramente (*vehr-rah-MEHN-teh*)

verity, truth verità *f.* (*vehr-ree-TAH*)
 ⓘ Important, related noncognates: **true** (*actual*) (adj.)—vero (*VEHR-roh*); **truthful** (adj.)—veritiero (*vehr-ree-TYEH-roh*)

vernacular vernacolo *m.* (*vehr-NAH-koh-loh*) ⊃(adj.)⊂

versatile (adj.) versatile (*vehr-sah-TEE-leh*)

verse verso *m.* (*VEHR-soh*)

version versione *f.* (*vehr-ZYOH-neh*)

vertical (adj.) verticale (*vehr-tee-KAH-leh*)

vertigo, dizziness vertigini *f.* (*vehr-TEE-jee-nee*)

very (adj.) vero (*VEHR-roh*)
 ✒ This adjective does NOT apply to the usage of **very** = "selfsame" (e.g., "the very one"). In that instance, the noncognate *stesso* (*STEHS-soh*) is used. In adverbial form, **very**—molto (*MOHL-toh*), or is connoted via the suffix –issimo. Thus, **beautiful**—bello becomes **very beautiful**—bellissimo, and so forth.

vestiments, clothes, clothing vestiti *m.* (*veh-STEE-tee*), abiti (*AH-bee-tee*), vestimento (*veh-stee-MEHN-toh*)

ⓘ Just as in English the terms *clothes* and *clothing* are used interchangeably, so are plural *vestiti* and *abiti* in Italian. The meaning of *vestimento* as *vestiti* and *abiti* is antiquated, found in literature. Closely related: **dress** (*garment*)—vestito *m.* (*veh-STEE-toh*); and **to dress, to get dressed**—vestirsi (*veh-STEER-see*).

veteran (*experienced doer* OR *military*)   veterano *m.* (*veh-tehr-RAH-noh*)

veterinarian   veterinario *m.* (*veh-tehr-ree-NAHR-ryoh*)

veternary (adj.)   veterinario (*veh-tehr-ree-NAHR-ryoh*)

veto   veto *m.* (*VEH-toh*)

veto (to)   vietare (*vyeh-TAHR-reh*) 💣

viaduct   viadotto *m.* (*vyah-DOHT-toh*)

vibrate (to)   vibrare (*vee-BRAHR-reh*)

vibration   vibrazione *f.* (*vee-brah-TSYOH-neh*)

vicinity, neighborhood, immediate area   vicinato *m.* (*vee-chee-NAH-toh*), vicinanza *f.* (*vee-chee-NAHN-tsah*)
ⓘ Related noncognates: **neighbor**—vicino *m.* (*vee-CHEE-noh*), prossimo *m.* (*PROHS-see-moh*); and **(in the) vicinity, nearby, neighboring** (adj.)—vicino (*vee-CHEE-noh*)

vicious (adj.)   vizioso (*vee-TSYOH-zoh*) 💣

victim   vittima *f.* (*VEET-tee-mah*) 💣

victory   vittoria *f.* (*veet-TOHR-ryah*)

vigilant, watchful (adj.)   vigilante (*vee-jee-LAHN-teh*)

vigor, stamina   vigore *m.* (*vee-GOHR-reh*)

vigorous, forceful (adj.)   vigoroso (*vee-gohr-ROH-soh*)

vile (adj.)   vile (*VEE-leh*)

villa (*small*), **cottage**   villetta *f.* (*veel-LEHT-tah*), casetta *f.* (*kah-SEHT-tah*)

village   villaggio *m.* (*veel-LAHD-joh*)

vindicate (to)   rivendicare (*ree-vehn-dee-KAHR-reh*) 💣

vineyard   vigneto *m.* (*vee-NYEH-toh*), vigna *f.* (*VEE-nyah*) 💣

viola   viola *f.* (*VYOH-lah*)

violate, rape (to)   violare (*vyoh-LAHR-reh*)

violation   violazione *f.* (*vyoh-lah-TSYOH-neh*), contravvenzione (*kohn-trahv-vehn-TSYOH-neh*)

violator   violatore *m.* (*vyoh-lah-TOHR-reh*), contravventore (*kohn-trahv-vehn-TOHR-reh*)

violence   violenza *f.* (*vyoh-LEHN-tsah*) ⊃**violent** (adj.) -nto C

violet (*flower*)   violetta *f.* (*vyoh-LEHT-tah*) ⊃(adj.) -to C

violin   violino *m.* (*vyoh-LEE-noh*)

VIP   VIP *m. & f.* (*VEEP*)

virgin   vergine *f.* (*VEHR-jee-neh*) ♦

virile (adj.)   virile (*veer-REE-leh*)

virility, manliness   virilità *f.* (*veer-ree-lee-TAH*)

virtual (adj.)   virtuale (*veer-too-AH-leh*)

virtue   virtù *f.* (*veer-TOO*)

virtuous (adj.)   virtuoso (*veer-TWOH-soh*)

virus   virus *m.* (*VEER-roos*)

visa   visto *m.* (*VEE-stoh*)

viscous, thick (*semiliquid*), sticky (adj.)   viscoso (*vee-SKOH-soh*)

visible (adj.)   visibile (*vee-ZEE-bee-leh*)

vision (*sense of sight*), (viewed) sight   vista *f.* (*VEE-stah*)

vision (*mental sight, apparition*)   visione *f.* (*vee-ZYOH-neh*)

visit   visita *f.* (*VEE-zee-tah*)

visit (to)   visitare (*vee-zee-TAHR-reh*)

visitor   visitatore *m.* (*vee-zee-tah-TOHR-reh*) ⊃*f.* -trice C

vista, view   vista *f.* (*VEE-stah*), veduta *f.* (*veh-DOO-tah*)

visual (adj.)   visuale (*vee-SWAH-leh*)

vital (adj.)   vitale (*vee-TAH-leh*)
　　① As here and below, the concepts of **life** and **liveliness** are embraced, in Italian, in terms beginning with *vita-* and *viva-*. Importantly related *vita-*

noncognates are: **life**—vita *f.* (*VEE-tah*); and **(one's) livelihood**—la vita *f.* (*lah VEE-tah*).

vitality   vitalità *f.* (*vee-tah-lee-TAH*)

vitamin   vitamina *f.* (*vee-tah-MEE-nah*)

vivacious, lively (adj.)   vivace (*vee-VAH-cheh*)
> ⓘ The notable *viva-* noncognates are: **to live, to be alive**—vivere (*vee-VEHR-reh*); **live** (adj.)—vivo (*VEE-voh*); **alive, living** (adj.)—vivente (*vee-VEHN-teh*); and **lifestyle**—modo (*m.*) di vivere (*MOH-doh dee VEE-vehr-reh*).

vivaciously, briskly   vivacemente (*vee-vah-cheh-MEHN-teh*)

vivacity, liveliness, briskness   vivacità *f.* (*vee-vah-chee-TAH*)

vivid (adj.)   vivido (*VEE-vee-doh*)

vocabulary   vocabolario *m.* (*voh-kah-boh-LAHR-ryoh*)

vocal (adj.)   vocale (*voh-KAH-leh*)

vocation, calling   vocazione *f.* (*voh-kah-TSYOH-neh*)

vogue   voga *f.* (*VOH-gah*)

voice, rumor   voce *f.* (*VOH-cheh*) ♠※

volcano   vulcano *m.* (*vool-KAH-noh*) ♠※

voltage   voltaggio *m.* (*vohl-TAHD-joh*)

volume (*of space*), bulk   volume *m.* (*voh-LOO-meh*)

voluminous, bulky (adj.)   voluminoso (*voh-loo-mee-NOH-soh*)

volunteer   volontario *m.* (*voh-lohn-TAHR-ryoh*) ⊃**voluntary** (adj.)⊂

vomit, discorge (to)   vomitare (*voh-mee-TAHR-reh*)

vortex, whirlpool, eddy   vortice *m.* (*VOHR-tee-cheh*)

vote   voto *m.* (*VOH-toh*)

vote (to)   votare (*voh-TAHR-reh*)

voter   votante *m. & f.* (*voh-TAHN-teh*), elettore (*eh-leht-TOH-reh*) ⊃*f.* -trice⊂

voters, (the) electorate   votanti *m.* (*voh-TAHN-tee*), elettorato (*eh-leht-toh-RAH-toh*)

voting   votazione *f.* (*voh-tah-TSYOH-neh*)

voyage, journey, trip, travel (*in general*)   viaggio *m.* (*VYAHD-joh*) 🖝
   ⓘ Two related noncognates are: **travel agency**—agenzia (*f.*) di viaggi (*ah-jehn-TSEE-ah dee VYAHD-jee*); and **travel agent**—agente (*m.*) di viaggi (*ah-JEHN-teh____*).

voyage, travel (to)   viaggiare (*vyahd-JAHR-reh*) 🖝

voyager, traveler   viaggiatore *m.* (*vyahd-jah-TOHR-reh*) 🖝

vulgar, common, vernacular (adj.)   volgare (*vohl-GAHR-reh*) 🖝

vulgarity   volgarità *f.* (*vohl-gahr-ree-TAH*) 🖝

vulnerable (adj.)   vulnerabile (*vool-nehr-RAH-bee-leh*)

—W—

   ⓘ No native-Italian word begins with the letter *w*, and almost none contain it even in component form. Thus, excepting only a few imports from other languages, this entire alphabetic section is notable for the phonetic similarity of terms that uniformly display that one negative characteristic: the missing initial *w*. The essential (*WH*) or (*V*) pronunciation of these terms is dependent largely on the initial source of each, and / or the degree to which it has been absorbed into the Italian vocabulary.

waltz   valzer *m.* (*VAHL-tsehr*) 🖝

weekend   fine settimana *m. or f.* (*FEE-ne seht-tee-MAH-nah*), weekend *m.* (*WEE-kehnd*)

west   ovest *m.* (*OH-vehst*) 🖝

western (*movie*)   western *m.* (*WEH-stehrn*)

whiskey   whiskey (*WEE-zkee*) 🖝

widow   vedova *f.* (*VEH-doh-vah*) 🖝

widower   védovo *m.* (*veh-DOH-voh*) 🖝

worm   verme *m.* (*VEHR-meh*) 🖝

—X—

   ⓘ No native-Italian word begins with the letter *x*, and few contain it even in component form. Thus, excepting only a few imports from other languages, this entire alphabetic section is notable for the phonetic similarity of terms that uniformly display that one negative characteristic: the missing initial *x*.

X-ray (*beam or process*)   raggio X *m.* (*RAHD-joh eeks*) 🔊

X-ray (*plate or image*)   radiografia *f.* (*rah-dyoh-grah-FEE-ah*) 🔊

X-ray (to)   radiografare (*rah-dyoh-grah-FAHR-reh*) 🔊

xylophone   silofono *m.* (*see-LOH-foh-noh*) 🔊

—Y—

ⓘ No native-Italian word begins with the letter *y*, and almost none contain it even in compoent form. Thus, excepting only a few imports from other languages, this entire alphabetic section is notable for the phonetic similarity of terms that uniformly display that one negative characteristic: the missing initial *y*.

yard (*English measure*)   iarda *f.* (*YAHR-dah*) 🔊

yellow (adj.)   giallo (*JAHL-loh*) 🔊

yogurt   yogurt *m.* (*YOH-goort*)

—Z—

zeal   zelo *m.* (*DZEH-loh*)

zealous (adj.)   zeloso (*dzehl-OH-soh*)

zebra   zebra *f.* (*DZEH-brah*)

zephyr   zeffiro *m.* (*DZEHF-feer-roh*)

zero   zero *m.* (*DZEHR-roh*)

zinc   zinco *m.* (*TSEENG-koh*)

zone   zona *f.* (*DZOH-nah*)

zoology   zoologia *f.* (*dzoh-oh-loh-JEE-ah*)

zoological (adj.)   zoologico (*dzoh-oh-LOH-jee-koh*)

LISTA DI TERMINI "SIMILI FALSI"
List of "Falsely Similar" Terms

The preceding list of cognates and near-cognates is so extensive that an incautious learner might be led to assume that virtually any Italian term that looks or sounds highly similar to an English word is, in fact, a cross-language twin. But several hundred Italian words clearly break that rule: either in spelling or sound they seem English-like, but in fact bear little or no relationship whatsoever to the words that they appear to mirror. They are, in short, false cognates—sometimes called "deceitful," "unfaithful," "specious," or "untrue" cognates—and should be carefully noted lest the learner assume erroneous meanings for their misleading appearances or sounds.

The only way to fully master these misleaders is to carefully memorize them by rote. The learner who does not want to be slowed in his or her development of the substantial vocabulary offered in the preceding pages should at least give this list a single careful review, in hope that the more egregious deceivers herein may become at least subconsciously flagged in his or her memory.

affluente *m.* (*ahf-floo-EHN-teh*)   tributary
   NOT *affluent*, which is ***opulento*** (*adj.*)

affrontare (*ahf-frohn-TAHR-reh*)   to face directly, to confront
   NOT *to [give] affront*, which is ***insultare***; or *to [give] offense*, which is ***offendere***

   ◆ This is a particularly confusing verb, in that the closely related noun ***affronto*** does mean *affront*. The learner will do well to limit him- / herself to the verb ***confrontare***, which means the same as ***affrontare***, minus the confusion!

agenda *f.* (*ah-JEHN-dah*)   notebook
   NOT *program outline*, which is ***ordine del giorno***

ago *f.* (*AH-goh*) needle
  NOT *in the past,* which is *fa*

ammenda *f.* (*ahm-MEHN-dah*) fine (*penalty*)
  NOT *amendment,* which is **emendamento** (*m.*)

annoiarsi (*ahn-noh-YAHR-see*) to be bored
  NOT *to be annoyed,* which is **avere a noia**
  ☛ This is another term with high confusion potential, in that the closely related verb **annoire** DOES include the denotations *to annoy* and *to harrass,* as well as that of *to bore.*

ape *f.* (*AH-peh*) bee
  NOT *ape,* which is **scimmia** (*f.*)

argomento *m.* (*ahr-goh-MEHN-toh*) (specific) logical point, thesis
  NOT *dispute,* which is **disputa** (*f.*); or *quarrel,* which is **lite** (*f.*)
  ☛ The subtlety embodied in this false cognate is considerable: whereas in English we can define either the entirety of a dispute and /or a specific position within same as an *argument,* in Italian the general concept is embraced by the terms noted above, and only it's component parts are referred to as **argomenti.**

arme *f.* (*AHR-meh*) weapon
  NOT *army,* which is **esercito** (*m.*); or *forelimb,* which is **braccio** (*m.*)

armi *f.* (*AHR-mee*) weapons
  NOT *army,* which is **esercito** (*m.*); or *forelimbs,* which are **bracci** (*m.*)

assente *m. & f.* (*ahs-SEHN-teh*) absentee; absent (*adj.*)
  NOT *assent,* which is **assenso** (*m.*); or *ascent,* which is **salita** (*f.*)

assorto (*adj.*) (*ahs-SOHR-toh*) absorbed
  NOT *assorted,* which is **assortito** (*adj.*); or *assortment* (*m.*), which is **assortimento**

atlante *m.* (*aht-LAHN-teh*) atlas
  NOT *Atlantic,* which is **atlantico** (*adj.*)

attaccamento *m.* (*aht-tahk-kah-MEHN-toh*) attachment
  NOT *attack,* which is **attacco** (*m.*)

attendere (*aht-tehn-DEHR-reh*) to await, to expect, to attend to business
  NOT *to be present at,* which is **assistere;** or *to pay attention,* which is **fare attenzione**

attimo *m.* (*AHT-tee-moh*) instant
   NOT *atom*, which is **atomo** (*m.*)

attitudine *f.* (*aht-tee-TOO-dee-neh*) aptitude
   NOT *attitude*, which is **atteggiamento** (*m.*)

atto *m.* (*AHT-toh*) act, deed
   NOT *auto*, which is **auto** (*f.*) or **automobile** (*f.*)

attuale (*adj.*) (*aht-TWAH-leh*) here and now, present
   NOT *actual* (nonimaginary), which is **vero** or **concreto** (*adj.*); or *actual*
   (proven), which is **effettivo** (*adj.*)

avvertire (*ahv-vehr-TEER-reh*) to warn, to alert
   NOT *to advertise*, which is *fare* **pubblicità, reclamizzare**

avvocato *m.* (*ahv-voh-KAH-toh*) advocate, lawyer
   NOT *avocado*, which is **pera** (*f.*) **avocado**

banchina *f.* (*bahn-KEE-nah*) pier
   NOT *bank* (financial institution), which is **banca** (*f.*); or *embankment*,
   which is **argine** (*m.*)

barba *f.* (*BAHR-bah*) beard
   NOT *barber*, which is **barbiere** (*m.*)

barbaro *m.* (*bahr-BAHR-roh*) barbarian (*noun & adj.*); barbarous (*adj.*)
   NOT *barber*, which is **barbiere** (*m.*)

barca *f.* (*BAHR-kah*) boat
   NOT *bark* (of tree), which is **scorza** (*f.*); or (of dog), which is **abbaia-
   mento** (*m.*)

battello *m.* (*baht-TEHL-loh*) boat
   NOT *battle*, which is **battaglia** (*f.*)

benda *f.* (BEHN-dah) bandage, blindfold, headband
   NOT *bend*, which is **curva** (*f.*)

bimbo *m.* (*BEEM-boh*) baby, child
   NOT *empty-headed young woman of easy virtue*, which is **sudiciona**
   (*f.*)

bisogno *m.* (*bee-ZOH-nyoh*) want, need
   NOT *bison*, which is **bisonte** (*m.*)

bollo *m.* (*BOHL-loh*) stamp
   NOT *bowl*, which is **scodella** (*f.*)

bottino *m.* (*boht-TEE-noh*) booty, loot, plunder
NOT *button,* which is **bottone** (*m.*)

brama *f.* (*BRAH-mah*) ardent longing, eagerness
NOT *Brahma* (bull or cow), which is **brahma** (*m.*)

brano *m.* (*BRAH-noh*) (musical or literary) excerpt, passage
NOT *brain,* which is **cervello** (*m.*)

bravo (adj.) (*BRAH-voh*) (especially) artful, clever, good; bravo, villain, hired assassin (*n.*)
NOT *brave,* which is **coraggioso** (*adj.*)

bruttezza *f.* (*broot-TEHT-tsah*) ugliness
NOT *brutality,* which is **brutalità** (*f.*)

brutto (adj.) (*BROOT-toh*) ugly
NOT *brute* which is **bruto** (*m.*); or *brutal,* which is **brutale** (*adj.*)

buco *m.* (*BOO-koh*) hole
NOT *book,* which is *libro* (*m.*)

bulletta *f.* (*bool-LEHT-tah*) tack, hobnail
NOT *bullet,* which is **pallottola** (*f.*)

burro *m.* (*BOORR-roh*) butter
NOT *ass, burro, donkey,* or *jackass,* which is **asino** (*m.*) or **somaro** (*m.*)

busta *f.* (*BOO-stah*) envelope
NOT *bust* (sculpture), which is **busto** (*m.*); or *bosom,* which is **petto** (*m.*) or **seno** (*m.*)

C (*on water faucets*), caldo (adj.) (*KAHL-doh*) hot
NOT *cold,* which is *F—freddo*
🖝 This is, in practical terms, perhaps the most dangerous of all Italian-English false cognates, as many an accidentally scalded traveler can attest! All Italian words relating to heat derive from the masculine noun **calore** (*heat*—closely related to the English term *calorie*: heat unit), and thus are anti-intuitive to any English speaker in both spelling and sound.

caffettiera *f.* (*kahf-feht-TYEHR-rah*) coffeepot
NOT *serve-yourself eating establishment,* which is unknown to Italy

camera *f.* (*KAH-mehr-rah*) room (*of structure*)
NOT *picture-taking device,* which is **macchina** (*f.*) **fotografica**
ⓘ Although most Italians now understand, in context, what an English speaker usually means by use of this term, to them the word retains its original meaning. An Italian *room* can be defined by several

terms, principal among which are **sala** (*SAH-lah*), **stanza** (*STAHN-tsah*), and **camera**. A **sala** is a hall, reception room, or other larger-than-average public space; in a particularly large private house, the living and dining rooms may be referred to as **sale**. The word **stanza** generally applies, or can be modified to apply, to virtually any sort of Italian room, with the implication that it is at least semiprivate. The term **camera** is equivalent to *chamber*, and is used only in those instances where quiet privacy is required and assumed.

campo *m.* (*KAHM-poh*) field, small plaza (*dialect form*)
NOT *camp*, which is **accampamento** (*m.*)

cane *m.* (*KAH-neh*) dog
NOT *cane* (walking aid), which is **bastone** (*m.*); or *tropical plant*, which is **canna** (*f.*)

capello *m.* (*kah-PEHL-loh*) hair (*one*)
NOT *chapel*, which is **cappella** (*f.*); *hat*, which is **cappello** (*m.*); or *cap*, which is **berretto** (*m.*)

capo *m.* (*KAH-poh*) chief, headman, leader
NOT *cap*, which is **berretto** (*m.*)

carburante *m.* (*kahr-boo-RAHN-teh*) fuel
NOT *carburetor*, which is **carburetore** (*m.*)

carta *f.* (*KAHR-tah*) card, paper, chart, map
NOT *cart*, which is **carro** (*m.*)

cartone *m.* (*kahr-TOH-neh*) cardboard, cartoon
NOT *carton*, which is **scatola** (*f.*) or **scatola di cartone**

cascata *f.* (*kah-SKAH-tah*) cascade, waterfall
NOT *casket*, which is **cassettina** (*f.*)

cassetto *m.* (*kahs-SEHT-toh*) drawer
NOT *cassette*, which is **cassetta** (*f.*)

casto (*adj.*) (*KAH-stoh*) chaste
NOT *cast* (of actors), which is **complesso** (*m.*); or *throw*, which is **getto** (*m.*)

catino *m.* (*kah-TEE-noh*) basin
NOT *cat*, which is **gatto** (*m.*); or *kitten*, which is **gattino**

cavo *m.* (*KAH-voh*) hollow (*noun & adj.*)
NOT *cave*, which is **caverna** (*f.*)

celare (*cheh-LAHR-reh*)   to conceal
   NOT *celery,* which is **sedano** (*m.*); or *cellar,* which is **cantina** (*f.*)

cespuglio *m.* (*cheh-SPOO-lyoh*)   bush
   NOT *cesspool,* which is **pozzo nero**

circo *m.* (*CHEER-koh*)   circus
   NOT *circle,* which is **circolo** (*m.*); *circular,* which is **circolare** (*adj.*); or
   approximately, which is **circa**

clero *m.* (*KLEHR-roh*)   clergy
   NOT *clear,* which is **chiaro** (*adj.*)

coda *f.* (*KOH-dah*)   tail, (musical) ending
   NOT *code* (law), which is **codice** (*m.*); or *code* (secret writing), which
   is **cifrario** (*m.*)

colare (*koh-LAHR-reh*)   to strain
   NOT *collar,* which is **colletto** (*m.*)

colazione *f.* (*koh-lah-TSYOH-neh*)   light meal, lunch
   NOT *collection,* which is **collezione** (*f.*) or **raccolta** (*f.*)

collant *m.* (*kohl-LAHN-teh*)   pantyhose
   NOT *coolant,* which is **refrigerante** (*m.*)

colto (adj.) (*KOHL-toh*)   cultured, cultivated, educated
   NOT *colt,* which is **puledro** (*m.*)

comodo *m.* (*KOH-moh-doh*)   convenience, comfort; convenient, comfortable (*adj.*)
   NOT *toilet fixture,* which is **latrina** (*f.*)

comprare (*kohm-PRAHR-reh*)   to purchase
   NOT *to compare,* which is **comparare**

compreso (adj.) (*kohm-PREH-soh*)   comprised of, included, including
   NOT *compression,* which is **compressione** (*f.*); or *compressed,* which is
   compresso (*adj.*)

comune (adj.) (*koh-MOO-neh*)   common
   NOT *commune,* which is **comune** (*m.*)

confezione *f.* (*kohn-feh-TSYOH-neh*)   clothing industry; garment, article of
   clothing (*for man, woman, or child*)
   NOT *confection,* which is **confetto** (*m.*) or **confettura** (*f.*)

contendere (*kohn-tehn-DEHR-reh*)   to contend, to vie for
   NOT *to claim or assert a viewpoint,* which is **asserire**

☛ This is an especially nettlesome verb, in that *one* of the two English denotations of *contend* is in fact reflected by the Italian look-alike, while the other is not embraced at all.

contesa *f.* (*kohn-TEH-sah*)   contest
NOT *countess*, which is **contessa** (*f.*)

contesto *m.* (*kohn-TEH-stoh*)   context
NOT *contest*, which is **contesa** (*f.*)

contribuente *m.* (*kohn-tree-BWEHN-teh*)   taxpayer
NOT *contributive*, which is **contributivo** (*adj.*); or *contributory*, which is **contributario** (*m.*)

corridore *m.* (*kohr-rree-DOHR-reh*)   runner
NOT *corridor*, which is **corridoio** (*m.*)

corto (adj.) (*KOHR-toh*)   short
NOT *court*, which is **corte**

costa *f.* (*KOH-stah*)   coast
NOT *cost*, which is **costo** (*m.*)

crudele (*kroo-DEH-leh*)   (adj.) cruel
NOT *crude*, which is **crudo** (*adj.*)

cupo (adj.) (*KOO-poh*)   sullen, moody
NOT *cup*, which is **coppa** (*f.*) or **tazza** (*f.*)

dare (*DAHR-reh*)   to give
NOT *to dare*, which is **osare**

data *f.* (*DAH-tah*)   date (*of year, not social engagement*)
NOT *data* (information), which is **dati** (*m.*)

deferente (adj.) (*deh-feh-REHN-teh*)   deferent, deferential
NOT *different*, which is **differente** (*adj.*)

deferenza *f.* (*deh-feh-REHN-tsah*)   deference
NOT *difference*, which is **differenza** (*f.*)

delitto *m.* (*deh-LEET-toh*)   crime
NOT *to delete*, which is **cancellare**

deludere (*deh-LOO-dehr-reh*)   to disappoint
NOT *to delude*, which is **ingannare**

ⓘ Some authorities assert that this is in fact a word in transition, and that the English denotation of disillusionment is increasingly being embraced by this Italian term. For the time being, however, the student is advised to understand and use it in its traditional sense, and learn *ingannare* as more surely indicating the act of delusion, trickery, leading astray.

deserto *m.* (*deh-ZEHR-toh*)   desert, wilderness
NOT *dessert,* which is ***dessert*** (*m.*)
ⓘ Italians rarely use *dessert* to indicate a meal's sweet last course, and when they do, it is with the term's original French pronunciation (*dey-ZEHR*). Rather, the term for sweets (*dolci*) is almost invariably employed.

destrezza *f.* (*deh-STREHT-tsah*)   dexterity, skill
NOT *distress,* which is ***afflizione*** (*f.*)

disimballare (*dee-zeem-bahl-LAHR-reh*)   to unpack
NOT *to disembowel,* which is ***sventrare***

dopo (*DOH-poh*)   after, afterward
NOT *dope* (stupid person), which is ***idiota*** (*m.*); or *narcotic drug,* which is ***narcotico*** (*m.*)

doppio (adj.) (*DOHP-pyoh*)   double; duplex
NOT *dope* (stupid person), which is ***idiota*** (*m.*); or *narcotic drug,* which is ***narcotico*** (*m.*)

dove (*DOH-veh*)   where
NOT *dove,* which is ***colombo*** (*m.*)

due (*DOO-eh*)   two
NOT *due* (owing), which is ***dovuto*** (*adj.*)

ecco (*EHK-koh*)   here (is / are), there (is / are), Behold! Lo!
NOT *echo,* which is ***eco*** (*m.*); or *to echo,* which is ***echeggiare***

errare (*ehr-RRAHR-reh*)   to err, to make a mistake
NOT *error,* which is ***errore*** (*m.*)

estate *f.* (*eh-STAH-teh*)   summer
NOT *estate,* which is ***beni*** (*m.*) or ***patrimonio*** (*m.*)

etichetta *f.* (*eh-tee-KEHT-tah*)   label, sticker, tag
NOT *etiquette,* which is ***galateo*** (*m.*)

evento *m.* (*eh-VEHN-toh*)   outcome
NOT *event,* which is ***avvenimento*** (*m.*)

fabbrica *f.* (*FAHB-bree-kah*)   factory, mill
   NOT *fabric,* which is *stoffa* (*f.*)
   ⓘ In referring to the general appearance and constructive makeup of an
   architectural structure, which in English is often called the building's
   "fabric," Italians also speak of its *fabbrica.* That is the only instance,
   however, in which this look-alike term corresponds to its English
   usage; all other Italian *fabb-* constructions relate in one way or another
   to the activity and process of fabrication.

fame *f.* (*FAH-meh*)   hunger, starvation
   NOT *fame,* which is *fama* (*f.*)

fanale *m.* (*fah-NAH-leh*)   lamp, light
   NOT *finale,* which is *finale* (*m.*)

fare (*FAHR-reh*)   to do, to make
   NOT *fare* (price), which is *tariffa* (*f.*); or *food,* which is *cibo* (*m.*)

fastidio *m.* (*fah-STEE-dyoh*)   annoyance, bother, nuisance
   NOT *fastidious,* which is *fastidioso* (*adj.*)

fato *m.* (*FAH-toh*)   fate
   NOT *fat* (grease), which is *grasso* or *grosso* (*adj.*); or *obese,* which is
   grassoccio (*adj.*)

fatto *m.* (*FAHT-toh*)   fact, deed, feat
   NOT *fat* (grease), which is *grasso* or *grosso* (*adj.*); or *obese,* which is
   grassoccio (*adj.*)

fermamente (*fehr-mah-MEHN-teh*)   firmly
   NOT *firmament,* which is *firmamento* (*m.*) or *cielo* (*m.*)

filo *m.* (*FEE-loh*)   string, thread, wire
   NOT *file* (of documents), which is *archivio* (*m.*); *aligned row,* which is
   fila (*f.*); or *the tool,* which is *lima* (*f.*)

fine *m. & f.* (*FEE-neh*)   end, finish (*f.*); purpose (*m.*)
   NOT *fine* (penalty), which is *multa* (*f.*); *fine, subtle, delicate*—which is
   fine (*adj.*); *extremely good,* which is *bravo* (*adj.*); or *beautiful,* which
   is *bello* (*adj.*)

firma *f.* (*FEER-mah*)   signature
   NOT *firm* (commercial organization), which is *compagnia* (*f.*); or
   steady, which is *fermo* (*adj.*)

firmare (*feer-MAHR-reh*)   to sign, to endorse
   NOT *to firm up, to solidify,* which is *solidificare*

foggia *f.* (*FOHD-jah*)   shape, guise
   NOT *haze* or *mist*, which is *foschia* (*f.*); or *foggy,* which is **nebbioso** (*adj.*)

foglio *m.* (*FOH-lyoh*)   sheet (*of paper*)
   NOT *folio,* which is *folio* (*m.*)

forestiero *m.* (*fohr-reh-STYEHR-roh*)   foreigner; foreign (*adj.*)
   NOT *forester,* which is **selvicoltore** (*m.*)

fornitura *f.* (*fohr-nee-TOOR-rah*)   supply
   NOT *furniture,* which is **mobilio** (*m.*)

ginnasio *m.* (*jeen-NAH-zyoh*)   high school
   NOT *gymnasium,* which is **palestra** (*f.*)

giù (*JOO*)   down
   NOT *Jew,* which is **ebreo** or **israelita** (*m.*)

giunco *m.* (*JOON-koh*)   rush
   NOT *junk,* which is **rottame** (*m.*) **commerciabile** or **rottami**

gola *f.* (*GOH-lah*)   throat
   NOT *goal,* which is **meta** (*f.*), **fine** (*m.*), or **scopo** (*m.*)

Iddio *m.* (*eed-DEE-oh*)   God
   NOT *idiot,* which is **idiota** (*m.*)

immagine *f.* (*eem-MAH-jee-neh*)   image
   NOT *to imagine,* which is **immaginare**

imparare (*eem-pahr-RAHR-reh*)   to learn
   NOT *to impair,* which is **danneggiare** or **menomare**

influsso *m.* (*een-FLOOS-soh*)   influence
   NOT *influx,* which is **affluenza** (*f.*)

ingiuria *f.* (*een-JOOR-ryah*)   insult, (verbal or emotional) abuse
   NOT (*physical*) *injury,* which is **danno** (*m.*) or **ferita** (*f.*)

ingiuriare (*een-joor-RYAHR-reh*)   to insult, to abuse
   NOT *to (physically) injure,* which is **danneggiare**, **nuocere**, or **ferire**

ingiurioso (*adj.*)(*een-joor-RYOH-soh*)   insulting, abusive
   NOT *injurious,* which is **dannoso** or **nocivo** (*adj.*)

intendere (*een-tehn-DEHR-reh*)   to understand
   NOT *to intend* or *to plan* or *to mean to do a particular thing,* which is
   aver intenzione di

♦ This is another term that the student would do well *not* to add to his / her early vocabulary, lest it promote the easy habit of misuse. Better idea: stay with the already familiar **capire**. The expression of intention in Italian is via the cumbersome construct noted above ("to have the intention of") which, for all its clumsiness, remains the only dependable means of conveying the concept of definitive purpose.

istantanea *f.* (*ee-stahn-TAH-neh-ah*) snapshot
NOT *instantaneous*, which is **istantaneo** (*adj.*)

kohl *m.* (*KOHL*) mascara
NOT *coal*, which is **carbone** (*m.*) *fossile*

lampo *m.* (*LAHM-poh*) lightning flash
NOT *lamp*, which is **lampada** (*f.*)

lettura *f.* (*leht-TOOR-rah*) reading
NOT *lecture*, which is **conferenza** (*f .*); or *(alphabetic) letter,* which is **lettera** (*f.*); or *(communicative) letter,* which is **lettera** or—jokingly— *epistola*

libero (adj.) (*LEE-behr-roh*) free
NOT *library*, which is **biblioteca** (*f.*); or *librarian*, which is **bibliotecario** (*m.*)

libraio *m.* (*lee-BRAH-yoh*) bookseller
NOT *library*, which is **biblioteca** (*f.*); or *librarian*, which is **bibliotecario** (*m.*)

libreria *f.* (*lee-brehr-REE-ah*) bookstore
NOT *library*, which is **biblioteca** (*f.*)

lillà *m.* (*leel-LAH*) lilac
NOT *lily*, which is **giglio** (*m.*)

lino *m.* (*LEE-noh*) linen
NOT *line*, which is **linea** (*f.*)

locale (adj.) (*loh-KAH-leh*) local
NOT *locale*, which is **località** (*f.*); or *locality*, which is also **località** (*f.*)

lordo (adj.) (*LOHR-doh*) soiled
NOT *lord*, which is **signore** (*m.*)

lungo (adj.) (*LOON-goh*) long, along
NOT *lung*, which is **polmone** (*m.*)

lussuoso (adj.) (*loos-SWOH-soh*)   luxurious
NOT *lustrous,* which is **lucido, luminoso, splendente** (*adj.*)

male *m.* (*MAH-leh*)   ache, evil, hurt, pain
NOT *male,* which is **maschio** (*m. noun & adj.*)

malizioso (adj.) (*mah-lee-TSYOH-soh*)   mischievous
NOT *malicious,* which is **maligno** (*adj.*)

mano *f.* (*MAH-noh*)   hand
NOT *man,* which is **uomo** (*m.*)

marca *f.* (*MAHR-kah*)   brand (*of manufacture*)
NOT *mark,* which is **segno** (*m.*)

marcio (adj.) (*MAHRR-choh*)   rotten, decayed
NOT *march,* which is **marcia** (*f.*)

marcire (*mahr-CHEER-reh*)   to rot, to decay
NOT *to march,* which is **marciare**

mare *m.* (*MAHR-reh*)   sea
NOT *mare* (female horse), which is **cavalla** (*f.*)

media *f.* (*MEH-dyah*)   average, mean
NOT the press and other means of information or entertainment distribution, which is a collective unknown to Italian.

memore (adj.) (*MEH-mohr-reh*)   mindful
NOT *memory,* which is **memoria** (*f.*)

mirare (*mee-RAHR-reh*)   to aim
NOT *mirror,* which is **specchio** (*m.*); or *to mirror,* which is **riflettere**

misto (adj.) (*MEE-stoh*)   mixed, coeducational
NOT *mist,* which is **foschia** (*f.*)

misura *f.* (*mee-ZOOR-rah*)   measure
NOT *misery,* which is **miseria** (*f.*)

mite (adj.) (*MEE-teh*)   gentle, meek, mild
NOT *mite* (insect), which is **baco** (*m.*)

mondo *m.* (*MOHN-doh*)   world
NOT *mound,* which is **tumulo** (*m.*)

moneta *f.* (*moh-NEH-tah*)   coin
NOT *money,* which is **denaro** (*m.*)

morbido (adj.) (*MOHR-bee-doh*)   soft
NOT *morbid*, which is **morboso** (*adj.*)

naso *m.* (*NAH-soh*)   nose
NOT *nasal*, which is **nasale** (*adj.*)

nave *f.* (*NAH-veh*)   ship
NOT *nave*, which is **navata** (*f.*); or *navy*, which is **marina** (*f.*)

negoziante *m.* (*neh-goh-TSYAHN-teh*)   dealer
NOT *negotiator*, which is **negoziatore** (*m.*)

negozio *m.* (*neh-GOH-tsyoh*)   shop, store
NOT *negotiation*, which is **negoziazione** (*f.*) or **trattativa** (*f.*)

noleggio *m.* (*noh-LEHD-joh*)   rental
NOT *knowledge*, which is **conoscenza** (*f.*)

nostro (adj.) (*NOH-stroh*)   our; ours (*pronoun*)
NOT *nostril*, which is **narice** (*f.*)

notizia *f.* (*noh-TEE-tsyah*)   news
NOT *notice* (printed or broadcast news item or advisory), which is **avviso** (*m.*)

nozze *f.* (*NOHT-tseh*)   wedding
NOT *nozzle*, which is **imboccatura** (*f.*)

occorrere (*ohk-kohr-RREHR-reh*)   to be necessary *or* required
NOT *to occur*, which is **accadere**

occupato (adj.) (*ohk-koo-PAH-toh*)   occupied, busy
NOT *occupation*, which is **occupazione** (*f.*)

offesa *f.* (*ohf-FEH-sah*)   offense
NOT *office*, which is **ufficio** (*m.*)

ogni (adj.) (*OH-nyee*)   each, every
NOT *only*, which is **unico** or **solo** (*adj.*)

omnibus *m.* (*OHM-nee-boos*)   local train
NOT *large bus*, which is **pullman** (*m.*)

onere *m.* (*OH-nehr-reh*)   burden, onus
NOT *honor*, which is **onore** (*m.*)

ordinare (*ohr-dee-NAHR-reh*)   to ordain, to order, to arrange, to trim
NOT *ordinary*, which is **ordinario** (*adj.*)

orefice *m.* (*ohr-REH-fee-cheh*) goldsmith
NOT *orifice,* which is ***apertura*** (*f.*)

ospitale (adj.) (*oh-spee-TAH-leh*) hospitable
NOT *hospital,* which is ***ospedale*** (*m.*)

oste *m.* (*OH-steh*) innkeeper
NOT *host,* which is ***ospite*** (*m.*)

ostrica *f.* (*OH-stree-kah*) oyster
NOT *ostrich,* which is ***struzzo*** (*m.*)

pace *f.* (*PAH-cheh*) peace
NOT *pace,* which is ***passo*** (*m.*)

paga *f.* (*PAH-gah*) pay
NOT *page* (book leaf), which is ***pagina*** (*f.*); or *errand runner,* which is
paggio (*m.*)

paio *m.* (*PAH-yoh*) pair, couple
NOT *pay,* which is ***paga*** (*f.*)

papa *m.* (*PAH-pah*) pope
NOT *Papa* (Dad, Daddy, Pa, Pappy, Pop), which is ***babbo*** (*m.*)

pappa *f.* (*PAHP-pah*) gruel
NOT *Papa* (Dad, Daddy, Pa, Pappy, Pop), which is ***babbo*** (*m.*)

parente *m.* (*pahr-REHN-teh*) relative
NOT *parent,* which is ***genitore*** (*m.*)

parentela *f.* (*pahr-rehn-TEH-lah*) kindred, relationship
NOT *parental,* which is ***genitoriale, dei genitori***

partita *f.* (*pahr-TEE-tah*) game
NOT *party,* which is ***partito*** (*m.*)

parto *m.* (*PAHR-toh*) childbirth
NOT *part,* which is ***parte*** (*f.*)

pasto *m.* (*PAH-stoh*) meal
NOT *past,* which is ***passato*** (*m. noun & adj.*)

pavimento *m.* (*pah-vee-MEHN-toh*) floor
NOT *pavement,* which is ***selciato*** (*m.*)

pesante (*peh-SAHN-teh*) (adj.) heavy
NOT *peasant,* which is ***contadino*** (*m.*)

petto *m.* (*PEHT-toh*)   chest, bosom, brisket
   NOT *pet,* which is ***animale domestico*** (*m.*)

piano *m.* (*PYAH-noh*)   story, floor (*of building*)
   NOT *piano* (musical instrument), which is ***pianoforte*** (*m.*)
   ⓘ While in English the term *floor* can refer to either the base surface or
   the level (1st, 2nd, 3rd, and so forth) within a multistory structure, in
   Italian the two concepts are pointedly distinct. ***Pavimento*** (*pah-vee-*
   MEHN-toh) is an interior supporting surface (*not* street or sidewalk
   material); a ***piano*** is one or another level within a building.
   Furthermore, what Americans consider the second floor is in Italy considered the first floor, or ***piano nobile*** (____*NOH-bee-leh*). Related:
   upstairs—al piano superiore (*ahl*____*soo-peh-RYOHR-reh*); **down-**
   stairs—in basso (*een BAHS-soh*).
   ⓘ *Piano* as a masculine noun also denotes *plan, plane;* and as an adjective, *level* and *flat.*
piccolo (adj.*) (*PEEK-koh-loh*)   little, small, petty
   NOT *(musical instrument) piccolo,* which is ***ottavino*** (*m.*)
pigione *f.* (*pee-JOH-neh*)   rent
   NOT *pigeon,* which is ***piccione*** (*m.*)
pila *f.* (*PEE-lah*)   battery
   NOT *pile* (heap), which is ***ammasso*** (*m.*)*, **mucchio*** (*m.*)*; or driven post,*
   which is ***palafitta*** (*f.*)

pizzo *m.* (*PEET-tsoh*)   lace
   NOT *piece,* which is ***pezzo*** (*m.*); or *pizza,* which is ***pizza*** (*f.*)

polizza *f.* (*poh-LEET-tsah*)   policy
   NOT *police,* which is ***polizia*** (*f.*)

pollo *m.* (*POHL-loh*)   chicken, fowl
   NOT *polo,* which is ***polo*** (*m.*)

ponte *m.* (*POHN-teh*)   bridge, span, deck
   NOT *point,* which is ***punto*** (*m.*)

poppa *f.* (*POHP-pah*)   breast, stern
   NOT *Papa* (Dad, Daddy, Pa, Pappy), which is ***babbo*** (*m.*)

porco *m.* (*POHR-koh*)   hog, pig, swine
   NOT *pork,* which is ***maiale*** (*m.*)

porre (*POHRR-reh*)   to lay, to place, to put, to set
   NOT *to pour,* which is ***versare***

portare (*pohr-TAHR-reh*)   to bring, to bear, to carry, to wear
   NOT *porter,* which is ***portiere*** (*m.*) or ***portabagagli*** (*m.*)

portatore *m.* (*pohr-tah-TOHR-reh*)   carrier, bearer
   NOT *porter,* which is *portiere* (*m.*) or *portabagagli* (*m.*)

pretendere (*preh-tehn-DEHR-reh*)   to claim, to assert, to have claim upon
   NOT *to pretend* (feign, play act, or assume an untrue role), which is
   fingere

   ⓘ If the learner will keep the concept of a pretender to the throne in
   mind, he / she will be aided in remembering this term's actual focus,
   and avoiding its easily misconstrued meaning.

privo (adj.) (*PREE-voh*)   devoid, void, lacking, destitute
   NOT *private,* which is *privato* (*adj.*); or *previous,* which is *precedente*
   (*adj.*)

procuratore *m.* (*proh-koor-rah-TOHR-reh*)   attorney, proxy
   NOT *procurer,* which is *mezzano* (*m.*) or *ruffiano* (*m.*)

proprietà *f.* (*proh-pryeh-TAH*)   property, belongings
   NOT *propriety,* which is *convenienza* (*f.*) or *correttezza* (*f.*)

prospettiva *f.* (*proh-speht-TEE-vah*)   perspective
   NOT *prospective,* which is *prospettivo* (*adj.*)

prossimo *m.* (*PROHS-see-moh*)   neighbor; next, nearest, forthcoming (*adj.*)
   NOT *approximate,* which is *approssimativo* (*adj.*)

provare (*proh-VAHR-reh*)   to rehearse, to test, to try
   NOT *to prove,* which is *comprovare*

pulizia *f.* (*poo-lee-TSEE-ah*)   cleanliness
   NOT *police,* which is *polizia* (*f.*)

pullman *m.* (*POOHL-mahn*)   (large, comfortable) bus
   NOT *pullman* (railway sleeping coach), which is *vagone letto*
puzzo *m.* (*POOT-tsoh*)   stench, smell
   NOT *puzzle,* which is *indovinello* (*m.*)
quando (*KWAHN-doh*)   when
   NOT *quandary,* which is *perplessità* (*f.*)
quanto (*KWAHN-toh*)   how much, how many
   NOT *quantity,* which is *quantità* (*f.*)
quarto *m.* (*KWAHR-toh*)   quarter; fourth (*adj.*)
   NOT *quart,* which does not exist in Italian
questa *f.* (*KWEH-stah*)   this
   NOT *quest,* which is *ricerca* (*f.*)

queste *f.* (*KWEH-steh*)   these
  NOT *quest,* which is ***ricerca*** (*f.*)

questo (adj.) (*KWEH-stoh*)   this
  NOT *quest,* which is ***ricerca*** (*f.*)

ragione *f.* (*rah-JOH-neh*)   reason
  NOT *region,* which is ***regione*** (*f.*)

rancio *m.* (*RAHN-choh*)   mess
  NOT *ranch,* which is ***fattoria*** (*f.*)

rapina *f.* (*rah-PEE-nah*)   robbery, plunder
  NOT *rape,* which is ***violazione*** (*f.*) or ***violenza*** (*f.*) ***carnale***

rapinare (*rah-pee-NAHR-reh*)   to rob
  NOT *to rape,* which is ***violare***

rapire (*rah-PEER-reh*)   to abduct, to kidnap
  NOT *to rape,* which is ***violare***; or *rapist,* which is ***violatore*** (*m.*)

rapitore *m.* (*rah-pee-TOHR-reh*)   abductor, kidnapper
  NOT r*apist,* which is ***violatore*** (*m.*)

rasentare (*rah-zehn-TAHR-reh*)   to skim, skirt
  NOT *to resent,* which is ***risentirsi di, prendersela per***

raso *m.* (*RAH-soh*)   satin
  NOT *razor,* which is ***rasoio*** (*m.*)

rata *f.* (*RAH-tah*)   installment
  NOT *rate* (price), which is ***prezzo*** (*m.*); *speed of,* which is ***velocità*** (*f.*);
  or *rat,* which is ***ratto*** (*m.*)

recipiente *m.* (*reh-chee-PYEHN-teh*)   container, holder, vessel, bin
  NOT *recipient,* which is ***ricevente*** (*adj.* or *m. & f. noun*)

reclamare (*reh-klah-MAHR-reh*)   to claim
  NOT *to reclaim,* which is ***redimere*** or ***bonific***

reclamizzare (*reh-klah-meed-DZAHR-reh*)   to advertise
  NOT *to reclaim,* which is ***redimere*** or ***bonificare***

reclamo *m.* (*reh-KLAH-moh*)   claim
  NOT *reclamation,* which is ***bonifica*** (*f.*)

recluta *f.* (*REH-kloo-tah*)   recruit
  NOT *recluse,* which is ***eremita*** (*m.*)

regalare (*reh-gah-LAHR-reh*)   to present, to give (as a present)
NOT *to regulate,* which is ***regolare***; or *to regale,* which is ***festeggiare***
or ***intrattenere***

restare (*reh-STAHR-reh*)   to stay, to remain
NOT *to restore,* which is ***restaurare***

ricordare (*ree-kohr-DAHR-reh*)   to remember, to recall, to recollect
NOT *to record,* which is ***registrare***

ricordo *m.* (*ree-KOHR-doh*)   remembrance, souvenir, (written) record
NOT *(phonograph) record,* which is ***disco*** (*m.*)

ricovero *m.* (*ree-KOH-vehr-roh*)   shelter
NOT r*ecovery,* which is ***recupero*** (*m.*) or ***guarigione*** (*f.*)

riferire (*ree-fehr-REER-reh*)   to refer
NOT r*eferee,* which is ***arbitro*** (*m.*)

rifiutare (*ree-fyoo-TAHR-reh*)   to refuse, to decline
NOT *to refute,* which is ***confutare***

rifiuto *m.* (*ree-FYOO-toh*)   refusal
NOT *refutation,* which is ***confutazione*** (*f.*)

riga *f.* (*REE-gah*)   line (*of things or persons*), row, file
NOT *rig,* which is ***equipaggio*** (*m.*)

rimandare (*ree-mahn-DAHR-reh*)   to postpone
NOT *to remind,* which is ***rammentare, (far) ricordare (a qualcuno)***

rissa *f.* (*REES-sah*)   fight, brawl
NOT *rice,* which is ***riso*** (*m.*)

ristoro *m.* (*ree-STOHR-roh*)   refreshment
NOT *to restore,* which is ***restaurare***; or *restoration,* which is ***restaurazione*** (*f.*)

roba *f.* (*ROH-bah*)   stuff, miscellany
NOT *robe,* which is ***veste*** (*f.*)

rock *m.* (*RAAHK*)   rock music
NOT *rock* (stone), which is ***roccia*** (*f.*)

rompere (*ROHM-pehr-reh*)   to break
NOT *to romp,* which is ***giocare vigorosamente***

rubare (*roo-BAHR-reh*)   to steal
NOT *to rub,* which is *****fregare*** or ***strofinare***; or r*ubber,* which is ***gomma*** (*f.*)

rullare (*rool-LAHR-reh*) to roll
  NOT *ruler* (head of state), which is ***sovrano*** (*m.*); or *measuring device,* which is ***regolo*** (*m.*)

rumore *m.* (*roo-MOHR-reh*) noise, clatter, din
  NOT *rumor,* which is ***diceria*** (*f.*)

salato (adj.) (*sah-LAH-toh*) salty
  NOT *salad,* which is ***insalata*** (*f.*)

sale *m.* (*SAH-leh*) salt
  NOT *sale,* which is ***vendita*** (*f.*) or ***spaccio*** (*m.*)

salire (*sah-LEER-reh*) to go up, to ascend, to mount
  NOT *sailor,* which is ***marinaio*** (*m.*)

saltare (*sahl-TAHR-reh*) to jump, to leap, to bound, to hop, to skip, to spring
  NOT *to salt,* which is ***salare***

salto *m.* (*SAHL-toh*) jump, leap, bound, hop, vault
  NOT *salt,* which is ***sale*** (*m.*)

salute *f.* (*sah-LOO-teh*) health
  NOT *salute,* which is ***saluto*** (*m.*); or *to salute,* which is ***salutare***

scalo *m.* (*SKAH-loh*) station (*freight handling implied vs.* stazione)
  NOT *scale* (hardened residue), which is ***scala*** (*f.*); *weighing device,* which is ***bilancia*** (*f.*); *fish covering,* which is ***squama*** (*f.*); or *musical measure,* which is ***gamma*** (*f.*)

scolare (*skoh-LAHR-reh*) to drain
  NOT *scholar,* which is ***studioso*** (*m.*), ***erudito*** (*m.*), or ***scolaro*** (*m.*)

scopa *f.* (*SKOH-pah*) broom
  NOT *scope,* which is ***portata*** (*f.*)

scopo *m.* (*SKOH-poh*) aim, purpose
  NOT *scope,* which is ***portata*** (*f.*)

scrigno *m.* (*SKREE-nyoh*) safe, strongbox
  NOT *screen* (privacy furniture), which is ***paravento*** (*m.*); *woven metal,* which is ***crivello*** (*m.*); or *film or television display surface,* which is ***schermo*** (*m.*)

sellare (*sehl-LAHR-reh*) to saddle
  NOT *to sell,* which is ***vendere***

sensibile (adj.) (*sehn-SEE-bee-leh*) sensitive, sympathetic
  NOT *sensible,* which is ***assennato*** (*adj.*)

simpatico (adj.) (*seem-PAH-tee-koh*)   agreeable, congenial, likeable, pleasant
   NOT *simpatico* (in accord with one's feelings, beliefs, outlook), which
   is ***armonioso*** (*adj.*)
   ◐ This word has become subtly but importantly transformed in its otherwise intact adoption into English. Italian usage does not connote the
   same intensity of emotional bond and appreciation as is now implied in
   the American and British employment of the term.

spada *f.* (*SPAH-dah*)   sword
   NOT *spade*, which is ***vanga*** (*f.*)

spiritoso (adj.) (*spee-ree-TOH-soh*)   witty
   NOT *spirited*, which is ***vivace*** or ***brioso*** (*adj.*)

spugna *f.* (*SPOO-nyah*)   sponge
   NOT *spoon*, which is ***cucchiaio*** (*m.*)

stalla *f.* (*STAHL-lah*)   stable
   NOT *stall*, which is stallo (*m.*) or ***stalla*** (*f.*)

stampa *f.* (*STAHM-pah*)   printing press, printing
   NOT *stamp* (postage), which is ***francobollo*** (*m.*); *embossed mark*,
   which is ***timbro*** (*m.*); or *impressing device*, which is ***stampo*** (*m.*)

stampare (*stahm-PAHR-reh*)   to print
   NOT *to stamp*, which is ***bollare*** or ***timbrare***

stare (*STAHR-reh*)   to stand, to be
   NOT *to stare*, which is ***guardare fisso***

stile *m.* (*STEE-leh*)   style
   NOT *steel*, which is ***acciaio*** (*m.*)

stirare (*steer-RAHR-reh*)   to iron
   NOT *to stir*, which is ***agitare*** or ***muovere***

strano (adj.) (*STRAH-noh*)   strange, odd, peculiar, weird
   NOT *strain*, which is ***tensione*** (*f.*)

tacere (*tah-CHEHR-reh*)   to be quiet, to keep quiet
   NOT *to tack*, which is ***attaccare***

tale (adj.) (*TAH-leh*)   such
   NOT *tale*, which is ***racconto*** (*m.*)

tappare (*tahp-PAHR-reh*)   to plug, to stop up
   NOT *to tap*, which is ***percuotere***

tappo *m.* (*TAHP-poh*)   plug, stopper, cork
   NOT *tap* (water faucet), which is ***rubinetto*** (*m.*)

targa *f.* (*TAHR-gah*)   plate
NOT *target,* which is **bersaglio** (*m.*)

tasca *f.* (*TAH-skah*)   pocket
NOT *task,* which is **compito** (*m.*) or **incarico** (*m.*)

tasto *m.* (*TAH-stoh*)   (piano or organ) key
NOT *taste,* which is **gusto** (*m.*)

temperare (*tehm-pehr-RAHR-reh*)   to temper
NOT *temporary,* which is **provvisorio** (*adj.*)

tenente *m.* (*teh-NEHN-teh*)   lieutenant
NOT *tenant,* which is **inquilino** (*m.*)

terra *f.* (*TEHRR-rah*)   earth, ground, land
NOT *tear* (rip in fabric), which is **strappo** (*m.*) or **rottura** (*f.*)

testa *f.* (*TEH-stah*)   head
NOT *test,* which is **prova** (*f.*)

testimone *m. & f.* (*teh-stee-MOH-neh*)   witness
NOT *testimony,* which is **testimonianza** (*f.*)

testo *m.* (*TEH-stoh*)   text
NOT *test,* which is **prova** (*f.*)

tiro *m.* (*TEER-roh*)   draught; throw, cast; shooting; shot; trick
NOT *tire,* which is **pneumatico** (*m.*)

tonno *m.* (*TOHN-noh*)   tuna
NOT *tone,* which is **tono** (*m.*)

trota *f.* (*TROH-tah*)   trout
NOT *trot,* which is **trotto** (*m.*)

trucco *m.* (*TROOK-koh*)   trick
NOT *trot,* which is **trotto** (*m.*)

tutore *m.* (*too-TOHR-reh*)   guardian
NOT *tutor,* which is **insegnante privato** (*m.*)

vacanza *f.* (*vah-KAHN-tsah*)   vacation, holiday
NOT *vacancy,* which is **stanza** (*f.*) **libera**

vagone *m.* (*vah-GOH-neh*)   (railway) car, coach
NOT *wagon,* which is **carro** (*m.*)
 ♦ Note the *exact reversal* of these terms between the two languages!

vento *m.* (*VEHN-toh*)   wind
    NOT *vent,* which is ***foro*** (*m.*)

viale *m.* (*vee-AH-leh*)   avenue, boulevard, driveway
    NOT *vial,* which is ***fiala*** (*f.*) or ***boccetta*** (*f.*)

vigilia *f.* (*vee-JEE-lyah*)   vigil, eve
    NOT *village,* which is ***villaggio*** (*m.*)

vigna *f.* (*VEE-nyah*)   vineyard
    NOT *vine,* which is ***vite*** (*f.*); or *vagina,* which is ***vagina*** (*f.*)

villano (*veel-LAH-noh*)   (adj.) inconsiderate
    NOT *villain,* which is ***furfante*** (*m.*)

visone *m.* (*vee-ZOH-neh*)   mink
    NOT *vision,* which is ***visione*** (*f.*)

vuotare (*vwoh-TAHR-reh*)   to empty
    NOT *to vote,* which is ***votare***

zotico *m.* (*ZOH-tee-koh*)   boor (*n.*); boorish (*adj.*)
    NOT *exotic,* which is ***esotico*** (*adj.*)

LISTA DI TERMINI E FRASI UTILI

List of Helpful Terms and Phrases

The thousands of cognates and near-cognates that exist between English and Italian do not, of course, embrace the whole of either tongue. A sea of additional terminology rounds out each language, most of which bears little or no cross-lingual similarity at all. Many such words are basic and vitally important to conversational richness and full information exchange, and thus must be incorporated into the vocabulary of any learner who aspires to communicate on a full and ever-broadening basis.

In this section, several hundred such terms are listed, arranged in topical groupings. Few of these are cognates or even close to "English-sounding," and thus will be somewhat more difficult to master than those that have gone before. They will be markedly easier to take in, however, than they would have been had the learner not already become acquainted with many of the cognates that precede them in this book.

Following these categorized word lists is a collection of everyday phrases and representative conversational constructions that will also be invaluable to study and absorb. An additional series of simple "fill-in" phrases allows the learner to employ his / her newly acquired cognate vocabulary in a practical manner.

CLOCK & CALENDAR

clock, timepiece   orologio *m.* (*ohr-roh-LOH-joh*)
> **moment**—momento *m.* (*moh-MEHN-toh*); **second**—secondo *m.* (*seh-KOHN-doh*); **minute**—minuto *m.* (*mee-NOO -toh*); **half-hour**—mezz'ora f. (*mehd-DZOHR-rah*); **hour**—ora f. (*OHR-rah*). A **wristwatch**—orologio (*m.*) da polso (____dah POHL-soh)

time (*in general, NOT specific o'clock or instance*), **weather**   tempo *m.* (*TEHM-poh*)
> ⓘ Amazingly, Italian employs the same word for both **time** and **weather**, a situation that would seem certain to create endless confusion. The

problem resolves when it's understood that Italians *never* ask "What time is it?" but rather "What *hour* is it?" (Che ora è?), or by indentifying a specific time in terms of the day, part of the day (this evening, tomorrow morning, next Tuesday), and / or hour at which an event is scheduled to take place, or previously occurred, without reference to the general concept of **time**. Thus *tempo* in everyday conversation refers, far more often than not, to **weather**, *never* to a *specific* time. As exemplified by such constructions as "**They left at the same time**," "**In time, I hope to see the pyramids**," "**I have no time to waste**," or "**Once** [as a rule, in the past], **barbers performed surgery**"—all of which would employ the word *tempo*—this Italian term is general, abstract, and philosophical rather than specific and practical.

time (*specific instance*)   volta *f.* (*VOHL-tah*)

ⓘ This term further exemplifies the limitations of the term *tempo*. Where in English one might refer to a past event as "**One time, I saw a tremendous fire**," or "**Once** [one time: in a specific instance], **I heard a priest scream**," an Italian would employ the term *una volta* rather than *un tempo*. Similarly, "**I hit my thumb twice**," would call up *due volte*; "**I called her three times**," would employ *tre volte*, and so forth.

(the) time (*specific hour*)   ora *f.* (*OHR-rah*)

timetable, (printed) schedule   orario *m.* (*oh-RAHR-ryoh*)

◆   ◆   ◆

calendar   calendario *m.* (*kah-len-DAHR-ryoh*)

century   secolo *m.* (*SEH-koh-loh*)

daily (adj.)   quotidiano (*kwoh-tee-DYAH-noh*)
    dawn—alba *f.* (*AHL-bah*); **to awaken**—svegliare (*zveh-LYAHR-reh*); **awake** (adj.)—sveglio (*ZVEH-lyoh*); **early** (*in the day*)—di buon'ora (*dee bwoh-NOHR-rah*);   **breakfast**—prima colazione *f.* (*PREE-mah koh-lah-TSYOH-neh*); **morning / forenoon**—mattina (*maht-TEE- nah*); **noon**—mezzogiorno *m.* (*MEHD-dzoh JOHR-noh*); **lunch / light meal**— colazione *f.* (*koh-lah-TSYOH-neh*); **afternoon**—pomeriggio *m.* (*poh-mehr-REED-joh*); **snack**—spuntino *m.* (*spoon-TEE-noh*); **evening**— sera *f.* (*SEHR-rah*); **dinner**—pranzo *m.* (*PRAHN-dzoh*); **night**—notte *f.* (*NOHT-teh*);   **midnight**—mezzanotte *f0.* (*meht-tsah-NOHT-teh*); **to sleep**—dormire (*dohr-MEER-reh*); **sleep**—sonno *m.* (*SOHN-noh*)

day   giorno *m.* (*JOHR-noh*)
    Sunday—domenica *f.* (*doh-MEH-nee-kah*); **Monday**—lunedì *m.* (*loo-neh-DEE*); **Tuesday**—martedì *m.* (*mahr-teh-DEE*); **Wednesday**—mer-

coledì *m.* (*mehr-koh-leh-DEE*); **Thursday**—giovedì *m.* (*joh-veh-DEE*); **Friday**—venerdì *m.* (*veh-nehr-DEE*); **Saturday**—sabato *m.* (*SAH-bah-toh*); **holiday**—giorno (*m.*) festivo (*JOHR-noh feh-STEE-voh*)

decade decennio *m.* (*deh-CHEHN-nyoh*)

month mese *m.* (*MEH-seh*)
January—gennaio *m.* (*jehn-NAH-yoh*); **February**—febbraio *m.* (*fehb-BRAH-yoh*); **March**—marzo *m.* (*MAHR-tsoh*); **April**—aprile *m.* (*ah-PREE-leh*); **May**—maggio *m.* (*MAHD-joh*); **June**—giugno *m.* (*JOO-nyoh*); **July**—luglio *m.* (LOO-lyoh); **August**—agosto *m.* (*ah-GOH-stoh*); **September**—settembre *m.* (*seht-TEHM-breh*); **October**—ottobre *m.* (*oht-TOH-breh*); **November**—novembre *m.* (*noh-VEHM-breh*); **December**—dicembre *m.* (*dee-CHEM-breh*)

monthly (adj.) mensile (*mehn-SEE-leh*)

season stagione *f.* (*stah-JOH-neh*)
spring—primavera *f.* (*pree-mah-VEHR-rah*); **summer**—estate *f.* (*eh-STAH-teh*); **autumn, fall**—autunno *m.* (*aow-TOON-noh*); **winter**—inverno *m.* (*een-VEHR-noh*)

this evening, tonight stasera *f.* (*stah-SEHR-rah*)

today oggi *m.* (*OHD-jee*)

tomorrow domani *m.* (*doh-MAH-nee*)

week settimana *f.* (*seht-tee-MAH-nah*)

weekly settimanale (adj.) (*seht-tee-mah-NAH-leh*)

year anno *m.* (*AHN-noh*)

yesterday ieri *m.* (*YEHR-ree*)

◆ ◆ ◆

a while (*short time*) un tempo (*oon TEM-poh*)

after, afterward dopo (*DOH-poh*)

again, over again di nuovo (*dee NWOH-voh*)

ago fa (*FAH*)

already già (*JAH*)

anymore più (*PYOO*)

at (*time, place, or price*)   a (*AH*), (before vowels—especially *a*) ad (*AHD*)

before, ahead of (*in time*)   prima (*PREE-mah*)

beforehand   in anticipo (*een ahn-TEE-chee-poh*)

most recent   ultimamente (*ool-tee-mah-MEHN-teh*)

never   mai (*MAHY*)

next   prossimo (adj.) (*PROHS-see-moh*)
> ① Thus, **next week**—settimana prossima (*seht-tee-MAHN-nah____*);
> **next month**—mese prossimo (*MEH seh____*); **next time**—prossima volta (____ *VOHL-tah*); **next year**—anno prossimo (*AHN-noh____*).

now   ora (*OHR-rah*), adesso (*ah-DEHS-soh*)

not now   ora no (*OHR-rah noh*)

often   spesso (*SPEHS-soh*), frequentemente (*freh-kwehn-teh-MEHN-teh*)

previous (adj.)   anteriore (*ahn-tehr-RYOHR-reh*), precedente (*preh-cheh-DEHN-teh*)

since   da (*DAH*), da allora (*dah ahl-LOHR-rah*)

sometimes   qualche volta (*KWAHL-keh VOHL-tah*)

soon   presto (*PREH-stoh*), fra poco (*frah POH-koh*)

then (*at that time*)   allora (*ahl-LOHR-rah*)

then (*afterward*)   poi (*POY*)

thereafter   da allora in poi (*dah ahl-LOHR-rah een POY*)

throughout (*from start to finish*)   durante tutto (*door-RAHN-teh TOOT-toh*)

until   fino a (*FEE-noh AH*)

when   quando (*KWAHN-doh*)

whenever   quandunque (*kwahn-DOON-kweh*)

while   mentre (*MEHN-treh*)

yet   ancora (*ahn-KOHR-rah*)

PLACE & POSITION

above, over, upon sopra (*SOH-prah*)

ahead, forward, onward avanti (*ah-VAHN-tee*)

amid, amidst, among, between in mezzo a (*een MEHD-dzoh AH*), fra (*FRAH*), tra (*TRAH*)

away (*from specific place*) via (*VEE-ah*), lontano (*lohn-TAH-noh*)

back, backward indietro (*een-DYEH-troh*)

before (*in front of*) davanti (*dah-VAHN-tee*)

behind di dietro (*dee DYEH-troh*), dietro a (*DYEH-troh AH*)

below, beneath sotto (SOHT-toh)

beside (*next to*) acconto a (*ahk-KOHN-toh AH*)

between fra (*FRAH*), tra (*TRAH*)

by (*near*) presso a (*PREHS-soh AH*)

by (*through*) via (*VEE-ah*)

down giù (*JOO*), in basso (*een BAHS-soh*)

elsewhere altrove (*ahl-TROH-veh*)

everywhere dappertutto (*dahp-pehr-TOO-toh*)

far (adj.) lontano (*lohn-TAH-noh*)

forward avanti (*ah-VAHN-tee*)

from da (*DAH*)

here qui (*KWEE*)

here is ecco (*EHK-koh*)

high, tall alto (*AHL-toh*)

in in (*EEN*)

in the, into nel (*NEHL*), nello (*NEHL-loh*), nella (*NEHL-lah*)

indoors, inside, within dentro (*DEHN-troh*)

left (*side or direction*) sinistra *f.* (*see-NEE-strah*)

① **left** (adj.)—sinistro (*see-NEE-stroh*); (to the) **left / leftward**—a sinistra (*ah see-NEE-strah*)

near   vicino (adj.) (*vee-CHEE-noh*)

on   su (*SOO*)

place   luogo *m.* (*LWOH-goh*)

right (*side or direction*)   destra *f.* (*DEH-strah*)
   ① **right** (adj.)—destro (*DEH-stroh*); (to the) **right / rightward**—a destra (*ah DEH-strah*)

south   sud *m.* (*SOOD*)

straight ahead—sempre diritto (*SEHM-preh dee-REET-toh*)

there   là (*LAH*) / lì (*LEE*)

through   per (*PEHR*)

to (*re direction*)   a (*AH*), (before vowel) ad (*AHD*)

toward   verso (*VEHR-soh*)

under   sotto (*SOHT-toh*)

underneath   disotto (*dee-SOHT-toh*)

up   su (*SOO*)

upside down   sottosopra (*soht-toh-SOH-prah*)

upstairs   di sopra (*dee SOH-prah*)

upward   in alto (*een AHL-toh*)

where   dove (*DOH veh*)
   ① The question **Where is?** contracts to—Dov'è? (*doh-VEH?*)

QUANTITY & SIZE

all, everything, (the) whole of   tutto *m.* (*TOOT-toh*)

another (adj.)   un altro (*oohn AHL-troh*)

any   alcuno (*ahl-KOO-noh*)

average   media *f.* (*MEH-dyah*)

both   ambedue (*ahm-beh-DOO-eh*)

every ogni (*OH-nyee*)

few (adj.) pochi (*POH-kee*)

less (adj.) minore (*mee-NOHR-reh*)

less meno (*MEH-noh*)

mostly per lo più (*perh loh PYOO*)

much (adj.) molto (*MOHL-toh*)

none nessuno (*nehs-SOO-noh*), niente (*NYEHN-teh*)

nothing niente (*NYEHN-teh*), nulla (*NOOL-lah*)

number numero *m.* (*NOO-mehr-roh*)
ⓘ **zero**—zero (*DZEH-roh*); **one**—uno (*OOH-noh*); **first**—primo (*PREE-moh*); **two**—due (*DOO-eh*); **second**—secondo (*seh-KOHN-doh*; **three**—tre (*TREH*); **third**—terzo (*TEHR-tsoh*); **four**—quattro (*KWAHT-troh*); **fourth**—quarto (*KWAHR-toh*); **five**—cinque (*CHEEN-kweh*); **fifth**—quinto (*KWEEN-toh*); **six**—sei (*SEY*); **sixth**—sesto (*SEH-stoh*); **seven**—sette (*SEHT-teh*); **seventh**—settimo (*seht-TEE-moh*); **eight**—otto (*OHT-toh*); **eighth**—ottavo (*oht-TAH-voh*); **nine**—nove (*NOH-veh*); **ninth**—nono (*NOHN-noh*); **ten**—dieci (*DYEH-chee*); **tenth**—decimo (*DEH-chee-moh*); **eleven**—undici (*OOHN-dee-chee*); **twelve**—dodici (*DOH-dee-chee*); **thirteen** —tredici (*TREH-dee-chee*); **fourteen**—quattordici (*kwaht-TOHR-dee-chee*); **fifteen**—quindici (*KWEEN-dee-chee*); **sixteen**—sedici (*SEH-dee-chee*); **seventeen**—diciassette (*dee-chahs-SEHT-teh*); **eighteen**—diciotto (*dee-CHYOHT-toh*); **nineteen**—diciannove (*dee-chahn-NOH-veh*); **twenty**—venti (*VEHN-tee*); **twenty-one**—ventuno (*vehn-TOO-noh)*; **twenty-two**—ventidue (*vehn-tee-DOO-eh*); **thirty**—trenta (*TREHN-tah*); **forty**—quaranta (*kwahr-RAHN-tah*); **fifty**—cinquanta (*cheen-KWAHN-tah*); **sixty**—sessanta (*sehs-SAHN-tah*); **seventy**—settanta (*seht-TAHN-tah*); **eighty**—ottanta (*oht-TAHN-tah*); **ninety**—novanta (*noh-VAHN-tah*); **one hundred**—cento (*CHEN-toh*); **one hundred one**—cento uno (*CHEN-toh OOH-noh*); **two hundred**—duecento (*doo-eh CHEN-toh*); **two hundred one**—duecento uno (*doo-eh-CHEN-toh OOH-noh*); **three hundred**—trecento (*treh-CHEN-toh*); **one thousand**—mille (*MEEL-leh*); **one thousand one**—mille uno (*MEEL-leh OOH-noh*); **two thousand**—due mila (*DOO-eh MEE-lah*); **one million**—un milione (*oohn mee-LYOH-neh*); **one billion**—un bilione (*oohn bee-LYOH-neh*)

numerous (adj.) numeroso (*noo-mehr-ROH-soh*)

only (adj.)   unico (*OO-nee-koh*)

several (adj.)   parecchi (*pahr-REHK-kee*).l

size   grandezza *f.* (*grahn-DEHT-tsah*)

some (*singular*) (adj.)   qualche (*KWAHL-keh*)

some (*plural*) (adj.)   alcuni (*ahl-KOO-nee*)

PEOPLE & POSSESSIVES

anybody, anyone   chiunque (*kee-OONG-kweh*), qualcuno (*kwahl-KOO-noh*)

clerk   impiegato *m.* (*eem-pyeh-GAH-toh*)

darling (adj.)   carino (*kah-REE-noh*)

daughter   figlia *f.* (*FEE-lyah*)

dear, beloved (adj.)   caro (*KAHR-roh*)

everybody, everyone   ognuno (*oh-NYOO-noh*)

gentleman   galantuomo *m.* (*gah-lahn-TWOH-moh*)

husband   marito *m.* (*mahr-REE-toh*)

man   uomo *m.* (*WOH-moh*)

my (adj.), **mine**   mio (*MEE-oh*) ➔-iaᴄ

our (adj.), **ours**   nostro (*NOH-stroh*)

ourselves   ci (*CHEE*), noi stessi (*noh-ee STEHS-see*)

partner   compagno *m.* (*kohm-PAH-nyoh*), sòcio (*SOH-choh*)

same, self (adj.)   stesso (*STEHS-soh*)

    ⓘ Thus, **myself**—me stesso (*meh STEHS-soh*); **I myself**—io stesso (*EE-oh____*); **himself**—sè stesso (*seh____*), and so forth

sister   sorella *f.* (*sohr-REHL-lah*)

somebody, someone   qualcuno (*kwahl-KOO-noh*)

son   figlio *m.* (*FEE-lyoh*)

their (adj.), **theirs**   loro (*LOHR-roh*)

they loro (*LOHR-roh*), esse (*EHS-seh*) / essi (*EHS-see*)

those who coloro che (*koh-LOHR-roh keh*)

waiter, bellboy, steward, valet cameriere *m.* (*kah-mehr-RYEHR-reh*)
ⓘ Correspondingly, a **waitress, chambermaid, stewardess** is ɔ-raɔ

who, whom chi (*KEE*)

whoever, whomever chiunque (*kee-OONG-kweh*)

wife moglie *f.* (*MOH-lyeh*)

your (adj.), **yours** tuo (*TWOH*) / vostro (*VOH-stroh*)

PREPOSITIONS, CONJUNCTIONS & OTHER BASICS

all right, well va bene (*vah BEH-neh*)

almost, nearly quasi (*KWAH-zee*)

also, too anche (*AHN-keh*)

and e (*EH*), (before word beginning with vowel—especially *e*) ed (*EHD*)

apiece, each al pezzo (*ahl PETT-tsoh*), ogni (*OH-nyee*)

as come (*KOH-meh*)

bad (adj.) cattivo (*kaht-TEE-voh*)

because of a causa di (*ah KOW-zah dee*)

best better (adj.) migliore (*mee-LYOHR-reh*)

best, better meglio (*MEH-lyoh*)

but ma (*MAH*)

by (*agent of action*) da (*DAH*)

by (*means of*) a mezzo di (*ah MEHD-dzoh dee*)

can (*ability, capability*) potere (*poh-TEHR-reh*)

each (adj.) ogni (*OH-nyee*)

either, one or the other l' uno o l'altro (*LOO-noh oh LAHL-troh*)

else (adj.) altro (*AHL-troh*)

empty (adj.)   vuoto (*VWOH-toh*)

even   anche (*AHN-keh*)

excessive (adj.)   troppo (*TROHP-poh*)

heat   calore *m.* (*kah-LOH-reh*)

how   come (*KOH-meh*)

however, anyway, in any case   comunque (*koh-MOONG-kweh*)

however, though   però (*pehr-ROH*)

if   se (*SEH*)

> ⓘ **even if**—anche se (*AHN-keh seh*); **as if**—quasi (*KWAH-zee*), come se (KOH-meh seh)

instead of   invece di (*een-VEH-cheh dee*)

is   è (EH)

it is, it's   fa (*FAH*)

lacking, without   senza (*SEHN-tsah*)

larger, greater (*of two or more*) (adj.)   maggiore (*mahd JOH reh*)

light luce *f.* (*LOO cheh*)

maybe, perhaps   forse (*FOHR-seh*)

most (adj.)   maggiormente (*mahd-johr-MEHN-teh*)

must, ought to, have to (to)   dovere (*doh-VEHR-reh*)
> ⓘ This "auxiliary verb" is always followed—whether in an expressed or implied way—by the infinitive of the verb of the "action" that needs to be accomplished. The concept of **should** is similar: use *dovere* in conditional tense, followed by infinitive of the second verb.

of (*belonging to, associated with*)   di (*DEE*)

of (*from*)   da (*DAH*)

or   o (*OH*), (before word beginning with vowel—more especially *o*) od (*OHD*)

other (adj.)   altro (*AHL-troh*)

otherwise   altrimenti (*ahl-tree-MEHN-tee*)

overly, too much (adj.) troppo (*TROHP-poh*)

rain pioggia *f.* (*PYOHD-jah*)

raincoat impermeabile *m.* (*eem-pehr-meh-AH-bee-leh*)

rather piuttosto (*pyoot-TOH-stoh*)

reservation prenotazione *f.* (*preh-noh-tah-TSYOH-neh*)

short (*not long*) (adj.) corto (*KOHR-toh*)

shopping spesa *f.* (*SPEH-sah*)

slow, sluggish (adj.) lento (*LEHN-toh*)

slowly lentamente (*lehn-tah-MEHN-teh*)

so così (*koh-ZEE*)

something qualcosa (*kwahl-KOH-sah*)

than che (*KEH*)

> ⓘ In addition its use as a preposition, as noted above, *che* also serves as a multiuse pronoun, equating to **who, which,** and **what**. As a conjunction, it means **that**.

that (adj.) quel (*KWEHL*), quello (*KWEHL-loh*), quella (*KWEHL-lah*)

then (*in that case, therefore*) dunque (*DOON-kweh*)

thereby in tal modo (*een tahl MOH-doh*), così (*koh-SEE*), con ciò (*kohn CHOH*)

therefore, hence perciò (*pehr-CHOH*), quindi (*KWEEN-dee*)

these questi (*KWEH-stee*)

thing, matter *f.* cosa (*KOH-sah*)

this (adj.) questo (*KWEH-stoh*)

ticket (*for transport or admission*) biglietto *m.* (*bee-LYEHT-toh*)

tired (adj.) stanco (*STAHN-koh*)

to (*re purpose or action*) per (*PEHR*)

to the al (*AHL*)

together insieme (*een-SYEH-meh*)

too much, overly, excessive (adj) troppo (*TROHP-poh*); **too many** troppi (*TROHP-pee*)

unless a meno che (*ah MEH-noh keh*)

was ero (*EHR-roh*) / era (*EHR-rah*)

weather tempo *m.* [See **time.**]

what che (*KEH*), che cosa (*keh KOH-sah*)

whether se (*SEH*)

which (*of several*) quale (*KWAH-leh*)

without senza (*SEHN-tsah*)

worse (adj.) peggiore (*pehd-JOHR-reh*)

worthless senza valore (*SEHN-tsah vah-LOH-reh*)

writing scrittura *f.* (*skreet-TOOR-rah*)

VITAL VERBS

ask about (to) interrogare circa (*een-tehr-rroh-GAHR-reh CHEER-kah*)

be, exist (to) essere (*EHS-sehr-reh*)

> ① As in English, this verb embraces the whole of "is-ness" (I *am,* he *is,* they *were,* we will *be,* and so forth), and thus is one of the two most important of all Italian verbs; alas, like the other one (**to have**—avere), its conjugation is wildly irregular and difficult to master. The student aspiring to real fluency has no option, however: it simply must be learned.

be able to (to) potere (*poh-TEHR-reh*)

bring / carry (to) portare (*pohr-TAHR-reh*)

close / shut (to) chiudere (*KYOO-dehr-reh*)

> ① The very important related adjective: **closed**—chiuso (*KYOO-zoh*)

come, come to (to) venire (*veh-NEER-reh*)

do, make (to) fare (*FAHR-reh*)

drink (to) bere (*BEHR-reh*)

eat (to) mangiare (*mahn-JAHR-reh*)

find, come upon (to) trovare (*troh-VAHR-reh*)

forget (to) dimenticare (*dee-mehn-tee-KAHR-reh*)

give (to) dare (*DAHR-reh*)

go (to) andare (*ahn-DAHR-reh*)

happen (to) accadere (*ahk-kah-DEHR-reh*)

have to, be obliged to (to) dovere (*doh-VEHR-reh*)

hear (to) sentire (*sehn-TEER-reh*)

hold, keep (to) tenere (*teh-NEHR-reh*)

hope (to) sperare (*spehr-RAHR-reh*)

know (to) sapere (*sah-PEHR-reh*), conoscere (*koh-noh-SHEHR-reh*)
   ⓘ **Do you know?**—Sa lei? (*sah LEH-ee*); **I don't know**—Non so (*NOHN soh*); **Who knows?**—Chi lo sa? (*kee loh SAH*)

learn (to) imparare (*eem-pah-RAHR-reh*)

lose perdere (*PEHR-dehr-reh*)

need (to) aver bisogno di (*ah-VEHR bee-ZOH-nyoh dee*)

open (to) aprire (*ah-PREER-reh*)
   ⓘ Its related adjective: **open**—aperto (*ah-PEHRR-toh*)

pay, pay for (to) pagare (*pah-GAH-reh*)

purchase, buy (to) comprare (*kohm-PRAHR-reh*)

put, place, set (to) mettere (*MEHT-tehr-reh*)

read (to) leggere (*LEHD-jehr-reh*)

remember (to) ricordarsi (*ree-kohr-DAHR-see*)

say (to) dire (*DEER-reh*)

say again (to) ridire (*ree-DEER-reh*)

see, look at (to) vedere (*veh-DEHR-reh*)

seek cercare (*cher-KAHR-reh*)

send (to) inviare (*een-vee-AHR-reh*)

sense, feel (to)   sentire (*sehn-TEER-reh*)

ship (to)   spedire (*speh-DEER-reh*)

shop, go shopping (to)   fare compere (*FAHR-reh KOHM-pehr-reh*)

show (to)   mostrare (*moh-STRAHR-reh*)

sleep (to)   dormire (*dohr-MEER-reh*)

speak, talk (to)   parlare (*pahr-LAH-reh*)

stay (to)   stare (*STAHR-reh*)

stop (to)   fermare (*fehr-MAHR-reh*)

take, get, seize (to)   prendere (*prehn-DEHR-reh*)

teach (to)   insegnare (*een-seh-NYAHR-reh*)

tell (to)   dire (*DEER-reh*)

translate (to)   tradurre (*trah-DOOHRR-reh*)

understand (to)   capire (*kah-PEER-reh*)

wait, wait for (to)   aspettare (*ah-speht-TAHR-reh*)

walk (to)   camminare (*kahm-mee-NAHR-reh*)

want (to)   volere (*voh-LEHR-reh*)

write (to)   scrivere (*skree-VEHR-reh*)

PRACTICAL PHRASES

Glad to meet you!   Piacere di fare la sua conoscenza! (*pyah-CHER-reh dee FAHR-reh lah SOO-ah koh-noh-SCHENN-tsah!*)

How are you?   Come sta? (*koh-meh STAH?*)

I'm fine, thanks; and you?   Bene, grazie, e Lei? (*BEH-neh, GRAH-tsyeh, eh LEH-ee?*)

I am_____.   Io sono_____. (*EE-oh SOH-noh_____.*)

What's your name?   Come si chiama? (*KOH-me see KYAH-mah?*)

My name is_____.   Mi chiamo_____. (*mee KYAH-moh_____.*)

Let me introduce_____. Le presento_____. (*leh preh-ZEHN-toh_____.*)

I'm American. Sono americano / americana. (*SOH-noh ah-mehr-ree-KAH-noh / nah.*)

ⓘ ____**British.**—____inglese. (____*een-GLEH-zeh.*); ____**Canadian**—____canadese. (____*kah-nah-DEH-zeh.*)

Do you speak English? Parla inglese? (*pahr-lah een-GLEH-zeh?*)

I understand a little Italian. Capisco un po' italiano. (*kah-PEE-skoh oon poh ee-tah-LYAH-noh.*)

I understand you. La capisco. (*lah kah-PEE-skoh.*)

Tell me_____. Mi dica_____. (*mee DEE-kah_____.*)

What did you say? Come, prego? (*KOH-meh, PREH-goh?*)

I don't understand. Non capisco. (*non kah-PEE-skoh.*)

Please repeat. Ripeta, per favore. (*ree-PEH-tah, pehr fah-VOHR-reh.*)

Please speak more slowly. Per favore, parli più lentamente. (*pehr fah-VOHR-reh, PAHR-lee pyoo lehn-tah-MEHN-teh.*)

What time is it? Che ora è? (*keh OHR-rah EH?*)

It is six o'clock. Sono le sei. (*SOH-noh leh SAY.*)

It is half past three / three-thirty. Sono le tre e mezzo / le tre e trenta. (____*leh TREH eh MEHD-dzoh / leh TREH eh TREHN-tah.*)

It is ten past nine. Sono le nove e dieci. (____*leh NOH-veh eh DYEH-chee.*)

I'm late. Sono in ritardo. (*SOH-noh een ree-TAHR-doh.*)

I'm in a hurry. Ho fretta. (*oh FREHT-tah.*)

Hurry up! Presto! (*PREH-stoh!*)

When do you open? A che ora apre? (*ah keh OHR-rah AH-preh?*)

When do you close? A che ora chiude? (*ah keh OHR-rah KYOO-deh?*)

In a little while. Soon. Fra poco. (*frah POH-koh.*)

What fine weather! Che bel tempo! (*keh behl TEHM-poh!*)

It's hot! Fa caldo! (*fah KAHL-doh!*)

It's very cold today! Fa molto freddo oggi! (*fah MOHL-toh FREHD-doh OHD-jee!*)

Excuse me. OR Pardon me. Mi scusi. (*mee SKOO-zee.*)

Allow me_____. Mi permetta_____. (*mee pehr-MEHT-tah_____.*)

I'm sorry. Mi dispiace. (*mee dee-SPYAH-cheh.*)

I don't know. Non so. (*nohn SOH.*)

What's the matter? Che c'è? (*keh CHEH?*)

Why? Perché? (*pehr KEH?*)

Because_____. Perché_____. (*pehr KEH_____.*)

Regardless of (apart from) the fact that_____. Indipendentemente dal fatto che_____. (*een-dee-pehn-dehn-teh-MEHN-teh dahl FAHT-toh keh_____.*)

It's not important. OR Never mind. Non importa. (*nohn eem-POHR-tah.*)

That's fine. Va bene. (*vah BEH-neh.*)

Well,_____. Beh,_____. (*BEH_____.*)

Whose? Di chi? (*dee KEE?*)

How? Come? (*KOH-meh*)
  ① **How many?—**Quanti? (*KWAHN-tee?*); **How much?—**Quanto? (*KWAHN-toh?*)

Look! Guardi! (*GWAHR-dee!*)

Help! OR Assistance! Aiuto! (*ah-YOO-toh!*)

I appreciate your help. Apprezzo il suo aiuto. (*ahp-PREHT-tsoh eel SOO-oh ah-YOO-toh.*)

You have been very kind. È stato molto gentile. (*eh STAH-toh MOHL-toh jehn-TEE-leh.*)

What place is this? Che posto è questo? (*keh POH-stoh eh KWEH-stoh?*)

May I? (*general permission request*) Posso? (*Pohs-soh?*)

May I? OR Excuse me! (*Remark of courtesy when entering a room or when requesting permission to pass*) Permesso? (*pehr-MEHS-soh?*)

May I use your bathroom? Posso usare il gabinetto? (*POHS-soh oo-ZAHR-reh eel gah-bee-NEHT-toh?*)

What is this called? Come si chiama questo? (*KOH-meh see KYAH-mah KWEH-stoh?*)

This one. Questo. (*KWEH-stoh.*)

That one. Quello (*KWEHL-loh.*)

I'm just looking. Sto soltanto guardando. (*stoh sohl-TAHN-toh gwahr-DAHN-doh.*)

How much does this cost? Quant'è? (*kwahn-TEH?*) OR Quanto costa? (*KWAHN-toh KOH-stah?*)

FILL-IN PHRASES

The phrases below exemplify how to use your new Italian vocabulary from the main text to ask questions and make simple statements. They can also be used as a simple self-test to measure the strength and extent of your vocabulary, and / or as the basis upon which to model an expanding self-evaluation program. The three units offer unlimited potential to supply mastered nouns, adjectives, and infinitive verbs as fill-ins to complete the partial phrases.

Noun Phrases

Complete the following phrases with any noun in your new Italian vocabulary, together with its appropriate definite or indefinite article. For example, in the first instance you might complete the phrase with *l'hotel, la fontana, la stazione, il lago, la cucina,* and so forth.

Where is (*article + noun*)? Dov'è_____?

In which direction is (*article + noun*)? In che direzione è_____?

Please direct me to (*article + noun*). Per favore, potrebbe dirigermi verso_____.

Please point to (*article + noun*). Indichi, per favore,_____.

Please take me to (*article + noun*). Per favore, mi porti (a)_____.

How long does it take to get to (*article + noun*)? Quanto tempo ci vuole per andare (a)_____?

Is there (*article + noun*) nearby? C'è_____vicino?

Where can I find (*article + noun*)? Dove potrei trovare_____?

Do you have (*article + noun*)? Avete_____?

Is that (*article + noun*)? È_____?

I have (*article + noun*). Ho_____.

I need (*article + noun*). Ho bisogno di_____.

I want (*article + noun*). Desidero_____.

I would like some (*article + noun*). Vorrei (di)_____.

Please bring me (*article + noun*). Per favore, mi porti_____.

Some more (*noun*), please. Un poco più di (d')_____, per favore.

(*Article + noun*) is not working. _____ non funziona.

I have lost my (*article + noun*)! Ho perso_____mio / -a_____!

Adjective Phrases

Complete the following phrases with any appropriate adjective in your new Italian vocabulary. For example, in the first instance you might complete the phrase with *caldo, freddo, umido, bello,* and so forth.

It is very (*adjective*) here. Fa molto_____qui.

He is (*adjective*). Lui è_____.

She is (*adjective*). Lei è_____.

They are (*adjective*). Loro sono_____.

I am (*adjective*). Sono_____.

I feel (*adjective*). Sento_____.

Do you feel (*adjective*)? Senti_____?

Verb Phrases

Complete the following phrases with the infinitive—the "to + action" form—of any appropriate verb in your Italian vocabulary. For example, in the first instance you might complete the phrase with *celebrare, dominare, flirtare, improvvisare, negoziare, osservare, partecipare, semplificare,* or *sperimentare.*

I like (*infinitive*). Mi piace_____.

I would like (*infinitive*). Vorrei_____.

I want (*infinitive*) **about eight o'clock.** Voglio_____circa le ore otto.

I need (*infinitive*) **tomorrow.** Ho bisogno di_____. / Devo_____domani.

I have to (*infinitive*). Devo_____.

I prefer (*infinitive*). Preferisco_____.

I wish (*infinitive*). Desidero_____.